# American Government

# American Government

## Competition and Compromise

**Stephen J. Rockwell**
*Brandeis University*

**Peter Woll**
*Brandeis University*

Boston    Burr Ridge, IL    Dubuque, IA    Madison, WI    New York    San Francisco    St. Louis
Bangkok    Bogotá    Caracas    Kuala Lumpur    Lisbon    London    Madrid    Mexico City
Milan    Montreal    New Delhi    Santiago    Seoul    Singapore    Sydney    Taipei    Toronto

# McGraw-Hill Higher Education

*A Division of The* **McGraw-Hill** *Companies*

AMERICAN GOVERNMENT: COMPETITION AND COMPROMISE

Published by McGraw-Hill, a business unit of The McGraw-Hill Companies, Inc., 1221 Avenue of the Americas, New York, NY 10020. Copyright © 2001 by The McGraw-Hill Companies, Inc. All rights reserved. No part of this publication may be reproduced or distributed in any form or by any means, or stored in a database or retrieval system, without the prior written consent of The McGraw-Hill Companies, Inc., including, but not limited to, in any network or other electronic storage or transmission, or broadcast for distance learning.

Some ancillaries, including electronic and print components, may not be available to customers outside the United States.

This book is printed on acid-free paper.

1 2 3 4 5 6 7 8 9 0 QPF/QPF 0 9 8 7 6 5 4 3 2 1 0

ISBN 0-07-039212-9

Vice president and editor-in-chief: *Thalia Dorwick*
Editorial director: *Jane E. Karpacz*
Sponsoring editor: *Monica Eckman*
Marketing manager: *Janise A. Fry*
Senior project manager: *Jayne Klein*
Media technology senior producer: *Sean Crowley*
Production supervisor: *Enboge Chong*
Coordinator of freelance design: *Rick D. Noel*
Cover designer: *Jamie A. O'Neal*
Cover images: © *Corbis Images:* Volume 54 *Skylines of North America-Capitol steps;*
Volume 98 *American Destinations-Flag*
Senior photo research coordinator: *Carrie K. Burger*
Photo research: *Feldman & Associates, Inc.*
Supplement producer: *Jodi K. Banowetz*
Compositor: *Shepherd, Inc.*
Typeface: *10/12 Palatino*
Printer: *Quebecor Printing Book Group/Fairfield, PA*

The credits section for this book begins on page 327 and is considered an extension of the copyright page.

## Library of Congress Cataloging-in-Publication Data

Rockwell, Stephen J., 1966–
      American government : competition and compromise / Stephen J. Rockwell,
   Peter Woll. — 1st ed.
         p.   cm.
   Includes bibliographical references and index.
      ISBN 0-07-039212-9
      1. United States—Politics and government.  2. Democracy—United States.
   I. Woll, Peter, 1933–   .  II. Title.

JK31 .R56   2001
320.973—dc21                                           00-062495
                                                         CIP

www.mhhe.com

*For my brothers, David and Kenny—*
*the best reasons for my phone to ring at 2 AM*

*For the Grands and Their Future—*
*Monica Leshan, Wesley Peter, and Sabrina Mary*

# Brief Contents

# Contents

Part Two
COMPETITION BY DESIGN

Part Three
INSTITUTIONS AND GOVERNING

# List of Boxes

## Scholar Boxes

## Zip Boxes

## BriefCase Boxes

## Discussion Boxes

# Preface

*American Government: Competition and Compromise* combines the best aspects of traditional introductory textbooks with a timely new chapter progression and versatile new teaching tools. The book covers all of the familiar topics of American government and politics in a manner designed to capture and hold students' interest by building on their experience, by offering brief, provocative readings set off in boxes and tied closely to the concepts in the text, and by offering text-based assignments designed to serve as the basis for short papers, class discussions, and an understanding of the American system as a coherent whole.

## THEME

Competition and compromise lie at the heart of American government. This theme offers students a realistic understanding of the key dynamics that sustain and drive American political life. Further, because competition and compromise are such fundamental and prevalent parts of American government, this text provides a ready foundation for integrating the newest issues and events into the classroom.

## CHAPTERS

*American Government: Competition and Compromise* is distinguished by its timely and innovative chapter progression.

Part One examines Americans and politics: Chapter 1 covers the media, Chapter 2 examines interest groups, Chapter 3 looks at political parties, and Chapter 4 focuses on elections, campaigns, and voting.

Opening the book with examination of the news media and political participation in America has significant advantages over the more traditional method of starting with the Constitution and founding principles. First, the chapter progression of *American Government: Competition and Compromise* appeals to today's students and their interests from the outset, encouraging them to become careful and informed observers of the news—habits that will benefit their understanding of politics and government as they move through the book.

More importantly, though, this chapter progression enables *American Government: Competition and Compromise* to cover the media far more thoroughly and with better integration than traditional textbooks. Chapter 1 examines the competition and compromise involved in gathering and presenting news—topics often excluded from traditional texts. The relationship of media coverage to other aspects of the system like campaigns and elections, policymaking, and presidential leadership are then integrated throughout the book where appropriate, instead of being relegated to an isolated chapter on the media. In short, *American Government: Competition and Compromise* covers more issues related to the news media and better integrates that material throughout the chapters on political processes and institutions—and it does so in a chapter progression that immediately captures students' attention and interest.

The remainder of *American Government: Competition and Compromise* covers all of the important and familiar topics involved in introductory textbooks; this is not a textbook about the media and politics alone. Interest groups, parties, campaigns, elections, and voting are covered in Chapters 2, 3, and 4, rounding out Part One by offering students a thorough understanding of the diversity and complexity of participation in American political life.

Part Two turns to the foundation and principles of American government, with Chapter 5 centering on the Constitution and Chapter 6 addressing civil liberties and civil rights. Chapter 5 highlights the competitive design established by the framers at the Constitutional Convention and the continuing relevance of their efforts to promote competition and encourage compromise in American government. Chapter 6 addresses the inevitable competition over the meaning of constitutional principles, and the difficulty of forging compromises when fundamental principles are at stake. Students who have become familiar with the diversity and complexity of American politics covered in Part One will be in an excellent position to understand and appreciate the framers' difficult task as well as their remarkable success.

Part Three covers the institutions of American government. Chapter 7 focuses on the bureaucracy, offering students an initial understanding of the bureaucracy's powers and limitations in a competitive system. This gives students a foundation for understanding the main branches of government and the ways in which the bureaucracy often stands at the center of institutional competition and compromise. Chapter 8 looks at the presidency, highlighting the diverse and often contradictory demands Americans make on that office. Chapter 9 examines Congress and the competition and compromise involved in reelection, lawmaking, and oversight. Chapter 10 centers on the courts, with attention to the competing interests and judicial compromises that surround the activities of the federal judiciary.

# *FEATURES*

*American Government: Competition and Compromise* features many innovative teaching tools designed to enhance classroom participation and integrate assignments with the text itself.

**Discussion Boxes** and **BriefCase Boxes** throughout the book support the main text with provocative readings and deeper analysis of examples illustrating important points; these boxes are closely integrated with the main text. The selections are brief and can be read quickly, making them ideal for in-class reading and discussion. Each box also includes an introductory note and a series of questions designed as a foundation for overnight assignments, short essays, or pop quizzes.

**Scholar Boxes** throughout the text link critical ideas in political science to important scholars, encouraging students to associate certain concepts with particular authors and researchers. Examples include "Fenno: Home Style," "Heclo: Issue Networks," and "Neustadt: The Power to Persuade."

**Zip Boxes** provide information at-a-glance on a wide variety of topics, including election and voting data, the growing prominence of thinktanks, campaign finance rules and abuses, and the committee system in Congress.

Each chapter concludes with two assignment features. An **Overnight Assignment** links a short task, like gathering information from the Internet or from the news, to the themes and concepts discussed in the chapter. **Long-Term Integrated Assignments** at the end of each chapter create a connected series of assignments designed to illustrate the ways in which diverse aspects of American politics relate to each other and form a coherent governing system. Students follow a particular news source, interest group, and issue throughout the book; by focusing on a specific case, they see how participation, principles, and institutions relate to each other in the political process. These assignments can serve as the basis for term papers, essays on midterms and finals, and other class projects.

## *Other Important Features*

- Each chapter's introduction concludes with a "Bottom Line" feature summarizing the chapter's themes and concepts, providing a heads-up introduction to important points and also a convenient focus for review.
- Websites listed in the book's margins link concepts and ideas to information available on the Internet. Many of the feature boxes and discussions in the main text address the relationship of the Internet to American politics and government in areas like voting over the Internet, political parties and congressional "home style" on the web, and the effects of rapidly changing technologies on judicial review.
- Names of important scholars and political figures are set off by underlining to alert students to the importance of individuals in American politics and to provide for easy reference and review of concepts linked with particular individuals. This feature takes advantage of the familiar format for

Internet hyperlinks, which have made the underlined word stand out as an important path to further information.

- Each chapter includes a list of authors and sources for further research. Rather than list only specific works, we have supplemented our bibliographic lists with short lists of prominent scholars in specific fields. This feature helps students identify authors whose body of work is relevant to chapter topics, and it helps students pursue electronic database searches to uncover multiple works by important authors.

- Top Ten lists from *The Late Show with David Letterman* and similar entries update the concept of political humor, replacing traditional cartoons with contemporary political commentary.

- The text and boxes include discussion and data from the 2000 election, and so *American Government Competition and Compromise* is up-to-date and relevant for classes in the post-Clinton era.

## *ACKNOWLEDGMENTS*

The authors are grateful for the careful and thoughtful work of those who reviewed early drafts of the manuscript, including Thomas Yantek, *Kent State University;* Stephen J. Farnsworth, *Mary Washington College;* John W. Cavanaugh, *University of South Carolina;* Robert Spitzer, *SUNY–Cortland;* Matthew Kerbel, *Villanova University;* Frank J. Musumici, *Mohave Community College;* Zoe Oxley, *Union College;* Janet Frantz, *University of Louisiana at Lafayette;* Paul Davis, *Truckee Meadows Community College;* Mark Byrnes, *Middle Tennessee State University;* David Darmofal, *University of Illinois at Urbana–Champaign;* Larry Elowitz, *Georgia College and State University;* Harry R. Mahood, *University of Memphis;* George Kiser, *Illinois State University;* Lars Hoffman, *Lewis & Clark Community College;* and Mitch Gerber, *South East Missouri State University.* We are deeply appreciative of the excellent and committed work of Monica Eckman, Hannah Glover, Shannon Morrow, Jayne Klein, Cheryl DuBois, Judy Feldman, Carrie Burger, Janise Fry, and Rick Noel. Steve Rockwell also thanks family, friends, and colleagues for their advice and support. In particular, I am indebted to Patricia and Ronald Rockwell, Jean Glaab, Peter Skerry, Martha Bayles, Sidney Milkis, Shep Melnick, Stephanie Greco Larson, Stephanie Muravchik and Jon Shields, Patricia and John Schmitt and their family, Matt Rorke, Hank Lutton, Zoe and Sam Gedal, Cheryl and Tal Ninyo and their family, Ann Ginsberg and Glen Weiss, Doug Katz, Lonnie Meiner, and Nicole and Steve Pierce. Finally, my thanks always to Peter Woll.

# Introduction

Competition is good.

Competition drives American politics; every public debate in America involves competing interests, values, and viewpoints. The American system of government promotes participation, free speech, the organization of individuals into groups—and it works purposefully to multiply the diversity of ideas, interests, and attitudes coursing through American public affairs. Are corporate interests corrupting the news media? Are special interests taking over Congress, infesting the halls of the Capitol with selfish demands and tainted campaign contributions? Are American political parties too weak to govern? Have we delegated too much power to an unelected federal bureaucracy? Can the institutions of government remain relevant in the new century? All of these questions are answered by competing interests with competing values and viewpoints, and rarely does a yes or no answer satisfy; rarely does *any* answer satisfy for very long.

Because of the diversity of competing attitudes and interests involved in public affairs, public policy emerges as an endless series of compromises. By compromise, we mean accepting and being satisfied, even if only temporarily, with something other than an ideal resolution of political competition. The resolution might involve something less than somebody wanted, or maybe just something different. At every stage of the political process in America, individuals and organized interests are brought to compromise solutions by the nature of the constitutional system. The system demands negotiation, bargaining, trade-offs, and a constant reevaluation of interests, goals, and objectives. The system also holds out the promise of future efforts to achieve goals, making compromises safe way-stations—and making government a never-ending story of adaptations, ad hoc solutions, temporary setbacks, and forward-looking hopes.

Competition is good. The framers confidently built a governing system that promotes the competition of interests and that checks and balances the exercise of power. With fragmented power and the participation of a large and diverse public, compromise becomes the road to progress—and the dominance of compromise is why public debate never ends, because at any given time the system loves the middle-of-the-road solution. Competitors immediately begin to pursue better results, in the firm belief that the last compromise can be improved upon.

Competition and compromise create perpetual motion. For if the framers settled the question of whether competition is good, the question that drives American politics and reveals the heart of American affairs is always this: Are the compromises good enough?

## *THEMES*

Competition and compromise occur among, and within, the many different pieces of our political system. This book examines these pieces and the ways in which they interact. In the big picture, people, groups, and interests compete in the political system. That system provides rules and procedures designed to ensure that most interests will get something that they want, even if no interest gets everything that it wants—the core of compromise. Government is the mechanism that orders the competition, enforces the rules, and adjusts procedures to adapt to new circumstances. Aspects of government are powerful elements of this system, so the government itself is often an important competitor.

Each chapter in this text examines how a piece of our political system is involved in the competition for power and influence in governing. Each chapter also examines the ways in which competition takes place *within* individual parts of the system, such as when representatives in Congress compete with each other. Throughout the book, we will also look at the ways in which our governing system encourages compromise. Current and historical examples demonstrate how and why people and interests compromise in order to achieve at least some of their goals. We will see how the media, organized political groups, and individual voters compromise when they participate in the political system.

Throughout this book, the authors consider competition and compromise to be valued elements of American government. Competition and compromise stabilize the political system, they encourage participation by interested parties, and they lead to sensible, if incremental, progress. The authors strive to present the system as a balanced, fair, and ultimately successful mechanism for integrating diverse viewpoints and for producing workable solutions in pursuit of our national goals.

Yet deeper questions lurk behind this point of view, questions that are easily overlooked. Americans worry that the compromises we make are not good enough—that we should be more outraged at violations of our trust and ethics, that we should do more to protect civil rights, that we should do more to ensure the integrity of our nation's public life. Americans ask whether practical and political compromises on issues and policies compromise our values and ideals, and whether compromising too easily leads to complacency—a willingness to settle too quickly and for too little. Many careful and insightful observers, for example, fear that current trends—such as the rising cost of political campaigns, the power of special interest groups, and the decline of political parties—threaten the very foundations of our civic community. These observers worry that the competition in American politics isn't fair; they worry that convenient compromises subvert the pursuit of our ideals.

Compromises create risks. In particular, compromising on fundamental issues can obscure dangerous threats to our polity. Too much willingness to compromise risks dampening the spirit of reform and the political idealism that have inspired this country for more than two centuries. The cases and discussions in this book are designed to provide a foundation for evaluating the results of our system of competition and compromise.

## *MAJOR SECTIONS AND CHAPTER OUTLINE*

Part One of this book examines the relationship of the individual American citizen to American government. The media, interest groups, political parties, and electoral behaviors, such as voting, are some of the most important vehicles through which people compete for power and influence in government. These four aspects of American public life all have important effects on what citizens know about public affairs, and also on what happens in government. Chapter 1 centers on the media, the most fundamental linkage between people and government, and highlights the ways in which participants in public affairs try to bend the media to serve their interests. Chapter 2 focuses on interest groups, a critically important way in which people and organized interests participate in government. Chapter 3 examines American political parties and their changing relationship to the public and government. Chapter 4 addresses electoral campaigns and voting, still the cornerstones of our American system.

Part Two of this book looks at the goals of the American political system and at the careful effort by our nation's founders to understand and control the competition inherent in American society. These goals start with the Declaration of Independence: life, liberty, and the pursuit of happiness. Chapter 5 focuses on the framers' efforts to design a governing mechanism to secure these grand principles, an effort that culminated in the United States Constitution. The laws and court decisions that have followed the Constitution, and the amendments we have made to the Constitution itself, are a fundamental expression of our nation's never-ending effort to realize our ideals in changing circumstances. Chapter 6 looks closely at the protection and promotion of civil liberties and civil rights, the true heart of America's effort to realize its ideals in the world of practical politics and competing interests.

Part Three of this book analyzes the major institutions of our governing system. By the time we reach these chapters, we will have seen the diverse interests involved in American politics and some of the ways in which they compete; we will have seen the design that promotes competition, and the development of the rules that govern the competition. In Part Three, we will examine how the government itself contributes to the system, not only ordering and enforcing the competition but also taking part itself. Chapter 7 looks at the administrative bureaucracy, where much of the work of designing and implementing public policies takes place, and the target of competition among the three major constitutional branches of government. These major branches are the subject of the book's final three chapters. Chapter 8 analyzes the executive branch and the office of the presidency; chapter 9 focuses on Congress; and chapter 10 highlights the important role of the federal judiciary.

Together, these ten chapters provide an introduction to the American governing system, its inherently competitive nature, and the role of compromise in resolving differences and moving the nation forward.

## STRUCTURE: WHY COVER THE MEDIA FIRST?

A defining feature of *American Government: Competition and Compromise* is that we address the media, interest groups, parties, and voting in the first part of the book. Most introductions to American government begin with the Constitution and the "rules of the game," and follow with an examination of how people and interests act under those rules. The problem with this approach is that American government did not start with rules; it didn't even start with principles. It started with people who had differing ideas and who wanted different things from public affairs and politics. Public affairs were competitive long before the Declaration of Independence defined our ideals, and long before the Constitution established a governing system to try to secure those ideals. Even today, our efforts to put our ideals into practice and to uphold the rights and principles of the Constitution *follow* from how we understand and explain those ideals. These understandings derive from the diversity that has always characterized the American people and their interests.

American government, then, starts with American people and their desires. Government is secondary, designed to secure these ends. Thus it is that this book turns first to how we perceive our world, how we as citizens and as members of groups interact, and how we compete to get what we want, for ourselves and for others. Only after understanding the competing forces in play in American public life will we be prepared to understand the genius of the Constitution's design and the success with which it has ordered and controlled competition in America for more than two centuries. And only then, with a better understanding of our competing interests and of the system designed to manage that competition, will we be ready to appreciate the extraordinarily complex demands we make on our government and the remarkable success of our institutions.

The fact that we deal first with the media does not mean that this book is about the media and American government alone, nor does it mean that we believe the media to be the most important element in today's politics. We address the media first so that we can build on readers' familiarity with the media, and also so we can address at the outset popular misconceptions about how the media function in American politics. Chapter 1 clarifies the media's importance and how media dynamics affect the news we receive about government; we build on these principles throughout the other chapters. Throughout the book, we will see that the media are an important source of information and an indispensable link facilitating communication among citizens and government, but their effects on what issues government addresses and how those issues are addressed, as well as their influences on political activity like voting behavior, are often overestimated. Textbooks that relegate discussion of the media in politics to a single, isolated chapter in the back of the book unwisely delay examination of what is, and what is not, important about the media in contemporary American politics.

Our chapter progression also allows us to build on other aspects of American government that might be familiar to readers: interest groups, political parties, and voting. After reviewing and examining themes and scholarship on these topics, we are able to discuss the Constitution and governing institutions later in the book when readers have a more thorough understanding of the numerous competing interests involved in American government—the interests that those rules and institutions seek to organize.

## *AND WHY COVER THE THREE MAIN BRANCHES LAST?*

As citizens, we are familiar with the three main branches of government and the ways in which the Constitution separates and distributes power among them. In short, the founding fathers structured the American system of government to prevent any one person, or even any one part of the government, from gaining too much power. In its familiar conception, then, the Congress makes the laws; the president executes and enforces the laws; and the courts interpret the laws. Power, though, overlaps: though the president is commander in chief of the nation's military, for example, Congress allocates the money that keeps the military functioning. Though Congress can pass bills, the president can veto them and thus prevent them from becoming law, at least temporarily. Though federal judges interpret laws, those judges are appointed by the president and approved by the Senate. In each of these cases, no single branch of the government can assume all the power; in each case, power is shared by several interests.

The executive, legislature, and judiciary are the three main branches of government in the constitutional design. It may seem strange, then, that these critical areas are covered in the *last* three chapters of this book. There are several reasons for this. First, the functioning of these branches is very complex. The foregoing outline of the general duties of the three branches is true in a sense, but it is also vastly oversimplified, given the amount of overlap among the branches and the complexity of how these branches actually function. But we can use this basic framework to help us understand the other pieces of the puzzle, and then return to the major branches after we have examined the other forces in play.

Second, the branches' complexity is a response to the diversity of the American people and to the innumerable demands we make on government. We need to understand how people relate to each other and how they relate to the government before we can fully understand the genius inherent in our constitutional design. Only then can we appreciate why the major branches have become so complex and why the tasks they face in running our government are so difficult.

Finally, just as the media—and misconceptions about the media—have become so prevalent in American politics that it makes sense to discuss the media's influence up front and throughout the text, the administrative bureaucracy is now so fundamental to the functioning of the American government, and such a point of contention, that it makes sense to understand the potential and limitations of the bureaucracy before we discuss the branches that seek to exert power and influence over administration. In short, understanding the bureaucracy is now a prerequisite to understanding American governing institutions. The limitations of the presidency, the complexity of demands made on Congress, and the influence of the federal judiciary on public policy all come together in our public bureaucracies. Studying the nature of public administration in chapter 7, before we address the three main branches, helps clarify the strengths and weaknesses—and the power and influence—of the traditional branches of government in today's politics.

## THE BOOK'S BOTTOM LINES

The complexity and fragmentation of the American political system makes it very difficult to discuss that system, because learning about one piece almost always requires some knowledge about some other piece. How can one understand how interest groups function within Congress, without knowing about Congress? Alternatively, how can one understand Congress without an understanding of how groups exert pressure on that institution?

As an introduction to the themes we will develop in each chapter, here are ten core aspects of the American governing system. These "bottom lines" capture the chapters' themes, and one shows up in each chapter's introduction. Together, they summarize the major ideas of this book.

1. The news media are a critically important political institution; much of what we know and learn about politics and government comes to us through the news media. Competing expectations complicate evaluations of the media's role and how well they perform in the public sphere. Moreover, the media business is very competitive, raising questions about how consolidation among media organizations affects the information available to the public. The media try to satisfy professional goals and the demands of the marketplace by making practical compromises, which affect what and how information is delivered.

2. Interest groups are a normal part of our political system, enabling people and organizations with shared interests to be more effective competitors in public affairs. Interest groups compete with each other using a variety of resources, and they build coalitions and make compromises to further their agendas. Overreliance on interest group politics is risky if public policy is driven only by selfish bargaining, if groups do not represent interests fairly, and if some groups come to have undue influence on elections

and government. Compromises encourage interest group behavior while trying to control the threats groups pose to the system.

3. The dynamics of American politics perpetuate a system dominated by two major political parties. In the electorate, political parties work to organize interests, reconcile conflicts, and win elections; in government, parties help coordinate action, order government activity, and compete for power and influence. Serious problems threaten the parties' ability to achieve these objectives successfully, and American parties are notoriously "weak." They are forced to make compromises in the electorate that dilute their positions on issues and risk alienating members with strong beliefs; they are forced to make compromises in government that limit their ability to coordinate government policies and to control individuals' behavior. Despite predictions of their demise, though, political parties have adapted to new circumstances and continue to be an important and influential part of our political system.

4. Campaigns and elections are the core of regular public competition in America, providing stability as well as the opportunity for peaceful and regular change in our leaders and in the direction of government. Expensive campaigns driven by candidate-centered organizations and intimately related to the media characterize modern elections. Successful candidates forge effective compromises between their own goals, the demands of the media, and the necessities of fundraising. Voters and votes are the prizes of these competitions, with numerous factors influencing voter access to the ballot, voter turnout, and voter choices.

5. The Constitution, and the political ideas of the eighteenth century, are the keys to today's American government. The Constitution is a unique and brilliant attempt to realize the best and highest values, while protecting people from the worst and most self-interested behavior. Optimism arises from eighteenth-century philosophy and anchors deep in the principles of the Declaration of Independence and the Constitution. The institutional structures organized by the Constitution are designed to protect these values by fragmenting power and by setting myriad countervailing forces against one another. The framers accepted that people act in self-interested ways, and they carefully anticipated the worst actions by the worst people and sought to protect government and the people from themselves. At its core, the Constitution turns a philosophy of humanity into a complex and enormously successful framework that institutionalizes competition and encourages compromise.

6. The Higher Law, the common law, and the Constitution create civil liberties and civil rights that stand above the will of political majorities. The Supreme Court defines liberties and rights through constitutional interpretation, and it overrules legislation that infringes too far upon civil liberties and rights. The Court recognizes that individual liberties and rights are not always absolute: legitimate governmental needs can require restraints on individual freedoms, because civil societies and their governments have a justifiable interest in protecting themselves and the commu-

nity against certain individual actions. Efforts to weigh competing rights and interests complicate the protection of civil liberties and civil rights, and lead to some inconsistent, evolving, and even startling results.

7. Congress delegates significant authority to administrative agencies and executive departments; these organizations combine important legislative, executive, and judicial powers. The bureaucracy's extensive influence over how the government designs and administers policies and programs encourages the three main branches of government to compete with each other and with interest groups to influence the behavior of individual agencies. Agencies utilize their own competitive defenses to protect their autonomy. All of this competition has particular effects on the nature of American administrative and regulatory agencies. Finally, the actions and the efficiency of public agencies are complicated by the conflicting demands we make on their behavior.

8. Americans have high hopes and expectations for their presidents. At the founding, compromises regarding presidential selection aimed to satisfy diverse interests and create an office with a measure of independence and autonomy—but one that would nevertheless be checked in the exercise of its power. For the most part, the system has worked: today the office enjoys broad powers under the Constitution, the potential for energy, and a position of visibility and leadership without parallel in the American system. Yet other forces continue to limit the president's potential: Congress and the bureaucracy have their own interests and their own constituents, and they must be persuaded—not commanded—to work with the president toward his objectives. Leadership is more about bargaining and compromise with these forces than it is about striking out in new directions and hoping that the nation follows. Finally, presidents confront a fundamental dilemma in satisfying demands that the president serve simultaneously as the leader of the entire nation and as the leader of partisan initiatives.

9. Congress is the cornerstone of American government; its roles in representation, lawmaking, and overseeing government activities involve virtually every aspect of American politics. Congress's authority is expansive, a function of enumerated constitutional powers and helpful rulings from the Supreme Court, yet it is also checked and balanced by other institutions and by its own bicameral structure. Members strive for reelection, especially early in their careers, and for power and policy influence within Congress. In many ways, the activities and structure of the modern Congress are designed to maximize members' ability to meet these goals. Congress's lawmaking and oversight responsibilities endlessly multiply competition and the need for compromise across Capitol Hill, creating an open public policy process that produces change only incrementally.

10. With the courts as the venue for so many political disputes, the judiciary is as important, and sometimes more important, to the political process than the president or Congress. The courts can defer to or accommodate the compromises reached in the regular political process, or replace those compromises with judicially made compromises that weigh interests

differently. The role of the federal judiciary and its considerable independence in a competitive system become important aspects of American politics. In turn, the means by which judges receive and decide cases, and their political role in policy making, place the courts squarely within—and not outside—the American system of competition and compromise.

\* \* \*

With that introductory outline of *American Government: Competition and Compromise*, we turn first to one of the most familiar and frequently misunderstood aspects of today's politics: the media.

# Americans and Politics

# The Media

## CHAPTER OUTLINE

"We have a story that we think is solid. We don't think anybody could ever sue us for libel. There are some twists and turns, and if you get in front of a jury in some states where the people on that jury are all related to people who work in tobacco companies, look out. That's a $15 billion gun pointed at your head. We may opt to get out of the line of fire." So stated Don Hewitt, executive producer of CBS's esteemed newsmagazine program *60 Minutes*. Hewitt's statement at the National Press Club in Washington, D.C., in the fall of 1995 came as CBS and *60 Minutes* were making the controversial decision not to broadcast an interview with a high-ranking whistleblower from within the tobacco industry. One influence on the *60 Minutes* decision was a just-settled controversy between ABC News and the Philip Morris tobacco company, in which the tobacco company had sued ABC News and won a hefty settlement and an on-air apology. Observers worried that CBS and *60 Minutes* had looked into the face of a potentially long and very costly lawsuit—and blinked.

The circumstances surrounding the *60 Minutes* decision were so dramatic that they were made into a movie, *The Insider,* which was nominated for an Academy Award for best picture of 1999. The movie became almost as controversial as the original incident, though, with critics charging that it distorted the story and inaccurately portrayed participants. The circumstances surrounding the case are so complex and detailed that it is difficult to know exactly what combination of influences determined the *60 Minutes* decision. Despite condemnations of *60 Minutes* for "caving in" to corporate pressure, it is unlikely that the decision was merely an economic one in which public awareness and the show's journalistic integrity were sacrificed to avoid a costly lawsuit.

More likely, the decision was a compromise among the competing expectations and goals of the show and the people involved. The team at *60 Minutes* recognized the relevance of the story to important issues surrounding tobacco industry practices and their effects on public health. Attorneys for CBS feared that the network might be legally liable for encouraging the whistleblower to break his nondisclosure agreement with the tobacco company, in which the whistleblower had agreed not to discuss his work. Corporate interests at CBS worried about protecting both the reputation of its flagship news program and the economic health of the network in a competitive business environment. CBS was also in negotiations at the time to be purchased by Westinghouse, and a new multi-billion-dollar lawsuit against the network might have affected the deal.[1]

Despite these competing dynamics, however, the *60 Minutes* story has become a cautionary tale of how corporate influence can bully the news media. This chapter examines the competing expectations and dynamics facing journalists, news outlets, and corporations, and the compromises they make. These compromises affect what and how we learn about public affairs, government, and politics in America.

We open this textbook on American politics with an examination of the news media for a very simple reason: almost all that we know and learn about politics, government, and public affairs we learn through the media. They link people with government, and they are the conduits for information about issues, programs, plans, and public affairs. They are used as intermediaries to communicate messages; they are the witting or unwitting accomplices of interests trying to manipulate images and information. Yet the media play a number of different roles, and they face competing expectations based on those roles. Further, the media operate in a competitive environment that demands compromises between these roles and expectations, on the one hand, and business demands, on the other. Throughout this book, we will see different, specific relationships among the media and various aspects of the political system such as political parties, the presidency, and Congress. In this chapter, we will examine some of the fundamental issues surrounding the media in America and their relationship to government and to the public.

**The Bottom Line.** The news media are a critically important political institution; much of what we know and learn about politics and government comes to us through the news media. Competing expectations complicate evaluations of the media's role and how well they perform in the public sphere. Moreover, the media business is very competitive, raising questions about how consolidation among media organizations affects the information available to the public. The media try to satisfy professional goals and the demands of the marketplace by making practical compromises, which affect what and how information is delivered.

## COMPETING FOR CONTROL
## OF INFORMATION: WHOSE NEWS?

### "The Lifeblood of Politics"

The news media are the gatekeepers of information the public receives, which is why the decision-making process surrounding coverage of public issues like tobacco and health is so significant. Far beyond the importance of any particular story, the media's control over information is a critical element influencing public life and political affairs. The media raise issues, and they can increase or undermine public support for policies and initiatives. The media help spur change, and they help create or destroy programs and policies. The media help build agendas by encouraging a general political climate that serves to influence government, and they are especially influential agenda setters among audiences with lower education levels and low political interest and activity. The media are also influential agenda setters in contexts where people depend on the media—rather than on their own experience or other sources—for information, such as very technical policy topics or foreign affairs.[2] Finally, the news media affect public debate by deciding *not* to report certain stories. Scholar Doris Graber calls media coverage the "lifeblood of politics," "because it shapes the perceptions that form the reality on which political action is based. Media do more than depict the political environment; they *are* the political environment. Because direct contact with political actors and situations is limited, media images define people and situations for nearly all participants in the political process."[3]

Two principles govern the media's impact. First, *people pay attention to the news and learn from the news selectively* and in light of their own preconceptions: in other words, people are attracted to reports that agree with their beliefs or positions, and they tend to pay less attention to reports that challenge those viewpoints. Second, and related to the first principle, media coverage *is* most *influential when people are still forming their opinions and attitudes, and* least *influential in altering established attitudes and behaviors.*

The news media, then, are an important—but not dominating—part of the political process. They help set agendas and they help shape perceptions, especially in certain situations, but the news media have a limited ability to change people's minds or bring them to new understandings of familiar issues. The limits of the news media's impact on behavior and policy is a topic we will examine throughout this book. In Chapter 4, for example, we will look more closely at the news media's surprisingly limited effect on voters' choices during elections. The present chapter focuses instead on how the news media are active participants in American politics, and on how the news is gathered and presented. These dynamics are important to virtually all aspects of American government, and we will refer to them throughout the text.

## Competing to Control the Message: The Media and Government

Far from being mere observers looking "from the outside in" on government, the media are directly involved in determining what we know and learn of politics. Media scholar Timothy E. Cook argues that the media are not only a part of politics—they are a "political institution" in their own right (see Scholar Box 1.1). According to Cook, the news is a *"coproduction"* between the media and government officials, by which he means that public officials participate in gathering, presenting, and managing the information that appears

---

 **Scholar Box 1.1**
*Cook: The Media as a Political Institution*

The media's role in politics is a compromise: we expect the media to play an important role in public communication and to uphold certain journalistic standards, but we also accept that the choices made by the media are influenced by economic and other factors that affect the way the media operate. In the passages below, Timothy E. Cook identifies two problems with the media's role as a political institution in the United States. What are these two problems? Are these problems likely to be ameliorated by journalists' professional standards or by the public's expectations of news coverage? How are these problems likely to be affected by corporate mergers and consolidations among news organizations?

The governmental news media in the United States present a twofold problem. One is the *capacity* of the news media to perform the role that has devolved on it. Journalists are not well trained, nor are news organizations well equipped, to help weigh problems, set political agendas, examine alternatives, and study implementation. Journalistic criteria of importance and interest simply may or may not have much to do with societal concerns of politics and policy making. I have argued that the work of journalists favors news that is easily and regularly gathered, that is timely, terse, simply described, concrete, dramatic, colorful, and visualizable. So, to the extent that journalism organizes politics and wields power in the American political system, it directs attention: toward episodic outcroppings rather than continuing conditions; toward issues that fade quickly in

public consciousness as newspersons begin to assume that the audience is getting as bored as they are with the same old concerns; and away from abstract complexity toward simple if not simplistic renderings of problems, policies, and alternatives.

Another problem, at least equally important, is that of *accountability*. If . . . journalists end up wielding political influence, one can only wonder: Who elected them? And to whom are journalists responsible? Newspersons will rightly contend that they are answerable to their audiences. But on what grounds? As in other areas of capitalism, one can easily doubt that consumers gravitate toward the better mousetrap. Instead, the public makes such choices shaped by how a product is marketed, whether oligopolies provide openings for innovation, and how investors react to new or old products. . . .

If the American political system has become increasingly dependent on the news media, not merely to communicate with the American people but to communicate among elites and activists and to help in the very process of government, it has empowered an institution that is neither well-designed to do so nor effectively politically accountable. Political actors have become ever more conscious of the need to make news, and they have become skilled at it as well, but . . . the demands of the news do not match the needs of the polity.*

*Timothy E. Cook, *Governing with the News: The News Media as a Political Institution* (Chicago: University of Chicago Press, 1998), reprinted in *American Political Ideals and Realities*, ed. Peter Woll and Stephen J. Rockwell (New York: Longman, 2000), 37–38.

The media cover news, but they are also an important vehicle for communication among political actors. Here, New York Representative Rick Lazio (R) watches a videotaped interview involving New York City Mayor Rudolph Giuliani (R) on NBC's *Meet the Press.*

in the news. And as the media become an indispensable part of governing, journalists become one of the most important parts of our political system.

The media and government use each other. The media use politics to attract viewers, sell advertisements, and build careers. Officials in government use the media to further their careers as well as their policy initiatives, and to react to the actions of others. Officials are very savvy when it comes to trying to use and manipulate media coverage: they know that good media coverage can make them look powerful and effective, and that it can help generate support or opposition on specific issues.

### We'll Tell You What to Say: Influencing the News

The importance of the news media as a means of communicating information, especially on new issues and events, draws the attention of competing interests inside and outside of government. Participants in politics utilize a variety of methods to influence the messages carried by media outlets to the public. In short, news doesn't just "happen"—it is often constructed and packaged by the participants themselves.

Politicians try as hard as they can to *"manage"* the news. Officials' reactions to events are timed to coincide with national television news shows going on the air, such as when the president responds to a national disaster or when a presidential candidate speaks after an important primary win. Media consultants manage the time and décor of press conferences, and they establish the camera positions assigned to different news teams and the backdrops framing speakers. When a tank or an F-14 looms behind a "tough" speech by the president on foreign policy, it is no accident. Similarly, when a presidential candidate appealing to farmers makes a televised speech in front of waving grainfields and shiny tractors, chances are that the location, camera angles, and even the time of day (capitalizing on good sunlight) were carefully chosen by the candidate's media team.

Officials and other interests aren't satisfied with managing the news; they also try to *script the information* an audience receives. Press releases highlight particular parts of speeches, for example, in an effort to influence the next day's headlines and thereby control "the message" reported by the media. Officials and interest groups produce and deliver to news organizations prepackaged and ready-to-air videotaped segments on specific topics. "Experts" can be made available to defend certain positions or interpretations. Such techniques take advantage of the pressures on media outlets delivering the news in a competitive environment: time and cost constraints make it very attractive for some news outlets to use materials given to them by outsiders.

Public officials take advantage of media opportunities, in effect working within the medium itself to get their views across. Talk shows like *Meet the Press* and *Nightline,* for example, offer excellent opportunities to reach large and influential audiences. Appearances by top officials on these shows are often carefully scripted publicity pieces. When a major issue is dominating the news, dozens of officials and experts take to the talk shows to push various interpretations and ideas. For instance, the president's administration will coordinate appearances by cabinet members and top leaders to flood the shows with the president's official position. Talk shows and interviews are also good opportunities for officials to "float," or informally suggest, new ideas in order to gauge reactions.

### Competition and Media Independence: Can Government Control the News?

Can government *control* the news? The answer is no, and Cook's understanding of the news as a *co*production is significant. Because of the media's diversity, reporters' desire to break big stories, and the professional pride journalists take in not believing everything they hear—and also because our governing system creates so many public officials with different agendas—it is virtually impossible for "the government" to control the news to the extent of completely dominating what we learn of public affairs (see Discussion Box 1.1). After all, it was a little-known Internet site run by Matt Drudge, then an obscure investigator, that originally broke the story that President Bill Clinton had had improper relations with a White House intern.

The media are very diverse: hundreds of different organizations gather and deliver the news in different ways. In a single day, an average citizen might get information from any number and combination of sources. A person might turn on a daily, national morning television show as she makes breakfast, and listen to local news or National Public Radio on the car radio on the way to work or school. After arriving, she might read the local newspaper or the *New York Times,* or visit an online news site; she might surf the Internet or

# DISCUSSION BOX 1.1
### ROASTING A MEDIA CHESTNUT: WORDS, PICTURES, AND JOURNALISTS' CHOICES

An old adage in political science says that the pictures in a television news account speak louder than the words. This chestnut of modern journalism often accompanies a familiar tale told by Lesley Stahl of CBS News. Media expert Stephanie Greco Larson, however, argues that the Stahl story is something of a myth that masks reporters' responsibilities. Are reporters at the mercy of politicians? According to Larson, what risk accompanies media strategy stories? How does this incident illustrate the complexity of the media's interactions with government and other public figures?

As Stahl tells the story in her book, *Reporting Live,* after being asked to sum up the Reagan campaign of 1984 for the "CBS Evening News,' she created a hard-hitting piece criticizing Reagan for deceptive image-making. To her surprise, Richard Darman, the deputy chief of staff, called from the White House to thank her for the "[f]ive minutes of free media." When she reiterated some of the tough things she said in the report, he remarked that she and her colleagues still did not get the point: "When the pictures are powerful and emotional, they override if not completely drown out the sound." . . .

The story of Stahl's piece supposedly validates the truism that pictures speak louder than words. It is also invoked to support the cynicism of television journalists who feel that they are at the mercy of politicians who know how to create attractive photo opportunities. Not only are these arguments vulnerable when held up to scrutiny, but Stahl's news segment is a poor example of both of them because the strong pictures were accompanied by a flawed narration that was explicit in its recognition of Reagan's strengths and vague in its criticisms, thus lending reinforcement to the messages in the positive pictures. Rather than demonstrate that reporters are at the mercy of politicians, it shows the pitfalls of reporters' own preoccupation with campaign strategy, candidate images and the media. . . .

The lessons to be learned from the story of Lesley Stahl's 1984 campaign piece are not the ones that have so often been promoted. Reporters are not at the mercy of politicians who know how to present appealing images. Viewers do not mindlessly believe pictures and ignore words. However, when reporters use pictures orchestrated by well-run campaigns to talk about the candidates' media management, they need to be very careful. A media strategy story that skirts the issues at stake in the strategy and loses sight of the viewers and voters' perspective runs the risk of amplifying that strategy and confusing, or even alienating, the very citizens a reporter is trying to inform.*

*Stephanie Greco Larson, "Debunking a Myth: Lesley Stahl's Legendary 1984 Campaign News Segment," *Media Studies Journal* 14, no. 1 (Winter 2000): 116, 117, 121.

# DISCUSSION BOX 1.2
### I WANT MY CNN! HOW BADLY DO WE NEED NEWS?

Even before the advent of cable television and instant news on the Internet, historian Daniel J. Boorstin suggested that popular hunger for news drove journalists' searches for stories. What recent stories fit Boorstin's discussion in the following passage of "fabricated" news, answering "our demand for illusions"? Conversely, with international coverage around the clock, must the audience of the twenty-first century settle for fabricated news, or are we overwhelmed with "intriguing or startling occurrences"?

We need not be theologians to see that we have shifted responsibility for making the world interesting from God to the newspaperman. We used to believe there were only so many "events" in the world. If there were not many intriguing or startling occurrences, it was no fault of the reporter. He could not be expected to report what did not exist.

Within the last hundred years, however, and especially in the twentieth century, all this has changed. We expect the papers to be full of news. If there is no news visible to the naked eye, or to the average citizen, we still expect it to be there for the enterprising newsman. The successful reporter is one who can find a story, even if there is no earthquake or assassination or civil war. If he cannot find a story, then he must make one—by the questions he asks of public figures, by the surprising human interest he unfolds from some commonplace event, or by "the news behind the news." If all this fails, then he must give us a "think piece"—an embroidering of well-known facts, or a speculation about startling things to come.

This change in our attitude toward "news" is not merely a basic fact about the history of American newspapers. It is a symptom of a revolutionary change in our attitude toward what happens in the world, how much of it is new, and surprising, and important. Toward how life can be enlivened, toward our power and the power of those who inform and educate and guide us, to pro-vide synthetic happenings to make up for the lack of spontaneous events. Demanding more than the world can give us, we require that something be fabricated to make up for the world's deficiency. This is only one ex-ample of our demand for illusions.*

*Daniel J. Boorstin, *The Image: A Guide to Pseudo-Events in America* (New York: Atheneum, 1973 [1961]), 8–9.

## Zip Box 1.1
*Who's Reading What? Use of Television, Radio, and Newspapers, 1996*

Note how television network news viewership increases with age, and how employment, higher income, and higher education levels correlate with increased use of magazines and newspapers.

### Use of Television, Radio, and Newspapers, Cross-Section, 1996

| | Television Watchers | | | | Magazines/Newspapers | | | | | |
| | Total adult population (thousands) | Network News | | | | New York Times daily | Time | US News & World Report | USA Today | Wall Street Journal |
| | | Early eve.[a] | Late night[b] | Newsweek | | | | | | |
|---|---|---|---|---|---|---|---|---|---|---|
| **Age** | | | | | | | | | | |
| 18–24 | 24,848 | 7.3 | 0.8 | 11.5 | | 1.4 | 12.2 | 3.2 | 2.5 | 0.6 |
| 25–34 | 42,530 | 11.0 | 1.7 | 9.1 | | 1.4 | 11.5 | 4.0 | 2.5 | 1.4 |
| 35–44 | 41,652 | 12.3 | 1.5 | 12.3 | | 1.1 | 13.0 | 5.7 | 2.8 | 2.0 |
| 45–54 | 29,737 | 15.9 | 2.4 | 15.0 | | 1.7 | 14.6 | 7.0 | 2.5 | 2.9 |
| 55–64 | 21,537 | 18.2 | 2.4 | 10.4 | | 1.2 | 10.7 | 5.0 | 2.1 | 1.5 |
| 65 and older | 31,359 | 19.5 | 2.4 | 7.0 | | 1.0 | 8.8 | 5.6 | 1.1 | 1.3 |
| **Sex** | | | | | | | | | | |
| Male | 91,780 | 13.6 | 2.1 | 12.1 | | 1.7 | 13.0 | 6.2 | 3.6 | 2.6 |
| Female | 99,882 | 14.0 | 1.6 | 9.6 | | 1.0 | 10.9 | 4.2 | 1.1 | 0.9 |
| **Race/ethnicity** | | | | | | | | | | |
| White | 162,526 | 13.6 | 1.6 | 11.2 | | 1.4 | 12.0 | 5.4 | 2.5 | 1.8 |
| Black | 21,957 | 16.4 | 3.6 | 8.1 | | 0.8 | 11.2 | 3.3 | 1.6 | 0.9 |
| Spanish-speaking | 14,144 | 11.0 | 1.7 | 9.7 | | 0.7 | 10.9 | 3.7 | 1.3 | 1.0 |
| Other | 7,180 | 9.9 | 2.1 | 9.5 | | 1.8 | 11.0 | 4.4 | 0.4 | 1.4 |
| **Education** | | | | | | | | | | |
| College graduate | 39,600 | 13.2 | 2.1 | 19.7 | | 4.1 | 19.6 | 10.5 | 4.6 | 6.2 |
| Attended college | 51,083 | 13.0 | 1.6 | 13.1 | | 1.1 | 14.5 | 6.0 | 3.1 | 1.1 |
| High school graduate | 64,414 | 13.8 | 1.8 | 7.3 | | 0.4 | 8.3 | 2.8 | 1.5 | 0.3 |
| Not high school graduate | 36,567 | 15.5 | 1.7 | 4.2 | | 0.3 | 6.3 | 2.1 | 0.2 | 0.0 |
| **Employment** | | | | | | | | | | |
| Full-time | 104,602 | 12.3 | 1.9 | 12.8 | | 1.6 | 13.5 | 6.0 | 3.3 | 2.4 |

| | | | | | | | | | |
|---|---|---|---|---|---|---|---|---|---|
| Part-time | 18,438 | 14.4 | 1.4 | 10.3 | 1.6 | 11.6 | 3.7 | 1.5 | 1.1 |
| Not Employed | 68,622 | 15.9 | 1.8 | 7.9 | 0.8 | 9.5 | 4.2 | 1.0 | 0.7 |
| **Household Income** | | | | | | | | | |
| Under $10,000 | 18,491 | 14.4 | 1.3 | 5.1 | 0.5 | 6.9 | 2.5 | 1.1 | 0.7 |
| $10,000–19,999 | 28,635 | 15.8 | 1.8 | 6.0 | 0.4 | 7.5 | 3.0 | 0.8 | — |
| $20,000–29,999 | 29,109 | 15.9 | 2.4 | 6.3 | 0.5 | 9.5 | 3.8 | 1.3 | 0.2 |
| $30,000–39,999 | 26,273 | 13.7 | 1.4 | 9.7 | 1.0 | 10.7 | 4.9 | 2.3 | 0.8 |
| $40,000–49,999 | 21,774 | 13.1 | 2.0 | 12.2 | 1.1 | 11.9 | 4.4 | 2.9 | 1.2 |
| $50,000–59,999 | 17,867 | 12.7 | 1.8 | 12.0 | 1.2 | 13.6 | 6.8 | 2.8 | 1.8 |
| $60,000–74,999 | 18,628 | 12.8 | 1.3 | 15.6 | 2.0 | 15.9 | 5.9 | 2.8 | 2.0 |
| $75,000 or more | 30,884 | 11.4 | 2.2 | 19.3 | 3.5 | 18.8 | 9.2 | 4.3 | 6.1 |
| Total | 191,663 | 13.8 | 1.8 | 10.8 | 1.3 | 11.9 | 5.1 | 2.3 | 1.7 |

*Note:* "—" indicates data not available. Data for earlier years can be found in previous editions of *Vital Statistics on American Politics.* Early news, late news: the average percentage viewing at least one of these news programs the weeknight before the survey. All percentages are based on 20,079 interviews for their Spring 1996 report. Percentages subject to sampling error; see sources. Total percentages for other categories: viewing CNN in the last seven days, 39.4 (Headline News, 19.9); viewing Court TV in the last seven days, 3.9; subscribes to cable TV, 64.3 (cable available in neighborhood, 91.9): has pay-TV 29.7; has satellite dish, 3.8; listens to (any) radio weekday, 77.9; listens to (any) radio weekend, 60.4; reads any daily newspaper, 53.0; reads any Sunday newspapers, 62.9.
[a]Includes "ABC World News Tonight," "CBS Evening News," and "NBC Nightly News," Monday through Friday.
[b]Includes "ABC News Nightline," Monday through Friday.
*Source:* Table, data, and note from *Vital Statistics on American Politics, 1999–2000,* ed. Harold W. Stanley and Harold Watkins (Washington, DC: CQ Press, 2000), 171–172.

watch CNN during the day to catch updates on breaking stories. In the afternoon, the same person might read a newsmagazine like the *New Republic* or *Newsweek,* or watch a midday news or talk show. More headline news and local or national talk are available on the way home, followed by the national network news and a variety of review and analysis shows peppering the nighttime airwaves, from ABC's *Nightline* to *Politically Incorrect* and *Larry King Live* (see Zip Box 1.1).

The rise of the Internet means that the public has tremendous access to news and information. Individuals and organizations can easily post documents and reports that they have uncovered and reach a worldwide audience in a matter of moments. When a group devoted to uncovering the government's involvement in Gulf War syndrome posted government documents on its website, for example, hundreds of people had a chance to read or download the documents before they were removed. Similarly, when Congress posted Kenneth Starr's report on President Clinton, millions of people were able to download the report and read the charges and findings for themselves—without having to rely on the interpretation of the document offered by media personalities. The number and diversity of news outlets and sources, then, complicates efforts by officials to control what the public learns.

ON THE WEB
www.washingtonpost.com

ON THE WEB
www.CNN.com

ON THE WEB
slate.msn.com

ON THE WEB
www.salon.com

## COMPETING ROLES AND EXPECTATIONS: WHAT DO WE EXPECT FROM THE NEWS MEDIA?

What do we expect of journalists? If the news media are a political institution playing an important role in what and how things happen in government, then what guides and controls their behavior? Competing objectives complicate how the media pursue professional and business goals. The news media try to live up to high professional standards even as they struggle to survive in a competitive marketplace where attracting audiences and advertising revenue are crucial factors in decision making. Critics charge that business dynamics and the high costs of gathering and delivering the news cripple the media's ability to fulfill their role in society and public communication. We will return to the business side of the media's universe, but first we need to ask: What roles do the media play, and what can we expect of journalists?

The news media serve three major functions. First, they watch and report on events and activities in government and society: this is a *surveillance* function. Second, the media do more than just watch: they also *interpret* what happens in the world. Third, certain types of media reporting and investigative journalism serve a *watchdog* function, overseeing activities and rooting out improper behavior and corruption. These functions compete with each other, though, and a realistic understanding of the potential and limitations of the news media recognizes that we can't always have everything we want from the news.[4]

## Surveillance: Can Journalists Just Report the Facts?

At its foundation, the media's surveillance function is to gather, organize, and disseminate information; by doing so, the media facilitate public communication and debate. Should the media, then, "just report the facts"? Many people assume so, without considering how difficult a task this is. What "facts" should be reported? Which get reported first, and which later? Should a television report use video footage? Will the story run as the first segment, or after the first commercial break? Should a newspaper place an article on the front page? Should the story be above the fold, so it shows prominently when displayed in a sales rack? Should a media outlet's homepage display a story or a headline on the first screen, or will the visitor have to follow a link like "National" or "Politics" to get to the story?

All of these questions complicate the notion of just "reporting" the news. It is impossible to report news without making decisions about what to report and how to present the material, and this inevitably opens up some distance between the audience and events. Media expert <u>Austin Ranney</u> puts it this way:

> Every student of human communication knows that it is unavoidably a selective process. No observer can absorb and communicate every fact about any observed situation, and newspaper reporters and television correspondents are no exceptions. Moreover, no newspaper has the space to print everything that its reporters know about all the matters they cover; hence editing (choosing which of the many facts at hand will actually be published in the limited space available and deciding how they will be presented) is at least as essential as reporting for putting out a newspaper. And . . . the "newsholes" in television newscasts are much smaller than their newspaper counterparts, and so the editing process is even more central to the way television presents the news than it is to what newspapers do.[5]

Simply "reporting the facts," without sifting and judging and interpreting, is an unattainable ideal.

## Interpreting Events:
## Can Journalists Provide Us with "The Truth"?

If reporting "just the facts" is complicated by the media's need to make judgments about which facts are most important and how information and meaning should be presented, should we expect the media to find and report those facts that will give the audience "the truth"? Maybe as an ideal, but in reality reporting a single "truth" is virtually impossible. All stories contain the seeds of different interpretations: What caused a given event to happen? What motivated the people involved? What is the significance of the story? What does an expert say, and what does a different expert say?

Think of a debate over Social Security funds. If you ask fifteen expert analysts whether a problem exists with Social Security, what that problem is, and how it should be fixed, you might get fifteen different answers. Even asking those analysts to describe a specific congressional plan for the future of Social Security might result in different interpretations. Journalists can report what those fifteen experts said, but they cannot be expected to uncover and report "truth."

Relying on the media to uncover truth asks too much of the media and not enough of the audience. Walter Lippmann warned that citizens must not rely so heavily on the media that they forfeit their own responsibility to keep informed about their society. He also cautioned citizens not to rely on the media to solve the complicated problems for which we create government institutions. "The press is no substitute for institutions. It is like the beam of a searchlight that moves restlessly about, bringing forth one episode and then another out of darkness into vision. Men cannot do the work of the world by this light alone."[6] It is not the role of the media to find "truth" or simply "to report the facts." The media cannot meet such impossible demands (see BriefCase Box 1.1).

## What Do We Expect from Digging Deep?
## The Watchdog Role and Investigative Journalism

In addition to their surveillance and interpretive roles, the media work to uncover deeper or hidden information that the public needs. The media's role as a watchdog draws strength from Americans' traditional suspicion of government, and from the fact that people lack the time and resources to watch over all aspects of government by themselves. Suspecting that the government or people within the government might be hiding something, investigative journalists can engage public reaction and help foment public outcries leading to new policies or reform of old ones. Because public interest tends to wane after a story breaks, however, and because the general public has difficulty acting as a well-organized and effective political force, investigative reports aimed at triggering change by galvanizing the public have only limited potential. *Investigative reports are much more adept at effecting change when they aim at influencing specific leaders or other powerful elites. Investigative reports can also be effective when they are collaborative efforts between members of the media and officials in government.*[7]

Investigative reporters try to tell exciting stories with mass appeal, and investigative journalism is arguably the most exciting activity undertaken by

## BRIEFCASE BOX 1.1
*News, Analysis, and Editorials*

The news media distribute information in three key ways:

- *Straight news reporting* tries hard to stick to basic facts, giving the audience information essential to understanding a situation while striving for accuracy and objectivity.
- *Analysis* looks for trends, deeper meanings, impacts, and ramifications, and draws events and issues together to give the audience a better understanding of how events related to one another.
- *Editorials* reflect the opinions of particular authors or groups. Editorial content is not bound by the same goals of objectivity that drive news reporting and analysis.

These different ways of distributing information raise thorny issues for news organizations and personalities, particularly as the explosion of cable and Internet news outlets increases the opportunities available to celebrity newspeople and popular analysts. Many journalists are involved in reporting, offering analysis, and delivering editorial comments. As news personalities increasingly serve several different functions for different television and print outlets, keeping these competing roles separate gets tricky. Stuart Taylor, a legal analyst, and Doris Kearns Goodwin, a historian, both ran into difficulties meeting their responsibilities on PBS's esteemed *NewsHour with Jim Lehrer*. Les Crystal, executive producer of the *NewsHour*, outlined the situations on the *NewsHour*'s webpage. Passages from his remarks appear below. What was Taylor's role on the *NewsHour*, and why was the show concerned? Why were they concerned about Goodwin?

Mr. Taylor's sole function [on the *NewsHour*] was as a reporter. He reported on Supreme Court cases, detailing the circumstances and history of cases, describing arguments before the court, pinpointing the highlights of decisions and explaining their significance and potential impact. He never was asked about nor did he offer his opinions about the right or wrong, good or bad of what he was reporting. Ms. Goodwin served as a regular contributor—recounting history and offering her opinions and judgments. . . .

Stuart Taylor, in print and on other networks, and with increasing frequency was offering his opinions about the Paula Jones case, Independent Prosecutor Kenneth Starr's investigation and President Clinton. In private conversations with Mr. Taylor, we expressed our concerns about that, and we mutually agreed that he would not appear on the *NewsHour* in connection with those stories or any Supreme Court story related to the Starr investigations or sexual harassment. . . . Some viewers have accused us of letting Stuart go because he represented a conservative voice. This is absolutely untrue. He never expressed an ideological or political perspective on our program. The issue was not his views, but his role. . . .

Doris Kearns Goodwin, as a frequent contributor to the *NewsHour*, virtually always offers judgments and interpretations. That is and has been her stated role. However, her decision to participate publicly in a political campaign put her in the position of being an active political partisan. We felt this would compromise the credibility of her role, in our eyes and in the eyes of our viewers. When we spoke to Doris she readily agreed and immediately pulled the campaign commercial she had taped. . . . We believe her quick response and apology, and commitment not to cross that line into public partisan political activity negated the situation and any need to end her relationship with the *NewsHour*.*

*Les Crystal, "Editor's Notes," retrieved from the World Wide Web at *http://www.pbs.org/newshour/forum/april 98/editor.html* on July 21, 1999.

journalists. Popularized in movies like *The Insider* and the Watergate thriller *All the President's Men*, and in "hard-hitting" investigative reports on news shows and in newspapers around the country, investigative journalism involves journalists seeking the story behind a story, digging to find hidden motivations and explanations. Yet these are the stories that often inspire the most public wrath: they evoke questions about whether the president's love life is a suitable topic for discussion, whether a news crew should use hidden cameras to investigate grocery store food-handling practices, and whether a candidate's rumored past drug use is relevant to his prospects as a president. It is often only with the passage of time that the impact and relevance of investigative journalism can be judged; before that time arrives, ongoing investigative reports become the targets for public discontent with the standards and practices of today's media.

## What Should We Expect?

When we expect the media to fulfill its surveillance, interpretive, and investigatory functions simultaneously, we risk forgetting that these functions involve competing expectations. We want the media to report facts, for example, but a report investigating deep-seated corruption might not have all the facts yet: an investigatory report might rely on some facts and some informed guesses, prodding more investigation. Matt Drudge certainly didn't have all the facts when he reported the opening salvos that led to President Clinton's impeachment. Yet most people would agree that Drudge's reporting was important, serving the media's watchdog role. If we condemn the media for its zeal in investigating stories and digging deep, then we ignore demands that the media serve as watchdogs of the public interest. And if we expect the media to report "facts" unadulterated by editorial choices, or if we expect the media to uncover "truth," then we expect too much (See Zip Box 1.2).

---

### Zip Box 1.2
*Bias in the Media*

Observers and citizens sometimes worry about biases in the media. There are several types of bias, each with specific effects on the news and reasons why people are concerned about them.

#### TYPE OF BIAS: STRUCTURAL BIAS

**Effect on the News:** Stories and coverage are based on newsworthiness, not necessarily on political or social importance. Newsworthiness bases the choice of stories on the potential impact on the audience, familiar people and issues, conflict or scandal, timeliness and novelty, and proximity to people's homes and lives.

**Reasons for:** Time and space constraints limit depth of coverage and the number of stories that can be covered. Media are businesses, and they must seek to attract and hold audiences. Constraints are imposed by the dynamics of television, newspaper and other industries.

**Competing Dynamics:** Structural bias is well documented and affects the way stories are chosen and reported upon. (See the section "Practical Compromises in the Media" later in this chapter.)

#### TYPE OF BIAS: CONSERVATIVE BIAS

**Effect on the News:** Coverage supports the existing social and economic order, reinforcing acceptance of the status quo. Coverage thereby opposes significant change.

**Reasons for:** Reporters and media companies are part of the establishment; they therefore protect their interest in continuing the system as it is. The status quo is reinforced not only in news, but also in entertainment media like movies and TV shows.

**Competing Dynamics:** To a great extent, conservative bias affects the news in mainstream news outlets. Other organizations, though, rely on challenging the status quo as a means of informing the public and attracting audiences. The diversity of the news media, therefore, makes conservative bias more prevalent in some areas than in others.

TYPE OF BIAS: ADVERSARIAL BIAS

**Effect on the News:** Journalists display a cynical, skeptical attitude toward politics and public officials that establishes the media as a force in opposition, digging for information from a recalcitrant government.

**Reasons for:** Journalists have embraced the energy and importance of the watchdog role.

**Competing Dynamics:** Journalists still need to maintain access to government officials and other leaders. Too much adversarialism risks alienating information contacts as well as viewers.

TYPE OF BIAS: POLITICAL BIAS

**Effect on the News:** Slanted reporting, favoring some parties, people, and issues over others.

**Reasons for:** Journalists' personal attitudes. Surveys find that journalists' attitudes are often more liberal than the general public's attitudes, especially on social issues like abortion and prayer in public schools.

**Competing Dynamics:** There is little evidence to support the conclusion that journalists' personal attitudes consistently bias their reporting; factors tempering personal attitudes include the more conservative views of media ownership and managers; professional norms emphasizing fair and objective reporting; and the fear of alienating viewers with biased coverage.

---

ON THE WEB
www.spj.org

ON THE WEB
www.ijnet.org/code.html

ON THE WEB
csep.iit.edu/codes/media.html

ON THE WEB
www.freedomforum.org

Media organizations often have a code of conduct, ethics, or professional standards that journalists are expected to follow. These provide some guidelines for the expectations audiences should have for journalists and news stories. Although the codes of various organizations differ on specifics, they usually include the goals of *fairness, balance, and impartiality* toward all sides involved in a story; a goal of *accuracy and objectivity* in gathering and reporting information; and a *prohibition against misleading the audience,* including clearly labeling opinion-based reports and promptly acknowledging and correcting errors.[8] These standards, rather than "just the facts" or finding "truth," are the objectives for which most reputable journalists and news organizations strive.

## THE DEMANDS OF A COMPETITIVE MARKETPLACE: QUALITY NEWS VERSUS GOOD PROFITS?

The news media operate in a competitive marketplace that exerts considerable influence over the news. The best journalistic goals and objectives compete with the realities of that marketplace in ways that affect what we see and hear through the media. It is naive to think that this is somehow wrong, or that it can be avoided. What we need to consider is how business dynamics influence the media's ability to serve as a link between people and government.

The most sinister threat facing professional journalists in today's media marketplace is corporate control of news content. Many critics fear that corporate dynamics directly influence the content and quality of media investigations and coverage of important issues. ABC News and *60 Minutes,* for example, might have altered their coverage of stories critical of tobacco companies' practices when pressured by corporate interests, as we saw at the beginning of this chapter.

Corporate influence, though, is more likely to have less obvious effects. Fear of expensive lawsuits, for example, can make the media more timid—less willing to spend freely for long-term investigations, less willing to air contentious material, and less willing to take on giant corporations that can fight back through long and costly litigation. The decision by *60 Minutes,* one of the most respected and best-supported news shows on television, set a bad example for other media outlets that already lack the power and influence of CBS's flagship investigative program.

## Consolidation and Cost Cutting

In recent years, mergers and acquisitions of media and news outlets by giant multinational corporations have raised fears that the news may soon be in the hands of a few wealthy and powerful companies. While news outlets seem to be multiplying—more magazines tailored to specific audiences, more cable channels, new Internet services that bring personally tailored news to individuals' desktops—some observers worry that all of this apparent fragmentation masks the fact that fewer and fewer interests own and control them. In January 2000, for example, America Online (AOL) and Time Warner announced that they would be merging their operations. AOL trumpeted its new access to Time Warner's information, film collections, and news information, and to its cable and other information delivery systems; Time Warner celebrated its new access to cutting-edge Internet technology and to AOL's twenty-two million subscribers.

At the same time as corporations are merging, existing news outlets are combining their resources in an effort to be competitive. News gathering and the presentation of the news are both affected. In late 1999, the Washington Post Company and NBC News announced an alliance in which they would share news stories, create joint websites involving Post's *Newsweek* magazine and MSNBC.com, and coordinate efforts on network and local television to promote the work of Post and *Newsweek* journalists. Just a few weeks later, ABC, CBS, and Fox News announced that they and their affiliates would formally share video footage from breaking news stories. These three rivals, then, can all benefit from situations in which only one of them has a reporter or camera crew in the vicinity of a story; further, even if there are overlapping news crews, the networks can decide to use whichever crew is giving the best footage. CBS News president Andrew Heyward remarked, "I don't think we would have done it five years ago. It is based on a growing realization of how the business is changing." Analyst Jim Rutenberg concludes, "[A]t its heart, the agreement represents an admission by two of the Big Three networks that they are no longer so much in the news gathering business as in the news analysis and packaging business."[9]

Consolidation in the news-gathering business affects the news that gets gathered. Increasingly, news organizations don't uncover their own news—they rely on commercial firms and wire services like the Associated Press (AP) or Reuters for basic information. Large companies have reduced the size of

ON THE WEB
www.msnbc.com

ON THE WEB
www.newsweek.com

ON THE WEB
www.wire.ap.org

ON THE WEB
www.reuters.com

foreign news offices and severely cut budgets for on-the-ground news gathering. Often, research staff and the lowest rung of journalists, like beat reporters (who cover such things as the daily operations of the police or city government), are the first to be "downsized" as a company cuts costs and puts relatively more money into technology and high-priced on-air talent.

The result is a dwindling number of ground-level sources for new and investigative news. Radio news, in particular, has proven to be very profitable in recent years because most stations purchase coverage and reporting from syndicated services like Metro Networks and Shadow Broadcasting Services; relatively few employ reporters and cover news firsthand. This means that many radio stations offer the same content, and audiences have fewer options for coverage. One expert estimates that only about fifteen of approximately ten thousand commercial radio stations in the United States are all-news stations employing "substantial" news staffs to report firsthand on community affairs; thirteen of these fifteen are owned by CBS.[10]

These trends are likely to exacerbate the problem of "pack journalism," in which different media outlets follow the same stories and cover them in the same ways. In part, pack journalism results from the fact that media at different levels are groups of professionals who work closely together in the same business. A certain amount of like-mindedness is to be expected among the White House press corps, for example, or among reporters covering the Supreme Court. A desire for the respect of one's peers, together with a fear of being on the outside, helps keep everyone operating in roughly the same direction. Critics have long worried that pack journalism diminishes the quantity and diversity of news available to the public; consolidating media ownership poses similar risks (see Discussion Box 1.3 and Zip Box 1.3).[11]

## Hazards for the News

As the effort to contain costs forces some organizations to compromise their standards for news gathering, the news media are increasingly vulnerable to prepackaged news and questionable sources. As we saw earlier, government and private interests seize opportunities created by the high costs facing media organizations. As political actors and organizations become more savvy about the news business, and as media outlets cut back on resources committed to news gathering, the news is increasingly "gathered" and delivered to the media's doorsteps by the very groups who are the subject of news reports. These sources tailor information and shape its presentation to support their own point of view, and thereby take advantage of some media outlets' willingness to have the work done (and paid for) by someone else.

Increasingly, television and other media outlets report stories when a competitor has reported them, in an effort to stay competitive and avoid getting scooped. In these cases, the supporting evidence backing up the story might be merely the phrase, "The *New York Times* tonight is reporting. . . ." Mainstream news outlets with established reputations for journalistic integrity sometimes pick up stories from a tabloid source and report that *tabloids* are covering a particular story. This gives the mainstream outlet an opportunity to

Most observers believe that progress in telecommunications and Internet technology will advance, rather than retard, the amount and diversity of information available to the public—despite such media megamergers as Time-CNN-AOL and ABC/Disney. In the passages below, however, <u>Benjamin R. Barber</u> argues that the current compromise between more channels and fewer owners might not be good enough. How are the effects of technology and ownership different? What is the risk of consolidated ownership? Are you worried? Why, or why not?

[T]echnology is clearly capable of exerting a pluralizing influence on communications. Yet though the technology may be inherently disaggregating and devolutionary, ownership over the technology's hardware and software is aggregating and centralizing. As delivery systems diversify and multiply, program content becomes more homogeneous. . . .

The idea is to gather together the production companies turning out product, the phone and cable and satellite companies transmitting them, and the television sets and computers and multiplexes presenting them to the public all into the same hands. Synergy, however, turns out to be a polite way of saying monopoly. And in the domain of information, monopoly is a polite word for uniformity, which is a polite word for virtual censorship—censorship not as a consequence of political choices but as a consequence of inelastic markets, imperfect competition, and economies of scale. . . .

Conglomeration had reduced the number of mainstage telecommunications players from forty-six in 1981 to twenty-three in 1991. And of these, a handful like Time Warner/Turner, Disney/ABC, Bertelsmann, and Murdoch's News Corporation dominate—genuinely intermedia corporations with a finger in every part of the business. So that, for example, when Rupert Murdoch wanted to accommodate the Chinese on the way to persuading them to permit his Asian Television Network to broadcast, he was able to instruct HarperCollins (a News Corporation subsidiary) to withdraw its offer to Harry Wu—a dissident thorn in the side of the Chinese—for his political memoirs.*

Benjamin R. Barber, "The New Telecommunications Technology: Endless Frontier or the End of Democracy?" in *A Communications Cornucopia*, ed. Roger G. Noll and Monroe E. Price (Washington, DC: Brookings Institution Press, 1998), 78–80.

## *Zip Box 1.3*
### *Media Ownership in the United States*

Many citizens don't realize the connections in ownership among many of our most familiar companies, products, and media outlets. This list is adapted from a feature on the website of the *Columbia Journalism Review* called "Who Owns What,"* For an up-to-date listing and a search feature, go to the *CJR*'s website at *www.cjr.org*.

### BERTELSMANN

Bantam Doubleday Dell
Literary Guild
Doubleday Book Club, Science Fiction Book Club
Random House, Knopf, Fodors
*Family Circle* magazine, *McCall's*
AOL Germany (45%), AOL France (50%)
BMG Music Service, RCA, Arista, RCA Victor, Windam Hill Group

### CABLEVISION

Cablevision Cable System
Regional phone services
With NBC Cable: American Movie Classics, Bravo, Independent Film Channel, News 12 (NY, NJ, CT regional news), Romance Classics
Parts of regional Fox Sports networks
Parts of MSG Network, the New York Knicks, the New York Rangers, the New York Liberty
Radio City Music Hall
Nobody Beats the Wiz stores

## DISNEY

Hyperion Books
Miramax Books
Discover, ESPN Magazine, Family PC
ABC television network, Disney Channel, ESPN Inc. (80%), A&E (37.5%), History Channel, Lifetime (50%), E! Entertainment Television Inc. (34.42%)
Touchstone Pictures, Miramax Films, Buena Vista International
Mr. Showbiz, NFL.com, NBA.com, NASCAR.com, GO Network
Mighty Ducks of Anaheim, Anaheim Angels (25% general partner ownership)
Disneyland, Disney-MGM Studios, Epcot, Disney Cruise Line

## NEWS CORPORATION

HarperCollins Publishers
Fox Broadcasting, Fox Sports, Fox Kids, MSG Network, Golf Channel (33%), Fox News Channel, British Sky Broadcasting (40%)
*TV Guide, The Weekly Standard*
Twentieth Century Fox
*New York Post*
Los Angeles Dodgers

## SEAGRAM

Absolut, Captain Morgan, Chivas Regal, Crown Royal
Tropicana Beverage Group (Dole, Tropicana)
Universal Studios, October Films, USA Networks (45%)
MCA Records, Decca, Interscope, Geffen, Hip-O, A&M, Island, London, Mercury, Motown, Phillips Classics, Polydor, Verve
Cineplex Odeon Corporation (42%)

## TIME WARNER

Time Life Books, Book of the Month Club, Paperback Book Club, History Book Club, Little, Brown and Company
Time Warner Cable, HBO, Cinemax, CNN, Court TV, TBS, TNT, Cartoon Network, Turner Classic Movies
Warner Bros., Castle Rock Entertainment
*Time* magazine, *Fortune, Life, Sports Illustrated, Money, People, Entertainment Weekly, InStyle, DC Comics*
Atlantic Group (recording labels), Rhino, Elektra, Reprise
Columbia House direct marketing (with Sony)
New Line Cinema
Atlanta Braves, Atlanta Hawks, World Championship Wrestling (WCW), Good Will Games
Plans to merge with America Online, Inc. (AOL)

## VIACOM

UPN, MTV, Nickelodeon, VH1, Comedy Central, Showtime, Sundance Channel (joint venture with Robert Redford and PolyGram), The Movie Channel
Paramount Pictures, Spelling Films/Television
Blockbuster Video and Music
Paramount Kings Dominion, other theme parks
Star Trek franchise
Free Press, Simon & Schuster Books, Pocket Books, Scribner's, Washington Square Press, Paramount Theaters

*"Who Owns What," *Columbia Journalism Review,* available at *http://www.cjr.org/owners/,* retrieved June 10, 2000. Listings reflect full or partial ownership, and do not include all holdings. International holdings and local or regional holdings, in particular, are not reflected. For a complete, searchable listing, visit the *CJR* website.

cover an unverified but potentially explosive story without taking responsibility for the story's accuracy. *Piggybacked* stories become particularly dangerous when the initial investigation was not thorough or if the information was not reliable.

As news-gathering abilities dwindle, there is increasing overlap and complementary "synergy" in what outlets offer as news. Time Warner, CNN, and *Sports Illustrated*, for example, have combined efforts and are closely connected both on cable television and on the Internet, where links allow Web surfers to jump easily from CNN's news reporting to *SI*'s sports coverage. When Warner released the movie *Twister, Time* ran a cover story on tornadoes; when Fox tel-

**ON THE WEB**

www.cnnsi.com

evision tried to tap into ABC's success with "Who Wants to Be a Millionaire?", local news affiliates ran stories on how people could get on Fox's competing show, "Greed"; NBC affiliates sometimes investigate topics raised on medical shows like "ER," cross-promoting both news and entertainment programming. Such examples of "synergy" can come dangerously close to manipulation of news divisions to sell another part of a company's products.

*Media collaborations,* wherein several news organizations combine resources in an effort to expand audiences and take advantage of each other's prestige or market share, also pose certain risks. *Time* magazine, for example, ran into problems when it collaborated with CNN on the Operation Tailwind investigation: *Time*'s apparent failure to verify CNN's research and reporting involved it in controversy (see BriefCase Box 1.2).

---

## BriefCase Box 1.2
*I Trusted You!: Operation Tailwind and the Risks of Media Collaborations*

In an effort to meet a deadline for launching an ambitious new collaboration between CNN and *Time* magazine, CNN's *NewsStand* rushed to air a story alleging that American military forces had dropped the nerve gas sarin onto an enemy village base camp in a secret mission into Laos during the Vietnam War. Such action would have been considered a war crime under international law. A companion essay ran in *Time,* co-authored by the segment's producer and its lead anchor, war correspondent Peter Arnett. Charges quickly surfaced that the story was untrue, and controversy erupted over the extent to which CNN's evidence supported the story's allegations. A review conducted by CNN's attorney and an outside counsel found that while the story's producers did not fabricate material, their presentation of the story was unfair; the review called for a retraction of the Tailwind story and an apology by CNN. The producers stood by the story, however, and in a detailed rebuttal defended their reporting. The controversy over the Tailwind story illustrates several lessons about the modern media, regardless of the story's ultimate veracity.

- First, the producers' defense argues that the time restrictions imposed on TV reporting precluded them from broadcasting evidence backing up their claims, suggesting the ways in which the practical constraints of specific media can hinder thorough reporting.

- Second, and more importantly, business dynamics affected the research and reporting of the story. The *Columbia Journalism Review* argued that "the lust for ratings" was crucial: "Avid for a blockbuster *NewsStand* premiere, CNN became blind to the report's fatal flaws."* For their part, *Time* apparently did virtually no fact-checking of CNN's story, thereby lending (and risking) its reputation to the research of another organization.

- Finally, anchor Peter Arnett distanced himself from the story's content by arguing that he was hired primarily as a front man who conducted little substantial research for the story. This position, though, raises questions about the role of media personalities as journalists. Arnett claimed, in effect, that he lent his reputation and credibility as a war corespondent to CNN as a marketing tool.†

---

*Neil Hickey, "Ten Mistakes That Lead to the Great Fiasco," *Columbia Journalism Review* (September/October 1998): 62.
†For a review of this case, see Neil Hickey, "Ten Mistakes That Lead to the Great Fiasco," in *Columbia Journalism Review* (September/October 1998). See also Floyd Abrams and David Kohler, "Report on CNN Broadcast 'Valley of Death,'" *The Harvard International Journal of Press/Politics* 4, no. 1 (Winter 1999); Jack Smith and April Oliver, "Rebuttal to the Abrams/Kohler Report," *The Harvard International Journal of Press/Politics* 4, no. 1 (Winter 1999).

The media business is extremely competitive, illustrated by CBS News's controversial decision to superimpose a digitally-created CBS logo on background buildings during its live coverage of New Year's Eve festivities in New York City's Times Square, December 31, 1999. Critics argued that the move sacrificed journalistic integrity to the interests of advertising.

The jury is still out on the future of the news media in America. Diversity seems to increase with more available channels and as more people gain access to the Internet, giving people greater access to information on politics and public affairs, while corporate mergers and consolidated ownership simultaneously threaten to narrow news gathering and homogenize news content.

## *PRACTICAL COMPROMISES IN THE MEDIA: PROFITS AND PROFESSIONALISM*

The *60 Minutes* tobacco story, which we discussed at the start of this chapter, is a rare example of a major national story being significantly affected by corporate influence and pressure. More regularly, news organizations and journalists make the best compromises they can between the demand for the highest professional standards and the demands of the marketplace. It is too easy to dismiss the media as a cabal of self-interested, greedy corporations willing

**Ways CBS Will Be Different Now That It's Owned By Westinghouse**

10. Andy Rooney is now dishwasher safe.

9. My first question for each guest will be, "So, tell me about your appliances?"

8. CBS executive replaced by whole new batch of weasels.

7. CBS News to add a spin cycle.

6. Thanks to advanced refrigerator technology, Ed Sullivan Theater will dip down to 4 below zero.

5. Late Show replaced by hour-long shot of a washing machine.

4. 60 Minutes doing a lot more investigation of that Maytag outfit.

3. I get to use slightly-rewritten G.E. jokes from the late 80's.

2. Dan Rather's new co-anchor: a coffee pot.

1. Five words: "Dr. Quinn, Refrigerator Repair Woman."

Source: Reprinted by permission of CBS Worldwide, Inc.

to push journalists around to maximize profits. Much of what we see on television and read in the papers is the result of practical compromises in news gathering and presentation that are intended to accommodate the competing professional and business imperatives surrounding media activities. The news we see and hear is generally the result of the media's efforts to choose and present stories that will attract large audiences while simultaneously upholding journalistic standards.

## *Attracting Audiences*

### Choosing the News: Newsworthiness

Professionals in the news business make choices about what gets reported based on a story's "newsworthiness." Judgments about newsworthiness are, at heart, compromises between informing the public about important events and ensuring that a news program or newspaper maximizes its audience and its revenue. First and foremost, a newsworthy story must have *conflict*, especially violence or scandal, because these dynamics make a story dramatic. A story must also have *impacts that hit close to home,* and the information must be *timely or novel:* it must be news, after all. The story should also contain *situations and personalities familiar to the audience.* Media expert <u>Doris Graber</u> writes, "News is attractive if it pertains to well-known people or involves familiar situations of concern to many. This is why newspeople try to cast unfamiliar situations, like mass famines in Africa, into more familiar stories of individual babies dying from malnutrition."[12] Stories that do not meet these criteria usually do not make it into the news (see BriefCase Box 1.3).

### Presenting the News I: Personalization

Newsworthy stories are generally presented in particular ways. To make an issue more compelling, for example, journalists focus on individuals. "Personalized news," according to media scholar <u>W. Lance Bennett</u>, is "the journalistic bias that gives preference to the individual actors and human-interest angles in events while downplaying institutional and political considerations that establish the social contexts for those events."[13] For example, a story on the complexity of welfare rules might tell the story of a person who failed to collect benefits because of a bureaucratic maze in the welfare office. Stories on certain policies personalize aspects of the debate by identifying positions with key participants. A debate over changes in welfare policy, for example, might be presented as a battle between one senator who wants reform and another senator who opposes change. Likewise, coverage of a major presidential speech might focus more on the perceived impact of the speech on the president's personal and political fortunes, and less on the actual content of the speech.

Personalizing the news can make stories more accessible and entertaining for the audience, but the merits of different policies get lost in the glare of attention on personalities. Passage and defeat of bills become stories about the political successes and failures of particular politicians. Bennett writes that personalized news "encourages people to take an egocentric rather than a socially concerned view of political problems," and that a focus on personalities encourages "a passive attitude among a public inclined to let those personalities do their thinking and acting for them."[14]

### Presenting the News II: Polarization

Media outlets also tend to polarize issues, presenting two clear and distinct "sides." This technique draws clear distinctions in subjects under debate, and it makes for entertaining reporting. Polarization provides a clear model for journalists conveying a story: present Side A, find a quotation from an expert supporting Side A; present Side B, find a quotation from an expert supporting Side B; compare and contrast. Guests on discussion shows are often chosen because they have sharply contrasting viewpoints that match Side A and Side B, and they can be counted upon to express viewpoints quickly, clearly, and in a manner easily understood by the audience.

Polarizing stories can be misleading if there are more than two sides to an issue, as there often are. Third and fourth options might be ignored, and polarization encourages journalists to highlight stark contrasts and downplay gray areas. This oversimplifies many of the complex issues that arise in public

Journalists and editors choose stories based on newsworthiness, which is why some stories make it into the news and others don't. School shootings and the process of crafting gun control legislation provide a good contrast. School shootings are tailor-made for the news, whereas the latter is often reported only when major new gun control measures go into effect—the nuts and bolts of policymaking are virtually invisible. Consider the discussion in the text about the drawbacks of media coverage driven by newsworthiness. In the comparison below, what will audiences learn from media coverage? Does this seem like an adequate approach to covering public affairs? How does it relate to Lippmann's warning about relying too much on the media for information about public affairs?

| School Shootings | | Gun Control Legislation* |
| --- | --- | --- |
| High drama, violence, conflict<br>Recognizable villains<br>Sympathetic victims | **Conflict** | Complex issues, many participants<br>Difficult to define basic issues<br>Decades of complex laws and regulations<br>Even experts have trouble agreeing on or describing the issues involved |
| Everybody went to school, goes to school, has kids or friends in school, or has a school in the neighborhood | **Impacts on Audience** | Most people affected only indirectly<br>Gun control generally has low salience with the public, unless there's a current crisis |
| Every new shooting is a new crisis<br>Even copycat shootings are immediate<br>Every new school shooting has a new twist: Different weapons, more planning, different victims | **Timeliness** | Violence and related issues have always been with us<br>Problem will not be solved overnight<br>Gun control is not necessarily the most important avenue for addressing crime and crime-related issues |
| Schools are familiar; everyone knows what libraries, gyms, and lunchrooms are<br>A string of shootings has made basic issues familiar<br>It's politically safe to condemn school shootings, so familiar officials can be reached for comment easily | **Familiarity** | Specific weapons and their features are unfamiliar<br>Details of specific legislative proposals are unfamiliar<br>Though public opinion seems to support gun control, the results of polling data are complicated by the variety of remedies and their effects<br>Experts and familiar public officials are reluctant to comment on detailed and politically troublesome legislation |

*On public opinion, crises, and gun control politics, see Gary Kleck, *Point Blank: Guns and Violence in America* (New York: Aldine de Gruyter, 1991); David R. Harding, Jr., "Public Opinion and Gun Control: Appearance and Transparence in Support and Opposition," Samuel L. Patterson and Keith R. Eakins, "Congress and Gun Control," and Marcia L. Godwin and Jean Reith Schroedel, "Gun Control Politics in California," in *The Changing Politics of Gun Control*, ed. John M. Bruce and Clyde Wilcox (Lanham, Md: Rowman & Littlefield, 1998). On reporters' mistakes and the complexity of gun issues, see, for example, Scott Baltic, "Bang! Bang! You're Wrong! How the Hip-Shooting Press Reports on Guns," *Columbia Journalism Review* (January/February 1994).

Three current issues in journalism present journalists and media organizations with dilemmas as they try to stay a step ahead of the competition and gather timely and relevant information.

- *Leaks:* A leak occurs when a source in government or in any position with access to secret or hard-to-obtain information gives that information to a journalist with the agreement that the source will not be identified. *Risks:* Leaks usually promote the source's own self-interest somehow; the source might have obtained the information illegally or be legally prohibited from sharing it.
- *Anonymous Sources:* A prevailing trend is journalists' willingness to attribute information to an unidentified source, such as "a high-ranking official" or "a top official in the Gore administration." *Risks:* It is easy for journalists to fabricate information and attribute it to an anonymous source; journalists might search for on-the-record sources less aggressively. Further, anonymity makes it difficult for the public to decide, independently of the news organization, how much weight and credibility to give to crucial information; the journalist has assumed responsibility for the information's reliability, and laid her or his own vulnerable credibility on the line.
- *Checkbook Journalism:* Paying for information or interviews. *Risks:* Money can encourage sources to embellish or fabricate information in order to secure a deal or increase the payment. Paying is seductively easy for media organizations, and investigations might become less aggressive and thorough. The practice also sets bad precedents for future news gathering, either by establishing a practice of pay-for-information or promoting the withholding of information in the absence of payment.

Why would journalists and media organizations be tempted to use information that was leaked? Why would they pay for information, or attribute information to anonymous sources? Do you think these practices are dangerous, and how would you combat them in a competitive media marketplace?

Personalization, polarization, and conflict: all three are provided by the husband-and-wife team of Democratic strategist James Carville and Republican strategist Mary Matalin.

policy debates. Another problem with polarization is that presenting two sides can make both appear equally weighty or attractive. In situations where clear consensus exists on an issue, presenting two sides can create a debate when there really isn't much disagreement, or lend credence to opinions that might have very little support or merit.

### Presenting the News III: Dramatization, Crisis Reporting, and the Absence of History

We noted above that conflict is an essential element of newsworthiness. Conflict provides drama, and drama makes stories compelling. Polarization adds drama by focusing the conflict into two sides, and personalization provides the heart of any good drama: interesting characters.

Crisis, too, enhances drama, and the media often report news in crisis terms. In large part, this is driven by the need to find and hold an audience. The media present issues as new or pivotally important, when the issues might simply be continuations of other events or very similar to past events now forgotten by most of the audience. Crisis reporting emphasizes the drama surrounding an issue, and not the issue's substance or merits. Television is particularly well suited to crisis news and dramatic video footage.

Viewing events as crises tends to ignore the long-term roots of important social, political, and economic issues, as well as the long-term commitment and hard work necessary to address an issue adequately. An addiction to crisis coverage also discourages the media from following up on stories, because they are quickly off to cover the next new crisis. Finally, crisis reporting obscures and overlooks the everyday nuts and bolts of government operations. Crisis reporting is especially uninterested in the mundane, day-to-day details of public affairs. Bennett writes, "With actors at their center, news dramas emphasize crisis over continuity, the present over the past or future, and the impact of scandals on personal political careers rather than on the institutions of government that harbored them. Lost in the news drama . . . are the persistent problems of our time, such as inequality, hunger, resource waste, staggering levels of military spending, and political oppression."[15] Bennett argues that the combination of personalized and dramatized news produces stories that are fragmented, preventing audiences from understanding the big picture. "[T]he news comes to us in sketchy dramatic capsules that make it difficult to see the connections across issues or even to follow the development of a particular issue over time."[16] (See Scholar Box 1.2.)

## *IS THE CURRENT COMPROMISE GOOD ENOUGH? THE DEBATE OVER PUBLIC JOURNALISM*

The demand for newsworthiness and the media's tendency to personalize, polarize, and dramatize news have serious implications. Observers argue that current media dynamics alienate citizens from a public sphere presented as conflict-ridden and ineffective. Media scholars Kathleen Hall Jamieson and Joseph N. Cappella, for example, find that media coverage during Clinton's first term narrowed the debate over health care reform to

The media's sporadic attention to hot issues limits its attention to the deeper causes and ongoing resolution of complex issues. Political scientist Anthony Downs outlined what he called the "issue-attention cycle" in an article focusing on the public's attention to environmental issues.* Downs's analysis, summarized below, is an important way of understanding how the public gets interested in an issue, and why it loses interest. What recent issues have gone through the cycle? What current issues might be able to escape the cycle? How do the dynamics of newsworthiness contribute to the issue-attention cycle?

**The Pre-Problem Stage:** This stage exists when some "highly undesirable social condition" exists, but the public attention has yet to be captured. Downs notes that the problem is usually much worse in this period than it is by the time the public becomes interested.

**Alarmed Discovery and Euphoric Enthusiasm:** Some dramatic event or series of events grips public attention, and focuses efforts to "solve this problem" or "do something effective" about it. Downs notes two important aspects of this stage: First, it reflects "the great American tradition of optimistically viewing most obstacles to social progress as *external* to the structure of society itself." Second, "The implication is that every obstacle can be eliminated and every problem solved *without any fundamental reordering of society itself,* if only we devote sufficient effort to it."

**Realizing the Cost of Significant Progress:** The public comes to realize that "solving" the problem will have a high cost and might even demand that benefits enjoyed by millions be sacrificed. "For example, traffic congestion and a great deal of smog are caused by increasing automobile usage. Yet this also enhances the mobility of millions of Americans who continue to purchase more vehicles to obtain these advantages."

**Gradual Decline of Public Interest:** As realization of the costs and difficulty of "solving" the problem dawns, some people get discouraged, others feel threatened by thinking about the problem and suppress consideration of it, and still others just get bored. "Consequently, public desire to keep attention focused on the issue wanes." At the same time, some other issue has hit Stage 2—and begun to attract the public's attention.

**The Post-Problem Stage:** The issue moves into "a prolonged limbo"; it recurs sometimes, but attention is dimmer than it was. Institutions and programs designed to address the problem when it was in the spotlight continue.

Not all issues go through the issue-attention cycle. Those that do often exhibit three main characteristics:

1. "[T]he majority of persons in society are not suffering from the problem nearly so much as some [numerical] minority."
2. "The sufferings caused by the problem are generated by social arrangements that provide significant benefits to a majority or a powerful minority of the population."
3. "[T]he problem has no intrinsically exciting qualities—or no longer has them."

*Quotations from Anthony Downs are from his "Up and Down with Ecology—the 'Issue-Attention Cycle,' " in *The Public Interest* 28 (Summer 1972); 38–50.

two conflicting proposals, limiting consideration of alternatives and attention to common ground. They also find that roughly two-thirds of print and broadcast coverage of health care reform focused on strategy or legislative process, rather than on the issues involved. The authors conclude, "The same basic tendencies could be found in reports about reform of Medicare in 1994–1995 and the deliberations about the budget in 1997. These structures of reporting activate public cynicism and depress learning about important issues. Press behaviors are making public deliberation more difficult at a time when the problems facing the country are increasingly complex."[17]

Media compromises between informing the public, containing costs, and attracting audiences do not always sit well with the public. Compromise, by nature, creates less-than-ideal practical solutions—but compromise often holds the promise of better results in the future. The "public journalism" movement addresses some of the tendencies that have turned people against the press, specifically the charge that the media have abdicated responsibility for the effects of their actions. Public journalism aims to satisfy the competing demands made on news organizations by audiences, professional standards, and the requirements of the marketplace. The movement has attracted some notable supporters, like James Fallows and David S. Broder, yet it has also attracted some sharp criticism.

Public journalism's founder, New York University's Jay Rosen, rejects the notion that journalists are merely observers without a stake in what they report. Rosen suggests instead that journalists share with the public a vested interest in the outcome of the democratic process:

> Journalists . . . would do well to assume that their own fortunes depend on the fate of America's civic culture. The way to secure a vital future for the press is to strengthen, in any practical way that can be found, all the forces that pull people into civic affairs, engage them in the give-and-take of political dialogue, make participants out of spectators, and illuminate the promise of public life. . . . Without relinquishing their stance as observers and critics, [journalists] can try to nourish a particular understanding of American society: not an audience of savvy spectators nor a class of information-rich consumers, but a nation of citizens with common problems, an inventive spirit, and a rich participatory tradition.[18]

In short, Rosen argues that because the press is such an important player in politics, and because it is by necessity "involved," the right question to ask is not whether or not the press should be involved or detached, but what the proper nature of its involvement should be.[19]

By the mid 1990s, public journalism involved hundreds of newspapers and broadcast outlets. The movement's signature project involved a group of newspapers in North Carolina that worked together in an effort to identify issues of concern to the public during the 1996 election campaign. The newspapers' editors conducted public opinion polls and interviews with citizens, and then drew up questionnaires for candidates that focused on issues they believed citizens wanted their candidates to address. The papers then coordinated a series of in-depth interviews with candidates running for office in the state and ran the candidates' answers along with development of their positions in regular Sunday articles.

The public journalism movement illustrates the constant and shifting compromises the media make in serving as a link between the public and government. Participants in the public journalism movement, in effect, seek to attract audiences by giving the public what they believe the public wants; simultaneously, public journalism tries to improve the nature and amount of information

On the Web
www.pewcenter.org/
index.php3

On the Web
www.markovits.com/
journalism/

On the Web
www.annenberg.nwu.
edu/pubs/tabloids/
tabloids08.htm

available and useful to the public. Conceivably, success in this effort helps the newspaper increase advertising revenue as readership increases. Public journalism, then, seeks to forge compromises between audience desires, corporate necessities, and journalistic standards in an effort to satisfy all of the competing forces surrounding the media.

Critics of public journalism, however, argue that public journalism is an *unacceptable* compromise. They ask whether the media are right to become so actively involved in setting the agenda for discussion during a campaign. At least one North Carolina candidate argued that he did not want to discuss a particular issue during the early part of his campaign, and that his strategy involved addressing the issue later. Under pressure from the newspapers, the candidate ultimately decided to respond to the paper's questions sooner than he had planned. Critics complained that by developing an issue agenda to guide coverage of the campaign, and then demanding that candidates respond to these specific issues, the media usurped the candidates' right to direct their own campaigns as they saw fit. The journalist plays "Election God," according to Michael Kelly, when he or she advances the notion "that a self-selected group of reporters and editors somehow could or should determine the fit subjects for debate in an election."[20]

Other critics attacked the concept of a newspaper's coverage being driven by polling results, the underlying basis for the North Carolina papers' decisions about which issues interested their readers. The engine of polling might lead candidates away from developing new issues or from controversial ones, choosing instead to stay with the issues and ideas that arise regularly in polls. Observers noted the economic benefit to be had by newspapers styling their coverage to polling results in an effort to increase readership and revenue.[21] Finally, critics asked, did coordination among the newspapers, which included running the same stories based on the same interviews in the participating papers, sacrifice diversity and the different issues and viewpoints that might have been brought to the public's attention had the papers' coverage remained more independent? In short, did such extensive coordination homogenize the process, boring voters and narrowing discussion?

## Conclusion

Public journalism and other efforts to keep the media vibrant and responsive to public demands, while providing accurate and useful information, will always need to navigate among the competing demands of the economic marketplace. But even though profits and professionalism compete, that does not mean that they are mutually exclusive. Media attorneys interviewed for a study about the *60 Minutes* tobacco controversy, for example, believe that their responsibilities "include enhancing the journalistic process by working to get broadcast stories on the air"—not by working to keep stories under wraps in order to protect the corporation.[22]

Choices about what stories to run and how to report them are based on compromises between the professional and economic demands that face journalists and media organizations. As we move through this text, we will see how newsworthiness, personalization, polarization, and crisis reporting affect what we know and learn about American politics. Yet, as we will also see, the ability of the news media to set agendas, influence voters, and affect policies is often surprisingly limited. The point to remember is how the dynamics of competition and compromise affect what we see and hear in the news. Far from being merely observers, the media are involved in a competitive marketplace that demands compromises among costs, revenues, and journalistic standards. And far from being independent and outside of politics, the media are the battleground for numerous groups and individuals trying to influence what the public learns about government.

## Overnight Assignment

Watch a television news story or read a news story in the newspaper. Does the presentation of the story fit any of the characteristics discussed in this chapter? Does the story fit the media's surveillance, interpretive, or watchdog role, or a combination? Do you detect any biases in the story, as discussed in Zip Box 1.2 on pages 15 and 16? Is the story "newsworthy"? Why? Is the story personalized, polarized, or dramatized? How?

Get the same story from two or three different media outlets, and compare and contrast the information delivered. How was the story presented in each, and what elements of the presentation were the same or different? Did you get a different interpretation of the story from different outlets? Did you believe one outlet more than another?

## Long-Term Integrated Assignment

Choose a newspaper, television station, or newsmagazine, and find out more about it. Who owns it? What other news-related organizations does it own? What audience does it serve, and how large is that audience? Does it have direct connections to other types of media, like television, radio, print, or the Internet?

As you move through this book, you will be asked how your media subject covers specific issues and groups, and how it covers public officials and parts of the government. Make sure you pick a newspaper or other source of information that will have an ongoing relationship with national politics.

## Researching the Media?

### Try These Authors:

W. Lance Bennett          Timothy E. Cook          Michael Robinson
David S. Broder           Walter Lippmann

### Try These Sources:

*Columbia Journalism Review*
Davis, Richard. *The Press and American Politics: The New Mediator.* 2nd ed. Upper Saddle River, NJ: Prentice Hall, 1996.

EPSTEIN, EDWARD J. *Between Fact and Fiction: The Problems of Journalism.* New York: Vintage, 1975.

FALLOWS, JAMES. *Breaking the News: How the Media Undermine American Democracy.* New York: Pantheon, 1996.

GRABER, DORIS A. *Mass Media and American Politics.* 4th ed. Washington, DC: CQ Press, 1993.

GRABER, DORIS, DENIS MCQUAIL, and PIPPA NORRIS, eds. *The Politics of News/The News of Politics,* Washington, DC: CQ Press, 1998.

HACHTEN, WILLIAM A. *The Troubles of Journalism: A Critical Look at What's Right and What's Wrong with the Press.* Mahwah, NJ: Erlbaum, 1998.

*Harvard International Journal of Press/Politics*

KURTZ, HOWARD. *Media Circus: The Trouble with America's Newspapers.* New York: Times Books, 1993.

*Media Studies Journal*

SABATO, LARRY. *Feeding Frenzy: How Attack Journalism Has Transformed American Politics.* New York: Free Press, 1991.

SANFORD, BRUCE W. *Don't Shoot the Messenger: How Our Growing Hatred of the Media Threatens Free Speech for All of Us.* New York: Free Press, 1999.

SEIB, PHILIP, and KATHY FITZPATRICK, *Journalism Ethics.* Fort Worth, TX: Harcourt Brace, 1997.

## Endnotes

1. For a review of the *60 Minutes* controversy, see Lawrence K. Grossman, "Lessons of the Sixty Minutes Cave-In," *Columbia Journalism Review* (January/February 1996). See also Joseph A. Russomanno and Kyu Ho Youm, "The *60 Minutes* Controversy: What Lawyers Are Telling the Media," *Communications and the Law* 18, no. 3 (September 1996); and Grossman's review of *The Insider*, "*The Insider:* It's Only a Movie," *Columbia Journalism Review* (November/December 1999).
2. See Doris A. Graber, *Mass Media and American Politics,* 4th ed. (Washington, DC: CQ Press, 1993), 292, 182. The media is not the only influence on agendas; the nature of the audience and the nature of particular issues also influence agenda-setting.
3. Ibid., 292.
4. Ibid., 4.
5. Austin Ranney, *Channels of Power* (New York: Basic Books, 1983), 34.
6. Walter Lippmann, *Public Opinion* (New York: Simon & Schuster, 1950 [1922]), 362, 364.
7. Graber, *Mass Media and American Politics,* 172, 111,127.
8. See Philip Seib and Kathy Fitzpatrick, *Journalism Ethics* (Fort Worth: Harcourt Brace, 1997), appendix, for a collection of some organizations' legal codes.
9. Jim Rutenberg, "Odd Alliance: ABC, CBS and Fox Agree to Share TV News Footage," *The New York Observer,* January 10, 2000, pp. 1, 15.
10. Lawrence K. Grossman, "The Death of Radio Reporting: Will TV Be Next?" *Columbia Journalism Review* (September/October 1998): 62.
11. Graber, *Mass Media and American Politics,* 118–120.
12. Ibid.
13. W. Lance Bennett, *News: The Politics of Illusion,* 2nd ed. (New York: Longman, 1988), 26.
14. Ibid., 23.
15. Ibid.
16. Ibid., 24.

17. Kathleen Hall Jamieson and Joseph N. Cappella, "The Role of the Press in the Health Care Reform Debate of 1993–1994," in *The Politics of News/The News of Politics*, ed. Doris Graber, Denis McQuail, and Pippa Norris (Washington, DC: CQ Press, 1998), 111, 119, 130.

18. Jay Rosen, *Getting the Connections Right: Public Journalism and the Troubles in the Press* (New York: The Twentieth Century Fund Press, 1996), 5.

19. Ibid., 5–6 and chapters 6, 7.

20. Quoted in Michael Schudson, "The Public Journalism Movement and Its Problems," in *The Politics of News/The News of Politics*, ed. Doris Graber, Denis McQuail, and Pippa Norris (Washington, DC: CQ Press, 1998), 142.

21. William E. Jackson, Jr., "Save Democracy from Civic Journalism: North Carolina's Odd Experiment," *Harvard International Journal of Press/Politics* 2, no. 3 (summer, 1997): 109, 105 and 105 n. 13. See also Michael Gartner, "Public Journalism—Seeing through the Gimmicks", *Media Studies Journal* 2, no. 1 (winter 1997). For a response, see Jennie Buckner, "Public Journalism—Giving Voters a Voice," *Media Studies Journal* 2, no. 1 (winter 1997).

22. Russomanno and Youm, "The *60 Minutes* Controversy."

*CHAPTER 2*

# Interest Groups

## CHAPTER OUTLINE

In his campaign for the governorship of Minnesota, former professional wrestler Jesse "The Body" Ventura ran a television ad in which a Ventura action figure attacked and defeated another action figure: Evil Special Interest Man. In similar cases around the country (usually without the action figures, though), politicians and others take on the "evil" referred to as "special interests." This chapter is about who and what these interests are.

Special interest groups are groups people become involved in because they share common ideas about the world; they represent specific interests and groups of people, promote and oppose particular policies and people, and compete with other interests to get what they want or to have an influence on the course of events. Competition among interest groups is where a lot of the action in American politics occurs. Interest groups are not, however, evil. In fact, the American system is designed to multiply interests and set them in competition with each other. The framers knew that Americans were a diverse people with many interests and opinions; they anticipated that as the nation grew, the number of interests would also grow. Rather than try to limit the

Jesse "The Body" Ventura's innovative campaign to become governor of Minnesota boosted the state's voter turnout in 1998 and brought renewed attention to the Reform Party. Here, Ventura's action figure takes a break from fighting Evil Special Interest Man in order to spend time with his action figure family, first lady Terry Ventura and daughter Jade.

number of interests competing for influence in public affairs, the framers aimed to set groups against each other as they developed. They believed that this competition would prevent any single interest from dominating the country.

**The Bottom Line.** Interest groups are a normal part of our political system, enabling people and organizations with shared interests to be more effective competitors in public affairs. Interest groups compete with each other using a variety of resources, and they build coalitions and make compromises to further their agendas. Overreliance on interest group politics is risky if public policy is driven only by selfish bargaining, if groups do not represent interests fairly, and if some groups come to have undue influence on elections and government. Compromises encourage interest group behavior while trying to control the threats groups pose to the system.

## WHO IS THIS NEW MAN, THIS EVIL SPECIAL INTEREST MAN?

First of all, Evil Special Interest Man isn't new. The Constitution's guarantees of freedom of speech, association, and the right to petition the government for redress of grievances have always encouraged the formation of groups, as have cultural factors that have made Americans a nation of "joiners." One reason Special Interest Man attracts so much attention now is that interest groups have multiplied rapidly, especially since the 1960s, encouraged by a number of factors. *Changes in campaign finance laws* in the 1970s created new opportunities for corporations and trade groups to organize political action committees (PACs), and the number of these groups has mushroomed in the last twenty-five years. *Better awareness of how to utilize modern media and technology* to organize and activate individuals also encourages interest group activity, as have *changes that grant groups easier and more effective access to the courts.* Finally, the *decline of political parties and labor unions* as organizing units is intimately related to the rise in interest group activity.

Specific groups form for a variety of reasons. Some groups, like Ralph Nader's Public Citizen, emerge *from the dedication and conviction of individuals.* Some specialized groups form *as society and economic circumstances become more diverse:* For example, as computers and the Internet become increasingly prevalent and socially and economically important, groups like the Electronic Freedom Foundation and the Electronic Privacy Information Center (EPIC) form. Finally, some groups develop *when shared interests are threatened,* such as when street vendors organize in response to crackdowns on their activities by city governments.[1]

Groups are designed to combine, or *aggregate,* the shared interests of their members, making individual interests more organized and more influential. An interest group's role is to communicate the views of its members and work toward accomplishing those members' shared goals. It is not the job of individual interest groups to represent all points of view, nor are interest groups necessarily concerned with protecting or promoting "the national interest." When a special interest group acts selfishly, by promoting programs or policies that benefit the group or the group's members, the group is doing precisely what it is designed to do.

## What Are We Talking About? Types of Interest Groups

Political scientist David Truman characterizes interest groups as "shared attitude" groups. They share attitudes for interpreting events, and also toward "what is needed or wanted in a given situation."[2] There are several basic categories of interest groups:

- **Citizen groups** are "lobbying organizations that mobilize members, donors, or activists around interests other than their vocation or profession." Among these are groups like the American Civil Liberties Union (ACLU), the National Association for the Advancement of Colored People (NAACP), and the National Organization for Women (NOW). *Public interest groups* are citizen groups that seek "a collective good, the achievement of which will not selectively and materially benefit the membership or activists of the organization." Some of these are good-government groups, like Common Cause and Public Citizen; others are environmental groups like the Sierra Club or consumers' groups like Consumers Union. Political scientist Jeffrey Berry notes that allegiance to these organizations can be very strong: "[T]hese organizations are the means by which [millions of

 ON THE WEB
www.publiccitizen.
org/

 ON THE WEB
www.eff.org/

 ON THE WEB
www.epic.org/

 ON THE WEB
www.aclu.org

 ON THE WEB
www.naacp.org/
default.asp

 ON THE WEB
www.now.org

 ON THE WEB
www.commoncause.
org/

Rallies and marches help interest groups publicize their messages. This pro-life rally moved past the Supreme Court building in Washington, D.C.

Americans] support advocacy on the issues they care the most about. For many people an identity as a Republican or a Democrat is superficial—if they have any partisan identity at all. A more intensely held identity is often that of a feminist, an evangelical Christian, or an environmentalist. If so, people will feel more affinity for the National Organization for Women, the Christian Coalition, or the Sierra Club than they do for any political party."[3] (See Zip Box 2.1.)

- In addition to citizen groups, **professional interest groups** play an important role in organizing interests and competing for influence in government. Professional interest groups like the American Medical Association (AMA) or the American Bar Association (ABA) develop around groups of people who share professional interests, like teachers, lawyers, doctors, machinists, and social workers. Virtually all professions are represented by organized groups. Professional interest groups are by far the most common type of interest group, with more than 75 percent of all membership groups associated with occupations.[4]

- **Economic and business interest groups** are involved with certain aspects of the economy. Many are very well funded and enjoy excellent access to government. Some are involved with particular sectors of the economy; for example, the American Farm Bureau and the National Grange represent agricultural interests. Businesses or corporations with similar interests form groups like the Chamber of Commerce of the United States and the National Association of Manufacturers. Economic interests are represented by broad coalition groups like the Business Roundtable as well as

On the Web
www.sierraclub.org

On the Web
www.consumersunion.org

On the Web
www.cc.org

On the Web
www.ama-assn.org

On the Web
www.abanet.org

On the Web
www.naswdc.org

On the Web
www.fb.com

On the Web
www.nationalgrange.org

## Zip Box 2.1
*Interest in the Environment*

### Membership Trends among Selected National Groups, 1970–1992

| Group | 1970 | 1980 | 1985 | 1990 | 1992 |
| --- | --- | --- | --- | --- | --- |
| Sierra Club (1892) | 113,000 | 181,000 | 364,000 | 630,000 | 650,000 |
| National Audubon Society (1905) | 105,000 | 400,000 | 550,000 | 575,000 | 600,000 |
| Izaak Walton League (1992) | 54,000 | 52,000 | 47,000 | 50,000 | 53,000 |
| Wilderness Society (1935) | 54,000 | 45,000 | 147,000 | 350,000 | 313,000 |
| National Wildlife Federation (1936)[a] | 540,000 | 818,000 | 900,000 | 997,000 | 975,000 |
| Defenders of Wildlife (1947) | 13,000 | 50,000 | 65,000 | 75,000 | 80,000 |
| Nature Conservancy (1951) | 22,000 | n/a | 400,000 | 600,000 | 690,000 |
| World Wildlife Fund (1961) | n/a | n/a | 130,000 | 400,000 | 940,000 |
| Environmental Defense Fund (1967) | 11,000 | 46,000 | 50,000 | 150,000 | 150,000 |
| Friends of the Earth (1969)[b] | 6,000 | n/a | 30,000 | 9,000 | 50,000 |
| Environmental Action (1970) | 10,000 | 20,000 | 15,000 | 20,000 | 16,000 |
| Greenpeace USA (1972) | n/a | n/a | 800,000 | 2.35 million | 1.8 million |

*Note:* All figures rounded.
[a]Full members only. The Federation in 1992 also had affiliated memberships (e.g., schoolchildren) of 5.3 million.
[b]Merged in 1990 with the 30,000-member Oceanic Society and the non-member Environmental Policy Institute.
*Source:* Table from Christopher J. Bosso, "The Color of Money: Environmental Groups and the Pathologies of Fund Raising," in *Interest Group Politics,* 4th ed., ed. Allan J. Cigler and Burdett A. Loomis (Washington, DC: CQ Press, 1994), 104.

Union membership has declined since its height in the 1950s, but unions are still an important factor in American politics and affairs. This photo was taken at a Teamsters convention in Philadelphia in 1996.

by smaller, more narrowly focused groups and lobbies. Within the transportation industry, for example, groups represent the particular interests of railroads, the trucking industry, and the airline industry.

- Labor interests are represented by **labor unions.** Chief among these is the AFL-CIO, which encompasses the American Federation of Labor and the Congress of Industrial Organizations. According to the Bureau of Labor Statistics, there are about sixteen million union workers in the United States; this is about 12 percent of the total labor force. This number is significantly lower than during the peak of union strength in the 1950s, when roughly one-third of American workers were members of unions (see Zip Box 2.2).

- Interest groups are not limited to private interests. **Governmental interest groups** include organizations like the U.S. Conference of Mayors and the National Association of Counties. As we will see throughout this book, congressional subcommittees, administrative agencies, and executive offices within the White House are just some of the governing interests that act as interest groups when they have an interest in policies being handled by other parts of the government.

ON THE WEB
www.uschamber.com

ON THE WEB
www.nam.org

ON THE WEB
www.brtable.org

ON THE WEB
www.aflcio.org/home.htm

## Zip Box 2.2
*Labor Union Membership*

### The Largest Labor Unions–1952 and 1993 (Membership in thousands)

*1952*

1. United Automobile, Aircraft and Agricultural Implement Workers Union — 1,185
2. United Steelworkers Union — 1,100
3. International Brotherhood of Teamsters — 1,000
4. United Brotherhood of Carpenters and Joiners — 750
5. International Association of Machinists — 699
6. United Mine Workers of America — 600
7. International Brotherhood of Electrical Workers — 500
8. Hotel and Restaurant Employees' International Alliance — 402
9. International Ladies' Garment Workers' Union — 390
10. International Hod Carriers, Building and Common Laborers Union — 386

*1993*

1. National Education Association — 2,000
2. International Brotherhood of Teamsters — 1,700
3. American Federation of State, County and Municipal Employees — 1,300
4. United Food and Commercial Workers International Union — 1,300
5. Service Employees International Union — 1,000
6. United Automobile, Aerospace and Agricultural Implement Workers of America — 862
7. International Brotherhood of Electrical Workers — 845
8. American Federation of Teachers — 830
9. Communications Workers of America — 600
10. International Association of Machinists and Aerospace Workers — 550
  United Steelworkers of America — 550

Union membership has declined from roughly 22 million people in the 1970s to about 16 million today.
*Source:* Table from Byron E. Shafer, "Partisan Elites," in *Partisan Approaches to Postwar American Politics,* ed. Byron E. Shafer (Chatham, NJ: Chatham House, 1998), 131.

## Why Bother? Interest Group Benefits and Activities

On the Web
stats.bls.gov

On the Web
www.usmayors.org

On the Web
www.naco.org

Groups engage in a number of activities. First, people and other interests that form into groups generally expect groups to provide some combination of *benefits*. Interest groups provide *purposive* benefits when they pursue broad purposes, like stopping censorship, ending a war, or providing relief to the underprivileged. Groups also offer *solidary* benefits, like the social advantages of being among people with shared interests or goals. Groups provide *material* benefits like magazines or hard-to-find information; many interest groups now have their own websites containing information about the group and its positions on issues (see Zip Box 2.3).

Second, groups *strive to influence individual behavior*. Labor groups, for example, run campaigns urging consumers to patronize union shops or to buy American goods. Environmental interest groups may try to convince the general public to recycle and to dispose of hazardous waste products properly. Pro-life groups try to convince people of the benefits of adoption in order to discourage abortions. Advertisements and mailings solicit support, but they also give information on current issues that individuals can use in other forums—with their representatives, for example, regardless of whether the individual is a member of the group.

---

### DISCUSSION BOX 2.1
*EVIL SPECIAL INTEREST MAN'S FAMILY TREE: TOCQUEVILLE ON POLITICAL ASSOCIATIONS IN THE UNITED STATES*

As early as the 1830s, <u>Alexis de Tocqueville</u> noted Americans' propensity to form groups. According to the following passages from Tocqueville, why do Americans want to form groups to solve problems? Are these groups limited to a few issues? Why do interests in the minority form groups?

In no country in the world has the principle of association been more successfully used or applied to a greater multitude of objects than in America. Besides the permanent associations which are established by law under the names of townships, cities, and counties, a vast number of others are formed and maintained by the agency of private individuals.

The citizen of the United States is taught from infancy to rely upon his own exertions in order to resist the evils and the difficulties of life; he looks upon the social authority with an eye of mistrust and anxiety, and he claims its assistance only when he is unable to do without it. . . . In the United States associations are es-

tablished to promote the public safety, commerce, industry, morality, and religion. There is no end which the human will despairs of attaining through the combined powers of individuals united into a society.

. . .

In America the citizens who form the minority associate in order, first, to show their numeric strength and so to diminish the moral power of the majority; and, secondly, to stimulate competition and thus to discover those arguments that are most fitted to act upon the majority; for they always entertain hopes of drawing over the majority to their own side, and then controlling the supreme power in its name. Political associations in the United States are therefore peaceable in their intentions and strictly legal in the means which they employ; and they assert with perfect truth that they aim at success only by lawful expedients.*

*Alexis de Tocqueville, *Democracy in America*, vol. 1 (New York: Vintage, 1945), 198–199, 203.

## Zip Box 2.3
*Interest Group Benefits: The National Rifle Association*

### NRA Membership Benefits, 1981–1997

| Year | Benefits | Year | Benefits |
|---|---|---|---|
| 1981 | Year subscription to *American Rifleman* or *American Hunter* <br> $300 firearms insurance <br> $10,000 accidental death and dismemberment insurance <br> $300,000 to $1,000,000 shooter's liability insurance <br> NRA cap | | NRA cap <br> Sportsman's bonus book with discounts and rebates |
| 1983 | Year subscription to *American Rifleman* or *American Hunter* <br> $300 firearms insurance <br> $10,000 accidental death and dismemberment insurance <br> $100,000 shooter's liability insurance <br> NRA cap | 1989 | Year subscription to *American Rifleman* or *American Hunter* <br> $600 gun theft insurance <br> $10,000 accidental death and dismemberment insurance <br> Discounts for Hertz car rentals <br> NRA window decal <br> NRA cap |
| 1985 | Year subscription to *American Rifleman* or *American Hunter* <br> $300 firearms insurance <br> $100,000 hunting liability insurance <br> $10,000 accidental death and dismemberment insurance <br> Pocket pal 3" lockback knife or NRA cap | 1991 | Year subscription to *American Rifleman* or *American Hunter* <br> $600 gun theft insurance <br> $10,000 accidental death and dismemberment insurance <br> Law enforcement insurance benefits for officers <br> NRA window decal <br> NRA cap |
| 1987 | Year subscription to *American Rifleman* or *American Hunter* <br> $600 gun theft insurance <br> $10,000 accidental death and dismemberment insurance <br> Discounts for Hertz car rentals <br> NRA window decal | 1997 | Year subscription to *American Rifleman* or *American Hunter* <br> $10,000 in personal accident insurance <br> $1,000 in ArmsCare firearm insurance <br> A no-annual-fee NRA VISA card <br> 40% discount on interstate moves of household goods <br> NRA window decal <br> NRA cap |

*Source:* From Kelly Patterson, "The Political Firepower of the National Rifle Association," in *Interest Group Politics*, 5th ed., ed. Allan J. Cigler and Burdett A. Loomis (Washington, DC: CQ Press, 1996), 128.

Third, interest groups work *to influence campaigns and elections.* Interest groups sometimes target specific elected officials for support or opposition. Groups donate to individual candidates or to the candidate's party in order to help get a candidate elected, or in order to defeat an opponent. Individuals and interest groups can form and contribute to PACs, which generate funds for candidates and political parties. Groups and PACs also run "issue ads," which ostensibly do not support or oppose a particular individual but inform the public about a particular issue. (We will examine interest group activity in campaigns and elections more fully in chapter 4.)

# INTEREST GROUP COMPETITION:
## ACCESS, CREDIBILITY, AND MONEY, MONEY, MONEY

### The Variety of Resources

Interest groups do not limit their activities to making campaign contributions and mailing magazines, of course. They continue to try to *influence officials in government* before and after elections, pressuring members of Congress, officials at administrative agencies, and all other members of the public service to support, oppose, or consider various policies and ideas. Powerful interest groups are often directly involved in writing legislation for congressional subcommittees and in drafting rules for administrative agencies.

American government is very open and decentralized. This means that an interest group can influence politics from any number of "access points": A group can go to Congress, or to the courts, or to a public agency, and it can work through any of the various local, state, tribal, and federal levels of government. If doors close at one point, other doors might open elsewhere. Even within Congress, for example, numerous committees deal with the same issues. All a lobbyist representing an interest group needs to do to be heard is have a brief meeting with one of the hundreds of congressional aides and staffers on Capitol Hill. And as interest groups increasingly utilize the media to promote their views, a meeting might not even be necessary for a group to communicate with officials in government.

Interest groups often benefit from being intensely interested in a specific issue area while the general public is too busy with other things to keep abreast of developments. In some of these scenarios, groups work to obtain benefits for narrow or limited interests (such as cotton growers), with the costs being passed on to the general public or a widely dispersed group (such as people who buy cotton products): this is called "client politics."

As interest groups try to influence public policy and the workings of government, competition within and among these groups is a critical dynamic in American politics. Three key resources groups use are access, credibility, and money.

### Gaining Access

Access to people in influential positions and to the media is an important resource for interest groups. Some groups capitalize on knowledgeable lobbyists with contacts inside of government to gain direct *access to decision makers.* Many lobbyists are former government officials; experience in government affords specialized knowledge about particular issues, about who in government is involved in making important decisions, and about what kind of lobbying or information is likely to influence those decisions. Thus government experience can enhance the access and credibility of a lobbyist and, by extension, of the group represented by the lobbyist. Money helps buy access, because individuals who have held the highest, most influential posts in government, or those who have very specialized knowledge about complex issues like telecommunications policy, command enormous fees to serve as lobbyists.

Access and credibility help groups and individuals promote their points of view on issues. Actor Christopher Reeve and former White House Press Secretary James Brady (who was shot during John Hinckley's attempted assassination of President Reagan) joined Senator Jay Rockefeller (D-West Virginia) to support legislation that would increase the lifetime cap on health insurance.

As we saw in chapter 1, the media are a fundamental force in what the public and government know and learn about issues. *Access to the media* helps to publicize a group's message and influence behavior without the group ever having to contact a public official directly. Further, many groups have far-flung national memberships, and the media are an effective means of communicating the organization's activities and positions. One way public interest groups build access to the media is by collaborating on investigative reports. Collaboration divides the costs of doing research even as it provides the group with a public relations outlet for its findings: the media benefit when a group does the difficult tasks of research.[5] Even without a direct collaboration, organizations can build reputations for thorough and accurate information, giving them a preferred position when a news organization or journalist needs someone to comment on an issue or a story.

Celebrities also draw attention to particular issues: actor <u>Christopher Reeve</u>, for example, testified before Congress on behalf of funding for scientific research and helped convince the New Jersey State Senate to pass a $1 surcharge on motor vehicle fines to fund spinal cord research. As head of the National Rifle Association, actor <u>Charlton Heston</u> uses his celebrity status to promote the NRA's positions and programs. These celebrities are attractive to the media in part because they help personalize issues, allowing the media to tell an issue's story by referring to famous people or individual situations.

### Winning Credibility

Christopher Reeve's efforts on behalf of research and funding for spinal cord and brain injuries involves a second important resource, one that is often overlooked: credibility. Reeve's appeal builds on his access to the media and his familiarity to the public, but it also builds on his credibility as a paralysis victim with good intentions who is believed to be intimately acquainted with the issues he addresses. When a group's representative testifies before Congress, responds to an agency's proposed regulations, or appears in the media to make a point, credibility matters.

Credibility can also stem from a group's *research* into issues. A group's ability to support a particular position on an issue or a program with reliable research findings enhances the credibility of the group and its particular policy position. Business groups and philanthropic foundations (often associated with business interests) conduct their own research and distribute it to the press and to public officials, complete with press releases highlighting findings and explaining connections between the research and current issues. Citizen groups and labor unions also study issues and produce research findings to promote their views. Many interest groups conduct public opinion polls, or hire special polling companies like Gallup or Roper to conduct polls, in order to lend credibility to claims that the group's attitudes are shared by the public.

*New research and timely reports* help interest groups capture the attention of decision makers and manipulate the media's interest in novel stories. In chapter 1, we saw how the media are attracted to stories that are novel or involve crises. By producing new research and new polls and by seizing on hot issues, interest groups are able to place opinion articles in newspapers or gain interview time on television. Environmental groups, for example, capitalize on disasters like the Exxon Valdez oil spill in the waters off Alaska as springboards for making other arguments about the environment or to push for particular legislation. Similarly, business groups use new developments in the world economy, such as the Asian financial crisis in the late 1990s, to support particular positions on trade regulations and economic policy. (See Zip Box 2.4.)

Some groups, of course, have more credibility than others. A research study from the ACLU about police abuse of suspected criminals, for example, might have more credibility with the public and government officials than a report on cigarettes conducted by a wing of the tobacco industry. Fairly or unfairly, variations in credibility can affect media coverage of a group's positions. Liberal citizen groups tend to be treated very favorably by the national mainstream news media, whereas business groups are treated much more critically.[6] (See Zip Box 2.5.)

Groups also take advantage of the media's desire for conflict and polarized issues by characterizing their positions as direct responses to the other "side" of an issue. If an interest group can build a reputation for advocating a particular standpoint and for making a credible case clearly and dramatically, it stands a better chance of fitting into the media's preferred method of delivering stories. The dynamics of the media and their importance in public

ON THE WEB
www.policy.com /
community/ttank.html

ON THE WEB
www.aei.org

ON THE WEB
www.brookings.edu

ON THE WEB
www.cato.org

ON THE WEB
www.heritage.org

ON THE WEB
www.csis.org

ON THE WEB
www.urbaninstitute.
org

## Zip Box 2.4
*Experts, Schmexperts: "Think Tanks and the Politicization of Expertise"*

Number of Nationally Focused Think Tanks

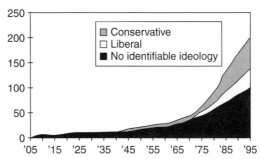

Interests give large sums of money to independent research "think tanks" that study issues and produce analyses and future projections. There are three basic types of think tanks:

- *University-without-students think tanks,* such as the Brookings Institution and the Russell Sage Foundation, are essentially small communities of university professors with doctoral degrees who produce books and scholarly articles with strict attention to complete and objective research.
- Whereas university-without-students think tanks are largely funded by private foundations and institutional endowments, *contract research think tanks,* like the RAND Corporation and the Urban Institute, draw funding from government contracts to study specific policy issues. At contract research think tanks, large teams of researchers examine narrow issues and produce detailed research reports rather than full-length books.
- Finally, *advocacy tanks,* a relatively new development, seek to influence policymakers on behalf of particular political positions and ideologies. Advocacy think tanks range from the libertarian Cato Institute and the conservative Heritage Foundation to liberal and labor-oriented tanks like the Economic Policy Institute.

Political scientists <u>Andrew Rich</u> and <u>R. Kent Weaver</u>, who have studied think tanks extensively, note that the recent rise of advocacy tanks presents older think tanks with a dual challenge. First, advocacy tanks compete for scarce funds, media attention, and access to policymakers. More importantly, though, Rich and Weaver note, the advocacy tanks pose a "challenge to the legitimacy of the older organizations' claim to provide impartial and highly credible expertise." Not only does the proliferation of advocacy tanks confuse policymakers and the public regarding what research and which organizations are more credible, advocacy tanks promote the notion that *all* research is value-based regardless of whether a particular think tank is open about its biases. "To the extent that these claims are accepted by policymakers and the public," Rich and Weaver write, "*all* think tanks risk having their expertise discounted or even dismissed as emanating from a hostile ideological camp."*

*Andrew Rich and R. Kent Weaver, "Advocates and Analysts: Think Tanks and the Politicization of Expertise," in *Interest Group Politics,* 5th ed., edited by Allan J. Cigler and Burdett A. Loomis (Washington, DC: CQ Press, 1998), 242ff. [italics added]. The figure, typology, and descriptions are adapted from this article.

## Research Featured in Newspapers

| Type of Organization | Percent Featured in Newspapers |
|---|---|
| Citizen groups | 19.4 |
| Think tanks | 5.6 |
| Corporations | 9.3 |
| Trade associations | 2.8 |
| Professional associations | .9 |
| Labor unions | .9 |
| Other advocacy groups[a] | 2.8 |
| Academe | 17.6 |
| Independent research institutions | 10.2 |
| Government | 30.6 |
| Total | 100.1 |

[a]Veterans, nonprofits, churches, and other groups.
*Source:* Jeffrey M. Berry, *The New Liberalism: The Rising Power of Interest Groups* (Washington, D.C.: Brooking Institution Press, 1999): Table 6-5, p. 135 [data from stories in the *New York Times* and the *Wall Street Journal* in 1995].

## Advocacy Organizations on the Op-Ed Page

| Type of Organization | Percent of All Op-Ed Columns Written by Someone from a Lobby or Think Tank |
|---|---|
| Citizen groups | 22.8 |
| Think tanks | 54.8 |
| Corporations | 15.4 |
| Trade associations | 3.3 |
| Professional associations | .4 |
| Labor unions | .8 |
| Other[a] | 2.5 |
| Total | 100.0 |

[a]Veterans, nonprofits, churches, and other groups.
*Source:* Berry, *The New Liberalism:* Table 6-6, p. 141 [data from the *New York Times* and *Wall Street Journal,* 1995].

## Authoritative Lobbyists According to Print Media

| Type of Group | Percent of All Quotations of Lobbyists, 1991 |
|---|---|
| Citizen groups | 46.2 |
| Think tanks | 0.5 |
| Corporations | 1.0 |
| Trade associations | 30.3 |
| Professional associations | 15.4 |
| Labor unions | 5.6 |
| Other[a] | 1.0 |
| Total | 100.0 |

[a]Veterans, nonprofits, churches, and other groups.
*Source:* Berry, *The New Liberalism:* Table 6-4, p. 132 [data from stories in the *New York Times, Wall Street Journal,* and *Congression/Quarterly Weekly Report,* 1991].

## Television News Coverage of Interest Groups, 1995

| Type of Interest Group | Percent of All Interest Group References |
|---|---|
| Citizen groups | 45.6 |
| Think tanks | 4.3 |
| Corporations | 24.3 |
| Trade associations | 13.0 |
| Professional associations | 3.8 |
| Labor unions | 4.0 |
| Other[a] | 5.1 |
| Total | 100.1 |

[a]Veterans, nonprofits, churches, and other groups.
*Source:* Berry, *The New Liberalism:* Table 6-1, p. 122 [data from 1995 broadcasts by ABC, CBS, *CNN Headline News,* and NBC].

Different types of interest groups have different relationships with the media. Note how successful citizen groups enjoy credibility as authoritative sources, and how successful they are in placing their research and opinions and in gaining television coverage relative to other types of groups.

*Zip Box 2.6*
*Interest Groups' Competitive Strengths and Weaknesses*

| Types of Internet Groups | Competitive Strengths | Competitive Weaknesses |
|---|---|---|
| Citizen groups (Sierra Club, ACLU, NOW, Planned Parenthood, NAACP) | Credibility and expertise on issues<br>Loyalty of members<br>Good relations with the media<br>Credibility with the public | Narrow focus limits versatility<br>Often not well funded<br>Often reliant on foundations and corporations for funding, rather than on members |
| Professional groups (AMA, Association of Trial Lawyers) | Credibility and expertise on issues<br>Loyalty of members<br>Often interested in specific issue areas that do not interest the general public | Narrow focus limits versatility<br>Varied credibility<br>Self-interest readily apparent |
| Business groups (Chamber of Commerce, Business Roundtable) | Well funded<br>Good access to decision makers and influential persons<br>Long relationship with government<br>Expertise on arcane details of tax code, other areas | Low credibility with public and media |
| Labor unions (AFL-CIO, American Federation of Teachers) | Well funded<br>Highly organized<br>Loyalty of members<br>Strong, historical ties to Democratic Party | Credibility varies<br>Opposition from business groups<br>Damaged by history and persistent rumors of corruption, criminal activity |
| Governmental interests | Often expert on issues, enhancing credibility<br>Good access to other parts of government<br>Dedicated employees | Obvious interest in their position, together with competition from other governmental interests and private interests, encourages strong competition<br>Often low credibility with public and other parts of government |

affairs, then, affect the ways in which interest groups try to disseminate information and influence behavior.

## Money, Money, Money

*Money*, of course, is an extremely potent and versatile resource. Well-funded interest groups are in a good position to contribute to candidates and campaigns, and to sponsor receptions, meetings, and seminars where influential officials and group representatives can discuss ideas. Money pays to produce slick and effective information packets, it funds polls to find out how best to promote certain positions, and it buys advertising time on television and radio. Money funds research to support a group's point of view, it pays for expensive lawsuits challenging public policies, and it intimidates opponents into moderating or forfeiting competing positions. To varying degrees, money can buy both access and credibility.[7]

An interest group's *funding,* therefore, is a crucial part of its operations—and an important window onto the group's support. Interest groups do not always receive the majority of their funding from members. Professional and trade associations receive about two-thirds of their funds from members, but most citizen groups receive only about a third of their funds from members—the bulk of their money comes from a variety of other sources, especially government grants and philanthropic foundations. Of interest groups surveyed by political scientist Jack L. Walker, 34 percent of profit-sector groups and a whopping 89 percent of citizen groups reported that they received start-up money from patrons, and citizen groups reported that about 35 percent of their budgets were funded by patrons.[8] The connection between funding and a group's activities is significant, because patrons have an influential say in how a group behaves and what issues it addresses. Foundation involvement is important, for example, because many important foundations supporting citizen groups are tied to major corporations and industries (see Zip Box 2.7).[9]

### Hitting the Best Shots Possible: The Dynamics of Different Resources

Different resources are good for different things, and groups possess varying combinations of resources and thus different strengths and weaknesses. Business groups tend to have the most money and possibly the best access to government, but Berry finds that citizen groups are about the only type of lobby group that has good credibility with the public.[10] Further, while groups maximize their influence in their own area of expertise, they often lack influence on other issues. For example, Consumers Union might be influential in consumer issues but have very little influence in debates on welfare policy. Because resources and their uses vary, groups try to match their resources to those activities in which they are likely to be most successful. A group with good access to the media, for example, might try to build public support for an initiative. On the other hand, a group with significant funds but lacking access and credibility might choose to pursue objectives through the courts, a strategy that can be very effective but also very costly.

Groups often pursue a number of strategies at once, playing one against another. Interests dissatisfied with the undercount of minorities in the decennial census, for instance, have participated in lawsuits aimed at forcing the government to use statistical measures to adjust for the undercount. At the same time, some of these same groups have used access to Congress to pressure representatives to order specific actions by the Census Bureau that support the same goal, even as they distribute research findings through the media to dramatize what they believe the effects of the undercount will be on minorities and cities across the country.

## Zip Box 2.7
*Interest Group Revenues*

### Sources of Revenues for Membership Groups Active in Environmental Issues

| Source Of Revenue | Mean Percentage |
|---|---|
| Membership dues | 32 |
| Individual contributions | 19 |
| Foundation grants | 17 |
| Sales | 8 |
| Corporate gifts | 4 |
| Capital assets | 3 |
| Federal grants and contracts | 2 |
| State grants and contracts | 2 |
| Other contracts | 2 |
| User fees | 2 |
| Other sources | 9 |

### Percentage of Revenues from "Individuals" and "Institutions" for Selected National Environmental Organizations, Fiscal Years 1987 and 1990

| | 1987 | | 1990 | |
|---|---|---|---|---|
| Group | Individuals | Institutions | Individuals | Institutions |
| Friends of the Earth[a] | 98 | 0 | 40 | 60 |
| Environmental Action | 73 | 22 | 74 | 17 |
| Greenpeace USA | 98 | 1 | 98 | 1 |
| Defenders of Wildlife | 91 | 0 | 92 | 0 |
| League of Conservation Voters | 100 | 0 | 100 | 0 |
| Sierra Club | 80 | 0 | 66 | 0 |
| Wilderness Society | 86 | 14 | 81 | 11 |
| National Audubon Society | 74 | 2 | 68 | 0 |
| Environmental Defense Fund | 53 | 35 | 64 | 30 |
| Natural Resources Defense Council | 44 | 45 | 49 | 42 |
| National Wildlife Federation | 38 | 18 | 47 | 0 |
| Izaak Walton Leaue | 52 | 40 | 39 | 56 |
| Nature Conservancy | 51 | 49 | 70 | 30 |
| World Wildlife Fund | 66 | 12 | 62 | 13 |

*Note:* "Individuals" includes member dues, individual contributions, gifts, bequests, and legacies. "Institutions" includes foundation, corporate, and government grants and donations. Figures do not add up to 100 percent in many cases because some groups generate revenues from publications, sales of goods and services, and investments, for example. Figures are compiled from annual reports. They are approximate and vary based on differing accounting practices.
[a]Friends of the Earth merged in 1990 with the Environmental Policy Institute, which relied on individual contributions for 23 percent of its year 1987 budget. The 1990 percentage reflects that merger.
*Source:* Tables from Christopher J. Bosso, "The Color of Money: Environmental Groups and the Pathologies of Fund Raising," in *Interest Group Politics*, 4th ed., ed. Allan J. Cigler and Burdett A. Loomis (Washington, DC: CQ Press, 1996), 107, 108.

It is important to note that interest group strategies are influenced not only by their available resources but also by the circumstances of a given policy debate at any particular time. Interest group experts <u>Frank R. Baumgartner</u> and <u>Beth L. Leech</u> put it this way: "The most effective groups may not be those that are best at a given strategy but rather those that have the greatest repertory of strategies available to them and who are most skillful at choosing the right strategy for the issue at hand. Asking what lobbyists do is like asking Pete Sampras whether he 'usually' hits backhands or forehands. It depends on the situation. The best players have all the shots, and they choose them wisely."[11] (See BriefCase Box 2.1.)

## FAST FRIENDS AND POLITICAL COMPROMISES: INTEREST GROUP POLITICS

Every day, thousands of organized groups compete to gather and disseminate information, influence behavior, and influence government. An important

---

### BRIEFCASE BOX 2.1
*Opposites Attract: Adversary Alliances in Action*

Interest groups can enhance their competitive positions by allying with traditional opponents. In the following passages, political scientists <u>Loree Bykerk</u> and <u>Ardith Maney</u> describe how such an "adversary alliance" between consumer groups and broadcasters (together with local governments) succeeded in influencing the re-regulation of cable television in the late 1980s and early 1990s. According to the authors, why are adversary alliances effective? How did the groups studied in this case use different resources to exert influence and complement the efforts of others?

"[C]onsumer groups on occasion join coalitions that include not just the usual allies, but also those who are ordinarily adversaries. The adversary coalitions combine competition and compromise. They are valuable because they offer real possibilities for resolving thorny issues, in part because they include members whose interests are ordinarily at odds. If that conflict can be surmounted, the resolution the coalition proposes has a greater chance of acceptance by formal decision makers, who must take notice of an alliance of strange bedfellows. . . .

Of particular interest is how the adversary coalition [in this case] behaved. Broadcasters provided most of the support for an expensive advertising campaign that defended "free TV"; consumer groups supplied extensive data on [cable] rates and service; and the cities reported on customer complaints and abuses. Broadcasters made political action committee contributions, but these represented only a fraction of cable interests' contributions. Each of the coalition partners had contacts with different members of Congress; the consumer groups, and particularly the Consumer Federation of America, took the lead in speaking to the print media. These groups could agree on an elevated public interest argument that defended the value of common media, accessible to most consumers, rather than a two-class system with cable available only to wealthier subscribers. . . .

The victorious adversary coalition probably could not have succeeded without the persistence of Rep. Edward J. Markey (D-Mass.), chair of the House Energy and Commerce Subcommittee on Telecommunication and Finance. . . . The alliance of consumer groups and the broadcast industry brought together the power of good ideas, defensible to viewer-constituents, and the lobbying influence derived in part from the broadcasters' great financial resources. By rounding up more than the usual suspects, the consumer/broadcasting coalition provided excellent cover for decision makers and thus achieved closure on a difficult, complex, high-stakes issue.*

*Loree Bykerk and Ardith Maney, "Consumer Groups and Coalition Politics on Capitol Hill," in *Interest Group Politics*, 4th ed., edited by Allan J. Cigler and Burdett A. Loomis (Washington, DC: CQ Press, 1996), 273, 274, 275.

strand of political thought holds that interest groups deserve their influential role in public policy decision-making. Under this argument, groups represent legitimate interests that government should take into account; collectively, they represent the will of the people. The national interest is defined as the sum of group interests and the outcome of bargaining among the groups. If groups accurately reflect individual interests, then group participation is democratic participation. Successful interest group activity involves long-term lobbying, commitment to coalition building and compromise, and acceptance of incremental progress.

## In It for the Long Haul: Lobbying Never Stops

One of the most important ways interest groups try to influence government is by lobbying. Interest groups marshal their money, access, and credibility throughout the policymaking process to educate officials and staff members on issues, hoping to make the group's positions convincing. Interest groups meet with officials and try to demonstrate why an issue is important, how it should be dealt with, and, perhaps most importantly, why it is in the interest of that official to deal with the issue at all. Issues usually find their way onto the national agenda only after years of effort by many individuals; a "current debate" on an issue is often the product of years of lobbying effort.

The lobbying process continues while Congress debates issues, and even *after* Congress passes legislation and after administrative agencies enact rules to govern behavior. Usually, putting laws and regulations into practice is as difficult, or more so, than writing them in the first place. As we will see in later chapters, implementing regulations and interpreting the meaning of laws are central components of the work done by the administrative bureaucracy and by the courts. Interest groups work hard to influence the decisions of these aspects of the government.

### Finding the Best Pressure Point: Focus on Congressional Subcommittees, the Courts, and Administrative Agencies

Interest groups aim their efforts at congressional subcommittees, the judiciary, and the bureaucracy. Congress is very decentralized, with hundreds of members and dozens of committees and subcommittees. *Congressional subcommittees* are popular targets for interest group activity because much of the important work in gathering information on an issue, hearing testimony, and drafting legislation occurs there. It is much easier to influence a small number of members and staffers at the subcommittee level than to influence large numbers of members, many of whom are unfamiliar with the details of particular bills and issues. By the time a bill is ready to be voted on by the entire House or Senate, much of the important work has already been done.

Interest groups also utilize *the court system* to push their views. Decisions by a court can have significant effects on how a law or a regulation is interpreted and implemented. The courts are popular interest group targets for two reasons: First, interest groups can bring cases directly to the courts, whether because of an allegedly illegal activity or to challenge laws and rules. The landmark decision in *Brown v. Board of Education of Topeka, Kansas* (1954), in which the Supreme Court ruled that racial segregation in public schools deprived minority children of equal educational opportunities, resulted directly from the court strategy of the NAACP. Second, interest groups can be effective in the court system by filing briefs on behalf of cases involving other groups. *Amicus curiae,* or "friend of the court," briefs allow interest groups a direct input into policymaking in the judiciary. The major drawback to litigation is its cost: beginning and pursuing a case through the courts can be tremendously expensive. The cost could be worth it, though, to a group that stands to lose huge profits, such as a major industry facing unfavorable regulation. The cost might also be worth it to a group, like the tobacco industry, that faces widespread public opposition to its goals and might not expect to generate much sympathy lobbying Congress.

Finally, interest groups target much of their activity at *administrative agencies.* Agencies, like the Environmental Protection Agency (EPA) and the Occupational Safety and Health Administration (OSHA), have very specialized functions and often have enormous influence over the design and implementation of rules and policies. Congress allows many agencies to make rules, carry them out, and adjudicate disputes, in effect giving agencies legislative, executive, and judicial powers all at once. Agencies rely on the input of experts and knowledgeable people and organizations to fulfill these roles—a service interest groups are happy to provide. Because implementation by agencies and interpretations by the courts are so important, interest groups also try to influence the appointment of individuals to posts in the bureaucracy or in the courts.

### Fast Friends and Coalition Building: Issue Networks

Lobbyists have to contact members of the government or their staffs, and they need to find cases to bring to court; they need to develop research and disseminate results to officials; research findings and attitudes need to be publicized through the media; and contacts need to be made with other groups to start the process of building coalitions and gathering momentum in pursuit of shared goals. Each part of the process sets groups against other groups with different agendas, who are also trying to woo the media, gain access to government, and gain the time and support of other influential groups. All of this activity creates a fluid environment where access, alliances, and coalitions change frequently. Interest group politics is a game, with each group trying to plan and adjust the use of its resources to fit opportunities in a constantly shifting political universe. To build on the Pete Sampras analogy used above, not only does an interest group need to use all of its varied resources at the appropriate times, but a group needs to adjust to new partners, changing opponents, and even new playing surfaces during the match itself.

Political scientist Hugh Heclo describes the politics surrounding interest groups as a process heavily influenced by "issue networks." These are networks of interested people and groups with expert knowledge, who share information and build coalitions to try and influence government action. Issue networks have formed as the number of interest groups has increased in recent decades, and as the techniques necessary for success have become more complex. Because there are so many interest groups with conflicting goals, groups operate in coalitions and share resources to increase their strength. (See Scholar Box 2.1.)

Issue networks are fluid and contentious, and most groups that get involved face opposition from other groups. Groups align, build coalitions, and make and reject allies with great rapidity, depending on the details of particular issues and on very complex calculations about chances for success, the nature of allies and opposition, and the resources available at any given time. Groups come and go at a moment's notice. Clusters do form, made up of like-minded groups in certain areas, such as leaders in telecommunications or major industries, but even groups in clusters can quickly turn against each

## Scholar Box 2.1
*Heclo: Issue Networks*

Heclo's notion of issue networks contrasts with the traditional concept of an iron triangle. *Iron triangles* in particular policy areas were characterized by three stable power centers: congressional committees, administrative agencies, and powerful interest groups. These elements dominated and controlled policymaking. Heclo, though, argues that as interest groups have proliferated and the federal government's role in providing services and regulating the economy has expanded, "issue networks" have come to overlay these iron triangles. Rather than being guided by stable and dominant policymakers, governmental policymaking is marked by the volatile activity of thousands of groups and players: participants move in and out; no one seems to be in control of policies and issues; and material interests are often subordinated to intellectual or emotional commitments on particular issues. Consultants, academics, and staffers add to the vast numbers of organized groups involved. In the following passage, Heclo portrays government activity in terms of a massive traffic jam waiting to happen. What causes such congestion? Is this the same cause identified by Tocqueville as the catalyst for group organizing (see Discussion Box 2.1)? What are the results of all this activity? What are the benefits and risks of so many groups mobilizing on behalf of issues?

Of course Americans' love affair with interest groups is hardly a new phenomenon. From abolitionists to abortionists there has never been a lack of issue-conscious organizations; in the 1830s, Tocqueville described how the tariff question generated an early version of local consumer groups and a national lobbying association. Yet if the current situation is a mere outgrowth of old tendencies, it is so in the same sense that a 16-lane spaghetti interchange is the mere elaboration of a country crossroads. With more public policies, more groups are being mobilized and there are more complex relationships among them. Since very few policies ever seem to drop off the public agenda as more are added, congestion among those interested in various issues grows, the chances for accidental collisions increase, and the interaction tends to take on a distinctive group-life of its own in the Washington community. One scene in a recent Jacques Tati film pictures a Paris traffic circle so dense with traffic that no one can get in or out; instead, drivers spend their time socializing with each other as they drive around in endless circles. Group politics in Washington may be becoming such a merry-go-round. . . .

In sum, new initiatives in federal funding and regulation have infused old and new organizations with a public policy dimension, especially when such groups are used as administrative middlemen and facilitators. Moreover, the growing body of compensatory interventions by government has helped create a climate of acceptance for ever more groups to insist that things be set right on their behalf. What matters is not so much that organizations are moving to Washington as that Washington's policy problems are coming to occupy so many different facets of organizational life in the United States.*

*Hugh Heclo, "Issue Networks and the Executive Establishment," in *The New American Political System*, ed. Anthony King (Washington, DC: American Enterprise Institute for Public Policy Research, 1978), 97–98.

other. Finally, some political fights are heavily influenced by unexpected players: political scientist <u>Laura R. Woliver</u>, for example, argues that abortion politics in coming years might be determined not by the "usual suspects" of pro-life and pro-choice groups deeply interested in the issue, but by interests that are only indirectly involved, like doctors trying to protect the privacy of doctor-patient relationships.[12]

## *Fast Friends but Slow Change: Incrementalism*

The result of interest group politics is often incremental policy development. Interest groups build coalitions and support, they make deals and bargain with other interests, all the while making compromises and softening demands as trade-offs for broader support. This moves policy forward little by little, instead of in big jumps. Incremental progress is often mistaken for gridlock, because only rarely are laws passed that radically alter existing arrangements in law or relationships among groups. Critics of interest group politics complain that it is much easier to defeat legislation than it is to pass it, and that this is one of the reasons government often has the appearance of being in "gridlock." Gridlock is hard to define and even harder to measure, though, and it is by no means clear that government functions less effectively when many interest groups are involved on a particular issue. <u>Jeffrey Berry</u>, for example, finds that in a case where there are ten interest groups involved on a bill in Congress and a case where there are no interest groups involved, only a trivial difference separates the chances that either bill will pass.[13]

Incrementalism characterizes American government by design. Supporters of interest group politics see in this system a natural brake on large-scale reforms and upheavals, which blocks efforts to enact untested or radical new programs. Supporters of interest group politics concede that government acts slowly and that passing new measures is a vastly complex and cumbersome process, but argue that the participation of so many interests with such attention to detail fortifies emerging compromises with broad-based support while posing little serious risk to the nation (see BriefCase Box 2.2).

---

## BRIEFCASE BOX 2.2
*Death of a Sales Plan: Tactics to Defeat Clinton's Health Care Proposal*

Many factors contributed to the failure of health care reform in Bill Clinton's first term, including the budget deficit, constraints imposed by Congressional Budget Office rules, the proposal's potential effect on Medicaid and Medicare, and what <u>Theda Skocpol</u> has identified as a fundamental conflict between the plan's ideal of democratic inclusiveness and the competing American ideal of individualism.\* Yet a fundamental obstacle to the Clinton plan, as with any sweeping reform in American government, was the number and diversity of American interests. Political analyst <u>E. J. Dionne Jr.</u> writes, for example:

[A]greeing on the principle of universal [health care] coverage was quite different from winning agreement on how it would be done, what procedures would be covered, how it would be paid for and how costs would be controlled. Optimistic reformers failed to realize going into the fight that there were good reasons universal coverage had eluded the grasp of even the nation's strongest and most skilled Democratic politicians. The American health care system, partly because of its strengths and partly because of its size, had created a dizzying array of competing interests. The constituencies that generally supported reform—organized labor, big business, hospitals, nurses, some physicians' groups, managed care providers, the elderly and the uninsured—had radically different goals and concerns going into the debate. Absent the most careful coalition management, almost any plan committed to paper was bound to split potential allies. On the other hand, those most skeptical of reform—small-business organizations, many insurance and drug companies, the majority of physicians and individuals who could afford the best coverage—needed only agreement on killing off any proposals that were not to their liking.[†]

The failure of Clinton's health care plan provides a good example of how different groups ally for different reasons, and how they use different resources and tactics. As you study the following table, keep these questions in mind: What resources did these groups use? What tactics did they use? Which groups used access to public officials or to the media? Which traded on their credibility?

*Theda Skocpol, *Boomerang: Clinton's Health Security Effort and the Turn Against Government in US Politics* (New York: W.W. Norton & Company, 1996).

[†]E. J. Dionne, Jr., *They Only Look Dead: Why Progressives Will Dominate the Next Political Era* (New York: Simon & Schuster, 1996), 123–124.

| Group | Position on Clinton Plan | Tactics for Influencing Health Care Reform |
| --- | --- | --- |
| Medical Rehabilitation Education Foundation | If rehabilatation were not covered under health care reform, rehabilitation employees might be out of work | Hired Hill and Knowlton to head lobbying effort; sent out a press package arguing that rehabilitation should be included in standard package of benefits available to all consumers; received funding from three hundred rehab hospitals and professional organizations that provided rehabilitation services |
| Large insurance companies, including Prudential, Aetna, and Cigna | Held a vested interest in any policy reforms affecting health insurance | Influenced debate through a group of physicians, academics, and businesspeople called the Jackson Hole Group |
| Pharmaceutical Manufacturers Association | Opposed the administration's effort to put price controls on drugs | Hired a Washington lobbying firm, which organized a grassroots letter-writing campaign to members of the House Ways and Means Committee and the Senate Finance Committee opposing price controls; sent some letters to employers; followed up with telephone calls |
| Consumers Union | Supported a health care system in which the government is the main insurer | Commissioned a Gallup poll to illustrate the lack of support for any plan that would limit people's choice of their doctors |

| Group | Position on Clinton Plan | Tactics for Influencing Health Care Reform |
| --- | --- | --- |
| Citizen Action | Supported a health care system in which the government is the main insurer | Got one million people to write postcards to Hillary Clinton; tracked contributions by the health care industry to members of Congress |
| Coalition to Preserve Health Benefits, representing hundreds of small and large employers, self-insured companies, and pension and health benefits administrators | Opposed the administration's plan to put most consumers into large pools of insurance purchasers | Held a news conference to describe its opposition |
| Members of Physicians for a National Health Program | Favored a system in which government pays for everyone's health benefits through taxes | Wrote to medical journals and argued against Clinton's plan |
| Christian Coalition | Opposed Clinton plan | Provided individuals with lists of questions to ask at town meetings |
| Citizens for a Sound Economy | Feared Clinton plan would lead to health care rationing and invasions of privacy | Ran sixty-second television advertisement |
| National Federation of Independent Business | Opposed Clinton plan | Members visited lawmakers at their homes |
| Congressional Black Caucus | Argued that Clinton plan posed financial risks for minority-owned businesses | Worked to protect interests from within Congress |
| Health Industry Manufacturers Association, representing three hundred firms that produce medical equipment | Wanted to protect interests of its members in any new system | Hired prominent Democrat Stuart E. Eizenstat, formerly of the Carter administration, to help the group gain access |
| Health Insurance Association of America | Believed Clinton plan threatened their interests | Spent $14 million to run "Harry and Louise" ads criticizing Clinton's plan; hired former representative and health care expert Bill Gradison (R.-OH) to gain access and credibility; ran a full-page ad in the *New York Times* promoting its positions |

*Source:* Adapted from "Case Study 1: Health-Care Reform," prepared by Colleen McGuiness from reports prepared by *Congressional Quarterly* editors and writers, in *Lobbying Congress: How the System Works*, 2nd ed., edited by Bruce C. Wolpe and Bertram J. Levine (Washington, DC: Congressional Quarterly, 1996), 104–115.

# IT'S ALL FUN AND GAMES UNTIL SOMEONE LOSES AN EYE: THE RISKS OF INTEREST GROUP COMPETITION

If groups compete in American politics by design, and if they contribute to incremental and safe policy development, then what's all the fuss about? Why does Jesse Ventura need to go after Evil Special Interest Man? What did he ever do to anybody?

Three fundamental aspects of interest group politics receive serious scrutiny by political scientists and other observers of American government: First, critics charge that interest group politics ignores higher goals and leads to incoherent and valueless policymaking. Second, critics attack the notion that interest groups represent the will of the people, arguing that groups unfairly represent some interests much more effectively than they represent others. Third, and perhaps most importantly, critics fear that interest groups have too much influence over campaigns and the actions of our government. The second and third criticisms lie at the heart of Ventura-style attacks on the influence of special interest groups. If we rely on group competition to produce policy outcomes, if groups represent some interests better than others, and if groups have undue influence over elections and government activity, then those groups with the most money, best access, and highest credibility might have unfair advantages in influencing what happens in government. And if money buys access and even credibility, then the groups with the most financial resources might have an unfair advantage over the politicians and policies that govern the country.

## Is Competition All There Is? Incoherence and the Absence of Values in Government

Critics of interest group politics fear that overreliance on competition and bargaining moves public affairs forward too coolly, as guiding American principles like fairness, equity, and justice give way to a simple acceptance of the outcome of self-interested negotiations. If it is the very *process* of bargaining that legitimizes the system, the competition takes place without attention to overriding national or principled goals. Political scientist Theodore Lowi writes that interest group politics, which he calls "interest group liberalism," demoralizes government by erasing values from the system. Without values, there can be no notion of justice: Lowi writes, "In order to weigh and assess the quality of justice in our government, it is not necessary to define justice, because there is something about [interest group] liberalism that prevents us from raising the question of justice at all."[14] The absence of guiding values, Lowi contends, leads to cynicism as government becomes little more than a bargaining machine. Eventually, strict adherence to the rules of government gives way to an anything-goes bargaining, unrestrained by higher principles, that bends and stretches laws and regulations as far as they will go.

There is a final twist to this critique. Lowi argues that overreliance on bargaining and compromises among competing groups leads to incoherent government, marked by a lack of planning and coordination in pursuit of long-term goals. Without values, government is set adrift: strong groups will have more influence, and weak groups or those individuals not represented by groups will be left behind. Because the pursuit of self-interest by interest groups is based on short-term decisions and selfishness, interest group politics precludes long-term planning, coherence in government activities, and adequate attention to the implementation of policies. In Lowi's interpretation, interest group liberalism renders government "impotent."

---

 ## DISCUSSION BOX 2.2
*INTEREST GROUPS, PARTICIPATION, AND THE WEB*

E-mail and the Internet provide wonderful new opportunities for activists and interest groups seeking to make their opinions known to officials in government. E-mail offers quick and easy communication, and the Internet provides information to Web surfers—who tend to have relatively high levels of education and income, fitting the profile of interest group leaders and activists. Consider the following passages, the first by political scientist Jeffrey Abramson and the second by Jack Bonner, president of a Washington, D.C., company specializing in grassroots mobilization campaigns aimed at influencing legislative and regulatory issues. Do you agree with Abramson's critique of electronic lobbying? How does Abramson's critique mirror Theodore Lowi's analysis of interest group politics, discussed in the text? Do Bonner's recommendations bear out some of Abramson's concerns? How?

**Abramson:**

It is true that the computer empowers groups to lobby more effectively at the mass level, thereby bringing public opinion to bear more immediately and more frequently on the acts of our representatives. But this kind of electrification of democracy, without more, short-circuits or bypasses the kind of deliberations and meetings and debates and considerations of opposing views that alone give democratic substance to the act of registering an opinion on an issue. Democracy demands a concern for, and a familiarity with, the views of others. When electronic democracy is envisioned as a way of permitting individuals, isolated in their own homes, to respond to direct mail stimuli while avoiding the meetings and conversations that alone permit an individual to find his interests in a public context, then the communications revolution threatens democracy with the historic ills of faction and balkanization—different interests competing for power with no sense of community or a common good, the winners bearing no responsibilities for the life of the losers in their midst.*

**Bonner:**

How do you recruit these proven activists [surfing the Web]? By creating an activation Web site, not an informational Web site that buried deep in its bowels has an activation portion to it—if anyone ever makes it that far—but a site that exists solely to create activists. A site that does not pretend to present a detailed wonklike discussion of the merits and intracacies of an issue, but a site that, in a very upfront manner, is an advocacy site, geared solely to recruit activists.

There is a definite need for speed. Remember most people on the Web are speed demons. They, like most of us, zoom through Web sites, and if you can't sell them on your side of an issue quickly they're out of there.

Your site must be a fast read, and a fast sell. As a campaign professional, you know your placard, TV or radio spot has seconds to make your client's case. The Web is an even more demanding place than traditional media. Users have to want to see, hear and send your message.†

*Jeffrey B. Abramson, "The New Media and the New Politics," *Aspen Institute Quarterly* (spring 1990): number 28.
†Jack Bonner, "The Internet and Grassroots Lobbying: The Next Wave," *Campaigns and Elections* (September 1998).

## What If Groups Represent Some Interests Better Than Others? The Limits of Interest Groups as Representative Organizations

The attractiveness of interest group politics rests, to a large extent, on the belief that all affected interests can and do pursue their objectives through competition in the political process. This implies that groups represent their members, and that the combined activities of all interest groups fairly represent all interests in society. If groups do not represent all interests, however, then relying on bargaining and competition among groups can place some interests at a disadvantage or leave some out entirely.

The interests represented by organized groups, in fact, are often *biased toward upper- and middle-class interests*, because it is members of the upper and middle classes who have both the money to support interest groups and the time to participate. And regardless of a group's membership, interest group agendas and strategies are often influenced more by their activist, elite leaders than by their members. Further, *economic and business groups have certain advantages* over public interest groups when squaring off on an issue. Business groups generally have greater financial resources, more established access to policymakers, and more stability than public interest groups, which rely more heavily on public support and use of the media to influence policymakers. Criticizing overreliance on pluralism, or the concept that *all* interests participate in politics to pursue their objectives, political scientist E. E. Schattschneider writes, "The flaw in the pluralist heaven is that the heavenly chorus sings with a strong upper-class accent."[15]

## And What If the Best-Represented Have Too Much Influence?

The third important risk associated with interest group activity is the possibility that an interest group, or a coalition of groups, will gain too much influence over the political system. Citizens often worry that politicians ignore the national interest, or the interests of ordinary citizens, in order to answer the pleas of well-funded or well-organized special interests.

*Growing numbers of well-funded and influential interest groups* fuel the fear of undue influence. Beginning in the 1960s and 1970s, the number of interest groups and their activities skyrocketed. The increase in the number of citizen groups was especially dramatic. In these years, the Civil Rights movement and anti–Vietnam War efforts demonstrated the potential of organized group activity to influence public affairs. Other social issues—abortion, family values, the environment—continue to spark organizing efforts. As government attention to issues such as environmental affairs created new regulatory agencies like the Environmental Protection Agency, businesses responded by increasing *their* lobbying and interest group efforts. Court decisions that allowed interest groups better access to the judiciary also encouraged group organizing.

Citizens worry that these multiplying special interests use their influence and the promise of financial contributions to hold government hostage. Direct payoffs for specific actions are rare in government, but groups can be very persuasive in using their various resources to affect policymaking. There is some evidence that giving by PACs, for example, can be influential in setting agendas, in gaining access to officials, and in important early votes in congressional subcommittees.

## *GUARDING THE GOALS AND POLICING THE PLAYING FIELD: ADDRESSING THE RISKS OF INTEREST GROUP POLITICS*

The dynamics of interest group behavior and groups' influence over public affairs and policymaking raise serious questions about the extent to which group competition produces valueless and incoherent government, the extent to which groups fairly represent American interests, and the prospect that certain influential groups exercise undue influence in our political system. Aspects of our political system address these concerns. We rely on a commitment to values and ideals, on dynamics of the political system, and on specific rules and regulations to control or at least diminish the risks of interest group behavior. The adequacy of our responses to these risks is debatable, though, and continues to attract attention from scholars, politicians, and citizens alike. Part of the criticism arises from the fact that our responses to the risks posed by interest groups are compromises: we sacrifice some attention to values and ideals in the hope that self-interest and competitive bargaining will foster acceptable responses to policy issues, and we encourage groups to participate even though we know some interests are better represented and more influential than others.

### *Avoiding Valueless Government and Incoherence*

An important control on interest groups is that interest groups are not the only forces in the political system; policies do not reflect *only* the outcomes of selfish and valueless competition. The American people remain deeply committed to the ideals and principles embodied in the Declaration of Independence and the Constitution. These principles underlie almost all aspects of the governing system, and one of the most remarkable aspects of interest group politics is the extent to which groups invoke higher principles to support their positions. The most heated public debates often involve competing interpretations of the meaning of these principles and how they should be translated into policy.

Further, though it is true that interest group conflict often makes it very difficult for the government to act, remember that American government is not designed to be efficient. We will examine this principle again in chapter 5, when we look at constitutional theory and the Madisonian framework of government. The aim of American democracy is as much the representation of interests as it is efficiency. Incoherence is part of the design.

### *Addressing Undue Influence*

Two specters of undue special interest influence in particular seem to worry the American public: influence by radical left-wing or right-wing groups whose views are too far out of the mainstream, and influence of upper-class and big business interests. Interest groups with radical or aberrant goals, however, face natural obstacles in the competition for power and influence. The farther an interest group's objectives stray from the mainstream, and the farther a group's competitive methods violate established standards of fair play, the more trouble a group can have pursuing its goals. Aberrant behavior affects a group's credibility, and credibility problems can lead to problems with financing and access. Radical values and objectives hinder access to the media, which favor stories that resonate with mainstream audiences. Members, too, might opt to decrease their support or involvement with a group that they feel has "gone too far," as when President George Bush resigned his membership in the National Rifle Association in response to the NRA's characterization of government agents as "jack-booted thugs."

The biggest risk posed by interest groups is that those groups with the most resources—generally upper-class and business interests—will come to have undue influence over candidates and over the government's activities. Though some groups are indeed better represented by organized interest groups than others, certain factors work to mitigate the effects of these dynamics. The "imperfect mobilization of interests," or the fact that people have diverse interests and belong to many groups with differing viewpoints, makes it unlikely that any one group can win the complete adherence of all of its members to all of the group's political goals. Further, though a special relationship often seems to exist between business interests and government officials, "business" is not always the winner in the competition to influence public policy decisions. First, not all businesses want the same things, and "business" does not always put forward a unified position. Moreover, Jeffrey Berry finds that citizen groups can hold their own against business interests when those two types of groups clash, contrary to the belief that business interests generally prevail in such conflicts. Berry also finds that in cases where a business group goes up against another business group, the winner of the conflict is often the one that is able to align with citizen groups (see Zip Box 2.8).[16]

Even though upper- and middle-class interests are generally better represented by interest groups than are other interests, the political system can still work to the benefit of unorganized interests. Some groups, like the National Coalition for the Homeless, work on behalf of interests that have difficulty organizing themselves. There are political incentives for "policy entrepreneurs" to gather support for initiatives on behalf of unorganized interests, and many opportunities exist for these entrepreneurs to prevail over the objections of even well-funded and well-organized interest groups.

Finally, a host of rules and regulations have been put in place in response to fears that certain groups are gaining undue influence over candidates and government officials. Interest group activity during campaigns, for example, is controlled by a detailed set of campaign finance regulations. The Federal Election Campaign Act of 1971 and the 1974 amendments to the act were designed to make the campaign finance system more ordered and accessible to public scrutiny by taking campaign funding out of back rooms where secret, wealthy contributors dominated. The rules require disclosure of funding sources, and they set maximum levels for some kinds of contributions, establish rules for

 ON THE WEB
www.fec.gov

 ON THE WEB
www.vote-smart.org

Notwithstanding their financial resources, business groups are not always the winners in Congress. In the 104th Congress, environmental groups won some important victories.

| Issue | Winning Side |
|---|---|
| Regulatory reform. House passes bill to mandate cost-benefit analysis and other reforms designed to limit environmental challenges. Senate fails to act. | Environmentalists |
| Clean water rewrite. House passes bill designed to weaken the Clean Water Act. Senate fails to act. | Environmentalists |
| 1995 Rescissions Bill. Contains timber salvage provision that may lead to overharvesting of old-growth forests. Signed into law. | Environmentalists |
| EPA appropriations. House first deletes and then passes restrictions on EPA's authority to enforce pollution control policies. Dropped from final bill. | Environmentalists |
| Endangered Species Act. House Resources Committee passes overhaul but bill fails to get to the floor. | Environmentalists |
| Rewrite of Superfund law. House Commerce subcommittee approves a bill that would weaken Superfund. Not brought up for vote in either house. | Environmentalists |
| Cattle grazing. Bill to overturn Clinton administration rules on grazing on public lands passes Senate but fails in House. | Environmentalists |
| Omnibus appropriations. Senate bill contains numerous environmental riders opposed by environmental groups. "Republicans are forced to retreat on almost all." | Environmentalists |
| Pesticides. Bipartisan rewrite of pesticide law supported by major environmental lobbies. | Environmentalists |
| Safe drinking water. Overhaul is a compromise and while environmentalists don't endorse the bill "they laud many of its provisions." Signed into law. | No clear winner |
| Fisheries management. Bill that is passed and signed into law is designed to protect U.S. fisheries. | Environmentalists |
| Omnibus parks and lands. Bipartisan bill protects and preserves more than 100 different areas. Signed into law. | Environmentalists |

*Source:* Table from Jeffrey M. Berry, *The New Liberalism: The Rising Power of Citizen Groups* (Washington, DC: Brookings Institution Press, 1999), 113.

how money can be raised and spent, and expand the role of interest groups by encouraging PACs. PAC donations can be scrutinized by the press and also by other candidates, and now information on PAC activities is readily available to the public through the Federal Election Commission's website. Interest groups, the media, and candidates competing for office are quick to point out large donations from labor unions, the gun lobby, or even certain professional interests like doctors or trial lawyers.

Such rules represent compromises between the goals of encouraging individual and group participation, on the one hand, and defending against undue influence, on the other. The rules multiply the number of interest groups and encourage their participation; and as the framers anticipated, multiplying groups makes it difficult for any to gain controlling influence. At the same time, though, and in recognition of the risks groups pose to the system, the rules try to regulate a system in which efforts to get around the rules are expected. Calls for reform of the campaign finance system hail from critics unhappy with the current compromise. As we will see in more detail in chapter 4, political parties, individual candidates, interest groups, and large contributors have all learned how to skirt existing campaign finance rules through legal loopholes—inflaming fears that candidates and government are beholden to certain wealthy and unduly influential special interest groups (see Discussion Box 2.3).

The fundamental problem associated with relying on rules and regulations to control undue influence by interest groups over campaigns and governing is that *the rules are subject to influence by these groups.* In other words, groups that have undue influence over the system will have undue influence over the very rules that are written to *govern* that system. Undue influence by special interests poses the threat of anchoring the status quo so deeply that reform is impossible—cementing a permanent advantage for today's most influential special interests.

---

## DISCUSSION BOX 2.3
*THE PAC MAN COMETH: THE CURRENT COMPROMISE ON CAMPAIGN FINANCE ISN'T GOOD ENOUGH*

Bill Bradley, former U.S. Senator from New Jersey, former New York Knicks basketball star, and former contender for the Democratic Party's presidential nomination in 2000, retired from the Senate in part because he was frustrated with the influence of money in American politics. What do you think of the depiction of the role of money in the following passage? Does money have a legitimate role in granting access to interests demonstrating support for politicians? Do politicians betray the public trust when they do favors for contributors who can afford to buy access?

Today, the flow of money into politics is more complicated [than in the nineteenth century] but equally destructive. Its biggest channels are the contributions of political-action committees, or PACs. There are corporate PACs, funded by the voluntary contributions of a company's employees; union or trade-association PACs funded by the contributions of members; and free-standing or cause PACs, funded by those who believe in the cause. PACs are a loophole in the 1974 law. Each can give a candidate five thousand dollars in the primary election and five thousand dollars in the general election.

Corporate PACs have replaced the corporate sinecures for senators and congresspeople. In some campaigns, they represent 50 percent of total contributions.

The five-thousand-dollar limit for PACs allows corporate interests to have a bigger impact on campaigns than individuals, with their thousand-dollar limitation. Many PACs buy access as insurance against changes in law adverse to their corporate interest. The contributor assumes that the corporation's Washington representative, who oversees the PAC allocations, can get an audience with the elected official, or at least with the official's staff, to make the special-interest case. Occasionally, their meeting results in report language that accompanies passage of a bill, or a colloquy on the floor between two senators, with the intent of directing the regulators to interpret a section of the law in a way that favors the special interest. In rare instances, the meeting produces an amendment that alters an effective date for a tax provision or a regulation in favor of the corporation. To assure a willing ear whatever the elective outcome, corporate PACs frequently give to both parties, like prudent businessmen hedging their risks. Those who control PACs are often blunt in their quest for any information that might affect their interests. Once, at a big PAC fund-raiser for the Democratic Party, a Washington PAC representative came up to me and said, "Senator, you've lost a lot of weight. What's the matter? Have you got AIDS?"*

*Bill Bradley, *Time Present, Time Past: A Memoir* (New York: Alfred A. Knopf, 1996), 176.

## Conclusion

Interest group support for candidates and participation in campaigns and government are not evil actions—they are the means by which many people and organizations with shared interests make their wishes known to public officials. When Jesse Ventura attacked "Evil Special Interest Man," he attacked a symbol representing many of the organized groups that were helping to put him in the Minnesota governor's mansion. This is not to say that interest groups are pure as driven snow—only that they are a normal and important part of American politics and government. Problems arise when interest group competition neglects higher principles in public affairs, and when groups have undue and unfair influence over our public leaders. Compromises like those regarding campaign finance regulations encourage interest group activity even as they try to control and channel behavior in ways that diminish the dangerous risks interest groups pose to the system. In the next chapter, we will look at how political parties try to combine and reconcile selfish interests, and how they serve to mitigate some of the more dangerous risks of interest group politics.

## Overnight Assignment ▬▬▬▬▬▬▬▬▬▬▬▬▬▬▬▬▬▬

Look over the media source you chose at the end of chapter 1. What examples are there of interest group activity? How are different groups portrayed in the news, and what activities are they engaged in? What tactics are they using, and what resources? Are some groups opposed by other groups? Are the groups using any rhetoric invoking values and ideals to support their positions?

## Long-Term Integrated Assignment ▬▬▬▬▬▬▬▬▬▬▬▬

Choose a group you are interested in. This can be a group in which you are already a member, or simply a group you'd like to learn more about. Your instructor might give you a few options to choose from. Then get information about the group: How many members does it have? How is the group funded? What are its positions on three specific issues? What kinds of benefits does the group offer? What, specifically, are those benefits? You can often get this information from the group's website, if it has one. You can also call the group—they will usually be very willing to talk with you, whether or not you are a member.

You will be following this group as you read the rest of this book and do the assignments at the end of each chapter, so make sure to pick a group that is involved in a current issue you care about.

## Researching Interest Groups? ▬▬▬▬▬▬▬▬▬▬▬▬▬▬▬

### Try These Authors:

| | | |
|---|---|---|
| Jeffrey M. Berry | Paul S. Herrnson | David Truman |
| Hugh Heclo | Theodore Lowi | Jack L. Walker |

CIGLER, ALLAN J., and BURDETT A. LOOMIS. *Interest Group Politics.* 5th ed. Washington, DC: CQ Press, 1998.

PETRACCA, MARK P., ed. *The Politics of Interests: Interest Groups Transformed.* Boulder, CO: Westview Press, 1992.

ROTHENBERG, LAWRENCE S. *Linking Citizens to Government: Interest Group Politics at Common Cause.* Cambridge, England: Cambridge University Press, 1992.

SABATO, LARRY. *PAC Power.* New York: Norton, 1984.

WILSON, JAMES Q. *Political Organizations.* New York: Basic Books, 1973.

WOLPE, BRUCE C., and BERTRAM J. LEVINE. *Lobbying Congress: How the System Works.* Washington, DC: CQ Press, 1996.

## *Endnotes* ▬▬▬▬▬▬

1. John Gaber, "Manhattan's 14th Street Vendors' Market: Informal Street Peddlers' Complementary Relationship with New York City's Economy,"*Urban Anthropology and Studies of Cultural Systems and World Economic Development* 23, no. 4 (winter 1994); John C. Cross, *Informal Politics: Street Vendors and the State in Mexico City* (Stanford: Stanford University Press, 1998).

2. David B. Truman, *The Governmental Process: Political Interests and Public Opinion.* 2nd ed. (New York: Alfred A. Knopf, 1971), 33–34.

3. Jeffrey M. Berry, *The New Liberalism: The Rising Power of Citizen Groups* (Washington, DC: Brookings Institution Press, 1999), 2; Jeffrey M. Berry, *Lobbying for the People* (Princeton: Princeton University Press, 1977), 7; Berry, *The New Liberalism*, 2. Berry draws a distinction between "public interest groups" and citizen groups. The latter are groups "that advocate material policies as part or all of their lobbying efforts," and these include the subset of "public interest groups" seeking collective goods "which will not selectively and materially benefit the membership or activists of the organization." See Berry, *The New Liberalism*, 190 n. 1.

4. Cited in Frank R. Baumgartner and Beth L. Leech, *Basic Interests: The Importance of Groups in Politics and in Political Science* (Princeton: Princeton University Press, 1998), 75.

5. Doris A. Graber, *Mass Media and American Politics,* 4th ed. (Washington, DC: CQ Press, 1993), 172.

6. Berry, *The New Liberalism,* chap. 6.

7. Simply having money does not guarantee success, however. Decisions about the allocation of resources and money management can be just as important to a group's effectiveness as how much money a particular group has to spend. Research suggests, for example, that citizen groups aligned on the Republican side of affairs might raise more funds than groups supporting traditional Democratic causes, but a larger proportion of these funds goes toward administrative overhead and activities like direct mail solicitations of more funds—inhibiting these groups' ability to target their resources for lobbying and other efforts. See Berry, *The New Liberalism,* chap. 5.

8. Cited in Baumgartner and Leech, *Basic Interests,* 74.

9. See Jeffrey M. Berry, *The Interest Group Society,* 3rd ed. (New York: Longman, 1997), 81ff.; Christopher J. Bosso, "The Color of Money: Environmental Groups and the Pathologies of Fund Raising," in *Interest Group Politics,* 4th ed., edited by Allan J. Cigler and Burdett A. Loomis (Washington, DC: CQ Press, 1996), 101ff.

10. Berry, *The New Liberalism,* 131.

11. Baumgartner and Leech, *Basic Interests,* 148.

12. Laura R. Woliver, "Abortion Interests: From the Usual Suspects to Expanded Coalitions," in *Interest Group Politics*, ed. Cigler and Loomis, chap. 15.

13. Berry, *The New Liberalism*, p. 116. For some examples of incremental progress and government activity that belie the concept of gridlock, see *The New Politics of Public Policy* (Baltimore: Johns Hopkins University Press, 1995), ed. Marc Landy and Martin A. Levin.

14. Theodore J. Lowi, *The End of Liberalism: The Second Republic in the United States*, 2nd ed. (New York: W. W. Norton & Company, 1976), 296.

15. E. E. Schattschneider, *The Semi-Sovereign People: A Realist's View of Democracy in America* (New York: Holt, Rinehart & Winston, 1960), 35.

16. Berry, *The New Liberalism*, 82–85.

# Political Parties

## CHAPTER OUTLINE

In November 1992, Bill Clinton became the first candidate representing the Democratic party to be elected president since Jimmy Carter in 1976. The Democrats suddenly controlled the White House and enjoyed majorities in both the House of Representatives and the Senate. Yet despite the appearance of Democratic control, many of President Clinton's early initiatives—most notably, reform of the nation's health care system—died in Congress.

In November 1994, the "Republican Revolution" saw Republican victories in House and Senate races across the country. For the first time in forty years, the Republican party enjoyed majorities in both houses of Congress. The Republican "Contract with America," skillfully promoted by soon-to-be Speaker of the House Newt Gingrich, articulated a clear plan of action for Republicans seeking to make the most of their new majority status. Yet despite the appearance of Republican control, most of the Contract's provisions—including term limits and a balanced budget amendment—failed to become law.

In November 1996, voters returned Democrat Bill Clinton to the White House for a second term; in 1996 and 1998, voters returned Republican majorities to both houses of Congress, even though those majorities were somewhat below 1994 levels. Finally, in November 2000, voters ushered in a new century by participating in one of the closest elections in United States history.

We saw in chapters 1 and 2 that Americans are linked to government by the media and its role in public discussion, and by interest groups, which organize shared interests to compete for influence in government. Americans and public officials are also connected to government by political parties, which compete for public offices and for influence in policymaking. But why are political parties, seemingly the beneficiaries of new public attitudes throughout elections in the 1990s, unable to shepherd policies successfully through government? Why did both parties have such problems governing when they possessed majorities in both houses of Congress? Why did the Democrats seem to face even *more* difficulties when they also controlled the White House? If political parties are unable to put popular agendas into practice, then what role do they play in the competitive American political system?

**The Bottom Line.** The dynamics of American politics perpetuate a system dominated by two major political parties. In the electorate, political parties work to organize interests, reconcile conflicts, and win elections; in government, parties help coordinate action, order government activity, and compete for power and influence. Serious problems threaten the parties' ability to achieve these objectives successfully, and American parties are notoriously "weak." They are forced to make compromises in the electorate that dilute their positions on issues and risk alienating members with strong beliefs; they are forced to make compromises in government that limit their ability to coordinate government policies and to control individuals' behavior. Despite predictions of their demise, though, political parties have adapted to new circumstances and continue to be an important and influential part of our political system.

## PARTY COMPETITION IN THE UNITED STATES: THEM AND THEM OTHERS, FOR BETTER OR WORSE

Political scientist E. E. Schattschneider writes, "[T]here are common interests as well as special interests. . . . To assume that people have merely conflicting interests and nothing else is to invent a political nightmare that has only a superficial relation to reality."[1] Unlike narrowly focused special interest groups, political parties are designed to bring together broad coalitions of interests under big "umbrellas." Parties compete with each other to maximize party interests, of course, but this competition is characterized by efforts to encourage diverse interests to work together toward compromise and the building of majority positions.

### Go One on One: Two-Party Dominance in the United States

American politics are dominated by two major political parties, the Democrats and the Republicans. In broad terms, the two parties are separated by philosophical views about government's role and the nature of American society.

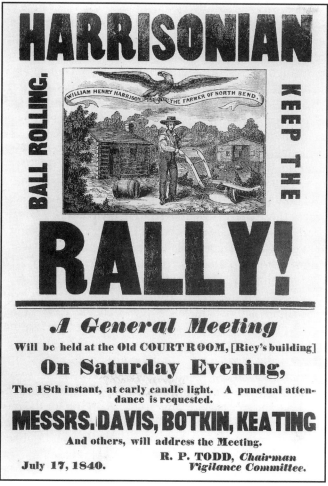

Nineteenth-century political rallies were exciting community events. This advertisement invited people to an event supporting William Henry Harrison's presidential campaign in 1840. Harrison won the election, but died a month after giving his inaugural address.

*Democrats* traditionally favor the active intervention of government to help solve public problems. They generally support government involvement in the economy and government spending for social programs—involvement that often demands higher taxes. Though the lineage of the Democratic party goes back as far as the nation's founding, the party's modern principles are rooted in Franklin Delano Roosevelt's presidency, which spanned the Great Depression and World War II, from 1933 to 1945. FDR's "New Deal" programs emphasized government involvement in the economy, government provision of jobs to the unemployed, the institution of Social Security, and the creation of a host of government agencies to facilitate and coordinate government activity.

Support for Roosevelt and the Democrats emanated from a broad "New Deal coalition" of urban residents, immigrants, northern blacks, the working

**ON THE WEB**
www.democrats.org/
index.html

class, labor unions, and the solidly Democratic South. Over time, this coalition has frayed somewhat, with the most noticeable change coming in the South's post-1960s shift toward the Republican party. The Democrats, though, continue to add new interests to their coalition. The party currently allies with many citizen groups representing environmentalists, civil rights and human rights organizations, consumers' groups, women's groups, and gay groups.

Critics charge FDR and later Democrats with building an expensive and oversized national government apparatus that fails to meet the needs of ordinary Americans, and with consistently raising taxes to pay for overblown programs and policies. Democratic programs from the "Great Society" of the 1960s, for example, have come under fire in recent years for being misguided and ineffective applications of time and money. Bill Clinton's promise to "end welfare as we know it," and his subsequent work with a Republican Congress, aimed to address these charges by redesigning the country's Great Society–era national welfare policy. Critics also charge Democrats with being inept in the conduct of foreign affairs. Democratic leadership of the failed war in Vietnam, as well as clumsy efforts to address recent situations in Bosnia, North Korea, and Kosovo, symbolize the Democrats' image in foreign policy. The Democrats' connections to groups representing interests like environmentalists, gays, and civil rights activists elicit charges that the party is beholden to a kaleidoscope of interests that diverge from the values of "ordinary" Americans.

ON THE WEB
www.rnc.org

*Republicans,* on the other hand, traditionally oppose government involvement in economic affairs and argue for smaller and less expensive government programs. Ronald Reagan's presidency (1981–1989) galvanized Republicans and embodied Republican ideas for governing. Working for the most part with a Democrat-controlled House and a Republican-controlled Senate, Reagan slashed government spending on programs like welfare and public housing for the poor. Reagan was particularly adept at making the case for a leaner, less intrusive federal government. At the same time as they advocate less government involvement in economic issues, though, Republicans have sought to expand government's involvement in certain social issues. Republicans often advocate restrictions on abortion, for example. In 1994, the party agenda outlined in the Republican "Contract with America" included welfare reform, term limits for federal representatives, and an amendment to the Constitution calling for a balanced budget. The Republican party also has a reputation for strength and effectiveness in foreign affairs: Reagan successfully advocated a muscular national military in the closing years of the Cold War, and President George Bush marshaled that military to quick victory over Iraq in the Gulf War.

Republicans generally draw support from the middle and upper classes, and from business interests. Republicans are aligned with "conservative" groups and groups supporting "traditional" social values and mores, like anti-abortion groups and fundamentalist Christians.

Critics charge Republicans with being dominated by business interests and with being unsympathetic toward the nation's less fortunate citizens. Republican reluctance to embrace the Civil Rights movement in the 1950s and 1960s, for example, continues to symbolize Republican lack of concern for minorities and the dispossessed. These views have been bolstered in recent years by the anti-immigrant rhetoric of Pete Wilson, former Republican governor of California, and Pat Buchanan, former Republican presidential candidate (now with the Reform Party). In a similar vein, critics argue that Republican pro-life positions ignore the difficult situations faced by many pregnant women, and that efforts to restrict access to abortions contradict Republican calls for less intrusive government. Critics also counter Republicans' reputation for fiscal conservatism by noting that the nation's debt tripled during the Reagan administration, a result of increased military spending and declining revenues resulting in part from tax cuts.

## Why Two Parties?

American politics have been dominated by two major parties throughout most of U.S. history (see Discussion Box 3.1). The parties have not always been the Republican and Democrat parties with which we are familiar, but for more than two centuries most Americans have aligned themselves with one of two partisan contenders. Several factors encourage two-party dominance in the United States, including the dynamics of our electoral system, the nature of the presidency, and the obstacles facing the development of strong third parties.

---

## DISCUSSION BOX 3.1
### WELCOME TO THE PARTY: EARLY THOUGHTS ON PARTIES AND POLITICS IN AMERICA

Within a few years of the start of government under the Constitution, two national parties were beginning to take shape. Historian John C. Miller writes:

While the Federalists and Republicans lacked the appurtenances of present-day political parties, they were true parties in the sense that they acted upon clearly formulated ideas, they had leaders of marked intellectual and political ability, and they aspired to administer the government for the benefit of sections and economic groups. It is significant that these political parties first manifested themselves in Congress, from whence they percolated down to the electorate.*

Parties developed slowly; some of the framers viewed parties with mistrust, seeing them as vehicles for political ambition and conflict. James Madison and Thomas Jefferson were both wary of parties and the threats parties posed to national unity and deliberative government, yet both acknowledged that ignoring the development of such important groups might nudge political competition in dangerous directions. In the passages below, what does Madison say could happen if citizens ignore the state of parties? Why does Jefferson believe his involvement with partisan politics is so important? Are these opinions still relevant today?

**Madison:**

As it is the business of the contemplative statesman to trace the history of parties in a free country, so it is the duty of the citizen at all times to understand the actual state of them. Whenever this duty is omitted, an opportunity is given to designing men, by the use of artificial or nominal distinctions, to oppose and balance against each other those who never differed as to the end to be pursued, and may no longer differ as to the means of attaining it.†

**Jefferson:**

Were parties here [in America] divided merely by a greediness for office, as in England, to take a part with either would be unworthy of a reasonable or moral man, but where the principle of difference is as substantial and as strongly pronounced as between the republicans & the Monocrats [Federalists] of our country, I hold it as honorable to take a firm & decided part, and as immoral to pursue a middle line, as between the parties of Honest men, & Rogues, into which every country is divided."‡

*John C. Miller, *The Federalist Era, 1789–1801* (New York: Harper & Row, 1963), 101–102.
†James Madison, "A Candid State of Parties", *National Gazette*, September 26, 1792, reprinted in *James Madison: Writings* (New York: Library of America, 1999), 530.
‡Thomas Jefferson to William Branch Giles, December 31, 1795, quoted in William Nisbet Chambers, *Political Parties in a New Nation: The American Experience, 1776–1809* (London: Oxford University Press, 1963), 93.

## The Winner-Take-All Electoral System

*The dynamics of the American electoral system* encourage two-party dominance. Our electoral system is a winner-take-all system, or what political scientists call a single-member district system. This means that no matter what office is at stake, no matter how large the constituency is, and no matter how many individuals run for the office, there will be only one winner. Further, in most cases a winner is chosen whether or not the winner receives a clear majority—more than 50 percent—of the votes. American candidates can win with a mere plurality of votes—meaning simply getting more votes than their opponents get. So in a race with three candidates, even if two receive 30 percent of the vote and the third gets only 40 percent, the candidate with the 40 percent wins and the other two candidates get nothing.

This system encourages coalition building, because there is no electoral benefit to winning a healthy percentage of the vote if you still lose the election. In the three-candidate race above, the two interests that each received 30 percent of the vote might have worked together to build a coalition, focused their efforts on electing one of their two candidates, and received 60 percent of the vote—winning the election. This system encourages groups without a clear chance for victory to forge compromises with other groups whereby they can back a winning candidate and meet some of their objectives; a candidate who holds too stubbornly to a position with weak support can wind up on election day with nothing to show for his or her efforts.

The single-member district system differs from the "proportional representation" system used in many countries to distribute seats in government. Under proportional representation, seats in a parliament or other governing body are distributed according to the proportion of the vote won by participating parties. This means that a party that receives one-third of the vote can expect to see that percentage translate into control of one-third of the seats in government. The results of the election example above, in which two candidates each received 30 percent of the vote and one received 40 percent, would look very different under a proportional representation system. Under American-style single-member districting, each of the two losers goes home; under proportional representation, with three parties each winning roughly one-third of the vote, the three parties might each receive one-third of the seats in government.

The difference in the results of the two systems leads to differences in the behavior of political parties. In a proportional representation system, parties that expect to win a relatively small part of the vote do not have the same incentive to form coalitions with other interests during the campaign as they would have under single-member districting. The incentive to compromise and build winning campaign coalitions in the American system works to draw diverse interests together, perpetuating electoral competition between two major contenders.

## The Nature of the Presidency and the Role of the Media

*The nature of the presidency* works in tandem with the dynamics of our electoral system to encourage two-party dominance. The presidency is the single most important jewel in the American political system, and it is the only office to which a candidate is elected in a national election. Presidents are elected by electoral votes, which are divided among the states; the candidate who wins a state's popular vote wins that state's electoral votes.[2] A candidate might win every state by one popular vote, and thereby win by a landslide in the electoral college; on the other hand, the candidate who lost each state by one popular vote gets no electoral votes at all. Presidential elections, then, require parties to organize and build winning coalitions state by state. The difficulty and expense of electing a single person to the presidency results in tremendous pressure for interests to pool resources and combine efforts, leading to coalition building on a massive scale and, usually, to competition between two dominant political parties.

Finally, we saw in chapter 1 how the media polarize discussions, drawing stark contrasts between two sides of an issue and highlighting conflict and competition between those two sides. Having two dominant parties compete for power fits that mold very nicely. Further, the two major parties benefit from well-established access to the media, from the credibility established over decades of influence in politics and government, and from being familiar to the media and to the public.

## Why Can't We Play, Too?
## Third Parties and Independents in America

Media dynamics and the nature of our electoral system not only promote two-party dominance, they actively discourage strong and lasting efforts by third parties and independents. Such candidacies can have important effects on elections and even on the nation's policy agenda, but their chances of electoral success at the national level and their chances for political longevity are both slim.

### Hey, Let Me In! Third Parties' and Independents' Problems with the Media

In chapter 1, we saw that the media are attracted to stories that are new and interesting to the public; to some extent, this dynamic works in favor of third parties and independents. Serious efforts outside of the dominant parties are often driven by important current issues or trends in government. Ross Perot's 1992 candidacy, for example, took advantage of a general belief that the two major parties and their candidates were not adequately serving the public interest. Third parties and independent candidacies can benefit from leadership by charismatic political newcomers like Perot and Jesse Ventura; they can also benefit from the public's interest in stories of comebacks by former officials dissatisfied with the established parties, like former President Theodore Roosevelt's presidential run for the Bull Moose party in 1912.

Yet third-party candidates and independents still need to contend with the media's desire to polarize issues and streamline conflict, and they need to contend with the fact that their very novelty can stand them at a *dis*advantage in terms of media access and credibility.[3] Perot enjoyed considerable access to the media, but many independent candidates have difficulty breaking into mainstream news coverage. Because the two-party system's dominance is so embedded in our history and our culture, it is relatively easy for third-party candidates to be marginalized as dangerous radicals or nutty kooks. Perot, for example, quickly gained a reputation as a wealthy outsider, and his unfamiliar style together with his huge personal fortune made him an easy target for late-night television one-liners. Many cast Perot as something of a lunatic, and this

ON THE WEB
www.fec.gov/pages/
ecmenu2.htm

ON THE WEB
www.reformparty.org

ON THE WEB
www.natural-law.org

ON THE WEB
www.greens.org/
gpusa

ON THE WEB
www.lp.org

ON THE WEB
www.political-parties.
com

ON THE WEB
www.politics1.com/
parties.htm

hampered his effort to gain the credibility necessary to become and remain a viable candidate for the presidency. After winning 19 percent of the popular vote in 1992, Perot won only 8 percent in 1996—a year in which he was excluded from nationally televised presidential debates. (See Zip Box 3.1.)

### I Just Can't Win: Disadvantages for Third-Party and Independent Candidates in the Electoral System

Our electoral system also creates obstacles to third-party and independent candidacies. Only the most committed and best organized third parties have the resources to place a presidential candidate on election ballots across the country. Because a candidate wins the presidency by winning state electoral votes, third parties must organize state by state to gain a place on presidential election ballots. A candidate who cannot win important states outright stands little chance of being elected. Winning the presidency, therefore, is much more difficult than simply generating a national following. As we will see in more detail in chapter 5, this is by design: the Constitution's framers insulated the presidency from charismatic demagogues who might capitalize on crises or popular passions to build strong but fleeting national support among the public. (See Zip Box 3.2.)

## Zip Box 3.1
*Fate of Third Parties and Independent Candidates*

| Year | Third Party | Percent of Popular Vote for President | No. of Electoral Votes | Status in Next Election |
|------|-------------|------------------------|------------------|------------------------|
| 1832 | Anti-Masonic | 7.8 | 7 | Endorse Whig candidate |
| 1848 | Free-Soil | 10.1 | 0 | Received 4.9% of vote |
| 1856 | American (Know-Nothing) | 21.5 | 8 | Party dissolved |
| | Republican | 33.1 | 114 | Won presidency |
| 1860 | Southern Democrat | 18.1 | 72 | Party dissolved |
| | Constitution Union | 12.6 | 39 | Party dissolved |
| 1892 | Populist | 8.5 | 22 | Endorsed Democratic candidate |
| 1912 | Progressive (T. Roosevelt) | 27.4 | 88 | Returned to Republican Party |
| | Socialist | 6.0 | 0 | Received 3.2% of vote |
| 1924 | Progressive (R. La Follette) | 16.6 | 13 | Returned to Republican Party |
| 1948 | States' Rights Democratic | 2.4 | 39 | Party dissolved |
| | Progressive (H. Wallace) | 2.4 | 0 | Received 0.23% of vote |
| 1968 | American Independent (G. Wallace) | 13.5 | 46 | Received 1.4% of vote |
| 1980 | John B. Anderson | 6.6 | 0 | Did not run |
| 1992 | Ross Perot | 18.9 | 0 | Received 8.4% of vote |
| 2000 | Ralph Nader | 3.0 | 0 | |

*Source:* John F. Bibby, *Governing by Consent* (Washington, D.C.: CQ Press, 1992), 190. Updated by the authors.

Other factors also hinder candidacies outside of the two dominant parties. In presidential and other federal elections, the two major parties automatically qualify for *federal funds* that they can use in their campaigns. Candidates not aligned with the two major parties struggle to qualify for federal funds, since they must have won at least 5 percent of the vote in the previous election, which most third parties will not have done. Third parties also have *trouble finding attractive candidates;* promising candidates are often more willing to tie their fortunes to established parties than to become associated with an upstart third party.

Finally, as we have just seen, the nature of our electoral system *encourages groups and movements to build coalitions* and work together to win elections. Third parties and strong independents usually become integrated into the major parties—the more successful they are, the more attractive they become to the two major parties. Knowing that their efforts will stand little chance of winning a plurality of votes, especially in a presidential election, a third party or an independent candidate eventually has an incentive to win attention and

## Zip Box 3.2
*Electoral Votes and Parties in America*

The wild and crazy 2000 presidential election highlighted the intricacies of the American electoral system. First, the election reminded voters that it is indeed possible to win the popular vote but lose the vote in the electoral college. Prior to 2000, this had happened in three presidential elections.

Second, third-party candidate Ralph Nader's impact on races in the key states of New Hampshire and Florida hurt Al Gore's overall chances. Nader won 4 percent of the vote in New Hampshire and about 3 percent of the vote in Florida. A shift of even a relatively small number of votes from Nader to Gore might have given Gore a convincing victory in either state. Third parties can play an important role in Americna presidential elections.

Finally, the importance of electoral votes turned the world spotlight on one state—Florida. Network news coverage on election night 2000 first gave Florida's large cache of 25 electoral votes to Al Gore, giving him an early lead in the electoral vote returns. Newscasts then stripped Gore's victory away, ruling Florida too close to call midway through the evening. Around 2:15 AM, vote projections and newscasts reversed and gave the state—and, by that time, the election—to George W. Bush. Projections shifted again, though, and by 4:00 AM viewers who had stayed up to watch the returns saw Florida, and the outcome of the presidential election, once again become "Too Close to Call." Counts, recounts, rumors and threats of lawsuits dominated the news as the nation awaited a final outcome.

political concessions from one of the major parties, and then hitch the wagon to a stronger horse. The Reform Party's recent history illustrates some of the difficulties facing third party movements. Founded by Ross Perot and surprisingly successful in the 1992 campaign, many of its themes were quickly co-opted by the major parties; the Reform Party had dramatically less impact in 1996. Bickering over the party's direction rendered the party all but irrelevant to the 2000 campaign and placed its future in serious jeopardy. Minnesota Governor Jesse Ventura left the party, disgusted with its disorganization and depriving the party of one of its most popular and successful members. The party suffered another blow when former Republican presidential candidate Pat Buchanan staged a hostile takeover, splitting the party and ousting many of its original supporters. The Buchanan-led Reform Party finished far back of the field in 2000.

## EVERYBODY'S INVITED: PARTY COMPROMISES AND WEAKNESS IN THE ELECTORATE

### Complex Roles and Party Compromises

If American politics are dominated by two major parties, what is it, exactly, that parties do? In the electorate, parties link people and interests with public officials, they work to combine as many interests as possible in order to forge winning majority coalitions, and they compete for power and influence. Taking these three roles together, parties are simultaneously expected to work for individuals, to build electoral majorities by smoothing and reconciling diverse interests, and to win elections by *highlighting* differences and conflicts. These competing goals make the parties' work very difficult.

Political parties in the electorate connect people to government by *serving as a means of political socialization.* They provide entry-level opportunities like canvasing and organizing for individuals who are interested in politics, and they help educate people about the political system. Parties traditionally make appeals to young people and recent immigrants in order to nurture party loyalty and support. Parties also connect people to government by *working on behalf of individuals.* Though this role was a bigger part of party behavior in the past, when parties and local party "machines" were a primary source of jobs and assistance to new immigrants and urban residents, parties remain avenues through which individuals can contact and attempt to influence the workings of government.

In the parties' electoral roles, we see the competing demands that lie at the heart of party activities. *Parties are designed to build influential coalitions* by attracting diverse interests, crafting compromises, and using the strength of those alliances to win elections. Unlike interest groups, which focus on narrow issues, parties are broadly focused and seek to draw support from as many different interests as possible. Interests disagree about aspects of policies and current issues, and parties must try to organize and reconcile competing opinions and interests. Part of this involves containing and integrating third-party and other movements taking place outside of the two major parties, and part asks the parties to bring together the numerous and diverse interests we examined in chapter 2.

Two fundamental problems arise from the party's role in organizing and reconciling competing interests. First, the very process of reconciliation is contentious, and that contention can make the parties appear ineffective. Media coverage of the parties contributes to this image. Media coverage emphasizes conflicts and divisions within the parties. This is understandable, given the demands for newsworthiness and conflict that we examined in chapter 1, but such coverage makes the parties look troubled, divided, and consumed by petty bickering—they look as though they are being torn apart from the inside. As political scientist <u>Matthew Robert Kerbel</u> writes,

> The dilemma this poses for parties is that differences are invariably portrayed as problematic and troublesome rather than healthy and inevitable, projecting the misleading impression that parties are unable to respond to the challenges of diversity. . . . Viewed with a wider lens, the presence of internal debate is a sign that the parties offer political shelter to a spectrum of interests whose inevitable disagreements antecede moderation and compromise. Interests are aggregated through shouting and shrugging; these are signs the party is functioning effectively. But it does not appear this way in the press.[4]

Second, the parties' role in combining and reconciling interests creates tension with their role in the electorate more generally. Parties *work for the election of particular candidates* by coordinating national and state political and campaign strategies, by outlining positions on issues, and by creating coordinated plans for action—activities that require parties to articulate *differences* between themselves and others. So even as political parties help stabilize and organize political activity in America, they serve as the engines of divisive, partisan competition. Political scientist <u>James L. Sundquist</u> has written that Americans hold an ambivalent attitude toward their political parties as a result of the competing demands we make on them:

> Political parties have always occupied an ambiguous position in American public life. They are profoundly mistrusted—yet accepted. Their constant maneuvering for petty advantage is reviled and ridiculed, but millions of people call themselves either Democrats or Republicans and cherish the ideals of their party with a religious fervor. Parties have been credited with such supreme achievements as saving the Union and rescuing the country from the Great Depression. But they have also been accused of placing partisan advantage ahead of the national good, of failing to conceive farsighted programs, of running away from problems and responsibilities, and sometimes of deep and pervasive corruption.[5]

In sum, parties struggle to appear effective and not torn by internal conflict, and they strive to combine and reconcile interests while simultaneously competing for partisan advantages. To meet these complex demands, parties often choose to take softer, compromising stands on issues, and they sometimes try to avoid contention on divisive issues altogether (see BriefCase Box 3.1). Such actions can dampen party allegiances and loyalties, and they can encourage partisans with strong commitments on particular issues to ally themselves more closely with narrowly focused interest groups.

The struggle over the Republican party's official platform stance on abortion illustrates a common dilemma facing American political parties: how to satisfy partisan activists whose ideological commitments can hurt the party's ability to attract broad and diverse support. The Republican dilemma begins with the fact that many of the party's strongest partisans and most active members are deeply committed to the party's traditional anti-abortion stance. Republican candidates rely heavily on these activists to get out the vote during elections. In recent years, though, more and more Republican candidates are voicing pro-choice positions, both as personal belief and as a political calculation based on evidence suggesting that most voters—even most Republicans—do not agree with the party's official platform stance opposing all abortions.

This situation created a dilemma for Bob Dole when he ran for president in 1996. Like any Republican candidate, Dole wanted to attract as many voters as possible—especially the pro-choice women and young urban professionals who had been key elements in the Republicans' 1980, 1984, and 1988 election success. At the same time, however, Dole knew that he was largely reliant on the active support of anti-abortion party members. Dole tried to broker a compromise as the split within the party headed toward the 1996 Republican National Convention, yet even a compromise on abortion risked alienating—and demobilizing—a substantial number of party members.

Consider the following statements from the months leading up to the convention.* Which side seems more willing to compromise, and why do you think they are? How do the others react to the prospect of a compromise? Why? What risk does a candidate run if he or she alienates party members deeply committed to a particular position? If you were running, which of these speakers would you like to have working for your campaign?

The more we suppress debate on this issue, the more it hurts the Republican Party.

We need to agree to disagree.

—Olympia Snowe, pro-choice
Republican Senator from Maine

Being a pro-life party is the right thing to do. We can't back off our values just because we think they may limit our membership. You end up running a poll to determine your values. We can be a party of values, or a valueless party.

—J. Randy Forbes, pro-life chairman
of the Virginia Republican Party

[Fighting over abortion] gets us bogged down with something that doesn't belong in the political arena. You create a disunity where people go home angry and say, "I'm not working with the Republican Party anymore."

—David N. Ott, pro-choice Republican
State Representative in Maine

We are saying no words can be changed [in the party's anti-abortion platform]. We will fight them [those who want to alter the platform] inside the convention hall. We will fight them outside the hall. We will fight them on radio, on TV, in the mail, on the phones. We will fight and fight and fight until we win. There is no compromise. There is no negotiating. There is no appeasement.

—Bay Buchanan, anti-abortion manager
of her brother Pat Buchanan's campaign
for the Republican nomination

*All quotations appeared in the *New York Times*: Snowe in "Abortion-Rights Supporters Fight for Their Say in G.O.P." by Francis X. Clines, May 6, 1996; Forbes and Ott in "In Many States, Abortion Feud Splits G.O.P." by Richard L. Berke, June 20, 1996; and Buchanan in "A Fundamental Problem" by Jason DeParle, July 14, 1996.

## Party Weakness in the Electorate

As we will see later in this chapter, if parties are too weak to fulfill their roles in socializing people, linking individuals with government, and reconciling interests, the entire political system can suffer—and key indicators suggest that individuals are now less connected to parties than they once were. First, *party identification has been declining.* Some studies suggest that a full third of registered voters today identify themselves as independents.[6] Second, the percentage of party members with *"strong" devotion to their parties has declined.* Third, *"split ticket" voting is on the rise.* In elections, "split-ticket" voting refers to a voter choosing candidates of one party for some offices and candidates of another party for other offices. According to one estimate, six out of ten voters split their ticket in presidential elections.[7] The rise in split-ticket voting suggests that voters increasingly base their choices on factors associated with individual candidates and issues, and less on the information offered by a candidate's party affiliation. (See Zip Box 3.3.)

## Zip Box 3.3
*Parties and Partisanship*

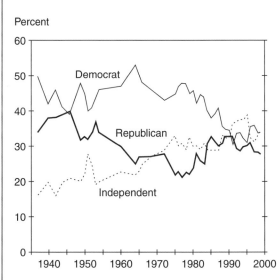

Percent

Note: Respondents who gave replies other than Democrat, Republican, or Independent are excluded. Question: "In politics, as of today, do you consider yourself a Republican, a Democrat, or an Independent?" Data from 1988 and later are from telephone surveys, which tend to report more Republican and fewer Democratic partisans than in-person interviews. See Larry Hugick, "Party Identification: The Disparity between Gallup's In-person and Telephone Interview Findings," *Public Perspective*, September/October 1991, 23–24.

**Partisan Identification, Gallup Poll, 1937–1999**

*Sources:* The Gallup Organization, "The Gallup Poll Party ID Trend to 1937," no date; and unpublished data from the Gallup Poll.

### Partisan Identification, Gallup Poll, Cross-Section, 1999 (percent)

|  | Republican | Independent | Democrat |
|---|---|---|---|
| Gender |  |  |  |
| Men | 28 | 45 | 27 |
| Women | 29 | 35 | 36 |
| Age |  |  |  |
| 18–29 | 23 | 52 | 25 |
| 30–49 | 31 | 37 | 32 |
| 50–64 | 26 | 39 | 35 |
| 65 and over | 32 | 33 | 35 |
| Race |  |  |  |
| White | 31 | 41 | 28 |
| Black | 13 | 25 | 62 |

|  | Republican | Independent | Democrat |
|---|---|---|---|
| **Education** | | | |
| No college | 24 | 43 | 33 |
| College incomplete | 33 | 37 | 30 |
| College graduate | 35 | 35 | 31 |
| Post graduate | 31 | 37 | 32 |
| **Household income** | | | |
| Under $20,000 | 20 | 46 | 34 |
| $20,000–29,999 | 21 | 47 | 32 |
| $30,000–49,999 | 33 | 38 | 29 |
| $50,000 and over | 33 | 35 | 32 |
| **Ideology** | | | |
| Conservative | 45 | 33 | 22 |
| Moderate | 7 | 43 | 34 |
| Liberal | 7 | 47 | 46 |
| **Region** | | | |
| East | 31 | 39 | 30 |
| Midwest | 25 | 45 | 31 |
| South | 30 | 38 | 32 |
| West | 28 | 38 | 34 |
| National | 29 | 40 | 32 |

*Note:* Question: "In politics, as of today, do you consider yourself a Republican, a Democrat, or an Independent?" Percentages are based on the 1,022 total respondents in a CNN/*USA Today*/Gallup Poll, June 1999.

## Partisan Identification, National Election Studies, 1952–1998 (percent)

| Year | Democrat | | | Inde-pen-dent | Republican | | | Apo-litical | Total | Number of Interviews |
|---|---|---|---|---|---|---|---|---|---|---|
| | Strong | Weak | Inde-pendent | | Inde-pendent | Weak | Strong | | | |
| 1952 | 22 | 25 | 10 | 6 | 7 | 14 | 14 | 3 | 101 | 1,784 |
| 1954 | 22 | 25 | 9 | 7 | 6 | 14 | 13 | 4 | 100 | 1,130 |
| 1956 | 21 | 23 | 6 | 9 | 8 | 14 | 15 | 4 | 100 | 1,757 |
| 1958 | 27 | 22 | 7 | 7 | 5 | 17 | 11 | 4 | 100 | 1,808 |
| 1960 | 20 | 25 | 6 | 10 | 7 | 14 | 16 | 2 | 100 | 1,911 |
| 1962 | 23 | 23 | 7 | 8 | 6 | 16 | 12 | 4 | 99 | 1,287 |
| 1964 | 27 | 25 | 9 | 8 | 6 | 14 | 11 | 1 | 101 | 1,550 |
| 1966 | 18 | 28 | 9 | 12 | 7 | 15 | 10 | 1 | 100 | 1,278 |
| 1968 | 20 | 25 | 10 | 11 | 9 | 15 | 10 | 1 | 101 | 1,553 |
| 1970 | 20 | 24 | 10 | 13 | 8 | 15 | 9 | 1 | 100 | 1,501 |
| 1972 | 15 | 26 | 11 | 13 | 10 | 13 | 10 | 1 | 99 | 2,694 |
| 1974 | 17 | 21 | 13 | 15 | 9 | 14 | 8 | 3 | 100 | 2,505 |
| 1976 | 15 | 25 | 12 | 15 | 10 | 14 | 9 | 1 | 101 | 2,850 |

| 1978 | 15 | 24 | 14 | 14 | 10 | 13 | 8 | 3 | 101 | 2,283 |
| 1980 | 18 | 23 | 11 | 13 | 10 | 14 | 9 | 2 | 100 | 1,613 |
| 1982 | 20 | 24 | 11 | 11 | 8 | 14 | 10 | 2 | 100 | 1,418 |
| 1984 | 17 | 20 | 11 | 11 | 12 | 15 | 12 | 2 | 100 | 2,236 |
| 1986 | 18 | 22 | 10 | 12 | 11 | 15 | 10 | 2 | 100 | 2,166 |
| 1988 | 17 | 18 | 12 | 11 | 13 | 14 | 14 | 2 | 101 | 2,032 |
| 1990 | 20 | 19 | 12 | 11 | 12 | 15 | 10 | 2 | 101 | 1,991 |
| 1992 | 17 | 18 | 14 | 12 | 13 | 15 | 11 | 1 | 101 | 2,487 |
| 1994 | 15 | 19 | 13 | 10 | 12 | 15 | 16 | 1 | 101 | 1,795 |
| 1996 | 19 | 20 | 14 | 9 | 11 | 15 | 13 | 0 | 101 | 1,695 |
| 1998 | 19 | 18 | 14 | 10 | 11 | 16 | 10 | 2 | 100 | 1,281 |

*Note:* Question: "Generally speaking, do you consider yourself a Republican, a Democrat, an Independent, or what?" If Republican or Democrat: "Would you call yourself a strong (R/D) or a not very strong (R/D)?" If Independent or other: "Do you think of yourself as closer to the Republican or Democratic party?"

## Split-Ticket Voting, 1952–1998 (percent)

| Year | President-House | Senate-House | State-Local |
|---|---|---|---|
| 1952 | 13 | 9 | 26 |
| 1956 | 16 | 10 | 29 |
| 1958 |  | 10 | 31 |
| 1960 | 14 | 9 | 27 |
| 1962 |  | — | 42 |
| 1964 | 14 | 18 | 41 |
| 1966 |  | 21 | 50 |
| 1968 | 17 | 21 | 47 |
| 1970 |  | 20 | 51 |
| 1972 | 30 | 22 | 58 |
| 1974 |  | 24 | 61 |
| 1976 | 25 | 23 | — |
| 1978 |  | 35 | — |
| 1980 | 28 | 31 | 59 |
| 1982 |  | 24 | 55 |
| 1984 | 25 | 20 | 52 |
| 1986 |  | 28 | — |
| 1988 | 25 | 27 | — |
| 1990 |  | 25 | — |
| 1992 | 22 | 25 | — |
| 1994 |  | 24 | — |
| 1996 | 18 | 19 | — |
| 1998 |  | 23 | — |

*Note:* "—" indicates not available. Entries are the percentages of voters who "split" their ticket by supporting candidates of different parties for the offices indicated. Those who cast ballots for other than Democratic and Republican candidates are excluded in presidential and congressional calculations. The state-local figure is based on a general question: "Did you vote for other state and local offices? Did you vote a straight ticket, or did you vote for candidates from different parties?"

## Changes in Mass Partisanship: A Summary

*(In percentages)*

|  | 1952–60 Average | 1988–96 Average | Change |
|---|---|---|---|
| *Party identification: traditional definition* | | | |
| Strong partisans | 36 | 31 | –5 |
| Weak partisans | 38 | 33 | –5 |
| Independents | 23 | 36 | +13 |
| *Party identification: revised definition* | | | |
| Strong partisans | 36 | 31 | –5 |
| Weak partisans | 38 | 33 | –5 |
| Independent leaners | 15 | 25 | +10 |
| Pure independents | 8 | 11 | +3 |
| *Party loyalty in presidential elections* | | | |
| Strong partisans | 92 | 93 | +1 |
| Weak partisans | 75 | 72 | –3 |
| Independent leaners | 81 | 75 | –6 |
| *Party loyalty in Senate elections* | | | |
| Strong partisans | 92 | 87 | –5 |
| Weak partisans | 82 | 76 | –6 |
| Independent leaners | 77 | 72 | –5 |
| *Party loyalty in House elections* | | | |
| Strong partisans | 92 | 87 | –5 |
| Weak partisans | 85 | 75 | –10 |
| Independent leaners | 78 | 73 | –5 |
| *Percentage seeing important differences between the parties* | 50 | 61 | +11 |
| *Percentage of split-party outcomes, presidential and congressional elections* | 25 | 27 | +2 |
| *Straight-ticket voting* | | | |
| Presidential-congressional | 86 | 71 | –15 |
| Senatorial-congressional | 90 | 76 | –14 |
| Presidential, senatorial, and congressional | 82 | 63 | –19 |

Tables and Figures from *Vital Statistics on American Politics, 1999–2000*, ed. Harold W. Stanley and Harold Watkins (Washington, DC: CQ Press, 2000), 114, 115, 133, 112; and from William G. Mayer, "Mass Partisanship," in *Partisan Approaches to Postwar American Politics*, ed. Byron E. Shafer (Chatham, NJ: Chatham House, 1998), 212.

In addition to the complex demands parties face in reconciling interests and winning elections, several other factors contribute to party weakness in the electorate. Chief among these is *the rise of individual, "candidate-centered" parties.* In part an offshoot of direct primaries and rules governing federal funding, a candidate-centered party is an organization specially designed to elect a particular individual. Candidates organize their own campaign staffs and strategies, produce their own advertising, and organize and raise their own contributions. The candidate's ability to coordinate tasks traditionally handled by the party grants the candidate great independence: she or he can take positions opposing the party's official stance, and any individual with enough backing can run for a party's nomination—whether or not the party wants the person to run. Once in government, the independence and freedom afforded by a candidate-centered organization makes it difficult for a party to control that individual's behavior.

This trend is closely related to *the influence of the media* on American politics. The personality-magnifying effects of the media, the desire of contributors to donate time and money to specific candidates, and the versatility with which officeholders manipulate media coverage increase the amount of attention paid to individuals, enhancing the visibility and independence of individuals at the expense of party organizations.

*Trends in election procedures* also weaken the parties. The direct primary process for nominating candidates now dominates presidential election campaigns. The direct primary grants much of the control over nominations to voters, weakening the influence of party leaders. In turn, because voters control the power to choose a nominee, direct primaries encourage candidate-centered campaigns for office—anyone can run for a party's nomination, regardless of the wishes of party officials. Public funding of candidates also weakens the parties, because significant funds go directly to individuals, helping separate the individual and the party as two distinct entities in elections. Finally, by losing control over who runs in primaries, parties lose their ability to reward loyal followers with nominations for office.

*Changes in voter registration rules* have expanded access to the ballot at the expense of the parties. Residency requirements that need to be met before an individual is eligible to register to vote have diminished, and in many cases a person can register to vote within a month or two of moving to a new state. Further, registering has become much easier: instead of having to journey to city hall, now a person can register at the Department of Motor Vehicles when receiving or renewing a driver's license. "Motor-voter" provisions have reportedly added as many as nine million new voters to the rolls since 1994.[8] Because new voters tend to be young voters, and young voters tend to have weaker partisan affiliations than older voters, expanding the suffrage in this way seems to reduce parties' connections to the electorate. Easier access to registration allows people to register without ever coming near a political party.

Finally, as we saw in the previous chapter, *the rise of interest groups* is an important factor in the decline of parties' importance. Citizens often feel much more closely connected to an interest group than to a party, because interest groups act on specific issues and can respond more effectively to particular concerns. A party by nature deals with a broader constituency and a larger number of issues, and therefore has a harder time attracting the same degree of commitment and loyalty.

Many of the dynamics that weaken parties in the electorate reflect competition between individuals and party organizations, as each seeks to control the direction of campaigns and of policymaking. Candidate-centered parties free candidates and officeholders and capitalize on the desire of the media to personalize stories, even as they replace party involvement in traditional organizing and coordinating roles. Direct primaries enhance the role of voters and of individual candidates at the expense of party leaders; easier voter registration makes it easier for people to register, but harder for parties to influence those voters. Interest groups attract individuals with the time and money to participate in politics, but they distract popular interest from broad coalition parties that fail to address specific issues in detail. Complex roles and the competition for influence all serve to weaken parties in the electorate.

A realignment of the electorate occurs when a new issue causes a major shift in voters' fundamental partisan loyalties. Some realignments create new parties and destroy old ones. Below is political scientist James L. Sundquist's outline of the realignment process. Do you see any current issues that might spark a realignment in today's politics? Some years ago, Laurence H. Tribe suggested that attitudes about abortion might trigger a realignment.* Do you think this is possible? How does abortion match up with Sundquist's requirements?

### SUNDQUIST'S VIEW
### OF THE REALIGNMENT PROCESS

1. A realignment has its origins in the rise of a new political issue (or cluster of related issues).
2. To bring about a realignment, the new issue must be one that cuts across the existing line of party cleavage.
3. To bring about a major political realignment, the new issue must also be one powerful enough to dominate political debate and polarize the community.
4. The realigning issue must be one on which major political groups take distinct and opposing policy positions that are easily dramatized and understood.
5. Whether a new issue becomes dominant depends not only on its intrinsic power but also on the extent to which the older issues underlying the party system have faded with the passage of time.
6. A new issue is likely to have greater inherent appeal to the voters of one of the major parties and thus potentially a more disruptive effect on that party than on the other.
7. The normal response of both major parties at the outset is to straddle the new crosscutting issue.
8. Within each of the parties, however, there form at each pole political groups that are more concerned with victory for their position on the new issue than with their party's electoral success.
9. The polar forces coalesce most rapidly if the party out of power is the one with the greater predisposition toward the new issue.

10. If both major parties persist in their straddle or come under the control of the polar forces opposing change, supporters of the new issue at some point form a third party.
11. A realignment crisis is precipitated when the moderate centrists lose control of one or both of the major parties—that is, of party policy and nominations—to one or the other of the polar forces.
12. If the polar forces supporting the new issue gain control of one major party and so precipitate a realignment crisis, realignment may still be averted if they also succeed in capturing the other major party simultaneously or shortly thereafter.
13. In any other circumstance, however, the crisis eventuates in a realignment. The form of the realignment is determined by the degree of difficulty encountered by the polar forces supporting the new issue in gaining control of one of the major parties.
14. The realignment reaches its climax in one or more critical elections that center on the realigning issue and resolve it, but the realigning process may extend over a considerable period before and after the critical election.
15. After the critical election or elections in which the voters make a clear choice on the issue that has polarized the country, polarization gives way to conciliation. As it does, the parties move from the poles toward the center and the distance between them narrows.
16. However, if new issues arise that coincide with the existing line of party cleavage, they strengthen party cohesion, increase the distance between the parties, and reinforce the existing alignment.†

*Laurence H. Tribe, *Abortion: The Clash of Absolutes* (New York: W.W. Norton & Company, 1992), 196.

† Adapted with permission from James L. Sundquist, *Dynamics of the Party System: Alignment and Realignment of Political Parties in the United States*, rev. ed. (Washington, DC: Brookings Institution, 1983), chap. 13. The passages above are direct quotations; we have omitted Sundquist's explanatory passages summarizing his analysis of party realignment in American history.

# PARTIES FOR ALL OCCASIONS: COMPETITION AND PARTY WEAKNESS IN GOVERNMENT

Let's return to this chapter's opening questions: Why do parties have such a tough time governing? Why was Bill Clinton, aided by a Congress in which both houses were controlled by Democrats, unable to pass sweeping health care reform in his first term? Why were the Republicans, once they recaptured Congress, unable to enact the lion's share of the Contract with America? The reason is that parties face competition when they operate in government, just as they do when they operate in the electorate. American parties are weak policymaking bodies, frustrated at every turn by the fragmentation of American government and by the independence of officials who rely on their own candidate-centered organizations more than they rely on the parties.

## *This Party's* **Weak:** *American Parties and Policymaking*

We saw above that candidate-centered parties have usurped much of the parties' traditional role in the electorate, by focusing attention on individuals and by delivering power into their hands. Once in government, elected officials remain largely independent of party support, because the parties have little leverage with which to influence individuals' behavior.

There is more to it than just the role of individuals, however. American government is designed to fragment power by creating different constituencies for different offices, and by setting the interests and goals of those offices

**ON THE WEB**
www.dccc.org/home/
index.cfm

**ON THE WEB**
www.dscc.org/index
pop.htm

**ON THE WEB**
www.democraticgov
ernors.org/dga/

**ON THE WEB**
www.nrcc.org

**ON THE WEB**
www.nrsc.org

**ON THE WEB**
www.rga.org

Partisanship in Congress is always evident during the State of the Union address. Members of the president's party offer frequent standing ovations while members of the opposition party remain seated.

## Zip Box 3.4
*Changes in Congress and the Parties*

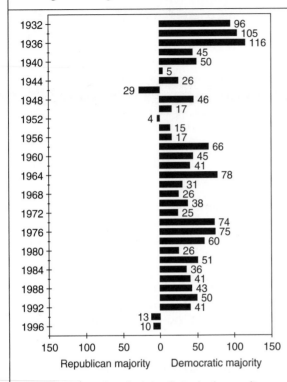

| Year | Republican/Democratic majority |
|------|-------------------------------|
| 1932 | 96 |
| | 105 |
| 1936 | 116 |
| 1940 | 45 |
| | 50 |
| 1944 | 5 |
| | 26 |
| 1948 | 29 |
| | 46 |
| 1952 | 17 |
| | 4 |
| 1956 | 15 |
| | 17 |
| 1960 | 66 |
| | 45 |
| 1964 | 41 |
| | 78 |
| 1968 | 31 |
| | 26 |
| 1972 | 38 |
| | 25 |
| 1976 | 74 |
| | 75 |
| 1980 | 60 |
| | 26 |
| 1984 | 51 |
| | 36 |
| 1988 | 41 |
| | 43 |
| 1992 | 50 |
| | 41 |
| 1996 | 13 |
| | 10 |

150   100   50   0   50   100   150

Republican majority     Democratic majority

*Note:* Numbers reflect the immediate election results.

**Party majorities in the House of Representatives, 1932–96**

100

100%   100
80%   92   85   85   House   76
Senate   65   64
60%
40%   54   47
42   40
31
20%
1955   1965   1975   1985   1995 1997

**Democratic strength in the South: U.S. House and Senate seats, 1955–97**

*Note:* Points are the percentage of southern U.S. House and Senate seats in a given year held by Democrats. "Southern" is defined as the 11 states of the Confederacy plus Kentucky and Oklahoma.
*Source:* Tables from Marjorie Randon Hershey, "The Congressional Elections," in *The Election of 1996: Reports and Interpretations,* ed. Gerald Pomper, et al. (Chatham, NJ: Chatham House, 1997), 207, 220.

The major stories of American parties in recent years have been the 1994 Republican takeover of the House and the transformation of the "Solid South" from a Democratic stronghold to a base of Republican support.

into competition with each other. We have an executive branch and a legislative branch—and the legislative branch is divided into two houses. The separation of powers encourages presidential and congressional parties; the two-house legislature encourages House and Senate parties. Each branch and each office has its own goals and interests to protect and promote, and each branch and office has its own constituency. Presidents have national constituencies; senators have statewide constituencies; and representatives have smaller constituencies located in their home districts. Federalism multiplies offices at the state and local levels. In response, national political parties in America are loose confederations of state and local organizations, complex amalgams of discrete organizational units dealing with executive and legislative offices at the local, state, and federal levels. It is very difficult to get hundreds of individuals to pull in the same direction when each has a different interpretation of his or her mandate and each must be responsive to different sources of support.

In chapter 2, we saw how interest groups used a variety of tactics to oppose the Clinton health care plan. Interest groups, though, were not the only impediment facing the plan. One of the more unexpected obstacles proved to be the Democrats themselves. Even though Democrats controlled the White House and both houses of Congress, competing Democrat factions and interests were unable to craft satisfactory compromises on health care and many more initiatives. According to the passage below, written by political analyst E. J. Dionne Jr., why were Democrats divided? What does he suggest were the key ingredients missing from the Democrats' efforts to govern? How are the separation of powers and decentralized government implicated in the Democrats' failure?

[T]he Democrats were simply not ready for . . . the discipline that governing demanded. Congress continued to operate under essentially feudal rules that ceded control of various patches of policy to long-serving committee and subcommittee chairs. The party's various factions struggled to defend particular regional, group, and programmatic interests for reasons that had nothing to do with philosophy. This made the task of reordering

the federal budget a nightmare. Conservatives in the party argued that Clinton's transformation [to a more conservative kind of Democrat] did not go far enough: They attacked his health plan, even though it made many concessions to the market, and even though national health insurance had been one of the oldest Democratic commitments. Liberals, on the other hand, feared that the Clinton renovation was going much *too far:* They accused the president of attacking welfare recipients, of embracing draconian criminal penalties, of spending too much on the Pentagon and too little on "domestic needs." Some also assailed his embrace of free trade and the priority he had given to deficit reduction. As one Clinton adviser lamented after the 1994 voting, "The only thing the Democratic Party needs is a *Party.*" He was not calling for a bacchanalia; he was saying that Democrats lacked the unity of purpose and the internal discipline to support the claim that they actually were a political party, a coherent political institution with a chance of governing the country. In the 103rd Congress, the Democrats were dysfunctional.*

*E. J. Dionne Jr., *They Only Look Dead: Why Progressives Will Dominate the Next Political Era* (New York: Simon & Schuster, 1996), 148.

The Democrats were unable to pass sweeping health care reform in part because there were so many different Democrats with different interests and constituencies, and because Bill Clinton was unable to build effective bridges to different wings of the party in Congress (see BriefCase Box 3.2). The Democratic party, nominally controlling the White House, the Senate, and the House, was unable to overcome the fragmenting forces of individuals' independence and the separation of powers, and thus was unable to entice and cajole party members into coordinated and successful action on health care.

While building bridges between parties in the White House and on Capitol Hill is difficult, building bridges between parties in the House and Senate has its own troubles. The presence of two houses in Congress weakens the parties because senators and representatives have different interests and different constituencies. Different rules in the two houses allow for some degree of centralized leadership in the House, but provide greater freedom and independence for senators. The Republican Contract with America exemplifies the ways in which these dynamics inhibit party control. The Contract's provisions and goals were clear; Newt Gingrich's leadership was also clear, and accepted by members of the House after the 1994 elections. The House passed Contract

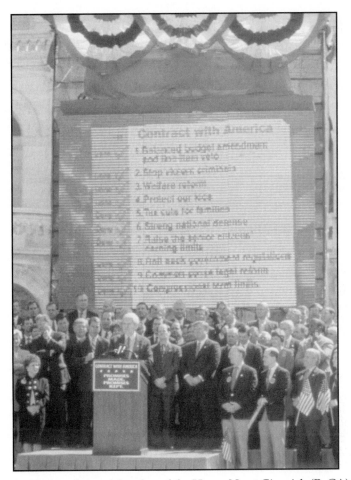

The Contract with America and Speaker of the House Newt Gingrich (R–GA) established an unusually coherent agenda for the Republican-controlled House of Representatives in the mid-1990s.

provisions quickly and effectively. But senators had their own objectives, their own constituencies, their own responsibilities—and the Contract was the brainchild of House Republicans alone. Republican senators blocked many measures because they had individual or institutional incentives to do so; and even though the Republicans had a majority in the Senate, there were enough Democrats to sustain presidential vetoes. Of course, President Clinton also had his own reasons for opposition, and he used his veto and his leadership abilities to block enactment of Contract provisions. These factors, then—separation of powers and diverse constituencies, a bicameral legislature, the effects of fragmentation and independence—combined to stymie the efforts of strong leadership and cohesive party action emanating from the House.

None of this should be taken to suggest that parties are irrelevant to the governing process. Parties in government continue to play important roles in

organizing action and voting in Congress, and in assigning committee and
subcommittee chairs. Such positions are granted to party members trusted to
act in committees and subcommittees according to the party's goals. Parties
also play a key role in filling posts like judgeships and other offices, an important function considering the extent to which such officeholders oversee the
day-to-day functioning and direction of government. Party favorites and party
veterans who lose elections are given plum assignments in diplomatic relations or in the president's cabinet. High-visibility posts on task forces, commissions, or within the party structure provide springboards for younger
party members by giving them access to the media and opportunities to network with the party's leading lights and leading donors.

The fact remains, however, that American political parties are notoriously
undisciplined and ill-prepared for designing, passing, and implementing coordinated programs and policies. Weak parties in government, like weak parties
in the electorate, raise issues about the potential for stability, effectiveness, and
coordination in American politics; it is to these questions and their implications for the health of the American polity that we now turn.

## FINDING A DESIGNATED DRIVER: ARE AMERICAN PARTIES RESPONSIBLE ENOUGH?

Political parties in American government are unlike parties in many other nations. In "party government" countries like England and France, for example,
parties have well-articulated governing philosophies and provide clear choices
regarding policy and candidates; they also exercise significant control over the
behavior of officeholders. The party that wins power elects a prime minister,
who then leads government initiatives and coordinates the behavior of others.
When several parties have significant shares of power, they form coalitions in
parliament to elect the prime minister; if they are unable to form such a coalition, a new election might bring to power a party or a coalition with enough
support to govern. The party out of power operates as a "loyal opposition,"
challenging the initiatives of the party in power but largely unable to block
their implementation. In short, party government in these countries organizes
government in support of the party in power, allowing that party and its programs to drive the actions of government. These parties are *responsible*, meaning that their goals and objectives are well-defined and they can be held accountable for policy outcomes—they can be turned out of office if they fail, and
continued in office as long as they have the support of the public.

Observers of the American political system are very interested in the health
of our parties. Because the parties have historically played an important role in
bringing citizens and government together, and because they hold the promise
of helping to organize choices and policies in government, parties are a perennial subject of debate among political scientists. American parties were once
characterized by their control over the candidates who ran for office, with the
party playing a large and important role in selecting candidates to run and
then in directing and organizing campaigns. Parties were influential places
where citizens, especially many new immigrants, could go for help in dealing

with the government and even for help in finding jobs; parties were a key ingredient in how people learned about their government, solved problems, and interacted in the public arena. Parties once were deeply involved in popular activities, like rallies and torchlight parades, which involved the electorate in party behavior and helped nurture voters' loyalty. American parties never were as strong or as coordinated as many European parties, but they once were very near the center of campaign activities and American political life.

When political scientists talk about parties being "weak," they usually mean that the parties are no longer able to play these traditional roles effectively. Parties today exercise only limited control over candidates' decisions to run for office, their positions on issues, or how candidates run their campaigns. Parties generally fail to put forward coherent plans for policy, and parties often fail to give voters clear choices between alternatives. Further, today's parties no longer serve as a strong link between people and government. As we saw in chapter 2, people often feel more allegiance to special interest groups than they do to political parties.

Scholars worry that American parties in decline are less able to fulfill their roles in organizing the electorate and coordinating government activities—in short, they are not responsible enough. Why does this matter? If we expect parties to play a role in socializing citizens and connecting them to government, then weaker parties mean that ties between the people and the government might be fraying. If we need parties to help reconcile competing interests as a counterweight to the actions of narrowly focused interest groups, then weaker parties could exacerbate the risks of interest group politics discussed in the previous chapter. And if we want "responsible" parties to put forward and enact, or systematically oppose, plans and alternatives for public policy, then weaker parties and more powerful individuals could destabilize the government. Power might shift rapidly and without purpose among competing interests, and we might lose the ability to hold parties accountable for outcomes. In sum, if we look to parties to help stabilize the long-term goals of government and for collective responsibility for political affairs, weaker parties create the danger of a fragmented system given over to battles among special interest groups.

Weak parties pose other risks. In 1950 a committee of the American Political Science Association (APSA) published an influential report on parties that outlined political scientists' concerns with weakening parties. The APSA committee feared that American parties were too weak to deal with the increasingly broad and complex problems facing cold war America, and the group warned that a further weakening of American parties might have several important and dangerous consequences for the presidency and for the government in general. The group predicted that fragmented parties would place undue burdens on the president, as the focus of national attention and policy organization. Not only might the president's tasks become overwhelming, but popular support without the parties—support focused on the president alone, and not organized, cultivated, and informed by parties—would be volatile and inconsistent, susceptible to rapid fluctuations as the public's opinion of the president shifted. Moreover, the APSA committee feared that a system reliant on the president's program and not the program of a party "favors a President who exploits skillfully the arts of demagoguery, who uses the whole country as his political backyard, and who does not mind turning into the embodiment of personal government."[9] (See Discussion Box 3.3 and Scholar Box 3.1.)

The APSA report argued that parties in government needed to be strong enough to provide clear choices on public policy and national programs, and that they needed to be strong enough to carry out their plans by controlling officeholders who held office under party banners. The report also argued that the party out of power needed to be strong and cohesive enough to set up an organized and critical opposition, by which policies and alternatives could be examined and debated. The goal, in short, was to have parties that were organized enough to articulate their programs, strong enough to carry them out, and responsible enough to be held accountable for outcomes.

## Recent Party Adaptation and Revival

The fact is, though, that the rise of candidate-centered parties, the related influence of the media, and especially the fragmented and decentralized American political system virtually preclude strong parties of the type seen in many

**Ways Al Gore Tried to Raise Money for the Democratic Party**

10. Competed in pay-per-view "ultimate fighting" match against Janet Reno.

9. For six months, did nothing but check pay phones for quarters.

8. Secretly sold the entire state of New Jersey to the Swedes.

7. Signed deal to turn the Bill of Rights into "the Frito Lay Bill of Rights."

6. Made a quick $300,000 by returning Ted Kennedy's empties.

5. For $20, let people sign their names to the Declaration of Independence.

4. Got Iraqi spies drunk and sold them the blueprints for a hair dryer.

3. Asked Hillary for a few investment tips.

2. Equipped Lincoln Bedroom with coin-operated condom machine.

1. Vice President by day, Hollywood hooker by night.

Source: Reprinted by permission of CBS Worldwide, Inc.

European countries. American parties fit our system well, and they have proven to be very adept at adapting to new circumstances in order to remain relevant. Strategically placed at the center of the campaign financing system, parties are a vital link in raising and distributing the funds required for today's costly elections. *Fundraising* by national parties has been liberalized under the Federal Election Campaign Act and subsequent amendments, and national parties raise and distribute tremendous fiscal resources to state parties and to candidates. Party-building "soft money" donations also make their way through the party as a central mediator.[10] Parties increasingly *provide "services"* to candidates in the form of technical assistance, production of advertising, and access to expensive and complex resources like direct mailing lists and computer databases. Providing services, especially the coordination and legwork necessary for fundraising, has helped parties remain relevant in the face of candidate-centered campaigns and despite the decline in traditional party organizing roles.

Federal election laws and rules within the parties have also increased the *coordination of activities* between state and national party units, integrating these levels more than they were in the past. Though state party organizations seem to be much more organized and influential than they once were, the national parties' control over massive funds enables them to assert themselves and their national goals in relation to the state parties.[11] In effect, state parties have become stronger and more influential than they had been, but at the cost

---

 ## Discussion Box 3.3
### *The Danger of Disintegration of the Two Parties*

More than fifty years ago, a committee within the American Political Science Association drafted a report outlining the weakness of American political parties and summarizing the risks that such weakness posed for American government and society. The committee's analysis remains relevant and is a classic defense of the importance of strong and responsible American parties. According to the following passage, what does the committee believe might be the outcome of alienation between voters and parties? To whom do voters increasingly pledge their loyalty?

It is a thing both familiar and deeply disturbing that many Americans have only caustic words or disdainful shrugs of the shoulder for the party system as it operates today. . . .

*A chance that the electorate will turn its back upon the two parties is by no means academic.* As a matter of fact,

this development has already occurred in considerable part, and is still going on. Present conditions are a great incentive for the voters to dispose of the parties as intermediaries between themselves and the government. In a way, a sizable body of the electorate has shifted from hopeful interest in the parties to the opposite attitude. This mass of voters sees itself as the President's or his opponent's direct electoral support.

Continued alienation between increasing numbers of voters and both major parties is an ominous tendency. It has a splintering effect and may lead to a system of several smaller parties. *American political institutions are too firmly grounded upon the two-party system to make its collapse a small matter.**

*American Political Science Association, "Toward a More Responsible Two-Party System: A Report of the Committee on Political Parties," in a *Supplement to the American Political Science Review*, Vol. XLIV, No. 3, Part 2, September 1950 (New York: Rinehart & Company, 1950), 95. [italics in original].

of some of their independence from the national party leadership. Political scientist <u>John F. Bibby</u> summarizes these developments:

> In effect, what has been occurring through national [party] committee transfers of funds and assistance programs for state parties is that the national party has been using its superior resources and legal authority to nationalize campaign efforts and integrate the national and state parties in an unprecedented manner. National money and resources tend to flow to state parties in conformity with the national party's campaign strategy and priorities (and in presidential election years, with the strategy and priorities of the presidential nominees). State parties are thereby being integrated into a national campaign structure in presidential, House, and Senate campaigns.[12]

These are momentous developments, and significant evidence of vitality among American political parties. Millions of people remain tied to their parties, taking pleasure and pride in partisan affiliations and participating in party activities. Members of the electorate still recognize and make decisions based on perceived differences between the two major parties, as well as on the performance of parties in government. Interest groups are drawn together under party banners, and even though individual ties to parties have weakened, the ties individuals have to groups can be used to generate support and activism during campaigns and elections. In some ways, then, parties remain the most important embodiment of collective responsibility in an American system fragmented by competing interests.

---

 ### Scholar Box 3.1
*Mayhew: Divided We Govern*

Political observers worry that weak parties and trends like split-ticket voting create an almost permanent state of divided government characterized by partisan bickering, gridlock, and paralysis at a time of increasing complexity in the issues facing American government. Recent critics echo the concerns of the APSA Committee on Parties (see Discussion Box 3.3). Political scientist <u>David Mayhew</u> has studied divided government and American parties in the twentieth century, and he argues that divided government works just as well as unified government. According to the passage below, why does Mayhew defend American parties? What "components of the American regime" give us the kinds of parties we have? Who in the system is responsible? Are Mayhew and the APSA Committee Report necessarily at odds with each other?

To demand more of American parties—to ask that they become governing instruments—is to run them up against components of the American regime as fundamental as the party system itself. . . . The government floats in public opinion; it goes up and down on great long waves of it that often have little to do with parties. There is the obvious structural component—separation of powers—that brings on deadlock and chronic conflict, but also nudges officials toward deliberation, compromise, and super-majority outcomes. And there is a component of deep-seated individualism among American politicians, who build and tend their own electoral bases and maintain their own relations of responsibility with electorates. This seems to be a matter of political culture—perhaps a survival of republicanism—that goes way back. Unlike most politicians elsewhere, American ones at both legislative and executive levels have managed to navigate the last two centuries of history without becoming minions of party leaders. In this complicated, multi-component setting, British-style governing by party majorities does not have much of a chance.*

*David R. Mayhew, *Divided We Govern: Party Control, Lawmaking, and Investigations, 1946–1990* (New Haven: Yale University Press, 1991).

## Conclusion

American parties have never approached European parties' ability to serve as engines of clarity and coordination. In our fragmented, volatile, and decentralized system, parties continue to adapt to new circumstances, new rules and regulations, new dynamics of media coverage, changes in fundraising laws and techniques, and alterations in how people choose to relate to government. They continue to struggle to meet conflicting demands: that parties build coalitions, reconcile competing interests, and organize government for coordinated action; and that they compete for power and influence, even if it means petty, divisive partisanship. In the next chapter, we turn to elections, campaigns, and voting: some particular battlefields involving the media, interest groups, and the parties.

## Overnight Assignment ▬▬▬▬▬▬▬▬▬▬▬▬▬▬▬▬▬▬▬▬▬▬

Find your representative in Congress on the Web. With which party is she or he affiliated? How prominent is the party affiliation on the website? Does the site refer to other party relationships, like issues or ties to party leaders? Alternatively, find a political party on the Web. What information on issues and candidates does the website provide? Is there a way to get from the party's website to your representative's site?

## Long-Term Integrated Assignment ▬▬▬▬▬▬▬▬▬▬▬▬▬▬▬▬▬

Consider the interest group you chose at the end of chapter 2: Is it traditionally aligned with either party? Which one, and why? Is there evidence of a close connection between the interest group and campaign activity, like advocating positions or supporting certain candidates? Are the concerns of your interest group addressed on the party's website?

## Researching Political Parties? ▬▬▬▬▬▬▬▬▬▬▬▬▬▬▬▬▬▬▬

### Try These Authors:

John F. Bibby           William T. Crotty        James L. Sundquist
Walter Dean Burnham     Paul S. Hernnson         Martin P. Wattenberg

### Try These Sources:

CHAMBERS, WILLIAM NISBET. *Political Parties in a New Nation: The American Experience. 1776–1809*. New York: Oxford University Press, 1961.

KEEFE, WILLIAM J. *Parties, Politics, and Public Policy in America*. 8th ed. Washington, DC: CQ Press, 1998.

MAISEL, L. SANDY, ed. *The Parties Respond: Changes in American Parties and Campaigns*. Boulder: Westview Press, 1998.

MAYHEW, DAVID R. *Divided We Govern: Party Control, Lawmaking, and Investigations, 1946–1990*. New Haven: Yale University Press, 1991.

MILKIS, SIDNEY M. *Political Parties and Constitutional Government: Remaking American Democracy.* Baltimore: Johns Hopkins University Press, 1999.

SCHATTSCHNEIDER, E. E. *Party Government.* New York: Holt, Rinehart and Winston, 1942.

SHAFER, BYRON E. with HAROLD E. BASS, JR. *Partisan Approaches to Postwar American Politics.* New York: Chatham House Publishers, 1998.

## Endnotes

1. E. E. Schattschneider, *Party Government* (New York: Rinehart & Company, 1942), 32.

2. In Maine and Nebraska, the candidate winning the popular vote does not necessarily receive all of the electoral votes.

3. Doris A. Graber, *Mass Media and American Politics,* 4th ed. (Washington, DC: CQ Press, 1993), 265.

4. Matthew Robert Kerbel, "Parties in the Media: Elephants, Donkeys, Boars, Pigs, and Jackals," in *The Parties Respond: Changes in American Parties and Campaigns,* ed. L. Sandy Maisel (Boulder: Westview Press, 1998), 254–255. Research suggests that the media also tend to personalize stories about the parties, reducing the diversity of interests represented by the parties to the faces of a few high-profile individuals.

5. James L. Sundquist, *Dynamics of the Party System: Alignment and Realignment of Political Parties in the United States,* rev. ed. (Washington, DC: Brookings Institution, 1983), 195.

6. William J. Keefe, *Parties, Politics, and Public Policy in America,* 7th ed. (Washington, DC: CQ Press, 1994), 291.

7. Ibid. Voters do not split their tickets for the purpose of dividing government as a control on government's actions, but usually in order to vote for an individual candidate or on a particular issue. See Barry C. Burden and David C. Kimball, "A New Approach to the Study of Ticket Splitting," *American Political Science Review* 92, no. 3 (September 1998).

8. See Jerry Calvert, "Election Law Reform and Turnout: What Works?" in *Engaging the Public: How Government and the Media Can Reinvigorate American Democracy,* ed. Thomas J. Johnson, Carol E. Hays, and Scott P. Hays (Lanham, MD: Rowman & Littlefield, 1998), 144.

9. "Toward a More Responsible Two-Party System," a Report of the Committee on Political Parties, American Political Science Association (New York: Rinehart & Company, 1950), 94.

10. John F. Bibby, "Party Organizations, 1946–1996," in *Partisan Approaches to Postwar American Politics,* ed. Byron E. Shafer (New York: Chatham House, 1998), 159.

11. Ibid., 155.

12. Ibid., 164.

# CHAPTER 4

# Elections, Campaigns, and Voting

## Chapter Outline

The 2000 election campaign ended with bizarre twists. Absentee and mail-in ballots in several states delayed the final tally of the national popular vote, and an extraordinarily tight race in the pivotal state of Florida clouded Vice President and Democratic candidate Al Gore's chances for success in the all-important electoral college. Long after election night, uncertainty about the outcome in Florida paralyzed both campaigns, delayed the transition to a new president, and riveted the attention of individuals around the world.

Yet despite the dramatic and almost unbelievable finish to what had been a largely passionless campaign, the results from November 2000 tell a familiar tale. The campaigns followed established channels, from early primaries through nominating conventions and the general election. The news media followed the candidates, and the candidates spent millions of dollars on their campaigns. Meanwhile, most voters voted in accord with their party affiliation; some switched because of a particular candidate; most did not cast a vote based on feelings about a single issue. Almost half of all eligible voters chose not to vote at all. There were no reports of violence, no threats of a military coup, no widespread reports of voter fraud or of illegal efforts to prevent people from voting. Bill Clinton vacated the White House in January 2001 and left the job to his successor; losers in other elections packed up their boxes and turned their offices over to newcomers. Despite the extraordinary closeness of many of the elections in 2000, and despite delays in resolving some of them, the business of government continued and the nation did not fall apart.

It is a testament to the American political system's stability that campaigns, elections, and voting so often seem to remain remarkably unremarkable. Yet consider the implications of the 2000 results: The president may have the opportunity to appoint three or more Supreme Court Justices, influencing the very peak of the nation's judicial system for years to come and directly affecting the way the nation handles issues like abortion, health care, minority rights, racial profiling by the police, the death penalty, and campaign finance laws. Leadership on environmental, regulatory, and health care policies will be vastly different than they might have been. The Social Security system, global warming, automobile emissions controls, technology and the Internet, and even the government's antitrust case against Microsoft will all be dealt with in unique ways. Even the priorities of the Congress will depend on results that change the character and composition of both houses every two years.

Elections, campaigns, and voting—as routine and unexciting as they may sometimes appear to be—are critically important parts of the American political system, bringing together the actions of the media, interest groups, political parties, voters, and officeholders. Even a dull campaign has important ramifications on the nation's course, and even elections with important ramifications eventually find resolution. This chapter is about the competition and compromise inside American campaigns, elections, and voting.

**The Bottom Line.** Campaigns and elections are the core of regular public competition in America, providing stability as well as the opportunity for peaceful and regular change in our leaders and in the direction of government. Expensive campaigns driven by candidate-centered organizations and intimately related to the media characterize modern elections. Successful candidates forge effective compromises between their own goals, the demands of the media, and the necessities of fundraising. Voters and votes are the prizes of these competitions, with numerous factors influencing voter access to the ballot, voter turnout, and voter choices.

## DON'T BLAME ME, I VOTED FOR HAGELIN: THE IMPORTANCE OF COMPETITIVE ELECTIONS

The popularity of bumper stickers like, "Don't Blame Me, I Voted for——" acknowledge the importance of elections by implying that the current state of affairs is the result of who we put into office; they also imply an acceptance of the winner, even though the person with the sticker supported the loser. Elections are a cornerstone of both change and stability in the American system. They can have profound effects on the course of the nation's policy, and they regularly draw public attention to the nation's public life. More than 100 million people voted in the 2000 election, or 51 percent of eligible voters—a slight increase over the 1996 election.

**ON THE WEB**
www.fec.gov

**ON THE WEB**
www.cnn.com/all
politics

**ON THE WEB**
fisher.lib.virginia.edu/
elections/maps

**ON THE WEB**
www.nytimes.com

**ON THE WEB**
clerkweb.house. gov/
elections/elections.
htm

Examples of important recent elections abound. Bill Clinton's defeat of incumbent George Bush in 1992 ended twelve years of Republican control of the presidency and *signaled a shift in the priorities addressed by the federal government:* in broad terms, the Republicans' attention to foreign policy and the end of the cold war, cutting taxes, and controlling social spending gave way to Democratic focus on domestic policies and reducing the national debt. The 1992 election also *signaled a change in the philosophy of governance* emanating from the White House: the antigovernment rhetoric of the Reagan-Bush years, which had emphasized getting government "off the backs" of people and businesses, gave way to Clintonism's celebration of government's promise and its potential to solve pressing social problems. The Republican takeover of Congress in 1994 also signaled a sea change in Congress's priorities and in the ways it addressed them: Forty years of governing in the House by Democrats gave way to a new class of Republican representatives driven to change the way Congress operated.

The 2000 election, of course, will stand forever as a landmark in American history—and for reasons that go far beyond the short-term implications of its gripping finale. Any close election affects the ways in which priorities in government are arranged and pursued. 2000 produced very tenuous control of the House and the Senate, for example; passing bills in a tight House or Senate is a much different matter from passing bills when wide majorities exist. Any close presidential election affects the political environment within which the president tries to exercise leadership, dynamics discussed in more detail in Chapter 8. Finally, the shadow of 2000 will extend over future elections and the activities of parties, voters, and governing institutions for many years to come.

Further, as corny as it may sound, regular elections are important in that they *register the consent of the governed*—an essential ritual in a country that prides itself on representing the interests of the public. In 1776, eleven years before the Constitutional Convention, Thomas Paine wrote:

> [T]hat the *elected* might never form to themselves an interest separate from the *electors,* prudence will point out the propriety of having elections often; because as the *elected* might by that means return and mix again with the general body of the *electors* in a few months, their fidelity to the public will be secured. . . . And as this frequent interchange will establish a common interest with every part of the community, they will mutually and naturally support each other, and on this (not on the unmeaning name of king) depends the *strength of government, and the happiness of the governed.*[1]

Finally, and this is easily overlooked, elections are important in perpetuating the *peaceful transfer of power.* Federalist John Adams's surrender of the White House to the victorious Thomas Jefferson following the election of 1800 remains one of the most momentous events in American political history. Jefferson's victory was significant in itself, signaling the transfer of executive power away from the Federalists, who favored a strong central government and the promotion of American business interests, and into the hands of the

Jeffersonians, who sought a less intrusive national government and who favored the development of agricultural interests over manufacturing. The real story relevant to the nation's long-term stability and survival, however, was that Adams accepted defeat by his opponent and left the office to his enemies—without a fight (see BriefCase Box 4.1).

---

## Scholar Box 4.1
### Key, Jr.: Critical Election Theory

Elections provide political scientists with a convenient tool for examining trends in the nation's politics and public life. In chapter 3, we examined the characteristics of a voter realignment (see Discussion Box 3.2). Realignments are part of V. O. Key, Jr.'s classic theory of critical elections, which is a useful shorthand for discussing elections and their significance and which we summarize below.

- **Critical election:** Signals a major shift in the electorate's views and party allegiances.
  Best Example: Democrat Franklin Roosevelt's victory in 1932. FDR's election not only ended Republican dominance in national politics, it set the stage for Democratic party dominance in Congress and the presidency that would last for a generation.
- **Maintaining election:** One that continues the dominant party's control.
  Best Example: The 1948 election of FDR's former vice president, Harry S Truman (who had risen to the presidency upon FDR's death in 1945), continued the Democrat's dominance in national politics.
- **Deviating election:** One in which public attitudes and party allegiances remain tied to the dominant party, despite the election of a president from the minority party. A deviating election does not signal a shift in public loyalty, despite the dominant party's defeat at the polls.
  Best Example: Republican presidential candidate Dwight D. Eisenhower defeats Democrat Adlai Stevenson in 1952, ending almost twenty years of Democratic control of the White House. Eisenhower's victory did not signal a major long-term shift in the electorate's attitudes, however. Eisenhower was a war hero, the supreme Allied commander of the forces in World War II. His election reflected a response to his character and his military service more than a shift in public attitudes about government and policies.

- **Reinstating election:** One that restores the majority party to power.
  Best Example: Following Eisenhower's two terms, Democrat John F. Kennedy defeats Republican Richard Nixon (Eisenhower's Vice President) in the 1960 election. Eisenhower's two victories were "deviations"; Kennedy's election signaled the reinstatement of Democratic dominance in national politics.*

Key's theory can be pushed only so far, and political scientists have had a difficult time fitting recent elections into the theory. Since 1968, government has been frequently divided: for years, Republican presidents squared off against a Democratic Congress; recently, the Democrats' hold on the White House has been countered by Republican control of Congress. As party identification among the electorate wanes, and as individual candidates grow more important to electoral outcomes than parties, it becomes increasingly difficult to understand elections in terms of party loyalties. Some scholars believe that the United States is in a period of "dealignment," in which partisan ties have weakened and independent voting has increased to the extent that party identification is no longer the best criterion for interpreting American elections.

* For his theory of critical elections, see V. O. Key, Jr., "A Theory of Critical Elections," *The Journal of Politics* 17 (February 1955).

Elections produce changes, but in the American system of separated powers and staggered elections they cannot overturn the entire government. Outgoing presidents generally try to ensure the continuation of their policies and principles, and appointing federal judges is a time-honored method of having an influence on the system long after leaving office. When <u>Thomas Jefferson</u> beat <u>John Adams</u> and the Federalists in the "Revolution of 1800," Adams responded in two important ways: First, he accepted his defeat as the valid outcome of a fair election and quietly surrendered the White House to his rivals. Second, he appointed <u>John Marshall</u> as Chief Justice of the Supreme Court. <u>Henry Adams</u>, John Adams's grandson, described the appointment in his history of the Jefferson administration. Judging from the passages below, why did Adams appoint Marshall? What were the implications of the appointment for politics in the Jefferson administration?

Jefferson was the first President inaugurated at Washington, and the ceremony, necessarily simple, was made still simpler for political reasons. The retiring President was not present at the installation of his successor. In Jefferson's eyes, a revolution had taken place as vast as that of 1776; and if this was his belief, perhaps the late President was wise to retire from a stage where everything was arranged to point a censure upon his principles, and where he would have seemed in his successor's opinion, as little in place as George III would have appeared at the installation of President Washington. . . .

In this first appearance of John Marshall as Chief-Justice, to administer the oath of office, lay the dramatic climax of the inauguration. The retiring President, acting for what he supposed to be the best interests of the country, by one of his last acts of power, deliberately intended to perpetuate the principles of his administration, placed at the head of the judiciary, for life, a man as obnoxious to Jefferson as the bitterest New England Calvinist could have been; for he belonged to that class of conservative Virginians, whose devotion to President Washington, and whose education in the common law, caused them to hold Jefferson and his theories in antipathy. The new President and his two Secretaries were political philanthropists, bent on restricting the powers of the national government in the interests of human liberty. The Chief-Justice, a man who in grasp of mind and steadiness of purpose had no superior, perhaps no equal, was bent on enlarging the powers of government in the interests of justice and nationality. As they stood face to face on this threshold of their power, each could foresee that the contest between them would end only with life.*

* Henry Adams, *History of the United States of America during the First Administration of Thomas Jefferson, 1801–1805* (New York: Library of America, 1986), 130–131.

## THE HEART OF THE COMPETITION: CAMPAIGNS FOR CONGRESS AND THE WHITE HOUSE

### If You Were Already in Congress, You'd Be Home by Now: Congressional Campaigns and the Incumbency Effect

Campaigns are competitions, but that doesn't mean that everybody lines up at the same starting line. Perhaps the most dominating factor in congressional elections these days is *the incumbency effect:* the vast majority of incumbents were returned to the House in 2000, and this is by no means unusual. Senate incumbents also win at high levels, although Senate races tend to be a little more competitive than House races. Even the "Republican revolution," which gave the Republican party majorities in both houses of Congress for the first time in four decades, witnessed considerable success among incumbent candidates (see Zip Box 4.1).

**Incumbent Reelection Rates: Representatives and Senators, General Elections, 1960–1998**

| Year/Office | Number of Incumbents | | | Incumbents Winning Election | Incumbent Reelected with 60+ Percent of the Major-Party Vote |
| | Ran | Won | Lost | | |
| --- | --- | --- | --- | --- | --- |
| **1960** | | | | | |
| House | 400 | 374 | 26 | 93.5% | 58.9% |
| Senate | 29 | 28 | 1 | 96.6 | 41.3 |
| **1962** | | | | | |
| House | 396 | 381 | 15 | 94.3 | 63.6 |
| Senate | 34 | 29 | 5 | 85.3 | 26.4 |
| **1964** | | | | | |
| House | 389 | 344 | 45 | 88.4 | 58.5 |
| Senate | 32 | 28 | 4 | 87.5 | 46.8 |
| **1966** | | | | | |
| House | 402 | 362 | 40 | 90.1 | 67.7 |
| Senate | 29 | 28 | 1 | 96.6 | 41.3 |
| **1968** | | | | | |
| House | 401 | 396 | 5 | 98.8 | 72.2 |
| Senate | 24 | 20 | 4 | 83.3 | 37.5 |
| **1970** | | | | | |
| House | 391 | 379 | 12 | 96.9 | 77.3 |
| Senate | 29 | 23 | 6 | 79.3 | 31.0 |
| **1972** | | | | | |
| House | 380 | 367 | 13 | 95.6 | 77.8 |
| Senate | 25 | 20 | 5 | 80.0 | 52.0 |
| **1974** | | | | | |
| House | 383 | 343 | 40 | 89.6 | 66.4 |
| Senate | 25 | 23 | 2 | 92.0 | 40.0 |
| **1976** | | | | | |
| House | 381 | 368 | 13 | 96.6 | 69.2 |
| Senate | 25 | 16 | 9 | 64.0 | 40.0 |
| **1978** | | | | | |
| House | 378 | 359 | 19 | 95.0 | 76.6 |
| Senate | 22 | 15 | 7 | 68.1 | 31.8 |
| **1980** | | | | | |
| House | 392 | 361 | 31 | 90.7 | 72.9 |
| Senate | 25 | 16 | 9 | 55.2 | 40.0 |

| | | | | | |
|---|---|---|---|---|---|
| **1982** | | | | | |
| House | 381 | 352 | 29 | 92.4 | 68.9 |
| Senate | 30 | 28 | 2 | 93.3 | 56.7 |
| **1984** | | | | | |
| House | 407 | 391 | 16 | 96.1 | 78.9 |
| Senate | 29 | 26 | 3 | 89.7 | 65.5 |
| **1986** | | | | | |
| House | 391 | 385 | 6 | 98.5 | 84.5 |
| Senate | 28 | 21 | 7 | 75.0 | 50.0 |
| **1988** | | | | | |
| House | 409 | 402 | 6 | 98.3 | 87.3 |
| Senate | 27 | 23 | 4 | 85.0 | 60.9 |
| **1990** | | | | | |
| House | 406 | 391 | 15 | 96.3 | 79.5 |
| Senate | 32 | 31 | 1 | 96.9 | 66.7 |
| **1992** | | | | | |
| House | 349 | 325 | 24 | 93.1 | 65.0 |
| Senate | 28 | 24 | 4 | 85.7 | 46.4 |
| **1994** | | | | | |
| House | 384 | 349 | 35 | 90.9 | 63.0 |
| Senate | 25 | 23 | 2 | 92.0 | 48.0 |
| **1996** | | | | | |
| House | 381 | 361 | 20 | 94.5 | 68.0 |
| Senate | 20 | 19 | 1 | 95.0 | 30.0 |
| **1998** | | | | | |
| House | 400 | 394 | 6 | 98.5 | 77.2 |
| Senate | 29 | 26 | 3 | 89.7 | 65.5 |

*Note:* Percentage gaining more than 60 percent of the vote is calculated on the basis of the vote for the two major parties. "Off-off" year gubernatorial elections, held in Kentucky, Louisiana, Mississippi, New Jersey, and Virginia, are not included in the above totals. For these gubernatorial election outcomes, see *Congressional Quarterly's Guide to U.S. Elections.*
Source: Table adapted from *Vital Statistics on American Politics, 1999–2000,* ed. Harold W. Stanley and Harold Watkins (Washington, DC: CQ Press, 2000), 51–52.

Note the high percentages of incumbent victories, and also the difference between House and Senate races in which the incumbent winner was reelected with more then 60 percent of the vote.

Why is incumbency such an important factor in congressional races? First, incumbents raise large sums of money because they are known quantities: donors, especially political action committees (PACS), prefer to back familiar and predictable candidates rather than newcomers. Current officeholders are also able to deliver concrete benefits to their districts—a dynamic that, as we will see in chapter 9, goes a long way toward generating and reinforcing electoral support. Finally, incumbency usually affords better name recognition. Incumbents not only have been winning at astounding rates, but they have been winning by ever-greater margins of victory—which might indicate that challengers are increasingly unlikely to enter races against what seem to be over-whelming odds.

## Running the Long Road to the White House: Presidential Campaigns

Presidential elections are the centerpiece of the American electoral system. Presidential primaries and national nominating conventions are scenes of competition and compromise in American campaigns, and they serve as important mileposts: success in primaries can provide momentum and legitimacy to winners, and underachievement can severely damage campaigns by high-profile losers.

### The Primaries

The presidential nominating process is dominated by *direct primaries*, in which voters select a candidate to run in the general election (see Zip Box 4.2). Nominating procedures and voter eligibility requirements in primaries are generally regulated by state laws. In some states, *"open primaries"* allow all voters to participate; the risk is that a party's primary election can be "raided" by an opposing party or influenced by independent voters. During the 2000 primaries, Republican candidate John McCain successfully reached out to independents and Democrats in Michigan's open Republican primary. Exit polls clearly showed that even though McCain won in Michigan, his opponent, George W. Bush, received roughly two-thirds of the votes cast by Republicans. In other words, the open primary gave McCain the edge, and kept his insurgent campaign afloat deep into the primary season. As a result, Bush was forced to spend valuable time and resources beating back McCain's challenge in the primaries that followed Michigan. Bush's spending, together with McCain's continued attacks, probably hurt Bush's chances in the general election.

Most states use *"closed primaries,"* in which only voters registered as members of a particular party may vote in that party's primary; usually, voters register months in advance of the primary. In these states, candidates' efforts focus on winning the support of party members who will turn out in the primary. Bush rebounded from his defeat in Michigan's open primary, winning handily in the closed primaries in Ohio and New York, propelling him to the party's nomination. McCain's appeal to independents and Democrats could not help him in closed primary states.

Even record turnout in several Republican primaries in 2000 did not reverse the fact that far fewer voters participate in the primaries than vote in the general election; primary turnout is often around 20 to 25 percent of eligible voters (see Zip Box 4.2).[2] With such low turnout, candidates must appeal to strong partisans and activists who do not represent the majority of their party's members. Activists tend to be more conservative (in the case of Republicans) or more liberal (in the case of Democrats) than other party members; as a result, candidates sometimes run in the primaries with exaggerated conservative or liberal positions—even though doing so risks alienating other voters whose support will be important for success in later rounds of the campaign.

## Zip Box 4.2
*Presidential Primary Elections*

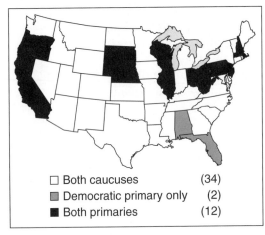

Both caucuses (34)
Democratic primary only (2)
Both primaries (12)

**Presidential primary elections, 1946**

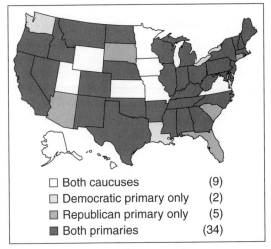

Both caucuses (9)
Democratic primary only (2)
Republican primary only (5)
Both primaries (34)

**Presidential primary elections, 1996**

Direct primaries have come to dominate presidential nominations, even though only a small percentage of eligible voters participate in them.

### Turnout in Major Party Primaries, 1972–1996

| Year | Democratic Primaries | Republican Primaries |
|------|----------------------|----------------------|
| 1972 | 19.7% | 18.1% |
| 1976 | 17.5 | 11.1 |
| 1980 | 14.8 | 11.0 |
| 1984 | 16.1 | 6.6 |
| 1988 | 15.9 | 8.6 |
| 1992 | 13.2 | 8.2 |
| 1996 | 8.1 | 8.6 |

Figure from Harold F. Bass Jr., "Partisan Rules," in *Partisan Approaches to Postwar American Politics*, ed. Byron E. Shafer (Chatham, NJ: Chatham House, 1998), 240–241; table from *Congressional Quarterly's Guide to the Presidency,* 2nd ed., ed. Michael Nelson (Washington, DC: CQ Press, 1996), 89.

### The National Nominating Conventions

After the early campaign and primaries, national conventions are venues for more competition as factions compete to influence the parties' official positions on issues and as former candidates and others position themselves for important future roles. Behind the scenes, conventions and advance planning for conventions sometimes involve the same kinds of competition and compromise that characterize the system as a whole. As we saw in chapter 3 when

At left, Texas governor George W. Bush emphasizes his western roots at the Republican party's 2000 nominating convention. At right, "the kiss" between Democratic nominee Al Gore and his wife, Tipper, becomes one of the most memorable moments of the 2000 campaign.

we examined the Republicans' 1996 efforts to reconcile anti-abortion and pro-choice factions within the party, diverse interests compete to influence party platforms and the party's general direction and image (see Briefcase Box 3.1). Official positions are often compromises among these factions, and the conventions are milestones in parties' efforts to draw together their coalitions, heal old wounds, and focus on the competition of the general election. At the convention, still more compromises are made in writing rules that will govern the allocation and selection of delegates for the next convention. The choice of the nominee's vice presidential running mate is often used to shore up support from some wing or faction within the party.

In spite of conflict over party platforms, national nominating conventions are no longer pervaded by tense excitement. Many conflicts over platform and positions are resolved before the convention begins, as was the case with the Republicans in 1996. More importantly, the conventions are no longer the site where the party chooses its nominee. Now, the primaries usually result in the party's nominee being known long before the convention begins. As a result, conventions have become highly orchestrated public events designed to present particular messages, often emphasizing the unity of the party and the party's appeal to ordinary Americans. Because the conventions are such media events, they are also important opportunities for rising stars. Mario Cuomo's 1984 speech at the Democratic convention seemed at the time like a prelude to a future presidential run (which never materialized); Elizabeth Dole's speech in 1996 was so well received that it encouraged her campaign for the Republican nomination in 2000. (See Briefcase Box 4.2.)

By the end of the national conventions, as many as two-thirds of eventual voters have already settled on a choice for the general election—a fact that indicates the importance of the early stages in the campaign. In a close race, though, the remaining one-third can have a heavy impact on an election's outcome—especially because this last third are predominantly weak partisans or independents, and more susceptible to campaign messages. (See Zip Box 4.3.)

Even though parties plan and coordinate the public face of their conventions, with the aim of presenting a winning image to the public watching on television, awkward mistakes still happen. In 1992, Republicans chose two speakers to make presentations at critical times. The party gave these important roles to former president <u>Ronald Reagan</u>, icon of the party and leader of its broad national appeal, and to journalist-turned-candidate <u>Pat Buchanan</u>, who had failed to win the party's nomination but had drawn surprising support in the primaries. Choosing Buchanan for a critical speech was an olive branch presented to the conservative wing of the party, intended to draw his supporters back to the fold and win their enthusiastic support for George Bush in the general election. This effort at internal compromise backfired, however, when the party chose Buchanan to lead

off the night's activities while Reagan waited in the wings. A national television audience saw Buchanan give a radically conservative and confrontational speech; many never saw Reagan's much more inclusive and optimistic speech. The party's convention, targeted at drawing the party together and launching the party's national campaign, instead set an uncomfortably aggressive tone for the upcoming election and, by association, for a future Republican administration.

In 2000, the Democrats made their own miscue: Bill Clinton's speech on the opening night of the convention started so late that many viewers missed it. Another unplanned moment—"the kiss" between Al Gore and his wife, Tipper, just prior to his acceptance speech—garnered both accolades and condemnation from observers.

## COMPETING FOR COINS AND COVERAGE: CAMPAIGNS, MONEY, AND THE MEDIA

### The Money Chase and Campaign Finance

Campaigns spent roughly $700 million on the presidential race in 1996; House and Senate races combined added close to another $800 million (see Zip Box 4.4). Candidates scrape and scrounge for contributions, making the "money chase" one of the more grueling aspects of campaigning. Candidates complain that they spend too much time raising money and not enough time considering people and issues—and raising money does not stop once a candidate is elected, either. Representatives, senators, and presidents continue to raise funds even when they are in office. Raising enough money to run successfully is a full-time proposition, and one that, if done correctly, can scare off potential challengers. Full coffers and a hefty war chest advertise success and commitments for the next election, disheartening outsiders.

As one might expect in the United States, the current campaign finance system is a compromise among competing sets of beliefs and values about the place of money in the political system. Between those who believe that money corrupts politics and those who believe money is a legitimate means of participating in and influencing the political system, lies a maze of PACs, soft-money contributions, spending on issue advertisements, and controversial interpretations of the Constitution. (See Discussion Box 4.1.)

Political action committees (PACs) are one controversial compromise. Political scientist <u>Frank J. Sorauf</u> describes the chief purpose of most PACs as being "to raise money in voluntary individual contributions for a separate

## Zip Box 4.3
*Television, Voter Choices, and the National Conventions*

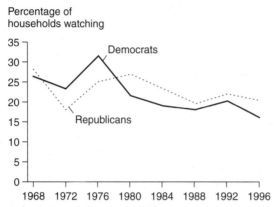

Percentage of households watching

**Television Audiences for Major Party Conventions, 1968–1996**

*Note:* The ratings for 1968–1988 are for the combined three-network (ABC, CBS, and NBC) average number of all TV households tuned in. For 1992 the rating is based on the five-network (ABC, CBS, NBC, CNN, and PBS) average number of TV households tuned in. For 1996 the Democratic convention rating is based on the five-network average number of all TV households tuned in, while the Republican convention rating is based on the six-network (ABC, CBS, NBC, CNN, PBS, and Family Channel) average. Data for 1968–1992 are for the percentage of TV households watching in an average minute during convention coverage; 1996 data are for the percentage of TV households watching in an average minute during the final evening of convention coverage.

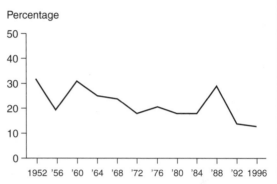

Percentage

**Voters Who Decided Their Vote During the Party Conventions, 1952–1996**

Though the television audience for the major conventions has declined over the last two decades and fewer voters make up their minds during the conventions, convention coverage still attracts a large number of viewers.

Figures from *Congressional Quarterly's Guide to the Presidency*, 2nd ed., ed. Michael Nelson (Washington, DC: CQ Press, 1996), 51.

**ON THE WEB**
www.lib.umich.edu/lib home/documents. center/psusp.html

political fund from which to support the interests of the sponsoring organization with campaign contributions." In other words, a PAC collects contributions from individuals and contributes the amounts to campaigns, in effect combining individual efforts to form a more powerful aggregate that supports the organization's goals. Because the PAC's sponsor can pay for administrative costs and can run the operation at its own expense, virtually all of the money raised can go for contributions, making the PAC very efficient and very effective at gathering and distributing money.[3] Even though the number

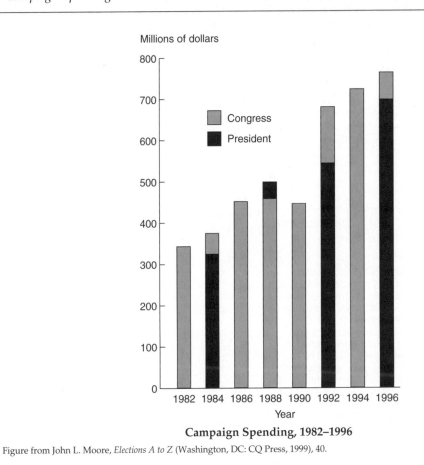

Millions of dollars

Congress
President

**Campaign Spending, 1982–1996**

Figure from John L. Moore, *Elections A to Z* (Washington, DC: CQ Press, 1999), 40.

of PACs has stabilized somewhat in the 1990s, their influence and the amount of money they raise continues to increase dramatically. (See Zip Box 4.5.)

PAC contributions are problematic because they raise the danger of undue influence over candidates and officeholders, because *PACs work to the advantage of some groups (like corporations) over others (like unorganized interests)*, and because *PAC contributions support incumbents* far more than they support challengers. PACs, though, are not some evil offspring of a system gone horribly wrong. PACs grew sharply after changes were made in the campaign finance laws in the 1970s. These changes were designed as compromises among the competing goals we have for our electoral system: encouraging participation, controlling abuses, and promoting the fair representation of diverse interests. The new rules sought to reduce the impact of back-room campaign contributions by bringing contributors under public scrutiny and limiting the amounts

# DISCUSSION BOX 4.1
### HELP, I'M IN A NUTSHELL: CAMPAIGN FINANCE AND THE CONSTITUTION

In *Buckley v. Valeo* (1976), the Supreme Court ruled on the constitutionality of government-imposed limits on campaign expenditures and campaign contributions. The Court's ruling continues to dominate campaign finance activity, hindering some reform efforts because of its determination that campaign expenditures are a protected form of free speech. In the following two passages, what distinction does the Court draw between expenditures and contributions? Do you agree with the Court's reasoning?

### Expenditures: a protected form of free speech

A restriction on the amount of money a person or group can spend on political communication during a campaign necessarily reduces the quantity of expression by restricting the number of issues discussed, the depth of their exploration, and the size of the audience reached. This is because virtually every means of communicating ideas in today's mass society requires the expenditure of money.

### Contributions: government can limit

By contrast with a limitation upon expenditures for political expression, a limitation upon the amount that any one person or group may contribute to a candidate or political committee entails only a marginal restriction upon the contributor's ability to engage in free communication. A contribution serves as a general expression of support for the candidate and his views, but does not communicate the underlying basis for the support. . . . While contributions may result in political expression if spent by a candidate or an association to present views to the voters, the transformation of contributions into political debate involves speech by someone other than the contributor.*

In February 2000, the Supreme Court upheld state limits on campaign contributions to state political candidates. *Nixon v. Shrink Missouri Government PAC* involved a candidate for state office, Zev David Fredman, who argued that he could campaign effectively only with contributions larger than those allowed by Missouri law; the law, he argued, infringed upon his rights under the First and Fourteenth Amendments. The Court upheld Missouri's limits on contributions, extending its ruling in *Buckley v. Valeo* to the state level, but Justice Anthony Kennedy's dissent criticized the Court's compromises on campaign finance issues. Accord-

ing to the following passages from Kennedy's dissent, what was the compromise view the Court took in reviewing Congress's campaign finance laws? What was the result of the Buckley decision? What has happened to "straightforward" speech? What does Kennedy imply, at the end of this passage, might be a better solution?

Zev David Fredman asks us to evaluate his speech claim in the context of a system which favors candidates and officeholders whose campaigns are supported by soft money, usually funneled through political parties. The Court pays him no heed. The plain fact is that the compromise the Court invented in *Buckley* set the stage for a new kind of speech to enter the political system. It is covert speech. The Court has forced a substantial amount of political speech underground, as contributors and candidates devise ever more elaborate methods of avoiding contribution limits, limits which take no account of rising campaign costs. The preferred method has been to conceal the real purpose of the speech. Soft money may be contributed to political parties in unlimited amounts, and is used often to fund so-called issue advocacy, advertisements that promote or attack a candidate's positions without specifically urging his or her election or defeat. Issue advocacy, like soft money, is unrestricted, while straightforward speech in the form of financial contributions paid to a candidate, speech subject to full disclosure and prompt evaluation by the public, is not. Thus has the Court's decision given us covert speech. This mocks the First Amendment. The current system would be unfortunate, and suspect under the First Amendment, had it evolved from a deliberate legislative choice; but its unhappy origins are in our earlier decree in *Buckley*, which by accepting half of what Congress did (limiting contributions) but rejecting the other (limiting expenditures) created a misshapen system, one which distorts the meaning of speech. . . .

Whether our officeholders can discharge their duties in a proper way when they are beholden to certain interests both for reelection and for campaign support is, I should think, of constant concern not alone to citizens but to conscientious officeholders themselves. There are no easy answers, but the Constitution relies on one: open, robust, honest, unfettered speech that the voters can examine and assess in an ever-changing and more complex environment.†

---

*Buckley v. Valeo* (424 V. S. 1(1976).
†Kennedy, dissent in *Nixon v. Shrink Missouri Government PAC* (161 F. 3d 519 (2000)).

| Individual contributions under $200 18% ($138,688) | Individual contributions of $200 or more 35% ($259,590) | PAC contributions 39% ($294,792) | Party contributions and coordinated expenditures 2% ($15,812) | Candidate contributions 1% ($6,328) | Miscellaneous 5% ($34,702) |

**Sources of House Incumbents' Campaign Receipts in the 1996 Elections, N = 356**

| Individual contributions under $200 22% ($61,784) | Individual contributions of $200 or more 32% ($88,712) | PAC contributions 19% ($53,556) | Party contributions and coordinated expenditures 7% ($20,772) | Candidate contributions 16% ($44,222) | Miscellaneous 3% ($9,473) |

**Sources of House Challengers' Campaign Receipts in the 1996 Elections, N = 356**

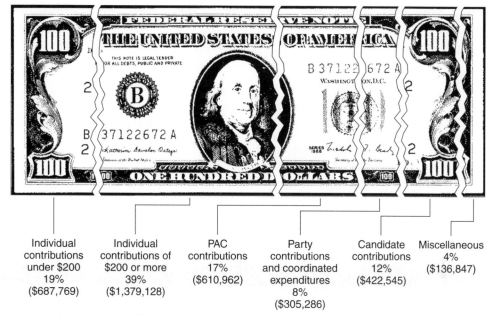

| Individual contributions under $200 19% ($687,769) | Individual contributions of $200 or more 39% ($1,379,128) | PAC contributions 17% ($610,962) | Party contributions and coordinated expenditures 8% ($305,286) | Candidate contributions 12% ($422,545) | Miscellaneous 4% ($136,847) |

**Sources of Senate Candidates' Campaign Receipts in the 1996 Elections, N = 68**

These images give a breakdown of House and Senate candidates' funding sources. Note that the amounts raised vary from Senate campaigns (which raise the most), to House incumbents' campaigns, to House challengers. Also note the significant difference between PAC contributions and candidate contributions depending on whether a candidate for the House is an incumbent or a challenger.

*Notes:* The dollar values in parentheses are averages. Candidate contributions include loans candidates made to their own campaigns. Miscellaneous includes interest from savings accounts and revenues from investments. Figures are for general election candidates in major-party contested elections, excluding a small number of atypical races that were decided in runoffs or won by independents.

Images adapted from Paul S. Herrnson, *Congressional Elections, Campaigning at Home and in Washington,* 2nd ed. (Washington, DC: CQ Press, 1998), 133, 142, 153.

that groups could give. Defending PACs against charges that they are intrusions onto the political scene, Sorauf writes:

> Like political parties, PACs are instruments of representation in a representative democracy. They organize individuals around interests, ideologies, and policy options. By bringing individuals together, they create aggregates of political influence greater than the mere sum of the individuals they bring together. Organized political action has always been more purposeful, better informed, and more resourceful than the actions of scattered individuals. For those reasons, it has also always been more influential.[4]

Campaign finance and campaign finance reform are such hot topics because of the importance of keeping the electoral system free of corruption, and because

## Zip Box 4.6
*All That and a Bag of Chips: Campaign Spending in Context*

Political scientist <u>Bradley Smith</u> estimates that Americans spend two to three times more money each year for potato chips than they do for political campaigns. By Smith's analysis, in the two years prior to November 1996 *all* congressional candidates in the 1996 general election spent a total of $800 million—or about $4 per eligible voter, spread over two years. Smith finds that total campaign outlays for all candidates in local, state, and federal election campaigns amounted to about $12 per voter. He concludes by noting that the nation's two largest advertisers, Philip Morris and Procter & Gamble, budget about the same amount for advertising.*

*Bradley A. Smith, "Faulty Assumptions and Undemocratic Consequences of Campaign Finance Reform," *Yale Law Journal* 105 (January 1996).

encouraging participation cannot help but draw potential corrupting influences into the system. As the boxes in this section suggest, PACs are not the only current compromise: the Supreme Court, for example, has tried to draw compromises between the goals of campaign finance regulation and constitutional rights. Nor are PACs the only threat present in the current system: abuses involving soft money and issue advocacy tainted the 1996 presidential campaign, and little has been done to close legal loopholes that allow illegal activity (see Zip Box 4.7).

### The Money Chase and the Media

Comedian Dennis Miller once remarked that Ross Perot's 1992 running mate, Admiral James Stockdale, committed an unforgivable sin in American politics during that year's vice presidential debate: he was bad on television. Stockdale's credentials for integrity and intelligence were impeccable: he was a decorated war hero, a former college professor, and a fellow at the Hoover Institution of War, Revolution and Peace. Nevertheless, on television he came across as an aging crank so inept that he turned his hearing aid off during the debate. Vicious parodies of Stockdale included a skit on *Saturday Night Live* in which Dana Carvey's Perot drove Phil Hartman's Stockdale deep into the countryside—and abandoned him in the woods. Stockdale's performance in the debate helped fuel the Perot campaign's image as a coterie of kooks lacking the credibility and common sense necessary to serve in the nation's highest offices. Other factors certainly affected Perot's chances, but his campaign never recovered from the caricatures and Perot remains a ready punchline even today. But if Perot is the joke, the relationship between modern campaigns and the media certainly isn't. Aspects of this relationship inflate campaign costs, influence the nature of campaigns, and focus attention on individual candidates to the detriment of political parties and coverage of issues.

The importance of money in campaigns is not new, and campaign finance rules are not the only forces inflating the cost of campaigns. The tools of modern campaigning—such as computers, polls, phone banks, and mailing lists—

Current campaign finance system compromises have resulted in loopholes that have been exploited in recent campaigns. A group of leading experts wrote that in 1996, the campaign finance system "went from the political equivalent of a low-grade fever to Code Blue—from a chronic problem needing attention sooner or later to a crisis, with a system clearly out of control."*

TWO BIG LOOPHOLES

*Soft money:* Soft money is money raised and spent by the major parties' national committees, not by individual candidates, and is meant to be used for "party-building activities" like voter registration and get-out-the-vote drives. In reality, soft money is easily coordinated with campaigns to help elect particular candidates. Soft money is so called because it is not subject to the "hard" regulations of campaign finance laws.

*Issue ads:* "Issue ads," which stop short of expressly advocating the election or defeat of specific candidates, are not subject to strict federal spending limits. Ads that *expressly* advocate the election or defeat of specific candidates *are* subject to strict spending limits. The courts and the FEC have taken very narrow views of what distinguishes "express" ads: in effect, only ads that use "magic words" such as "vote for or against," "elect," "defeat," or "Smith for Congress" are considered express advocacy ads. Any ad that *avoids* those magic words ostensibly informs the public about an issue.

1996 ABUSES

The soft money loophole allows contributions of hundreds of thousands of dollars which wouldn't be allowed under the "hard" campaign finance laws. The major parties raised about $83 million in soft money in 1992, and about $262 million in 1996.[†] Estimates for 2000 predict that soft money may top $500 million. In 1996, the Democrats and Republicans combined the two loopholes, raising and spending millions of dollars in soft money for envelope-pushing "issue ads" that stopped just short of using the magic words advocating defeat or election of specific candidates. Other groups also got involved: the AFL-CIO, for example, targeted $35 million to defeat vulnerable Republican members of Congress in 1996, with $20 to $25 million spent for issue ads.[‡] Other scandals involved fundraising calls made by Vice President Gore from the White House, in apparent contravention of law, and large foreign contributions to the Clinton-Gore campaign.

After the 1996 elections, FEC auditors ruled that both parties had coordinated campaign spending with supposedly independent expenditures, in violation of the law. The auditors suggested that the Dole campaign should have to return $17.7 million in federal matching funds, and the Clinton campaign should return $7 million. The FEC rejected that recommendation.

*Norman J. Ornstein, Thomas E. Mann, Paul Taylor, Michael J. Malbin, and Anthony Corrado, "Reforming Campaign Finance," reprinted in *Campaign Finance Reform: A Sourcebook,* ed. Anthony Corrado, Thomas E. Mann, Daniel R. Ortiz, Trevor Potter, and Frank J. Sorauf (Washington, DC: Brookings Institution Press, 1997), p. 379.

†Anthony Corrado, "Party Soft Money: Introduction," in *Campaign Finance Reform: A Sourcebook,* ed. Anthony Corrado, et al. (Washington, D.C.: Brookings Institution Press, 1997), 1975.

‡Frank J. Sorauf, "Political Parties and the New World of Campaign Finance," in *Partisan Approaches to Postwar American Politics,* ed. Byron E. Shafer (New York: Chatham House, 1998), 232; see also Gary C. Jacobson, "The Effect of the AFL-CIO's 'Voter Education' Campaigns in the 1996 House Elections," *Journal of Politics* 61, no. 1 (February, 1999).

are all tremendously expensive. Yet one of the most expensive tools of campaigning is also one of the most important: media advertising. Between April 1, 1996, and the November 1996 election, for example, the Clinton and Dole campaigns spent roughly $130 million on television ads—or roughly two-thirds of their campaign money. This paid for almost 168,000 ads running for a

# DISCUSSION BOX 4.2
*I'M RUBBER AND YOU'RE GLUE (I HOPE): NEGATIVE ADS AND PERSONAL ATTACKS*

Campaign advertisements spend more time covering issues than do television network newscasts, yet many campaign ads that cover issues are perceived as "negative advertising." And though many observers assume that negative ads make voters apathetic, debate is heating up in political science circles over the possibility that negative advertising actually draws *more* voters to the polls by getting them involved in campaigns and raising issues. Going negative is controversial, but in part this is because different people have different ideas about what "going negative" actually means. The passages below are by E. J. Dionne, Jr., a longtime observer of American politics, and Alan Keyes, who ran for the Republican presidential nomination in 1996 and 2000. Keyes's reference to "cheap ploys" immediately followed a handshake and a pledge by candidates George W. Bush and John McCain not to use negative advertisements. Are Dionne and Keyes talking about the same thing? Do you think negative ads have a role in politics and campaigns?* Can ads be negative without being personal? How would you define "negative advertising?"

## E. J. Dionne, Jr.:

If one operates on the reasonable assumption that human nature is rather constant, it's hard to believe that today's politicians are demonstrably more venal than those of a generation or a century ago—especially since formal ethics codes are stricter now, and politicians have to live by tougher rules. Whatever their real failings—and politicians *do* have real failings—something more profound is going on. American politics is mired in recrimination, mistrust and accusation. . . .

The United States has fallen into a politics of accusation in which the moral annihilation of opponents is the ultimate goal. It is now no longer enough to simply defeat, outargue or outpoll a foe. Now, the only test of victory is whether an adversary's moral standing is thoroughly shredded and destroyed. A political rival or philosophical adversary cannot be mistaken, foolish, impractical or wrongheaded. He or she has to be made into the moral equivalent of Hitler or Stalin, the Marquis de Sade or Al Capone.†

## Alan Keyes:

I think when we get beyond the kind of cheap ploys, we ought to consider the fact that in a court of law, if the prosecution presents its case and the defense doesn't bother, we don't get to the truth. Some people might want to pretend that we don't have an adversarial political system—but we do. And therefore, if the folks who are running against each other don't, in an honest, clear way, speak about the differences on issues—and if you're going to run on your record, they get to speak about your record, and it's going to be their interpretation of your record, not your own—that is not negative advertising. That is sharing with people your views and the truth, and they're not going to get at it any other way. And so, if we're honest with ourselves, we not only have to tolerate it, we should *encourage* that kind of exchange of viewpoints, so that the voters get the maximum information on which to base their choice.‡

*On the impact of negative ads, see, for example, the forum on negative advertising in the *American Political Science Review* 93, no. 4 (December 1999).
†E. J. Dionne, Jr., *They Only Look Dead: Why Progressives Will Dominate the Next Political Era* (New York: Simon & Schuster, 1996), 20.
‡Alan Keyes, speaking at Calvin College, January 10, 2000, broadcast live on CNN.

total of fifty-eight days, or close to 1,400 hours. Candidates for the Senate in 1992 spent 42 percent of their campaign funds on TV advertising; House candidates in competitive races spent more than 30 percent of their funds for TV ads.[5]

Despite the attention to advertising, though, ads generally fail to influence viewers' evaluations of candidates. Media scholar Doris Graber puts it this way:

Although people learn facts about campaign issues from commercials, most ads fail to influence viewers' evaluations of the candidates. Commercials are

Fundraising is a time-consuming yet critically important part of modern campaigns. Here, Bill Clinton speaks to donors at a Democratic National Committee fundraiser.

perceiver-determined. People see in them pretty much what they want to see—attractive images for their favorite candidates and unattractive ones for the opponent. If attempts to glamorize political actors and hide their weaknesses succeed, the effect lasts for only a short time. Commercials of opposing candidates, media exposes of deceptive messages, and people's cynicism about campaign propaganda see to that.[6]

The dynamics of media coverage are far more important in how they relate to the course of a campaign. Candidates run campaigns that will meet their own goals as well as draw favorable attention from the media. Candidates often compromise their vision of a campaign's course in order to meet the requirements of the media. In chapter 1, for example, we saw how the public journalism movement in North Carolina encouraged political candidates to address issues that journalists had determined to be of interest to their audiences. Some candidates bristled at the effort, because candidates and campaign teams expend considerable effort trying to control the messages involved in an election; yet most of the candidates responded anyway.

Just as interest groups use available resources in different ways, depending on allies, competitors, and political situations, candidates in campaigns utilize a variety of techniques to advance their cause. Campaign teams carefully *design an overall strategy*, taking into account the nature of the electorate, the type of election, and the resources available to the campaign. They decide

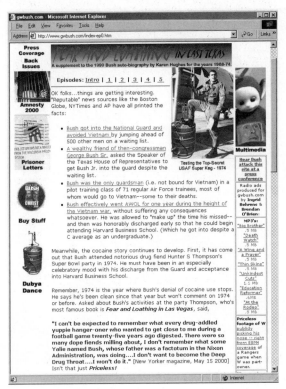

A candidate's control of her or his campaign message is complicated by the number and diversity of information sources available to potential voters. Moreover, Internet parody sites, like this one at www.gwbush.com, disseminate political opinions and commentary to unsuspecting websurfers who might be looking for official campaign sites. The information above is not necessarily true, but the U.S. Federal Election Commission dismissed the Bush campaign's complaint against the site, ruling that the issue was too low a priority to merit the use of the commission's resources.

which issues will be addressed and when, how the candidate will address those issues, and what the candidate's image will be. Changes are made depending on the relative success of different gambits. Consultants take polls to uncover public opinion on issues; speechwriters and consultants shape a candidate's words and physical appearance; advisors and assistants work to coordinate with interest groups, donors, party leaders, journalists, and media executives. Experts design and produce position papers, advertisements, and press releases for distribution through the media.

Campaign teams also work to *control the delivery* of campaign messages. Attention to successive topics progresses according to plan, matching the media's demand for novelty: thus a candidate might push domestic policy as an issue for a time, and then capture renewed attention by shifting gears with a "new" speech on foreign policy. Otherwise, because candidates are expected to have consistent views on issues, covering issue positions often doesn't qualify as "news." Part of controlling the campaign is *staying "on message,"* an effort designed to control the course of a campaign and also to avoid mistakes

The Internet promises some exciting new wrinkles in American politics, including wider access to political news and commentary and the possibility of Internet voting (see Discussion Box 4.6). Yet political scientists <u>Michael Margolis</u>, <u>David Resnick</u>, and <u>Chin-chang Tu</u> predicted in a 1997 article that the Internet was unlikely to have much impact on campaigning. Judging from the following passages from their article, why do they hold this opinion? What dynamics of participation generally do they apply to the prospects of citizens' Internet usage? Do you think their prediction was accurate?

First, we must remember that unless extraordinary events like a war or economic depression impinge on their daily lives, most people don't actively participate in politics and neither know nor care very much about it. Thus, even as the Internet lowers the information costs of learning about parties, candidates, and issues in a campaign, we cannot expect people to overcome their habitual indifference unless or until parties, candidates, or interests motivate them to follow electoral politics more closely and to care more about its outcomes. . . .

The Internet may have the potential to change the nature of American and indeed even world politics, but we doubt that it will. Cyberspace heralds neither a new world of egalitarian communalism and participatory democracy nor one of isolated computer-addicted pseudocitizens wandering a virtual reality that is manipulated by totalitarians. . . . When all is said and done, commercial interests and mainstream political interests will control the WWW or its successor in a manner similar to the control they presently exert over other mass media. Citizens who can afford it will have better access to information about a variety of products and services and about a multitude of subjects, including politics. However, we expect that most people will act as high-tech consumers rather than political activists. In sum: *plus ça change, plus c'est la meme chose.*\*

---

\*Michael Margolis, David Resnick, and Chin-chang Tu, "Campaigning on the Internet: Parties and Candidates on the World Wide Web in the 1996 Primary Season," *Harvard International Journal of Press/Politics* 2, no. 1 (winter 1997): 73, 75. See also Michael Margolis, David Resnick, and Joel D. Wolfe, "Party Competition on the Internet in the United States and Britain," *Harvard International Journal of Press/Politics* 4, no. 4 (fall 1999).

---

that can be magnified in the glare of media coverage. Candidates generally try to avoid offhand remarks, which might result in a mistake or distract an audience from the candidate's main point. Most candidates answer questions with prepared statements and mold their responses to uncommon or tricky questions in such a way as to make a prepared answer seem to fit the question.

To stay on message and avoid newsworthy gaffes and scandals, campaign teams strive to respond to unforeseen events quickly and effectively, eliminating distractions as quickly as possible so the candidate can return to the campaign's strategy. In the 1992 presidential campaign, for example, stories emerged repeatedly about then-Governor Bill Clinton's extramarital affairs and his alleged draft dodging during the Vietnam War. Clinton tried to parry these disclosures, responding with reactions designed to quash the rumors and refocus attention on his own agenda. Clinton's early inability to lead media attention away from such issues led his team to develop a full-scale campaign wing devoted to quick and decisive responses to unforeseen matters.

### Campaign Reporting and Newsworthiness: Media Focus on the Horse Race

The truth is that *voters learn very little specific information* about candidates and issues through the news media, and media coverage has yet to prove very influential in changing voters' choices. Media coverage of campaigns tends to be uniform across the various media, largely a result of pack journalism and the media's tendency to cover issues based more on "newsworthiness" than on a commitment to covering all issues or even those issues that could have the most serious impact on the nation. As we saw in chapter 1, complex social problems like poverty—long-term problems with diverse causes and complicated responses—do not feed the media's desire for new and interesting stories with easily understandable conflicts at their core.[7]

The dynamics of newsworthiness govern media coverage of campaigns, with important effects. *Horse race coverage* occurs when the media report on the competitive positions of the candidates, focusing on who is ahead, who behind, who might be gaining and who slipping. Polls are a significant part of horse race coverage, tracking candidates' fortunes and expectations as campaigns pass various milestones: early straw polls, primaries, conventions, Labor Day, and so on right up to the election itself. About half of the stories on presidential campaigns are related to the horse race; this percentage is even higher during the nominating season (see Zip Box 4.8).

Horse races, especially when there are only two major candidates competing, satisfy the media's desire for a polarized story with competition and conflict. Horse race coverage also satisfies the need for novelty, since advances, declines, and even stagnation in the polls or in the perceived momentum of a campaign can all be covered as new developments. Horse race coverage allows the media to focus on the fortunes of interesting personalities, too, whether they are candidates themselves, advisors who might be on the way out due to declining fortunes, or consultants on the way in to jumpstart a campaign.

Horse race coverage has important ramifications. First, this kind of coverage takes time away from consideration of candidates' qualifications and their positions on issues. *Media coverage of candidates generally exceeds coverage of issues* by roughly a 60 percent to 40 percent margin.[8] Media coverage during primaries is particularly skewed toward covering personalities and personal traits more than professional qualifications and positions on issues. Second, horse race coverage tends to *focus attention on the frontrunners,* giving the media power in what Doris Graber calls the "kingmaker" role.[9] Attention to frontrunners can work to the disadvantage of those trying to catch them, especially as the media are often quick to craft a candidate's reputation as a "winner" or a "loser." Because media coverage, monetary contributions, and momentum in public opinion polls can all reinforce each other, good early coverage can be critical to a candidate's ultimate success.

In the campaign for the 2000 Republican presidential nomination, for example, a group of candidates—Elizabeth Dole, John McCain, Lamar Alexander, and Dan Quayle among them—watched as Texas Governor George W. Bush jumped out to an early lead in polls and saturation coverage by the media. Dole, Alexander, and Quayle failed to survive the early race, as Bush's frontrunner advantages helped him build familiarity with the public, capture important endorsements, and rake in impressive campaign contributions. Early success does not always translate into *continued* success, however: in the early days of the 2000 race, both Al Gore and George W. Bush watched as favorable coverage, positive results in public opinion polls, key endorsements,

## Focus of Television News Coverage, 1996 Presidential Election

| Period | Dates | Policy Issues (percent) | Campaign Issues (percent) | Horse Race (percent) | Number of Stories |
|---|---|---|---|---|---|
| Nomination contest | | | | | |
| 1995 | 1/1–12/31 | 44 | 14 | 42 | 485 |
| Pre-Iowa | 1/1–2/11 | 42 | 18 | 40 | 192 |
| New Hampshire | 2/12–2/19 | 25 | 33 | 42 | 98 |
| Arizona | 2/20–2/27 | 32 | 20 | 48 | 89 |
| South Carolina | 2/28–3/1 | 55 | 10 | 35 | 18 |
| Junior Tuesday | 3/2–3/4 | 29 | 0 | 71 | 32 |
| Super Tuesday | 3/5–3/11 | 18 | 13 | 70 | 48 |
| Midwest | 3/12–3/18 | 30 | 10 | 60 | 23 |
| California | 3/19–3/26 | 52 | 12 | 36 | 34 |
| Total nomination contest | | 39 | 16 | 45 | 1,019 |
| Rest of nomination period | | | | | |
| End of March | 3/27–3/31 | 80 | 20 | 0 | 8 |
| April | 4/1–4/30 | 76 | 3 | 21 | 38 |
| May | 5/1–5/31 | 50 | 27 | 23 | 102 |
| June | 6/1–6/30 | 55 | 35 | 9 | 115 |
| July | 7/1–7/31 | 54 | 24 | 21 | 112 |
| Pre-convention | 8/1–8/9 | 94 | 0 | 6 | 55 |
| Republican convention | 8/10–8/18 | 34 | 33 | 33 | 188 |
| Interim | 8/19–8/23 | 59 | 24 | 17 | 40 |
| Democratic convention | 8/24–9/1 | 50 | 27 | 23 | 151 |
| Total for period | 3/27–9/1 | 53 | 27 | 21 | 809 |
| General Election | | | | | |
| Pre-debates | 9/2–10/5 | 50 | 33 | 17 | 197 |
| Debates | 10/6–10/16 | 24 | 45 | 31 | 98 |
| Final days | 10/17–11/4 | 32 | 36 | 32 | 188 |
| Total general election | | 39 | 36 | 25 | 483 |
| Nomination and general election total | | 43 | 24 | 33 | 2,311 |

*Note:* "Policy issues" involve concerns such as those detailed in Table 4-9; "campaign issues" concern candidate character; "horse race" coverage focuses on the contest—who's ahead, who's behind. Stories may be classified in more than one category. In addition, presidential campaign coverage can be other than policy, campaign, or horse race. Comparable data for earlier elections can be found in previous editions of *Vital Statistics on American Politics.*

Source: Adapted from *Vital Statistics on American Politics, 1999–2000,* ed. Harold W. Stanley and Harold Watkins (Washington, DC: CQ Press, 2000), 179.

Note the percentage of "horse race" coverage stories, especially during the nomination contest and the general election.

and sound financial support failed to beat back challenges from Bill Bradley and John McCain, respectively.

The second important ramification of horse race coverage arises from its *focus on individuals.* Candidate-centered reporting reinforces the role of individuals and their personal organizations, weakening the control of political parties over candidates and nominations. Media coverage enhances name recognition and voter awareness of candidates, especially in congressional elections and elections at lower levels. Further, candidate-centered reporting encourages the media to develop a shorthand with audiences to facilitate and influence future coverage. The media seized quickly on John McCain's temper, George W. Bush's frat-boy past, Al Gore's woodenness, and Bill Bradley's "above politics" image. Once attached to a candidate, characterizations like these are very hard to overcome. In Bradley's case, what looked like a positive attachment became problematic when early primary defeats presented him with a dilemma: remaining "above politics" and maintaining his aloof campaign style put him at risk of being trounced by an aggressive Gore, whereas fighting Gore with more traditional tactics threatened to paint Bradley as a hypocrite who was really "just another politician." Media images, coproduced by the Bradley campaign and the media, backed Bradley into a corner; Bradley ultimately kept his image intact but lost the nomination.

## VOTES AND VOTERS: THE COMPETITION'S PRIZES

So who is watching the horse race? Why do campaigns and candidates raise all this money and expend all this effort? The answer of course, is voters and their votes—they are the competition's prizes.

### Voting Rights

James Madison emphasized in *Federalist 10* that the United States is a republic characterized by representation, or "the delegation of the government . . . to a small number of citizens elected by the rest"—it is decidedly *not* a democracy, wherein the members of a small society can gather and administer the government in person. This is not merely semantic nitpicking; it is, rather, crucial to understanding the nature of voting in the United States. Citizens are not asked to run the government, nor are they even forced to vote. In fact, the framers constructed a number of mechanisms to *limit* the effects of popular votes. Presidents, as we saw in the previous chapter, are selected by winning a majority of electoral votes, not directly by popular vote—this was designed to insulate the presidency from popular passions and demagogic manipulation.

Originally, United States senators were chosen by state legislatures; only since the 1913 ratification of the Seventeenth Amendment have senators been elected directly by the people. And although it was not part of the framers' original design, for most of our history nominees for the presidency were chosen by party leaders—not through the direct primaries that dominate the current nominating system.

Access to the ballot has also been limited throughout American history. Early on, property-holding and tax-paying requirements excluded roughly three-quarters of the country's white men from voting. Women did not gain the vote fully until passage of the Nineteenth Amendment in 1920. Only in 1971 did the vote extend to eighteen-year-olds with passage of the Twenty-sixth Amendment. Finally, extension of voting rights to blacks has a long and troubled history (see Discussion Boxes 4.4 and 4.5). So while the United States has moved steadily toward universal suffrage, it has not always moved speedily or easily.

---

 ## DISCUSSION BOX 4.4
*VOTING RIGHTS: NO COMPROMISES ON PRINCIPLE . . .*

---

The Fifteenth Amendment (1870) guarantees that "The right of citizens of the United States to vote shall not be denied or abridged by the United States or by any State on account of race, color, or previous condition of servitude." The Amendment left the door open to voting restrictions of many kinds, though, and most blacks still could not vote ninety-five years after the Amendment's ratification. The Voting Rights Act of 1965 suspended literacy tests and other "tests and devices" used to determine voter qualifications in states where fewer than 50 percent of eligible voters had been registered in 1964. The Act authorized federal registrars to register voters and to supervise elections in those states, and it required any changes in the states' election laws to be approved, or "pre-cleared," by the federal Department of Justice before they could go into effect. The Voting Rights Act was an unprecedented extension of federal power to protect voting rights.

Few have made the case for voting rights more passionately than the Reverend Martin Luther King, Jr., and President Lyndon Johnson, speaking amid the turmoil of the civil rights era of the 1960s. Judging from the passages below, did King and Johnson leave room for compromise on the right to vote? How did Johnson respond to those who see voting as a local concern?

**Dr. King:**

And as we walk, we must make the pledge that we shall march ahead. We cannot turn back. There are those who are asking the devotees of civil rights, "when will you be satisfied?" We can never be satisfied as long as the Negro is the victim of the unspeakable horrors of police brutality. We can never be satisfied as long as our bodies, heavy with the fatigue of travel, cannot gain lodging in the motels of the highways and the hotels of the cities.

We cannot be satisfied as long as the Negro's basic mobility is from a smaller ghetto to a larger one. We can never be satisfied as long as a Negro in Mississippi cannot vote and a Negro in New York believes he has nothing for which to vote. No, no we are not satisfied, and we will not be satisfied until justice rolls down like waters and righteousness like a mighty stream."*

**President Johnson:**

Many of the issues of civil rights are very complex and most difficult. But about this there can and should be no argument. Every American citizen must have an equal right to vote. There is no reason which can excuse the denial of that right. There is no duty which weighs more heavily on us than the duty we have to insure that right.

Yet the harsh fact is that in many places in this country men and women are kept from voting simply because they are Negroes. . . .

To those who seek to avoid action by their National Government in their home communities—who want to and who seek to maintain purely local control over elections—the answer is simple. Open your polling places to all your people. Allow men and women to register and vote whatever the color of their skin. Extend the rights of citizenship to every citizen of this land. There is no constitutional issue here. The command of the Constitution is plain. There is no moral issue. It is wrong—deadly wrong—to deny any of your fellow Americans the right to vote in this country. There is no issue of States rights or National rights. There is only the struggle for human rights.†

*Martin Luther King, Jr., "I Have a Dream" Speech, August 28, 1963, reprinted in *Great Issues in American History: From Reconstruction to the Present Day, 1864–1969,* ed. Richard Hofstadter (New York: Vintage, 1969), 486–487.

†Lyndon B. Johnson, Speech on the Voting Rights Act of 1965, March 15, 1965, reprinted in *Great Issues in American History: From Reconstruction to the Present Day, 1864–1969,* ed. Richard Hofstadter (New York: Vintage, 1969), 489–490.

Protecting the right to vote in practice is much more difficult than proclaiming that the right exists. One way of protecting the impact of votes cast by minorities is to create "majority-minority" voting districts, which concentrate racial minorities in electoral districts to promote the election of minority candidates. Such a plan is designed to ensure that minority votes are not wasted in districts where minorities are a small percentage of voters. Yet such plans have been challenged as unconstitutional "racial gerrymanders" that hurt communities by segregating the votes of black and white citizens. The most controversial of these districts has been North Carolina's Twelfth District, which snakes its way along Interstate 85, expanding to encompass black neighborhoods and contracting to avoid white ones. The district creates a safe seat for a black representative, but it also isolates many black votes from impacting other elections throughout the state. (See map below.)

The Supreme Court ruled in *Shaw v. Reno* (1993) that state redistricting statutes can be challenged under the Fourteenth Amendment's Equal Protection Clause if the statute "rationally cannot be understood as anything other than an effort to separate voters into different districts on the basis of race, and that the separation lacks sufficient justification." A district based solely or predominantly on racial classifications, Justice Sandra Day O'Connor wrote, "bears an uncomfortable resemblance to political apartheid."* Justice Clarence Thomas wrote, in *Holder v. Hall,* that "few devices could be better designed to exacerbate racial tensions than the consciously segregated districting system currently being constructed in the name of the Voting Rights Act."†

Scholars disagree vehemently on the impact and wisdom of majority-minority districts. Elaine Jones, director of the NAACP Legal Defense Fund, said that Supreme Court rulings like *Shaw* "really torch the fundamental right of African-Americans, Hispanics and others to be included as participatory citizens in this democracy."‡ Do you think racial minorities should be grouped in districts that virtually guarantee the election of a minority representative? Does such a district rest too heavily on the assumption that race links voters together more than other factors such as income, geography, or occupation? Are majority-minority districts the best way to ensure that minority voters can compete effectively in the electoral system?

*Shaw v. Reno (509 U.S. 630 (1993)).

†Holder v. Hall (129 L Ed 2d 687 (1994), 711).

‡Quoted in Stephan Thernstrom and Abigail Thernstrom, *America in Black and White: One Nation, Indivisible* (New York, Simon & Schuster, 1997), p. 482.

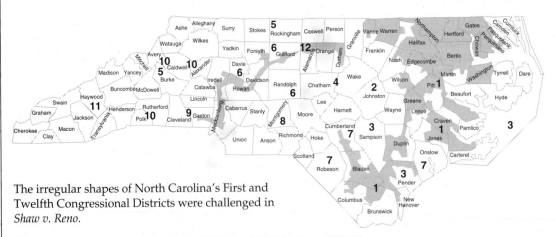

The irregular shapes of North Carolina's First and Twelfth Congressional Districts were challenged in *Shaw v. Reno.*

Source: Map from John L. Moore, *Elections A to Z* (Washington, DC: CQ Press, 1999), 405.

## Voter Turnout

Despite the battles fought to extend voting rights, voter turnout continues to be a source of concern for many observers. 51 percent of eligible voters cast votes in the 2000 presidential election, a slight increase over the 1996 election. Yet voter turnout in America has been steadily declining since World War II. Part of the explanation for this might be that the American voting system imposes *high costs* on potential voters, meaning that voting can be a practical burden: an individual must take positive action to register to vote, and many individuals must take time off from work to vote or somehow fit voting into tight daily schedules. In contrast, some countries automatically register all citizens to vote; some allow elections to take place over time, instead of on a single day; and some have easier procedures than the United States for absentee voting or voting by mail. Turnout also depends on the *type of election*: presidential elections, for example, attract more voters than other elections. Congressional elections see far fewer voters in off years than during a presidential campaign. Finally, turnout can be affected by calculations of "political *efficacy*," or the extent to which an individual believes her or his vote will matter.

There are several basic rules of thumb about voter turnout in the United States:

- People with *higher education* levels tend to vote more than people with lower education levels. Many other factors are relevant, but education level seems to be the most significant factor correlated with whether a person votes or not.

ON THE WEB
www.census.gov/
population/www/
socdemo/voting.html

ON THE WEB
www.fec.gov/pages/
electpg.htm

ON THE WEB
www.igc.apc.org/cvd/
graphics.html

ON THE WEB
www.umich.edu.~nes

Waiting in a voting line brings people into close contact with their neighbors and gives them a chance to discuss political issues and community affairs face-to-face.

Voting over the Internet is a hot topic with growing support. Two important practical concerns have been raised regarding e-voting: First, some worry that access will be skewed toward people with higher levels of income and education, mirroring the bias in access to the Web generally. Second, any e-voting plans must be able to protect against voter fraud. In the first passage below, New York Governor <u>George Pataki</u> lists some of the advantages of e-voting; in the second, political analyst <u>Rick Valelly</u> raises fundamental concerns about the very *nature* of e-voting. Do you find Pataki's argument attractive? What does Valelly fear might be the result of increased e-voting? Are Pataki and Valelly addressing the same concerns? Which case do you find more persuasive, and why?

**Governor Pataki:**

You have rural areas [in New York and California] where people, on a [snowy] day like today, simply will not be able to get to the polls, even if they want to, and couldn't vote. You have other urban areas where you have a large population base, where they might come down and face a line where you have to wait 45 or 50 minutes to be eligible to have the opportunity to vote. We have handicapped people who cannot get to the polls despite our best efforts. And certainly one of the most frustrating things as an elected official is, we have elections where we don't know for eight to ten days after the election who has won because we're waiting for mailed-in ballots from overseas or out of the state to arrive. All of that can change with Internet voting. All of that can change when people have the opportunity to

simply, from their homes, use an electronic signature, be a participant in the process.*

**Valelly:**

Now is the time to stop and think before we make what could be a big mistake. Not only will e-voting fail to reverse electoral apathy, it will actually lead us in the wrong direction. Voting is more than the simple act of indicating one's political preference. It's a vital public ritual that increases social solidarity and binds citizens together. The history of voting in America clearly shows that the physical mechanics of voting have a huge impact on the quality of our public life. . . .

The problem is that e-voting will transform voting, an inherently public activity, into a private one. Even with the secret ballot, the mechanics of voting are still explicitly designed to remind us that, in principle, we are all equal members of a political community. On Election Day, we must leave our homes and offices, travel to a polling place, and physically mingle with people who are plainly our equals that day, no matter what other differences we have. Voting, as we currently do it, is a civic ritual, however brief it may be.†

*George S. Pataki, from a transcript of "The Future of Internet Voting," a symposium co-sponsored by The Brookings Institution and Cisco Systems, Inc., January 20, 2000, retrieved from *http://www.brook.edu/comm/events/20000120.htm*, February 13, 2000.

†Rick Valelly, "The Case against Virtual Ballot Boxes: Voting Alone," *New Republic*, September 13–20, 1999, pp. 20–22. See also Thomas J. Johnson and Barbara K. Kaye, "A Vehicle for Engagement or a Haven for the Disaffected? Internet Use, Political Alienation, and Voter Participation," in *Engaging the Public: How Government and the Media Can Reinvigorate American Democracy*, ed. Thomas J. Johnson, Carol E. Hays, and Scott P. Hays (Lanham, MD: Rowman & Littlefield, 1998).

- People with *higher incomes* tend to vote more than people with lower incomes.
- *Older citizens* tend to vote more than younger citizens. In fact, younger people have the lowest turnout rates.
- People who are *employed* report higher levels of voting participation than those who are unemployed.

American voter turnout is notoriously lower than turnout in other western democracies, a fact often used to suggest the ill health of the American system. However, several very important factors suggest that the worry over low turnout might be misplaced. First, comparing turnout with other countries can

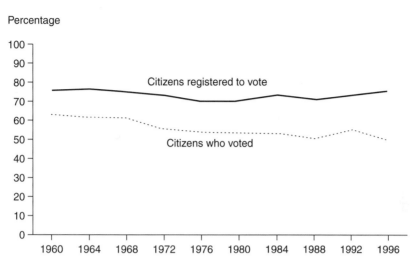

Percentage

Note: Registration and voting as a percentage of the voting age population.

The National Voter Registration Act of 1993 (the "motor voter" bill) eased requirements for registering to vote. Voter registration increased two percentage points between 1992 and 1996, and the Federal Election Commission estimates that as many as 80 or 90 percent of eligible voters might be registered by the year 2000. However, it is not yet clear that these newly registered voters will actually turn out to vote in elections.*

## Voting-Age Population Registered and Voting, Cross-Sections, 1978–1996 (percent)

| | Percentage Reporting They Registered | | | | | | | | | | Percentage Reporting They Voted | | | | | | | | | |
| --- | --- | --- | --- | --- | --- | --- | --- | --- | --- | --- | --- | --- | --- | --- | --- | --- | --- | --- | --- | --- |
| | Presidential Election Years | | | | | Congressional Election Years | | | | | Presidential Election Years | | | | | Congressional Election Years | | | | |
| | 1980 | 1984 | 1988 | 1992 | 1996 | 1978 | 1982 | 1986 | 1990 | 1994 | 1980 | 1984 | 1988 | 1992 | 1996 | 1978 | 1982 | 1986 | 1990 | 1994 |
| Race/ethnicity | | | | | | | | | | | | | | | | | | | | |
| White | 68 | 70 | 68 | 70 | 72 | 64 | 66 | 65 | 64 | 64 | 61 | 61 | 59 | 64 | 60 | 47 | 50 | 47 | 47 | 47 |
| Black | 60 | 66 | 65 | 64 | 64 | 57 | 59 | 64 | 59 | 58 | 51 | 56 | 52 | 54 | 51 | 37 | 43 | 43 | 39 | 37 |
| Hispanic origin[a] | 36 | 40 | 36 | 35 | 36 | 33 | 35 | 36 | 32 | 30 | 30 | 33 | 29 | 29 | 27 | 24 | 25 | 24 | 21 | 19 |
| Hispanic citizen[a] | 54 | 59 | 57 | 59 | 59 | 48 | 52 | 54 | 52 | 53 | 44 | 48 | 46 | 48 | 44 | 34 | 37 | 36 | 34 | 34 |
| Sex | | | | | | | | | | | | | | | | | | | | |
| Male | 67 | 67 | 65 | 67 | 64 | 63 | 64 | 63 | 61 | 61 | 59 | 59 | 56 | 60 | 53 | 47 | 49 | 46 | 45 | 44 |
| Female | 67 | 69 | 68 | 69 | 67 | 63 | 64 | 65 | 63 | 63 | 59 | 61 | 58 | 62 | 56 | 45 | 48 | 46 | 45 | 45 |
| Region | | | | | | | | | | | | | | | | | | | | |
| Northeast | 65 | 67 | 65 | 67 | 65 | 62 | 63 | 62 | 61 | 61 | 59 | 60 | 57 | 61 | 54 | 48 | 50 | 44 | 45 | 45 |
| Midwest | 74 | 75 | 73 | 75 | 72 | 68 | 71 | 71 | 68 | 69 | 66 | 66 | 63 | 67 | 59 | 51 | 55 | 50 | 49 | 49 |
| South | 64 | 64 | 66 | 67 | 66 | 60 | 62 | 63 | 61 | 61 | 56 | 57 | 55 | 59 | 52 | 40 | 42 | 43 | 42 | 41 |
| West | 63 | 65 | 63 | 64 | 61 | 59 | 61 | 61 | 58 | 58 | 57 | 59 | 56 | 59 | 52 | 48 | 51 | 48 | 45 | 46 |

# Voting-Age Population Registered and Voting, Cross-Sections, 1978–1996 (percent)

| | Percentage Reporting They Registered | | | | | | | | | | Percentage Reporting They Voted | | | | | | | | | |
|---|---|---|---|---|---|---|---|---|---|---|---|---|---|---|---|---|---|---|---|---|
| | Presidential Election Years | | | | | Congressional Election Years | | | | | Presidential Election Years | | | | | Congressional Election Years | | | | |
| | 1980 | 1984 | 1988 | 1992 | 1996 | 1978 | 1982 | 1986 | 1990 | 1994 | 1980 | 1984 | 1988 | 1992 | 1996 | 1978 | 1982 | 1986 | 1990 | 1994 |
| **Age** | | | | | | | | | | | | | | | | | | | | |
| 18–20 | 45 | 47 | 45 | 48 | 46 | 35 | 35 | 35 | 35 | 37 | 36 | 37 | 33 | 38 | 31 | 20 | 20 | 19 | 18 | 17 |
| 21–24 | 53 | 54 | 51 | 55 | 51 | 45 | 48 | 47 | 43 | 46 | 43 | 44 | 38 | 46 | 33 | 26 | 28 | 24 | 22 | 22 |
| 25–34 | 62 | 63 | 58 | 61 | 57 | 56 | 57 | 56 | 52 | 52 | 55 | 55 | 48 | 53 | 43 | 38 | 40 | 35 | 34 | 32 |
| 35–44 | 71 | 71 | 69 | 69 | 67 | 67 | 68 | 68 | 66 | 63 | 64 | 64 | 61 | 64 | 55 | 50 | 52 | 49 | 48 | 46 |
| 45–64 | 76 | 77 | 76 | 75 | 74 | 74 | 76 | 75 | 71 | 71 | 69 | 70 | 68 | 70 | 64 | 59 | 62 | 59 | 56 | 56 |
| 65 and older | 75 | 77 | 78 | 78 | 77 | 73 | 75 | 77 | 80 | 76 | 65 | 68 | 69 | 70 | 67 | 56 | 60 | 61 | 66 | 61 |
| **Employment** | | | | | | | | | | | | | | | | | | | | |
| Employed | 69 | 69 | 67 | 70 | 67 | 63 | 66 | 64 | 63 | 63 | 62 | 62 | 58 | 64 | 55 | 47 | 50 | 46 | 45 | 45 |
| Unemployed | 50 | 54 | 50 | 54 | 53 | 44 | 50 | 49 | 45 | 46 | 41 | 44 | 39 | 46 | 37 | 27 | 34 | 30 | 28 | 28 |
| Not in labor force | 66 | 68 | 67 | 67 | 65 | 63 | 64 | 66 | 63 | 62 | 57 | 59 | 57 | 59 | 54 | 46 | 49 | 48 | 47 | 45 |
| **Education (years)** | | | | | | | | | | | | | | | | | | | | |
| 8 or less | 53 | 53 | 48 | 44 | 41 | 53 | 52 | 51 | 44 | 40 | 43 | 43 | 37 | 35 | 30 | 35 | 36 | 33 | 28 | 23 |
| 1–3 of high school | 55 | 55 | 53 | 50 | 48 | 53 | 53 | 52 | 48 | 45 | 46 | 44 | 41 | 41 | 34 | 35 | 38 | 34 | 31 | 27 |
| 4 of high school | 66 | 67 | 65 | 65 | 62 | 62 | 63 | 63 | 60 | 59 | 59 | 59 | 55 | 58 | 49 | 45 | 47 | 44 | 42 | 40 |
| 1–3 of college | 74 | 76 | 74 | 75 | 73 | 69 | 70 | 70 | 69 | 68 | 67 | 68 | 65 | 69 | 61 | 52 | 53 | 50 | 50 | 49 |
| 4 or more college | 84 | 84 | 83 | 85 | 80 | 77 | 78 | 78 | 77 | 76 | 80 | 79 | 78 | 81 | 73 | 64 | 67 | 63 | 63 | 63 |
| Total | 67 | 68 | 67 | 68 | 66 | 62 | 64 | 64 | 62 | 62 | 59 | 60 | 57 | 61 | 54 | 46 | 49 | 46 | 45 | 45 |

Note: Data for earlier years can be found in previous editions of *Vital Statistics on American Politics*.

a Persons of Hispanic origin may be of any race.

Note the drop-off in turnout during midterm elections, and how turnout increases with age and educational achievement.

*See Jerry Calvert, "Election Law Reform and Turnout: What Works?" in *Engaging the Public: How Government and the Media Can Reinvigorate American Democracy*, ed. Thomas J. Johnson, Carol E. Hays, and Scott P. Hays (Lanham, MD: Rowman & Littlefield, 1998).
Source: Figures from *Congressional Quarterly's Guide to the Presidency*, 2nd ed., ed. Michael Nelson (Washington, DC: CQ Press, 1996), 89; *Vital Statistics on American Politics, 1999–2000*, ed. Harold W. Stanley and Harold Watkins (Washington, DC: CQ Press, 2000), 16–17.

be misleading. American turnout rates are usually calculated by using the voting-age population as a baseline, whereas European rates are usually figured using *registered* voters as a baseline. When American turnout is figured as a percentage of *registered* voters, American turnout compares favorably with turnout in other countries. Second, though many believe that nonvoting is a result of increasing cynicism among the general public, the fact is that nonvoting is *not* statistically correlated with cynicism—in other words, people who report distrust of government and public officials are just as likely to vote as those with less cynical attitudes. Finally, participation in the United States in political activities other than voting—joining groups, contacting public officials, and so on—tends to be higher in the United States than in other countries.

## Voter Choices

Why does a voter choose one candidate over another? In general, voter choices are determined by *party identification, attitudes about the candidates' images,* and *positions on issues*—in that order. Choices are thus based primarily on long-

### Ways to Get Dumb Guys to Vote for You

**10.** Promise to replace presidential limo with monster truck.

**9.** Pass out campaign buttons and say, "Look, free shiny things!"

**8.** Promise that if you win, you'll help them get the mouse traps off their feet.

**7.** In "Nightline" interview, keep calling Ted Koppel "Mr. Snapple."

**6.** Say you'll bomb the ever-lovin' shorts off every country whose name ain't spelled U-S-A.

**5.** Promise to publish a "Where's Waldo" book in which the only thing on each page is Waldo.

**4.** Put bucket on head. Wander around parking lot.

**3.** New campaign slogan: "Uhhhhh..."

**2.** Begin every speech with, "I am like a box of chocolates!"

**1.** Free circus tickets.

Source: Reprinted by permission of CBS Worldwide, Inc.

term attitudes and relationships with a party, and only secondarily with short-term considerations regarding images and issues.

As with turnout, a few general rules of thumb help us predict how people will cast their votes.

- People with lower levels of education and income tend to vote Democratic more than they vote Republican.
- Women, minorities, Catholics, Jews, young voters, and union members all tend to vote Democratic more than they vote Republican.
- Protestants and the religious right tend to vote Republican, although religion is closely connected with social and economic factors as a determinant of voter choices.
- *Identification with a political party* remains the best predictor of how a person will vote. Despite cries that voter turnout is down and that parties are decaying, party identification continues to be a source of long-term stability in the way the electorate behaves— especially in nonpresidential elections. Some scholars argue that partisan attachments are "affective" ties picked up from parents and the environments in which people are raised;

**Presidential Vote in 2000 Election, by Groups**

| | 2000 | | | | 2000 | | |
|---|---|---|---|---|---|---|---|
| | Gore | Bush | Nader | | Gore | Bush | Nader |
| **Sex** | | | | **Religion** | | | |
| Male | 43 | 54 | 3 | Protestant | 40 | 58 | 2 |
| Female | 55 | 43 | 2 | Catholic | 53 | 46 | 1 |
| **Race/ethnicity** | | | | Jewish | 77 | 22 | 1 |
| White | 43 | 54 | 3 | **Political affiliation** | | | |
| Black | 90 | 9 | 1 | Democrat | 88 | 10 | 2 |
| Latino | 61 | 38 | 1 | Independent | 43 | 49 | 8 |
| **Education** | | | | Republican | 7 | 92 | 1 |
| High school or less | 54 | 44 | 2 | **Region** | | | |
| Some college | 45 | 51 | 4 | East | 58 | 37 | 5 |
| College degree or less | 49 | 48 | 3 | Midwest | 47 | 50 | 3 |
| **Age** | | | | South | 41 | 58 | 1 |
| Under 30 | 54 | 41 | 5 | West | 52 | 44 | 4 |
| 30–44 | 46 | 51 | 3 | | | | |
| 45–64 | 51 | 47 | 2 | **Total** | 49 | 48 | 3 |
| 65 or older | 46 | 52 | 2 | | | | |

Source: Data from the Los Angeles Times, November 9, 2000. Used by permission.

others argue that party identification is based on satisfaction or dissatisfaction with the performance of particular parties. Both arguments suggest, though, that an individual's party identification strengthens over the years.

Beyond these rules of thumb, a host of other factors influence voter choices. Retrospective considerations of the parties' and candidates' past performance are important, as are, of course, considerations surrounding the candidates and issues involved in any particular election. And if this seems like a fairly comprehensive list of factors, it is. Elections and voting choices are at bottom a complex collection of attitudes and opinions and calculations, and to an extent every election is different.

Yet even in the year 2000, voters tended to stay with their parties (see Zip Box 4.10). Even in a time of weakening party loyalties and growing numbers of independent voters, then, the key to voter choice continues to be party identification. In fact, some scholars have pointed out that if voting behavior depends so much on long-term affiliations and relatively stable identifications with a party, then what happens during a campaign might not be that significant. To an extent, this is true—we have seen that almost two-thirds of voters make up their minds before or during the conventions, for example, and many voters ultimately vote for a candidate they chose well before the convention even happened. At the same time, though, that last, procrastinating one-third that waits until the general campaign can be very important in a tight race.

## Conclusion

Voting, campaigns, and elections remain at the very center of American politics, reinforcing our national commitment to a government based on the consent of the governed. This notion that the true source of government's legitimate authority lies with the people, and that government is instituted by free people to secure their natural rights, is the subject of the next chapter—as we turn our attention to the United States Constitution.

## Overnight Assignment

Using the FEC's webpage, Project VoteSmart's webpage, or some other source, identify the major contributors to the most recent campaigns of your representative in Congress and your senators. Did they receive PAC money? What kind of PACs were involved? How did contributions differ for the House and Senate campaign? Besides PACs, where did campaign contributions come from?

## Long-Term Integrated Assignment

Return to the interest group you chose to follow at the end of chapter 2. Did the group play an active role in the last election, or is it playing an active role in the upcoming election? What appeals is the group making to get people to vote, and to get people to vote a certain way? Did the group make any campaign contributions? Is the group involved with a political action committee? Use the websites of the group, the parties, and the FEC, as well as your media source, to gather this information.

## Researching Elections, Campaigns, and Voting?

**Try These Authors:**

James E. Campbell          Warren E. Miller          Abigail M. Thernstron
Paul S. Herrnson          Mark Rozell          Clyde Wilcox
V. O. Key, Jr.

**Try These Sources:**

ABRAMSON, PAUL R., JOHN H. ALDRICH, and DAVID W. ROHDE. *Change and Continuity in the 1996 and 1998 Elections.* Washington, DC: CQ Press, 1999.

ANSOLABEHERE, STEPHEN, and SHANTO IYENGAR. *Going Negative: How Attack Ads Shrink and Polarize the Electorate.* New York: Free Press, 1995.

DENNIS, JACK. "The Study of Electoral Behavior." In *Political Science: Looking to the Future.* Vol. 3, *Political Behavior,* ed. William Crotty. Evanston, IL: Northwestern University Press, 1991.

GUINIER, LANI. *The Tyranny of the Majority: Fundamental Fairness in Representative Democracy.* New York: Free Press, 1994.

HERRNSON, PAUL S. *Congressional Elections: Campaigning at Home and in Washington.* 2nd ed. Washington, DC: CQ Press, 1998.

HOLBROOK, THOMAS M. *Do Campaigns Matter?* Thousand Oaks, CA: Sage, 1996.

JOHNSON, THOMAS J., CAROL E. HAYS, and SCOTT P. HAYS, eds. *Engaging the Public: How Government and the Media Can Reinvigorate American Democracy.* Lanham, MD: Rowman & Littlefield, 1998.

MILLER, WARREN E., and J. MERRILL SHANKS. *The New American Voter.* Cambridge, MA: Harvard University Press, 1996.

POMPER, GERALD M. *The Election of 1996: Reports and Interpretations.* Chatham, NJ: Chatham House Publishers, 1997.

TEIXEIRA, RUY A. *The Disappearing American Voter.* Washington, DC: Brookings Institution, 1992.

## Endnotes ▬▬▬▬▬▬▬▬▬▬▬▬▬▬▬▬▬▬▬

1. Thomas Paine, *Common Sense,* in *Thomas Paine: Collected Writings* (New York: Library of America, 1995), 8 [emphasis in original].
2. William J. Keefe, *Parties, Politics, and Public Policy in America,* 7th ed. (Washington, DC: CQ Press, 1994), 186.
3. Frank J. Sorauf, "Political Action Committees: Introduction," in *Campaign Finance Reform: A Sourcebook,* ed. Anthony Corrado, Thomas E. Mann, Daniel R. Ortiz, Trevor Potter, and Frank J. Sorauf (Washington, DC: Brookings Institution Press, 1997), 123.
4. Ibid., 129.
5. Fred Wertheimer, "TV Ad Wars: How to Cut Advertising Costs in Political Campaigns," *Harvard International Journal of Press/Politics,* 2, no. 3 (summer 1997): 94.
6. Doris A. Graber, *Mass Media and American Politics,* 4th ed. (Washington, DC: CQ Press, 1993), 248–249. Advertising has more of an effect in congressional campaigns, in part because the absence of saturation coverage makes advertising an important factor in building name recognition and public visibility. Spending on advertising in congressional campaigns seems to help both challengers and incumbents.
7. Ibid., 262, 278, 279. See also Robert Lichter and Ted Smith, "Why Elections Are Bad News: Media and Candidate Discourse in the 1996 Presidential Primaries," *Harvard International Journal of Press/Politics* 1 (fall 1996).
8. Graber, *Mass Media and American Politics,* 262. The two are related, though, so it is difficult to separate them completely. Further, horse race polls can increase voters' attention to other issues, in effect enhancing voter awareness of issues. See, for example, Xinshu Zhao and Glen L. Bleske, "Horse-Race Polls and Audience Issue Learning," and Philip Meyer and Deborah Potter, "Preelection Polls and Issue Knowledge in the 1996 U.S. Presidential Election," both in *Harvard International Journal of Press/Politics* 3, no. 4 (fall 1998).
9. Graber, *Mass Media and American Politics,* 251–255.

# PART TWO

# Competition by Design

CHAPTER 5

# *The Constitution*

## CHAPTER OUTLINE

★ Managed Competition:
The Ideals and Purpose of the Constitution   135

★ You Scratch My Back, I'll Scratch Yours:
Practical Compromises at the Framing   140

★ Balance in Wonderland:
The Constitution's Competitive Design   150

★ Brevity Is the Soul of Lit(igation):
Competing Interpretations of the Constitution
and Politics by Other Means   157

In the years leading up to the taking of the 2000 Census, the media portrayed the issue of the census undercount of minorities as a political issue pitting Democrats against Republicans. The media generally presented the debate as a choice between two methods of taking the census: a traditional headcount, which would perpetuate the undercount and benefit Republicans; and a census influenced by statistical counting measures, which would reduce the undercount and benefit Democrats.

Interest groups weighed in on the census issue. Some, particularly minority groups and civil rights groups, argued that the census disproportionately undercounted blacks and some inner-city residents like the homeless, depriving them of fair representation. Others, such as groups representing senior citizens (who have high rates of participation in the census), argued that statistically adjusting traditional headcounts was unfair to those citizens who fulfilled their legal responsibility to participate in the census. Government interests also weighed in: cities with high undercounts, like Los Angeles, argued that the undercount hurt them by unfairly reducing their share of federal funds for social programs; other cities, believing that an adjustment would redirect funds to cities like L.A., aligned against them.

The major political parties acted in the firm belief that statistical adjustment would benefit Democrats and hurt Republicans. For years, the Clinton White House pressured the Bureau of the Census and its parent, the Commerce Department, to promote such measures. The Republican-controlled House of Representatives brought suit in federal court against the Commerce Department to prohibit the Census Bureau from "sampling" the population, or artificially counting those who were missed by the traditional headcount; Democrats in the House responded by supporting efforts to defeat the suit. Cities and interest groups lined up on either side and joined the litigation.

Most of this activity, though, took place for the wrong reasons. Eliminating the undercount through statistical measures would have only a very limited effect on the apportionment of representatives in Congress, with at best only a few seats in the House shifting from some states to others. How these seats would affect party strength in Congress is unknown; the effects on parties in the states and localities is almost completely unpredictable. Further, given the complicated nature of federal funding programs, eliminating the undercount would have only a trivial impact on the sums going to cities like Los Angeles. And, finally, the proposition that not being counted in the census translates into a lack of representation is simply not true.[1]

It is not difficult to understand why the media, interest groups, and political parties responded to the census undercount issue as they did. As we saw throughout Part One, the media polarize issues and frequently overlook complicated details. Thousands of interest groups compete for influence through the media, Congress, and the courts to promote what they believe to be the interests of their members. The parties compete with each other as they strive to bring interests together and to win elections. Voting and elections register popular preferences and affirm the legitimacy of the system; to the extent that the census determines the apportionment of seats in the House, the census is an important component of our representative government.

The census issue captures the complicated constitutional design in action. The census is a fundamentally constitutional issue: taking a new census within ten years of the last is explicitly required by the Constitution, and the census count remains the cornerstone of popular representation in the House. The Constitution protects free speech and thus protects the media's right to report the census story however they want; the Constitution protects the right of association and thus encourages the formation of interest groups that compete to influence the method of taking the census; and the Constitution separates powers within government, encouraging parties and institutional interests to compete for control of how agencies like the Bureau of the Census do their jobs.

This chapter examines the formation and design of our Constitution. The work of the framers at Philadelphia in 1787 continues to be the single greatest factor determining the course of American politics. The competition and compromise that lie at the heart of American government were cemented in place in the Constitution, a grand and successful effort to build a governing framework strong enough to strive for the ideals of life, liberty, and the pursuit of happiness, yet not so strong as to pose a tyrannical threat to those ideals. The constitutional system is a brilliant mechanism of optimism and wariness, of balance and counterweight, and of practical compromise. The census is one example among thousands illustrating the continued relevance of the constitutional system to everyday lives.

**The Bottom Line.** The Constitution, and the political ideas of the eighteenth century, are the keys to today's American government. The Constitution is a unique and brilliant attempt to realize the best and highest values, while protecting people from the worst and most self-interested behavior. Optimism arises from eighteenth-century philosophy and anchors deep in the principles of the Declaration of Independence and the Constitution. The institutional structures organized by the Constitution are designed to protect these values by fragmenting power and by setting myriad countervailing forces against one another. The framers accepted that people act in self-interested ways, and they carefully anticipated the worst actions by the worst people and sought to protect government and the people from themselves. At its core, the Constitution turns a philosophy of humanity into a complex and enormously successful framework that institutionalizes competition and encourages compromise.

## MANAGED COMPETITION: THE IDEALS AND PURPOSE OF THE CONSTITUTION

The Constitution is our social compact, an agreement between the people and government. It is binding on both parties, although the people remain sovereign and can amend the Constitution or dissolve a government that does not adhere to the contract. The Constitution's ratification fulfilled the great seventeenth-century philosopher John Locke's requirement that legitimate government must be formed with the consent of the people. The Constitution remains our social compact after more than two hundred years because it is a flexible document that can and has been interpreted to meet ever-changing political demands and realities. The Constitution's basic principles stand, but within the framework of those principles governmental structures and processes have changed over the years. New events and issues, new technologies, new beliefs, and new Americans have all been included within the constitutional system.

### Getting from There to Here: John Locke, Natural Rights, and Higher Law

The United States Constitution is an eighteenth-century governing mechanism based on the ideas and ideals of that era. Eighteenth-century understanding of natural rights and higher law forms the foundation of American political thought.

Political philosophers have long tried to understand how people organize into societies and why people form governments. The concept of a "state of nature" is a cornerstone for such inquiries; the state of nature represents the place of individuals in a hypothetical time before the formation of government.

John Trumbull's famous oil painting of the signing of the Declaration of Independence.

English author <u>John Locke</u> argued that all individuals in the state of nature possessed *natural rights* to life, liberty, and property, and that all men were created equal. Locke describes the state of nature as a state of equality, and also a state of freedom: "To understand Political Power right, and derive it from its Original, we must consider what State all Men are naturally in, and that is, a *State of perfect Freedom* to order their Actions, and dispose of their Possessions, and Persons as they think fit, within the bounds of the Law of Nature, without asking leave, or depending on the Will of any other Man."[2]

The state of nature, though, was unpredictable: with no mechanisms to preserve natural rights, individuals were left to protect themselves against those who would violate those rights; the weak were at the mercy of the strong. Locke suggested that individuals in a state of nature formed governments for self-preservation, to protect natural rights, resolve disputes, repel foreign invasions, and carry out other tasks in the public interest. According to Locke, such governments were established by a social compact that could be abrogated if the government did not govern with the consent of the people. "The people" possessed the right to overthrow a government that did not act with the people's "consent."

American political philosophy owes much to Locke's work. <u>Thomas Jefferson</u> embodied Locke's ideas in the Declaration of Independence, in some places almost word for word. The Declaration outlined the reasons why the American colonies were justified in breaking their ties to England and striking out for independence, and the crucial opening paragraph of the Declaration perfectly reflects Locke's reasoning in support of a people's ability to break away from their government (see Discussion Box 5.1).

The Declaration of Independence followed the ideas outlined by English political theorist John Locke. Too easily and too often overlooked, the Declaration justifies the colonies' break with the crown and highlights the American commitment to natural rights and to higher law. According to the passages below, what justifies America's appeal to assume powers on earth? What argument supports the appeal to natural rights? Should the act of changing an established government be undertaken lightly?

When in the Course of human events, it becomes necessary for one people to dissolve the political bands which have connected them with another, and to assume among the Powers of the earth, the separate and equal station to which the Laws of Nature and of Nature's God entitle them, a decent respect to the opinions of mankind requires that they should declare the causes which inspired them to the separation.

We hold these truths to be self-evident, that all men are created equal, that they are endowed by their Creator with certain unalienable Rights, that among these are Life, Liberty, and the pursuit of happiness. That to secure these rights, Governments are instituted among Men, deriving their just powers from the consent of the governed. That whenever any Form of Government becomes destructive of these ends, it is the Right of the People to alter or to abolish it, and to institute a new Government, laying its foundation on such principles and organizing its powers in such form, as to them shall seem most likely to effect their Safety and Happiness.

Prudence, indeed, will dictate that Governments long established should not be changed for light and transient causes; and accordingly, all experience hath shown, that mankind are more disposed to suffer, while evils are sufferable, than to right themselves by abolishing the forms to which they are accustomed. But when a long train of abuses and usurpations, pursuing invariably the same Object, evinces a design to reduce them under absolute Despotism, it is their right, it is their duty, to throw off such Government, and to provide new Guards for their future security.—Such has been the patient sufferance of these Colonies; and such is now the necessity which constrains them to alter their former Systems of Government. The history of the present King of Great Britain is a history of repeated injuries and usurpations, all having in direct object the establishment of an absolute Tyranny over these States. To prove this, let Facts be submitted to a candid world. . . .

Eighteenth-century political philosophy also posited a *higher law,* what Locke called the Law of Nature, which governs even the state of nature. Locke wrote, "The State of Nature has a Law of Nature to govern it, which obliges every one: And Reason, which is that Law, teaches all Mankind, who will but consult it, that being all equal and independent, no one ought to harm another in his Life, Health, Liberty, or Possessions."[3] The higher law thus defines individual rights and the purpose of government. The higher law gives people natural rights, the freedom to consent to government and the right to revolution if governments act without popular consent. These rights and freedoms transcend constitutions and laws because no legitimate social contract can deny individual rights or establish government not based on the consent of the people. The higher law is significant because the concept of a higher law in the Anglo-American political and legal tradition is intertwined with important aspects of the American governing system. As we will see later in this chapter and throughout the rest of this text, the judiciary branch under the Constitution has the authority to review legislative and executive actions to assure their conformity with the higher law.

The Constitution is the social compact to which the American people have, in Lockean terms, consented. It constructs a governing mechanism designed to secure natural rights while remaining consistent with the higher law.

**137**

# Optimism and Wariness:
# The Madisonian Model of Government

The Constitution is driven by optimism surrounding the promise and potential of humanity, but it is also infused with wariness and skepticism. The Constitution embodies the framers' attempt to build a government that would protect natural rights and conform to higher law, striving for liberty, justice, and freedom, yet the framers also tried to ensure that no single interest or force in society ever possessed the power to tyrannize over others. In short, the task facing the framers was to put American ideals into practice in such a way that those ideals would be protected and furthered in a world of practical politics and dangerous, selfish interests.

To this end, two goals drive the Madisonian model of American government: preventing selfish interests, including a selfish majority, from gaining too much power; and assuring that government would still be powerful and competent enough to secure individual rights and the long-term interests of the nation as a whole. James Madison, Alexander Hamilton, and John Jay describe the core of the eighteenth-century governmental model in *The Federalist Papers,* written to persuade the voters of New York State to ratify the Constitution. *The Federalist* describes a symmetry to the Constitution that the other framers would have greatly admired. So compelling is *The Federalist* that the Supreme Court, historians, political scientists, and politicians of all kinds have used it as an authoritative guide to the Constitution's meaning.

**ON THE WEB**
lcweb2.loc.gov/const/
fed/fedpapers.html

**ON THE WEB**
www.yale.edu/law
web/avalon/federal/
fed.htm

### Controlling Self-Interest I: The Extended Republic

Madison and the other framers believed in the Enlightenment and had faith in reason, progress, and the ability of men to govern in a deliberative and selfless way. This view, though, was tempered by a very practical skepticism.

First of all, Madison understood that self-interested factions are inevitable in society. Madison defined a faction as "a number of citizens, whether amounting to a majority or minority of the whole, who are united and actuated by some common impulse of passion, or of interest, adverse to the rights of other citizens, or to the permanent and aggregate interests of the community."[4] Madison conceded that removing the causes of faction by destroying the liberty that motivates them would be worse than having factions in the first place; he also understood that all people in a society cannot be made to share the same interests and values. Factions would exist; they could not be eradicated. They would need to be controlled.

Madison's explanation of the extended republic, in *Federalist 10,* succinctly captures his philosophy for controlling the effects of factions. The United States would not be a "democracy," where citizens gathered to make decisions and administer the government. Instead the framers relied on *representative government* "to refine and enlarge the public views by passing them through the medium of a chosen body of citizens, whose wisdom might best discern the true interest of their country and whose patriotism and love of justice will be least likely to sacrifice it to temporary or partial considerations."[5]

The risk was that the representatives themselves, beholden to narrow interests, might betray the interests of the people. If Americans were to form together into a national union, that union had to deal with the diversity of interests in American society and also with the vast size of the American states. Size mattered because political philosophers had long believed that only small states could function successfully as republics. Madison turned this notion on its head, and argued that an *extended republic* could function successfully exactly *because* it would *multiply selfish factions,* setting them all against one another to such an extent that none could ever possess the power to tyrannize others. "Extend the sphere and you take in a greater variety of parties and interests; you make it less probable that a majority of the whole will have a common motive to invade the rights of other citizens.[6]

Madison's theory applied equally—perhaps even more so—to preventing the tyranny of the majority. Madison understood that majority factions might form, and that then minority interests would be at risk. He wrote, "When a majority is included in a faction, the form of popular government . . . enables it to sacrifice to its ruling passion or interest both the public good and the rights of other citizens. To secure the public good and private rights against the danger of such a [majority] faction, and at the same time to preserve the spirit and form of popular government, is then the great object to which our inquiries are directed."[7]

## Controlling Self-Interest II: The Constitution

The American system of government is specifically designed to fragment power, enabling good men to rule according to law—and preventing evil men and demagogues from gaining so much power that they might threaten the people's freedom. In effect, the self-interest of man was set against itself. By ensuring broad opportunities for people to be involved in public affairs, Madison expected different individuals, and different groups, to counteract the influence of each—preventing majority tyranny. Madison and the other framers also believed that balanced government would be deliberative government, one that would be capable of arriving at the national interest. The Constitution was as much about deliberative government as about limited government. Madison and the framers above all believed that statesmen should govern, that government and particularly a strong national government was essential for the preservation of the national interest.

Yet Madison and the framers were as wary of individual selfishness *within* government as they were wary of the power of factions to destroy the nation's society. In recognizing that the greatest threat of government is the concentration of power in the hands of a single branch or department of that government, Madison summarizes the philosophy of the constitutional system in a brilliant passage from *Federalist 51:*

> [T]he great security against a gradual concentration of the several powers in the same department consists in giving to those who administer each department the necessary constitutional means and personal motives to resist encroachments of the others. . . . Ambition must be made to counteract ambition. The interest of the man must be connected with the constitutional rights of the place.
>
> It may be a reflection on human nature that such devices should be necessary to control the abuses of government. But what is government itself but

the greatest of all reflections on human nature? If men were angels, no government would be necessary. If angels were to govern men, neither external nor internal controls on government would be necessary. In framing a government which is to be administered by men over men, the great difficulty lies in this: you must first enable government to control the governed; and in the next place oblige it to control itself. A dependence on the people is, no doubt, the primary control on the government; but experience has taught mankind the necessity of auxiliary precautions.[8]

Thus Madison captures the central difficulty of designing a government, and the central difficulty addressed by the framers in 1787. Living as we do in a free and open polity, we forget the extraordinary minds, events, and courage that ultimately produced our constitutional government with its intricate balance of powers and respect for freedoms of expression and natural rights. James Madison, Alexander Hamilton, Benjamin Franklin, John Adams, and George Mason were just some of the brilliant political theorists and practical politicians who came together in eighteenth-century America to design the new nation's governing structure. They gave us the free and open society we enjoy today, and their and our Constitution has endured with only a few significant formal changes for more than two hundred years. And while the Constitution reflected political philosophy, it also accommodated the political realities of the time. The rest of this chapter is about the formation and organic development of the Constitution.

## YOU SCRATCH MY BACK, I'LL SCRATCH YOURS: PRACTICAL COMPROMISES AT THE FRAMING

Delegates to the Constitutional Convention represented states with large populations and states with small populations; they represented slave states and free states; they represented manufacturing states fearful of foreign competition, and agricultural states dependent upon foreign trade. Not only would the new government have to be strong enough to govern and also able to control itself, as Madison wrote in *The Federalist*; all of these interests would have to agree on what that government should look like. The Constitution aims to protect natural rights, yet putting such idealistic goals into practice in the real world of politics and society is a difficult task. The Constitution's framers brilliantly accommodated conflicting political interests to create a national government.

### Framing the Constitution

The Articles of Confederation, which preceded the Constitution as the new nation's governing framework, gave no real power to Congress to establish a national army or navy, nor to raise taxes or duties, nor to provide a national currency, regulate interstate commerce and trade, or directly to enforce its laws. Congress thus had little power over the states or the American people. The states competed with each other for land and trade. This competition weakened the states and also failed to secure land borders or provide for a strong defense of the confederation. In the wake of the Revolution, national defense became a priority of the highest order; domestic anarchy seemed a possibility. In the winter of 1786–1787, for instance, Daniel Shays led a rebellion of Massachusetts debtors irate about being threatened with imprisonment and the loss of their property. Massachusetts had to put down the rebellion by using a private army supported by individual contributions. Further, the fledgling United States was threatened by powerful interests just outside its borders: Indian nations and European powers did not recede from the continent following the Revolution, but remained strong influences threatening the new nation's independence.

The framers realized that a stronger national government was needed to secure the principles of the Declaration of Independence. Nevertheless, state sovereignty and a wariness of centralized control dominated as the Constitutional Convention met in 1787. Alexander Hamilton, in addressing the Convention, pointed out that the states "constantly pursue internal interests adverse to those of the whole." A new national government, continued Hamilton, would require the "habitual attachment of the people," but the "whole force of this tie is on the side of the state government. Its sovereignty is immediately before the eyes of the people; its protection is immediately enjoyed by them." Similarly, James Madison declared: "In spite of every precaution, the general [national] government would be in perpetual danger of encroachments from the state government."[9] The majority of delegates agreed with the nationalistic views of Madison and Hamilton and voted for the creation of a national government that would have authority to carry out specific enumerated powers, but they faced an array of competing interests.

ON THE WEB
www.yale.edu/law
web/avalon/debates/
debcont.htm

ON THE WEB
www.constitution.org

## Convention Disputes

The key to drafting the Constitution was compromise. Without compromise among different personal, political, and economic interests, the national government as established by the Constitution would never have been possible. Because each state had interests that it wanted to protect against encroachment by the others and against potential national power, disputes arose over how the states would be represented in a new national government. Also debated was the balance of power between the states and the new national government. The large states were pitted against the small states, the Southern slave states opposed the Northern free states, and the merchant states were in conflict with the agrarian states.

### Large versus Small States

States with large populations and those with small populations argued for systems of appointing representatives to the national legislature that they believed would protect their own interests. Delegates from the larger, more populous states maintained that representation in the national legislature should be apportioned according to the population of each state. A plan to organize the government along these lines was presented by Edmund Randolph of Virginia. The Virginia delegation, strong nationalists all, included George Washington and James Madison in addition to Randolph. They had initially provided much of the impetus and guidance for the Convention.

Whereas the Virginia Plan was designed to establish a strong national government, the New Jersey Plan would have allowed continuation of a government more akin to the confederation already established. The New Jersey Plan was designed to advance the interests of the smaller states. The Articles of Confederation would have been maintained, and a few amendments would have been added that would have slightly increased the powers of the national government. The unicameral, or one-house, legislature of the Confederation government was to be retained, with each state possessing an equal number of representatives. The New Jersey Plan would have resulted in a weak national government with real power remaining in the hands of the states.

Alexander Hamilton expressed the views of delegates who opposed the New Jersey Plan. Addressing the Convention several days after <u>William Paterson</u> presented the New Jersey Plan, Hamilton declared: "We owed it to our country to do, on this emergency, whatever we should deem essential to its happiness. The states sent us here to provide for the exigencies of the Union. To rely on and propose any plan not adequate to these exigencies, merely because it was not clearly within our powers, would be to sacrifice the means to the end. . . . The great question is, what provisions shall we make for the happiness of our country?"[10]

### Slave versus Free States

Madison suggested that the major dispute was not between the large and the small states but between the free and slaveholding states, an issue related to apportionment of representatives in the legislature. Northerners, who did not possess great numbers of slaves, wanted slaves counted only as property for tax purposes. Southern states, on the other hand, would see their population numbers and thus their representation grow if slaves were counted for purposes of apportioning representatives.

### Manufacturing versus Agricultural States

Northern and Southern states also clashed over economic disputes. Most of the Northern states were involved with manufacturing and needed to import raw materials for factories; northern states thus wanted imports to be favored. Southern plantation owners, however, wanted the government to favor exports and to allow continuation of the slave trade as a source of cheap labor so that their products would have an advantage with overseas buyers. Naturally, each region wanted to control any government that would make decisions about treaties and taxes.

The differences between the large and small states, between free and slave states, and between commercial and agricultural interests, threatened to dissolve the Constitutional Convention as the heat of the Philadelphia summer intensified. During a particularly acrimonious session on June 30, <u>James Wilson</u>, a prominent Philadelphian who had signed the Declaration of Independence and had been a member of the Congress of the Confederation, admonished the delegates, "Can we forget for whom we are forming a government? Is it for men, or for the imaginary beings called states?"[11] <u>Benjamin Franklin</u>, the oldest delegate at eighty-one years of age, attempted to smooth the "ruf-

Independence Hall in Philadelphia as it appeared in the late eighteenth century.

fled feathers" of the younger delegates, a role he played throughout the Convention. He told them, "When a broad table is to be made, and the edges of planks do not fit, the artist takes a little from both, and makes a good joint. In like manner, here, both sides must part with some of their demands, in order that they may join in some accommodating proposition."[12]

## Convention Compromises

### The Great Compromise

The tension among the delegates was at a peak by July 2, when <u>Oliver Ellsworth</u>, a Connecticut lawyer and member of Congress, suggested a compromise to the issue of states and representation. To accommodate the interests of the small states, Ellsworth proposed that there be equal representation of states in the upper house of Congress, the Senate. This meant that in the lower house, representation would be driven by population; in the upper house, population would be irrelevant. The vote of the Convention on Ellsworth's proposal tied, with five states on each side (see Zip Box 5.1).

So the Convention was not dissolved, but it was still at an impasse. South Carolina delegates <u>Charles Pinckney</u> and General <u>Charles C. Pinckney</u> proposed the formation of a committee composed of one member from each state to study and make recommendations to resolve the disputes. Although Randolph, among others, had little hope for its success, the committee was duly appointed. Drawing and elaborating on the Ellsworth proposal, the committee quickly arrived at a solution known as the "Great Compromise." The plan called for a bicameral legislature, which most of the framers had already

It is an irony of history that if all the delegates had attended the Convention on the day Oliver Ellsworth offered his Great Compromise proposal, it would have been defeated and the Convention might have been dissolved by a walk-out of the small states' delegations. As historian Charles Warren writes:

The absence of two men changed the fate of the Constitution and the whole future history of the country. William Pierce of Georgia had gone to New York to attend Congress (and incidentally to fight a duel), Daniel of St. Thomas Jenifer of Maryland was late in taking his seat that morning. Both of these men were opposed to equality of representation. Had Pierce been present, the vote of Georgia . . . would have been cast with the large states. Had Jenifer been more prompt in his attendance, the vote of Maryland (actually cast by Luther Martin with the small states) would have been divided, and the large states would have prevailed on the motion.*

*Charles Warren, *The Making of the Constitution* (Cambridge, MA: Harvard University Press, 1947), 261–262.

---

accepted. Delegates to the lower house would be elected by the people from each state in proportion to the population. All states would have equal representation in the upper house, with two members chosen by each state legislature.

The Great Compromise carried on July 16 by a vote of five states to four. The Massachusetts delegation split and therefore did not cast a vote. Had Massachusetts voted no, the Great Compromise would have failed. Maryland delegate Luther Martin later commented, "We were on the verge of dissolution, scarce held together by the strength of a hair, though the public papers were announcing our extreme unanimity."[13]

Charles Warren notes both the significance of compromise over representation and the legitimate role played by forces demanding that their voices be heard. Warren writes,

The acceptance of the compromise by the Convention was not only a victory for the smaller states; but it was a deserved victory. Writers on the Constitution have been prone to regard the leaders of these states as a somewhat fractious minority, to pacify whom the nationalists were forced to yield their more valid principle of proportional representation. But the fact is that the small states were entirely right in believing that no such form of government as the nationalists, at that stage in the Convention, were supporting would ever be accepted by the people of the states—a government in which the national legislature was practically supreme, having power to elect the executive and the judiciary, and to negative all state laws which it deemed to infringe on its own and practically national powers. Students of the Constitution often forget now that at the time of the compromise the form of the government proposed was radically different from that which was finally adopted. The degree of the change marked the wisdom of the delegates in modifying their views after repeated discussions of the effects of their proposals upon the varying needs and conditions of the different states and the country at large.[14]

144

The Great Compromise saved the Convention, but other compromises were required to settle the controversies between the manufacturing North and the agrarian South, and between slave and free states.

Compromises temporarily satisfied manufacturing and agricultural state interests. The "commerce compromise" provided that the national government would have the power to regulate commerce, but that it could not tax exports nor could the states tax imports. The South exported agricultural products and feared that federal power to tax exports would be harmful to southern economic interests. On the other hand, those who favored a strong national union won a victory in this compromise by adding the provision prohibiting state taxation of imports from other states or from abroad. Undoubtedly such a power would have been used by many states against the products of their neighbors as well as against foreign goods. The ability of Congress to regulate commerce later became a potent weapon in the arsenal of those who favored the expansion of national power over the states.

Included in the Great Compromise was the Three-Fifths Compromise. Every five slaves would be counted as three persons in population counts used to apportion representatives in the legislature. The compromise worked to the satisfaction of northern states, which wished to see slaves discounted in order to limit southern representation and power in the legislature, but it did not go so far as to alienate southern delegations by discounting slaves completely. The framers also agreed that the slave trade could continue without interference until 1808, that fugitive slaves would be returned to their masters, and that whether or not slavery would be extended to new states would be determined by Congress—all decisions that sidestepped the explosive issue of slavery (see Discussion Box 5.2).

In appreciating the continued relevance of what happened in Philadelphia in 1787, we need to look beyond the obvious implications of the Great Compromise over representation and recognize the long-term implications of compromises that further political ends but fail to resolve important issues. The three-fifths compromise still casts a shadow over American history, and though all Americans have long since been counted as "whole" persons, the insult of the three-fifths compromise continues to be relevant to current policy debates. The census undercount, which we addressed at the beginning of this chapter, is sometimes discussed as an ominous echo of the federal government's willingness to count human beings as less than whole in order to satisfy political ends. Though the census undercount is not an intentional slight to any population, and though the undercount has little real impact on representation, the point here is to recognize the legacy of political compromises made over two hundred years ago. The disputes and compromises of the Constitutional Convention continue to electrify public debate.

ON THE WEB
mep.cla.sc.edu/rc/rc-table.html

ON THE WEB
www.constitution.org/afp/afp.htm

## *Accepting the Constitution*

Delegates to the Convention, with three exceptions, signed their names to the Constitution on Monday, September 17, 1787. Benjamin Franklin, the Convention's sage, sought the unanimity of all in support of the Constitution in an

Not everyone thought the convention compromises were good enough—or even good at all. Antifederalists opposed the Constitution, and numerous authors published criticisms of the Philadelphia Convention and its new plan for government. The antifederalist "Brutus" wrote a series of letters that appeared in the *New York Journal* during the same time that *The Federalist* papers were being published in New York. "Brutus" was probably <u>Robert Yates</u> of Albany. The letter below appeared in an issue dated November 15, 1787. What arguments does Brutus make against the Three-Fifths Compromise? What does he suggest, in the closing paragraph, are the two practical results of such a compromise?

The words are "representatives and direct taxes, shall be apportioned among the several states, which may be included in this union, according to their respective numbers, which shall be determined by adding to the whole number of free persons, including those bound to service for a term of years, and excluding Indians not taxed, three fifths of all other persons."—What a strange and unnecessary accumulation of words are here used to conceal from the public eye, what might have been expressed in the following concise manner[:] Representatives are to be proportioned among the states respectively, according to the number of freemen and slaves inhabiting them, counting five slaves for three free men.

"In a free state," says the celebrated Montesquieu, "every man, who is supposed to be a free agent, ought to be concerned in his own government, therefore the legislature should reside in the whole body of the people, or their representatives." But it has never been alledged that those who are not free agents, can, upon any rational principle, have any thing to do in govern-ment, either by themselves or others. If they have no share in government, why is the number of members in the assembly, to be increased on their account? Is it because in some of the states, a considerable part of the property of the inhabitants consists in a number of their fellow men, who are held in bondage, in defiance of every idea of benevolence, justice, and religion, and contrary to all the principles of liberty, which have been publickly avowed in the late glorious revolution? If this be a just ground for a representation, the horses in some of the states, and the oxen in others, ought to be represented—for a great share of property in some of them, consists in these animals; and they have as much controul over their own actions, as these poor unhappy creatures, who are intended to be described in the above recited clause, by the words, "all other persons."

By this mode of apportionment, the representatives of the different parts of the union, will be extremely unequal; in some of the southern states, the slaves are nearly equal in number to the free men; and for all these slaves, they will be entitled to a proportionate share in the legislature—this will give them an unreasonable weight in the government, which can derive no additional strength, protection, nor defence from the slaves, but the contrary. Why then should they be represented? What adds to the evil is, that these states are to be permitted to continue the inhuman traffic of importing slaves, until the year 1808—and for every cargo of these unhappy people, which unfeeling, unprincipled, barbarous, and avaricious wretches, may tear from their country, friends, and tender connections, and bring into those states, they are to be rewarded by having an increase of members in the general assembly.*

*Letter from "Brutus," *New York Journal*, November 15, 1787. Reprinted in Michael Kammen, ed., *The Origins of the American Constitution: A Documentary History* (New York: Penguin, 1986), 320–321 [second paragraph break added].

opening address that he had written but that was read by James Wilson. The statement reflects the willingness of the Convention delegates to accept less-than-perfect compromises to fulfill the demand of a new and effective government.

I confess that there are several parts of this Constitution which I do not at present approve, but I am not sure I shall never approve them. For having lived long, I have experienced many instances of being obliged by better information, or fuller consideration, to change opinions even on important subjects, which I once thought right but found to be otherwise. It is, therefore,

# DISCUSSION BOX 5.3
### DISNEY'S AMERICA? CORPORATIONS, THE MEDIA, AND OUR COMMON HISTORY

Some years ago, communities in Virginia worked to stop the Walt Disney Company from building a history theme park near a famous Civil War battlefield. Historians worried that Disney would be unwilling or unable to address the darker side of American history, and would choose to overlook the important struggles that mark our heritage. In the passage below, cultural historian <u>Michael Kammen</u> notes that we have entrusted many of our national symbols to major corporations. As the media and major corporations work more closely together, what are the benefits and risks to what we know of our past? Why might a major corporation want to ignore something like slavery or the three-fifths compromise? What benefit might a corporation see in addressing sensitive issues?

A pattern that began to appear in the 1970s became a major problem and issue by the later 1980s, namely, the utilization of historical commemorations as televised special events that got grossly commercialized through hefty sales of exclusive advertising rights to big corporate sponsors. Particular brands of cola, wine, sausage, hotel chains, and other products or industries bought into and "brought you" the centennial of the Statue of Liberty in 1986, and less flagrantly the bicentennial of the U.S. Constitution a year later. The United States had begun moving toward the commercial management of public memory. . . . [The] implications are quite extraordinary. As the historian Susan G. Davis has remarked, in "corporately sponsored events, live or televised, the way we experience the past and present, the very experience we have to interpret is being rebuilt for us through marketing strategies."*

*Michael Kammen, *Mystic Chords of Memory: The Transformation of Tradition in American Culture* (New York: Alfred A. Knopf, 1991), 669.

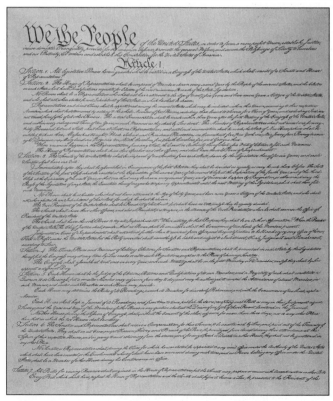

The first page of the Constitution of the United States of America.

that the older I grow, the more apt I am to doubt my own judgment, and to pay more respect to the judgment of others. . . . Thus, I consent, Sir, to this Constitution, because I expect no better, and because I am not sure, that it is not the best. . . . On the whole, Sir, I cannot help expressing a wish that every member of the Convention who may still have objections to it, would, with me, on this occasion doubt a little of his own infallibility, and to make manifest our unanimity, put his name to this instrument.[15]

Benjamin Franklin closed the signing session as he looked toward the painting of a sunrise behind the chair at the front of the chamber, which had been occupied by John Hancock as president of the Continental Congress and by George Washington in presiding over the Convention. "I have," he said, "often and often in the course of this session, and the vicissitudes of my hopes and fears as to its issue, looked at that [painting] behind the President, without being able to tell whether it was rising or setting; but now at length I have the happiness to know that it is a rising and not a setting sun."[16]

After the Constitution had been drafted and accepted by the framers, it had to be ratified by the states that would make up the new Republic. Ratification by nine states was required to put the document into operation. Conventions

---

 **DISCUSSION BOX 5.4**
*MEDIA BLACKOUTS AND DEMON BIRTHS IN THE EIGHTEENTH CENTURY*

The Constitutional Convention took place behind closed doors, to allow delegates to speak their minds—and change their minds—without being blasted in the press. Maryland delegate <u>Luther Martin</u> noted how the public received a distorted view of the Convention when he commented, "We were on the verge of dissolution, scarce held together by the strength of a hair, though the public papers were announcing our extreme unanimity."* Critics charged the Constitution's drafters and supporters with overstepping their mandate, usurping authority, and quashing dissent and discussion over the form of the new government. The ratification process further electrified opponents, including the antifederalist "Centinel." The following passage by Centinel is from the Philadelphia *Independent Gazette*, November 1787. Why is Centinel so upset? Would media blackouts of important gatherings today be a good idea? Why, or why not?

If you are in doubt about the nature and principles of the proposed government, view the conduct of its authors and patrons. That affords the best explanation, the most striking comment.

The evil genius of darkness presided at its birth, it came forth under the veil of mystery, its true features

being carefully concealed, and every deceptive art has been and is practicing to have this spurious brat received as the genuine offspring of heaven-born liberty. So fearful are its patrons that you should discern the imposition that they have hurried on its adoption with the greatest precipitation. They have endeavored also to preclude all investigation. They have endeavored to intimidate all opposition. By such means as these have they surreptitiously procured a convention in this state [Pennsylvania] favorable to their views. And here again investigation and discussion are abridged, the final question is moved before the subject has been under consideration; an appeal to the people is precluded even in the last resort, lest their eyes should be opened; the convention has denied the minority the privilege of entering the reasons of their dissent on its journals. Thus despotism is already triumphant, and the genius of liberty is on the eve of her exit, is about bidding an eternal adieu to this once happy people.†

---

*Quoted in Charles Warren, *The Making of the Constitution* (Cambridge, MA: Harvard University Press, 1947), 309.

†Letter from "Centinel," *Independent Gazette* (Philadelphia), November 1787. Reprinted in *The Essential Antifederalist*, ed. W. B. Allen and Gordon Lloyd (Lanham, MD: University Press of America, 1985), 248–249.

were called in twelve of the thirteen states in 1787 and 1788. Fierce debates over ratification took place within the states (see Discussion Box 5.4). Objections were made that the Constitution lacked a list of individual freedoms, that the executive was too powerful, and that the proposed new national government would be able to dominate state interests. Many state ratification conventions accepted the new Constitution only on condition that a Bill of Rights be added, to limit the authority of the national government to curtail the civil liberties and rights of citizens. All of the states had extensive lists of rights and

---

## DISCUSSION BOX 5.5
*FOUNDERS UNDER GLASS: COMPETING INTERPRETATIONS OF THE FRAMING*

---

While the accomplishments of the framers continue to influence the course and character of American government, the dynamics underlying their actions in Philadelphia have long been the subject of competing historical interpretation. Historians Charles A. Beard and John Roche, for example, offer very different explanations of how and why the Constitution was framed.

Beard offers an economic analysis intended to show that the framers were men of property and influence seeking to protect their own property and self-interest from the majority of Americans. Beard writes, "The makers of the federal Constitution represented the solid, conservative, commercial and financial interests of the country . . . ," and he argues that the framers "were anxious above everything else to safeguard the rights of private property against any leveling tendencies on the part of the propertyless masses."*

Roche, on the other hand, views the framers as practical politicians with nationalist leanings. He draws back from an interpretation of the framers as a collection of awesome geniuses, instead seeing them as "political men" driven to reach compromises necessary to gain agreement among themselves and the public in support of a new and stronger central government. Roche writes that the framers "were first and foremost superb democratic politicians . . . committed (perhaps willy-nilly) to working within the democratic framework, within the universe of public approval." Roche strikes directly at Beard's interpretation when he writes, "Charles Beard . . . notwithstanding, the Philadelphia Convention was not a College of Cardinals or a council of Platonic guardians working within a

manipulative, predemocratic framework; it was a nationalist reform caucus which had to operate with great delicacy and skill in a political cosmos full of enemies to achieve the one definitive goal—popular approbation."†

Much of Beard's evidence has been discredited, but the implications of his argument as well as those of Roche's interpretation are worth remembering. The framers designed the American government to control the pernicious effects of self-interest, but they institutionalized self-interest by crafting a system that depends upon self-interested competition and satisfactory compromise. While the system is admirably stable and while it disperses power among many interests remarkably well, Beard's underlying fear is still a real one, fueling complaints of government excess and special interest influence: those with power and access in the American system are in the best position to protect that power and access.

How could two historians emerge with such different interpretations of the Constitutional Convention? What might the implications be of accepting one or the other of these interpretations? Would constitutional issues today be interpreted differently if the founders were landed interests protecting their own property, as opposed to practical politicians trying to protect certain values and promote national power? For example, would these two interpretations of the founding lead you to different understandings of the motivations behind the three-fifths compromise?

*Quoted in *American Government: Readings and Cases,* ed. Peter Woll, 13th ed. (New York: Longman, 1999), 35, 36.

†Quoted in ibid., 11–12, 12.

liberties in their constitutions, and for most political leaders there was no reason the federal constitution should be different. Opponents agreed with the general concepts of individual rights and civil liberties, but feared that encoding an explicit list of them in the Constitution might enable government to trample on rights that were left off of the list. Arguments for a Bill of Rights failed during ratification, and the Constitution won ratification in nine states by 1788. Rhode Island, the only state that refused to call a ratifying convention at the time, finally ratified the Constitution in 1790—after it had been accepted by the other states.

## BALANCE IN WONDERLAND:
## THE CONSTITUTION'S COMPETITIVE DESIGN

The Constitution created a powerful national government marked by competing and balanced incentives. At the beginning of this chapter, we looked briefly at the decennial census as a constitutionally mandated function of the federal government. Census counts determine the apportionment of representatives in the House of Representatives, and so an astute observer might expect states to fatten their population numbers in order to increase the number of representatives they have. In an example of the practical common sense of the framers, though, the Constitution carefully balanced competing incentives in an effort to control the way states and federal interests approached the census. The Constitution originally tied census counts not only to apportionment of representation, but also to the apportionment of direct taxes: in other words, while a state had an incentive to increase its population to increase its representation, doing so would increase its tax burden. This was a very simple, and very clever, way of balancing incentives in order to encourage a fair and accurate count of state populations. Passage of the Sixteenth Amendment in 1913, authorizing the income tax, unbalanced the incentives surrounding the census count; since then, states and other interests have had much greater incentives to use outreach programs and statistical measures to maximize the number of census forms returned and minimize the undercount.

The balanced incentives surrounding census-taking provide a quick illustration of the Constitution's design. Countervailing incentives and interests balance and check each other at points throughout the governing mechanism. This balance, though, should not be mistaken for weakness. The framers filtered majority rule through the balancing mechanisms of the separation of power and checks and balances, but they did not prevent it. The framers wanted a balanced governmental process to promote a strong and vigorous government. Far too often, interpretation of the Constitution characterizes the separation of powers as a device to weaken the governmental process. Other descriptions describe the constitutional system as creating a "deadlock of democracy" by obstructing majority rule. Nothing could be farther from the truth. The framers did not deadlock democracy or government. The framers balanced government to make it *more,* not less, effective and powerful.

In *Federalist 47*, Madison states the premise of the separation of powers. He writes that "the accumulation of all powers, legislative, executive, and judiciary, in the same hands, whether hereditary, self-appointed, or elective, may justly be pronounced the very definition of tyranny."[17] He proceeds to acknowledge that the framers owed a debt to <u>Montesquieu</u>, whom Madison thought should be credited with authoring the doctrine of separation of powers. As an example of how separated powers disperse power and stabilize the government, the separate branches of government draw support from different constituencies and thus often work for separate interests. The president represents the nation as a whole, senators are responsible for the interests of their states, and representatives are responsible for local interests within their states; federal judges are not elected and thus have no electoral constituencies. The Constitution separates the president from Congress by selecting the president through a system of electors rather than by the legislature. In contrast, the Virginia and New Jersey Plans would have given to Congress the power of selecting the president. By separating constituencies, the framers ensured that

---

## DISCUSSION BOX 5.6
*COMPETITION AND CONFUSION? SIMPLIFY!*

"Centinel," an Antifederalist writing in Philadelphia's *Independent Journal,* argued that the complexity of the constitutional system would make it difficult for citizens to detect corruption and tyranny in the government. "Centinel" was <u>Samuel Bryan</u>. The passage below appeared in October 1787. What kind of society does Centinel favor? What characterizes the people, and what characterizes property holding? Who should be sovereign? Do you think Centinel's vision is realistic? How does Centinel's opinion recall the criticisms of interest group politics that we examined in chapter 2?

Suppose a government could be formed and supported on such principles [as are outlined in the Constitution], would it answer the great purposes of civil society? If the administrators of every government are actuated by views of private interest and ambition, how is the welfare and happiness of the community to be the result of such jarring adverse interests?

Therefore, as different orders in government will not produce the good of the whole, we must recur to other principles. I believe it will be found that the form

of government which holds those entrusted with power in the greatest responsibility to their constituents the best calculated for freemen. A republican or free government can only exist where the body of the people are virtuous and where property is pretty equally divided; in such a government the people are the sovereign and their sense or opinion is the criterion of every public measure. . . .

The highest responsibility is to be attained in a simple structure of government, for the great body of the people never steadily attend to the operations of government and for want of due information are liable to be imposed on. If you complicate the plan by various orders, the people will be perplexed and divided in their sentiments about the source of abuses or misconduct; some will impute it to the senate, others to the house of representatives, and so on, that the interposition of the people may be rendered imperfect or perhaps wholly abortive.*

*"Centinel" (Samuel Bryan), in *Independent Journal* (Philadelphia), October 1787. Reprinted in *The Essential Antifederalist*, ed. W. B. Allen and Gordon Lloyd (Lanham, MD: University Press of America, 1985), 96 [second paragraph break added].

it would be very difficult for the same powerful group of interests to control the various branches of government.

Yet neither Montesquieu nor Madison envisioned that the three branches of government should be completely separated. Rather, Madison interpreted Montesquieu as implying that the principles of a "free constitution" would be lost only in the extreme situation where "the *whole* power of one department is exercised by the same hands which possess the *whole* power of another department."[18] Thus some interconnection of responsibility, or sharing of functions, had to be expected among the branches of government. The framers believed that despotic or arbitrary government could be prevented only through a system of checks and balances between the president and Congress whereby both of these political branches would possess the ability to curtail excessive power by the other. It was feared that, without some shared functions, each branch would possess unlimited authority in its respective sphere.

### Congress and the President

There are several ways to illustrate the sharing of functions between Congress and the President (see Zip Box 5.2). First, the president's power to veto a bill is essentially a legislative function, because the president can stop a bill from becoming law. Presidential responsibility for recommending legislation and providing general information about the state of the union are other examples of the president's legislative function. Congress, for its part, can interfere at many points with the exercise of the executive function. For example, although the president has the authority to make treaties and appoint ambassadors and executive officers, the Senate must approve all treaties and appointments of public ministers and any other "inferior" officer to which the Senate has extended its advise-and-consent requirement.

The difficult situation of federal administrative agencies also illustrates the sharing of powers, as we will see in more detail in chapter 7. Because the Constitution failed to establish clear lines of authority over the bureaucracy, the bureaucracy is not clearly accountable to any one of the three regular branches of government. The president appoints many agency directors and can influence agency actions through executive orders, but the Constitution gives to Congress the power to create and structure the organization of the bureaucracy—and a jealous Congress rarely gives full supervision of these agencies to the executive. Congress, for example, retains control of agency budgets and can call for investigations into agency behavior. Furthermore, the decisions of independent agencies are subject to court review, and the judiciary can overturn agency decisions that it considers unconstitutional or beyond their legal authority. In fact, then, all three branches exercise some control over the bureaucracy.

### The Independent Judiciary

Though the judiciary stands independently and is part of the separation of powers,[19] the Supreme Court was not originally part of the checks and balances system of shared powers. The separation of powers makes the judiciary independent so that it can render impartial opinions, free from influence by political pressures. Only later development in judicial review, a concept

## Zip Box 5.2
*Shared Functions of Government*

SHARED LEGISLATIVE
FUNCTIONS
- Vetoes bills
- Suggests legislation
- Calls special sessions

SHARED EXECUTIVE
FUNCTIONS
- Declares actions of president or officials unconstitutional
- Interprets treaties
- Reviews administrative-agency cases

PRESIDENT

Administrative agencies

SHARED EXECUTIVE
FUNCTIONS
- Overrides vetoes
- Impeaches and removes officials including president
- Approves or denies appointments and treaties
- Sets up agencies and programs

SHARED JUDICIAL
FUNCTIONS
- Appoints judges
- Grants pardons for federal offenses

CONGRESS

JUDICIARY

SHARED LEGISLATIVE FUNCTIONS
- Determines constitutionality of laws
- Interprets laws and treaties

SHARED JUDICIAL FUNCTIONS
- Impeaches and removes judges
- Fixes number of justices who sit on Supreme Court
- Sets up lower courts
- Regulates types of appeals
- Approves and rejects presidential appointments

## Zip Box 5.3
*Federalism: Mmm . . . Marble Cake*

The national executive, legislative, and judicial branches are not the only governing bodies sharing powers in the American system. The national government shares powers with the states through federalism, an essential component of American government.

In chapter 4, we read that John Adams's appointment of John Marshall as Chief Justice of the Supreme Court aimed at perpetuating the Federalists' political views after their rivals' victory in the 1800 elections (BriefCase Box 4.1). Marshall rejected Jefferson's "strict constructionist" reading of the Constitution, which would have limited the federal government's powers to those clearly delegated by the Constitution. Instead, Marshall established, in *McCulloch v. Maryland* (1819), that the national government could act according to "implied powers" that reasonably followed the powers delegated to it by the Constitution. At the same time, in ruling a state tax on a federal bank unlawful because "the power to tax is the power to destroy," the Court helped establish federal supremacy over the states. Marshall's decisions, in effect, used the vagueness of the Constitution's text to expand the scope of federal authority. (For

more on the Court's role in expanding the constitutional authority of the federal government, see BriefCase Box 5.1.)

Where once federalism was portrayed as a layer cake of national, state, and local levels of government, political scientist Morton Grodzins describes contemporary relations under federalism as more of a marble cake, with governmental functions mixing and mingling among the levels.* The best examples of this are federal grants-in-aid, which are federal funds provided to state and local governments. Recipients must adhere to federal guidelines in carrying out policy, but they also enjoy flexibility under those guidelines to meet particular needs. All levels share some responsibility, although these programs have encouraged centralization of decision making authority at the national level. Such complex relations among different jurisdictional levels is the result of states' successful efforts to protect their independence during the framing of the Constitution.

*Morton Grodzins, ed., *Goals for Americans: The Report of the President's Commission on National Goals* (New York: The American Assembly, 1960), 265–282.

absent from the Constitution, expanded the role of the judiciary as a check against legislative or executive power. Yet even then, judicial review has not been an important check on Congress. The Supreme Court has ruled unconstitutional only about a hundred provisions of congressional laws since the founding. Only twice in our entire history has the Court raised political controversy because of judicial review of Congress, after the *Dred Scott* decision in 1857 and during the early New Deal in the 1930s.

### Obstacles to Majority Rule

The separation of powers helps to prevent the accumulation of political strength in an overpowering majority or faction at the national level. Because the various branches of the government are based on different constituencies and have different sources of authority, each branch has the means to resist encroachments by the other branches. This is exactly what Madison wanted, for he was wary of the potential power and divisiveness of factions. Yet the Madisonian framework goes beyond ensuring that the governing branches

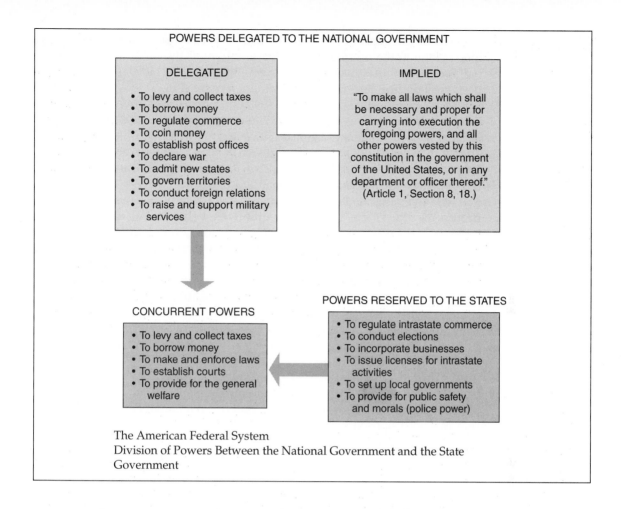

POWERS DELEGATED TO THE NATIONAL GOVERNMENT

**DELEGATED**

- To levy and collect taxes
- To borrow money
- To regulate commerce
- To coin money
- To establish post offices
- To declare war
- To admit new states
- To govern territories
- To conduct foreign relations
- To raise and support military services

**IMPLIED**

"To make all laws which shall be necessary and proper for carrying into execution the foregoing powers, and all other powers vested by this constitution in the government of the United States, or in any department or officer thereof." (Article 1, Section 8, 18.)

CONCURRENT POWERS

- To levy and collect taxes
- To borrow money
- To make and enforce laws
- To establish courts
- To provide for the general welfare

POWERS RESERVED TO THE STATES

- To regulate intrastate commerce
- To conduct elections
- To incorporate businesses
- To issue licenses for intrastate activities
- To set up local governments
- To provide for public safety and morals (police power)

The American Federal System
Division of Powers Between the National Government and the State Government

compete with each other. Madison and the framers believed that if a political party or faction, or even a popular majority, were to acquire too much power it would monopolize the government, suppress any disagreeing minorities, and replace the national interest with special interests. The framers thus built several obstacles to majority rule, whether that majority is represented by a party, a particularly large interest group, or a popular consensus.

**The Legislative Process**

First, the *bicameral nature of the legislature* itself is an important limitation to majority rule. To become law, a bill must pass both houses of Congress. Therefore, two majorities—one in each house—are needed for passage. The House of Representatives and the Senate have different constituencies, so passage is not always easy, and often the two houses are in sharp disagreement. The framers of the Constitution foresaw that the division of power in a bicameral legislature would be an important check upon Congress.

Second, the president's veto power enables him to block the legislation passed by Congress. A *presidential veto* can be overridden only by a two-thirds majority of Congress in both houses, and because most members of Congress who belong to the president's own party are reluctant to override a presidential veto, two-thirds majorities are very difficult to achieve. Once a bill has been vetoed, then, its chances of becoming law are slim.

Third, in almost all cases, after legislation has been approved by both Congress and the president, the authority to carry it out is delegated to a particular administrative agency. Agencies have acquired an extensive amount of *independent responsibility in the administration of laws*; therefore they are generally able to interpret and implement policy without referring back to Congress or the president for guidance. Because an administrative agency is for the most part able to ignore the broad constituencies of the branches that originally approved the legislation, a law might ultimately be given a shape not foreseen by its original proponents. Thus whereas majority opinion might have been expressed on the presidential or congressional level, it could be reshaped by an agency that responds to its own experts and to its own particular constituency, including special interests and congressional committees more than Congress as a whole. Agency independence and the power of narrow administrative constituencies can actually limit the effectiveness of majority rule.

Fourth, in some situations the Constitution insists on *extraordinary majorities*, or majorities well above 50 percent. A presidential veto, as we have just seen, can be overridden only by a two-thirds majority in both houses of Congress. An impeached president can be convicted in the Senate only on the approval of a two-thirds majority, a requirement that prevented the conviction of presidents Andrew Johnson and Bill Clinton. An amendment to the Constitution can be proposed by Congress only if there is a two-thirds majority in favor or upon the application of two-thirds of the state legislatures. To be ratified, amendments must have the approval of three-fourths of the state legislatures or conventions (depending upon which method of ratification is specified by Congress). Finally, treaties negotiated by the president can go into effect only with the approval of two-thirds of the Senate.

Such constitutional insistence on extraordinary majorities has occasionally defied the will of the majority in some important instances. Certainly the impeachment of President Andrew Johnson in 1868 would have resulted in his removal from office if a simple majority of the Senate had been permitted. (In this instance, the vote in the Senate was 35 to 19, only one vote short of the two-thirds majority required for conviction.) Another historical example is President Woodrow Wilson's unsuccessful attempt to win Senate approval for United States membership in the League of Nations in 1920. Acceptance of League membership required ratification of a treaty by a two-thirds majority in the Senate, and although a majority in the Senate approved of the League the vote was less than the required two-thirds majority. Extraordinary-majority provisions have also affected the amendment process: only twenty-seven amendments have been ratified since the Constitution went into effect—and only seventeen in the centuries since ratification of the Bill of Rights.

## Constitutional Factors

The Constitution also restrains the will of the majority by creating some "hands-off" areas in which even the government is not allowed to interfere.

The most notable of these are the freedoms and rights cited in *the Bill of Rights*. The Bill of Rights was not part of the original Constitution as drafted in 1787, but its addition was an implicit condition of ratification of the Constitution. Jefferson expressed the view of many state political leaders that the new national government threatened the civil liberties and rights of citizens of the states. Madison proposed the addition of a bill of rights to allay the fears of delegates to the ratifying conventions on this point.

The Bill of Rights was originally intended to limit only actions of the national government that abridged the enumerated rights and freedoms of individuals. It became the basis for a vast expansion of civil liberties and civil rights protections in the twentieth century, however, as most of its protections were gradually extended to state actions under the "due process" clause of the Fourteenth Amendment (adopted in 1868). Illustrating the anti-majoritarian potential of the Bill of Rights, the Supreme Court has made some unpopular and controversial decisions expanding civil rights and civil liberties. Decisions that banned school prayer, for example, beginning with *Engle v. Vitale* in 1962, have not been supported by a majority of people according to public opinion polls.

The Constitution contains *other specific prohibitions* on governmental exercise of power over individuals. Most of the prohibitions have to do with criminal law. For example, except in the case of rebellion or invasion, Congress is not permitted to suspend an individual's right to a writ of habeas corpus. This right directs that any official must show the reason for detaining or holding a person in custody. In addition, neither Congress nor a state government can pass a bill of attainder, that is, condemn and punish a person without a trial. The Constitution also prohibits the passage of an ex post facto law, which makes an act a crime after it has been committed. We will look more closely at civil rights and civil liberties in the next chapter.

## BREVITY IS THE SOUL OF LIT(IGATION): COMPETING INTERPRETATIONS OF THE CONSTITUTION AND POLITICS BY OTHER MEANS

The Constitution is brief, and vague, by design. It is a document of *enumeration:* it outlines more than it defines governmental structures, powers, and processes. The framers knew that the Constitution needed to be vague in order to be lasting. They hoped to preserve basic principles such as the separation of powers and checks and balances, yet they expected interpretation and formal amendment to give the document the flexibility necessary to accommodate the politics of the future.

Because the framers purposely did not define many parts of the Constitution, legal challenges have always been an effective tool for "politics by other means." By this we mean the pursuit of political ends through court action instead of through the traditional policymaking branches of the executive and legislature. As we will see throughout Part Three of this book, the Constitution's vagueness allows—even encourages—governmental forces to try to expand the scope of their powers. And because the Constitution is vague, acts of government inevitably inspire challenges based on competing interpretations of what the Constitution does, and does not, allow. Many of these challenges wind up in court, or even begin there, because the doctrine of judicial review gives courts authority to evaluate the constitutionality of government's actions. Further, the absence of political majorities and of disciplined political parties during most periods since the early days of the Republic—factors that limit the potential gains of working through the executive and legislative branches—has encouraged interests to seek their political goals through the courts.

The development of Congress's commerce power illustrates how the Constitution's vague prescriptions encourage resolution of competing political goals through the courts. The commerce power, one of the most important congressional powers enumerated in Article I of the Constitution, gives Congress the authority to regulate commerce among the states, with foreign nations, and with Indian tribes; the power to raise and support armies; and the power to tax and spend. Creating a national government capable of regulating commerce among the states was one of the major catalysts for drafting the Constitution.

As crucial as Congress's commerce power is, though, it requires interpretation to give it definition. The Constitution does not define what "commerce" is, nor does it say what the difference is between commercial and noncommercial activity. The Constitution also fails to define the boundaries separating interstate and *intra*state commerce. Moreover, the framers had no defined "intent" with regard to specific congressional commerce powers. They viewed the clause as a general grant of authority to Congress to do whatever it decided, after due deliberation, to be in the national interest. Alexander Hamilton wrote that the commerce power was open-ended. He implied that Congress, under its authority to make laws that are "necessary and proper," would interpret its own authority in this area.

Throughout American history, changing political, economic, and social circumstances have encouraged different actors in our political system to interpret the Commerce Clause in different ways, with competing views of how much authority Congress possesses in relation to state and private interests. Congress has used the commerce power to issue operating licenses that conflict with state actions, to control monopolistic businesses, to regulate workers' wages and hours, to desegregate motels and restaurants, and to ban guns near schools—actions that all inspired opposition from other interests. Taking on the task as a function of judicial review, the Supreme Court has struggled to moderate these disputes, vacillating among an array of standards and guidelines for clarifying the limits of the commerce power (see BriefCase Box 5.1). While the long-term trend of the Court's decisions have expanded the scope of the commerce power almost without limit, its halting interpretations perpetuate competition among would-be interpreters of the Constitution's meaning and encourage ever more litigation to resolve disputes.

ON THE WEB
www.findlaw.com/
casecode/

ON THE WEB
supct.law.cornell.edu:
8080/supct/

## BriefCase Box 5.1
*And Your Little Dog, Too! The Commerce Clause, Constitutional Interpretation, and the Expansion of National Power*

Interpretation of the Commerce Clause illustrates the common use of litigation as a political process, the vast authority of the Supreme Court as interpreter of vague constitutional provisions, and the important use of vague constitutional prescriptions as vehicles for the expansion of national power. Each of the major cases reviewed below involved competing interests with different interpretations of the Commerce Clause's meaning. Though the Court sometimes limits congressional powers under the Commerce Clause, the general trend of its decisions—the expansion of national power—is clear. Read through the following summary of the Court's interpretations of this clause. What do you think of the Court's decisions? Do some of the decisions appear contradictory? Why is this the case? If the Constitution had defined the commerce power more specifically, do you think there would be less litigation? Would the Supreme Court's job be any easier? Consider the wording of the Commerce Clause itself—how would you interpret it? Is there any activity that would *not* be considered interstate commerce, or that could *not* be tied to interstate commerce somehow?

| Case | Outcome |
| --- | --- |
| *Gibbons v. Ogden* (1824)<br>Faced with a dispute over rights to operate steam-powered vessels in the waters of New York State, Chief Justice John Marshall ruled that a federal permit issued under Congress's 1793 Coastal Licensing Act was valid—even though New York State had granted a monopoly to operate steamboats on New York waters to a different party. Marshall ruled that commerce is more than simply buying and selling; it also involves intercourse between and among states, and intercourse included transportation and navigation. Once an act like steamboat navigation is considered interstate commerce, Marshall ruled, the Constitution clearly gives Congress authority to regulate it. Finally, New York's law was invalid because it conflicted with a legitimate law of Congress; the Constitution clearly defines the supremacy of the Constitution and the laws made in pursuance of it. | Chief Justice Marshall offers expansive interpretation of Congress's powers under the Commerce Clause. |
| *United States v. E. C. Knight Co.* (1895)<br>The Court held that the federal Sherman Antitrust Act, designed to counter the nineteenth-century growth of corporate monopolies, could not be used against the American Sugar Refining Company, which had gained control over almost all of the nation's sugar-refining companies. The Court ruled that because the sugar-refining monopolies only *manufactured* refined sugar, they were intrastate activities and thus subject to state, not federal, control. The Court acknowledged that the sugar would ultimately find its way into interstate commerce— but until it did, its manufacture had only an indirect effect on interstate commerce and was therefore not a subject of congressional power under the Commerce Clause. | The Court imposes limits on federal power under the Commerce Clause. |

*Swift and Co. v. United States* (1905)
The Court outlined the concept of a "stream of commerce" to enable Congress to regulate acts that occur wholly within the confines of a state but that nevertheless are a part of interstate trade. Part of the passage of cattle from the field to the dinner plate took place wholly within the stockyards of midwestern states. These stockyards were controlled by three major meatpacking companies, which were in a position to fix meat prices and control the shipment of meat to consumers in other states. In *Swift*, however, the Court allowed federal regulation of interstate commerce from its point of origin to its termination, including all the steps in between—even if those steps were wholly within a particular state.

The Court upholds Congress's power to regulate aspects of interstate trade, even if they occur wholly within a state.

Under the principle laid down in *E. C. Knight*, the Court might have seen stockyard activity as an intrastate monopoly not subject to regulation by Congress.

*Hammer v. Dagenhart* (1918)
The Court held, in *Hammer v. Dagenhart*, that Congress's Keating-Owen Child Labor Act exceeded Congress's constitutional authority under the Commerce Clause by regulating child labor when that labor was involved in intrastate manufacturing.

The Court again limits Congress's authority.

*Schechter Poultry Corp. v. United States* (1935)
The Court ruled that Congress could not regulate commerce once the interstate movement of goods had ceased; at that point, the goods once again became the subjects of intrastate commerce. The case involved a local poultry-slaughtering company in Brooklyn, New York. Schechter purchased live chickens from local dealers, who brought the chickens to New York from other states. Schechter Poultry slaughtered the chickens, then sold them to restaurants and businesses in New York State. Under the National Industrial Recovery Act (NIRA), Congress sought to regulate businesses like the Schechter's with wage and hour standards, as well as health and inspection codes. When the Schechters were found in violation of these regulations, they were arrested.

The Court strikes down key parts of the New Deal, and limits Congress's power under the Commerce Clause.

FDR proposes Court-packing plan, which would enable him to appoint enough judges to ensure a pro–New Deal majority on the Court.

*National Labor Relations Board v. Jones & Laughlin Steel Co.* (1937)
The Court upheld the provisions of the National Labor Relations Act, or the Wagner Act, which sought to protect workers' right to bargain collectively for better hours and wages. The Act's primary goals were to protect the rights of employees to organize and join labor unions, and to establish a governmental regulatory system to protect those rights. When Jones & Laughlin, one of the nation's largest steel-producing companies, was ordered by the NLRB to reinstate several workers who had been dismissed because of their union activity, the company argued that because steel production was an intrastate manufacturing activity, Congress had no authority to regulate it; the company argued that the NLRA was unconstitutional. The Court upheld the NLRA and ruled against the steel producer.

FDR's Court-packing plan failed, but it made its point: the Court swings back to an expansive view of the commerce power, and upholds New Deal legislation.

*Wickard v. Filburn* (1942)
The Court ruled that even though wheat was produced and consumed completely within a state, this production and consumption had effects on interstate trade; therefore Congress had the authority under the Commerce Clause to regulate the production and sale of wheat that never moved across state borders.

In both *NLRB* and *Wickard*, the Court rules that Congress had expansive authority under the Commerce Clause. Ultimately, the Court's new direction in *NLRB* and *Wickard* has left very little activity that cannot be construed as interstate commerce, and thus very little activity that Congress cannot regulate under the Commerce Clause.

*Heart of Atlanta Motel, Inc. v. United States* (1964)
The Civil Rights Act of 1964, still the landmark civil rights legislation in American history, rests on Congress's authority to regulate interstate commerce. When the Civil Rights Act of 1964 was challenged by an Atlanta motel, which admitted discriminating on the basis of race, the Court ruled that racial discrimination affects interstate commerce and that Congress can use the Commerce Clause to regulate moral wrongs that occur in interstate commerce.

The Court accepts Congress's power to regulate social issues under the authority of the Commerce Clause.

The Court cited *Gibbons v. Ogden* in support of Congress's broad commerce powers.

*National League of Cities v. Usery* (1976)
Congress had extended the minimum wage and maximum hour provisions of the Fair Labor Standards Act to most state and municipal employees. The Court ruled that the extension violated tenets of federalism and was therefore unconstitutional.

*Garcia v. San Antonio Metropolitan Transit Authority* (1985)
The Court reversed its decision in *Usery*, and removed almost all constitutional limitations on the commerce power arising from federalism.

*United States v. Lopez* (1995)
The Court struck down portions of an anticrime law, by which Congress tried to ban guns within a thousand feet of schools, as an unconstitutional extension of the commerce power.

The Court continues to struggle with commerce clause interpretation, sometimes limiting the power and sometimes expanding it.

## Conclusion

The Constitution's system, its vagueness, and its adaptability to new circumstances perpetuate its relevance to current affairs. The separation of powers and federalism encourage competition among different interests vying to expand their own power and influence and to control encroachments by others. The vagueness of the Constitution ensures that there will be a multitude of justifications for, and challenges to, government actions. Litigation is a common and sensible political process, as different aspects of the system—Congress, state governments, small and large companies, and even groups representing different positions on the mechanics of census taking—look to the courts to resolve disputes about the Constitution's meaning. The next chapter turns to one particular area that never fails to inspire creative and fundamentally important interpretations of the Constitution: the relationship of American government to civil liberties and civil rights.

## *Overnight Assignment* ▬▬▬▬▬▬

Read the United States Constitution. Do you find it as vague as the authors of this chapter do? Or do you find it to be fairly explicit in its purpose and specific in the powers it grants, and does not grant, to parts of the federal government?

What constitutional issues are in the news lately? Check your media source for recent discussions of the Supreme Court, for example, or for other issues discussed in this chapter.

## *Long-Term Integrated Assignment* ▬▬▬▬▬▬

Consider the interest group and issues you've examined previously. Have you seen constitutional arguments or claims being made? Does the group you chose in chapter 2, or the party you looked at in chapter 3, use the Constitution to bolster its arguments? If so, what part of the Constitution do they use, and do you find their arguments convincing? Why, or why not? What passages in the Constitution might *counter* the arguments being made or the positions being taken? If the group or party is not using a constitutional argument, can you construct an argument supporting or opposing the issue, based on the terms of the Constitution?

## *Researching the Constitution?* ▬▬▬▬▬▬

### Try These Authors:

| | | |
|---|---|---|
| Merrill Jensen | Stanley N. Katz | Jack Rakove |
| Michael Kammen | Leonard W. Levy | Gordon S. Wood |

### Try These Sources:

*The Federalist Papers*

BEARD, CHARLES A. *An Economic Interpretation of the Constitution of the United States.* New York: Macmillan, 1913.

BEEMAN, RICHARD, STEPHEN BOTEIN, and EDWARD C. CARTER II, eds. *Beyond Confederation: Origins of the Constitution and American National Identity.* Chapel Hill: University of North Carolina Press, 1987.

FARRAND, MAX. *The Framing of the Constitution of the United States.* New Haven: Yale University Press, 1913.

LIPSET, SEYMOUR MARTIN. *The First New Nation: The United States in Historical & Comparative Perspective.* New York: Norton, 1979.

Morris, Richard B. *The Forging of the Union, 1781–1789.* New York: Harper & Row, 1987.

Warren, Charles. *The Making of the Constitution.* Littleton, CO: F. B. Rothman, 1993 [1928].

## Endnotes

1. Michael P. Murray, "Census Adjustment and the Distribution of Federal Spending," *Demography 29,* no. 3 (August 1992); Peter Skerry, *Counting on the Census? Race, Group Identity, and the Evasion of Politics* (Washington, DC: Brookings Institution Press, 2000).
2. John Locke, *Second Treatise on Government,* reprinted in *Locke: Two Treatises of Government,* ed. Peter Laslett (Cambridge: Cambridge University Press, 1998), 269.
3. Ibid., 271.
4. *Federalist 10,* reprinted in *The Federalist Papers,* ed. Clinton Rossiter (New York: Mentor, 1961), p. 78.
5. Ibid., 82.
6. Ibid., 83.
7. Ibid., 80.
8. *Federalist 51,* reprinted in *The Federalist Papers,* ed. Clinton Rossiter (New York: Mentor, 1961), 321–322 [paragraph break added].
9. Quoted in Max Farrand, *The Records of the Federal Convention of 1787* (New Haven: Yale University Press, 1911), 1:356.
10. Quoted in Charles Warren, *The Making of the Constitution* (Cambridge, MA: Harvard University Press, 1947), 223.
11. Quoted in ibid., 256.
12. Quoted in ibid., 257.
13. Quoted in ibid., 309.
14. Ibid., 310.
15. Quoted in ibid., 709.
16. Quoted in ibid., 717.
17. *Federalist 47,* reprinted in *The Federalist Papers,* ed. Clinton Rossiter (New York: Mentor, 1961), 301.
18. Ibid., 302–303 [italics in original].
19. As we will see in chapter 10, the judiciary is not completely independent of the other branches. Congress is empowered to decide the nature of the federal judiciary's organization, the number of courts and judges, their location, and their appellate jurisdiction, for example.

## CHAPTER 6

# Civil Liberties
# and Civil Rights

## CHAPTER OUTLINE

[T]he Government asserts that—in addition to its interest in protecting children—its "[e]qually significant" interest in fostering the growth of the Internet provides an independent basis for upholding the constitutionality of the CDA [Communications Decency Act]. The Government apparently assumes that the unregulated availability of "indecent" and "patently offensive" material on the Internet is driving countless citizens away from the medium because of the risk of exposing themselves or their children to harmful material.

We find this argument singularly unpersuasive. The dramatic expansion of this new marketplace of ideas contradicts the factual basis of this contention. The record demonstrates that the growth of the Internet has been and continues to be phenomenal. As a matter of constitutional tradition, in the absence of evidence to the contrary, we presume that governmental regulation of the content of speech is more likely to interfere with the free exchange of ideas than to encourage it. The interest in encouraging freedom of expression in a democratic society outweighs any theoretical but unproven benefit of censorship.[1]

The Communications Decency Act (CDA) of 1996 stands as the most important federal effort, to date, to attempt to regulate obscene and indecent material transmitted over the Internet. The CDA criminalized "knowing" transmission of sexually explicit materials to persons under the age of eighteen. With the language above, though, the Supreme Court ruled that the CDA cast a chilling effect on constitutionally guaranteed freedom of expression because violating the statute's vague standards could result in criminal penalties. The Supreme Court held major portions of the CDA to be unconstitutional scarcely a year after its passage, with six Justices joining John Paul Stevens's opinion. Challenges have also followed the government's follow-up effort, the Child Online Protection Act of 1998, and similar regulatory efforts at the state level. Opposition to these efforts comes from the American Civil Liberties Union and the Electronic Privacy Information Center, among other groups seeking to protect free speech rights; and from industry companies and mainstream businesses, which worry that successful efforts to regulate speech on the Internet will encourage efforts to regulate other aspects of the new medium.

Political majorities often try to suppress ideas that society considers to be beyond the pale of reason and morality, and so the application of constitutional principles and interpretation is alive and well along the information superhighway. The liberties and rights enumerated in the Bill of Rights are not necessarily absolute; perhaps Supreme Court Justice Oliver Wendell Holmes said it best when he wrote in *Schenck v. United States* (1917) that freedom of speech does not protect a person from falsely shouting "Fire!" in a crowded theater. In the case of the CDA, the Court did not strike down the law simply because it regulated speech. Rather, the Court ruled that the law was too vague and that the government had failed to show a strong enough interest in regulating free speech with this law. The competition between governmental interests and individual liberties of expression will continue as long as governments exist. As the twenty-first century begins, the Supreme Court and the political process continue to grapple with the struggle between individual liberties to express unpopular ideas and content and political majorities wishing to suppress them. The courts in our constitutional democracy have a unique role to play in protecting the cherished liberties and rights established by the Constitution, common law, and natural law.

**The Bottom Line.** The Higher Law, the common law, and the Constitution create civil liberties and civil rights that stand above the will of political majorities. The Supreme Court defines liberties and rights through constitutional interpretation, and it overrules legislation that infringes too far upon civil liberties and rights. The Court recognizes that individual liberties and rights are not always absolute: legitimate governmental needs can require restraints on individual freedoms, because civil societies and their governments have a justifiable interest in protecting themselves and the community against certain individual actions. Efforts to weigh competing rights and interests complicate the protection of civil liberties and civil rights, and lead to some inconsistent, evolving, and even startling results.

# IS THIS REALLY NECESSARY?
## THE CREATION OF THE AMERICAN BILL OF RIGHTS

### To List or Not to List?
### Competing Views on the Need for a Bill of Rights

Civil liberties and civil rights are not the same thing. *Civil liberties* are based on the idea that the government must be restrained from interfering with or encroaching upon the freedom of individuals to do certain things; First Amendment freedoms of speech, press, assembly, petition, and religion are the best examples. *Civil rights,* on the other hand, are specific interests possessed by individuals, like the right to a jury trial. Rights are based on constitutional or statutory grants, they can be claimed in court, and government must actively protect them against intrusion by government itself or by private individuals.

As they developed, American concepts of liberty became distinctly different from the common and statutory laws of England. In the English tradition, civil liberties that guarantee individuals areas of freedom from governmental interference were not parts of the common law or parliamentary law. Further, English civil rights were determined by the common law and interpreted by Parliament and the courts on a case-by-case basis. Because Parliament was supreme, it could overrule the courts and the common law at any time. So although common law due process defined certain rights, such as rights of the accused, these rights were not always protected in every case.

Building on their English heritage and striving for greater freedom through the rule of law, as historian <u>Robert Allen Rutland</u> writes,

> The Americans of 1776 were . . . drawing on a vast and rich background of legal knowledge accumulated in the mother country, but in going through their hands it was fused with newer ideas and the results of their own experiences. Somehow the events in America breathed a new spirit into men in search of personal and collective freedom. The spirit of liberty was not an overnight creation, however. It was nurtured, almost accidentally, by men on the Atlantic frontier who believed in the supremacy of the law.[2]

ON THE WEB
www.nara.gov/exhall/
charters/billrights/bill
main.html

ON THE WEB
its2.ocs.lsu.edu/
guests/poli/
public_html/bor.htm

ON THE WEB
www.findlaw.com/
casecode/
constitution

ON THE WEB
supct.law.
cornell.edu/supct/

Much of what ultimately emerged as the national Bill of Rights was designed to prevent the kinds of oppressive and arbitrary actions, many justified by common law, that King George III had used to rule the colonies. Even so, the Bill of Rights was almost an afterthought. By the time of the Constitutional Convention, most state constitutions in America either separately or in their main bodies listed all sorts of rights and liberties, including liberty of the press and, in at least one constitution, the right of revolution. Further, the politics of the period reflected state sovereignty more than national power, and the political culture of the time would not have supported the establishment of a national religion, national suppression of state militias, quartering soldiers in private homes, or writs of assistance used to search private property for contraband.

<u>Thomas Jefferson</u> argued that the absence of a national bill of rights was one of the Constitution's only great defects. <u>Alexander Hamilton</u> and many others, however, believed that attaching a bill of rights would be unnecessary and possibly even dangerous. In *Federalist 84,* for example, Hamilton mentions the Bill of Rights only to argue that it should not be attached to the Constitu-

tion: because every "Englishman" knows his rights under natural and common law, attaching a Bill of Rights to the Constitution was unnecessary. Much more importantly, many of the framers believed that a listing of rights might be interpreted as an *exhaustive* list—anything left off of the list might not be adequately protected. As James Wilson, a delegate to the Constitutional Convention, asked of the Pennsylvania ratifying convention, "[W]ho will be bold enough to undertake to enumerate all the rights of the people?—And when the attempt to enumerate them is made, it must be remembered that if the enumeration is not complete, everything not expressly mentioned will be presumed to be purposely omitted."

A final Hamiltonian worry was that enumerating rights and liberties would lead to the false assumption that the *definitions* of those rights and liberties were clear. What does "liberty" of the press mean, for example? No one

---

 ## DISCUSSION BOX 6.1
*HUMAN RIGHTS VERSUS HUMAN RITES: JEFFERSON AND SLAVERY*

Thomas Jefferson, author of the Declaration of Independence, struggled to reconcile his belief in human equality and the sanctity of liberty with the slave culture in which he lived and participated. Jefferson was not blind to the misery of slavery; in 1786, he wrote, "What a stupendous, what an incomprehensible machine is man! Who can endure toil, famine, stripes, imprisonment or death itself in vindication of his own liberty, and the next moment be deaf to all those motives whose power supported him thro' his trial, and inflict on his fellow men a bondage, one hour of which is fraught with more misery than ages of that which he rose in rebellion to oppose."*

Historian Joseph J. Ellis has called Thomas Jefferson the "American Sphinx" because his thoughts and beliefs can be so inscrutable, and it is impossible to convey the nuances and complexities of Jefferson's thoughts in a short statement. The following passage by historian Richard K. Matthews, though, conveys some of Jefferson's struggle to reconcile his ideals, his times, and the demands of practical politics. What was the basis of Jefferson's compromise on slavery? What was gained, and what was lost, in Jefferson's view? Do you accept his compromise? Consider Contemporary debates over abortion or over human rights abuses abroad: do people make similar compromises today? What is a leader's responsibility when his or her beliefs on an issue of fun-

damental civil rights conflict with prevailing public opinion?

Even while he was writing the Declaration of Independence, Jefferson was drafting model constitutions for his state of Virginia. In these models, slavery is expressly prohibited. In later models, the prohibition is maintained, with the proviso that the newly freed slaves must leave the state within one year. Refusing Jefferson's unsolicited advice, the Virginia Constitutional Convention reaffirmed the status of slavery. Once more, neither Jefferson nor his allies felt inclined to push the point. He explained his actions in this way: "The moment of doing it with success was not yet arrived, and . . . an unsuccessful effort, as too often happens, would only rivet still closer the chains of bondage, and retard the moment of delivery to this oppressed description of men." Similarly, as President of the United States, he was careful, above all, to do no harm to the cause of freedom. When asked to tacitly endorse an antislavery pamphlet entitled "A Tragical Poem on the Oppression of the Human Species," he refused, saying, "I have most carefully avoided every public act or manifestation on that subject. Should an occasion ever occur in which I can interpose with decisive effect, I shall certainly know & do my duty with promptitude & zeal. But in the meantime it would only be disarming myself of influence to be taking small means."†

*Jefferson to Jean Nicolas Démeunier, June 26, 1786, quoted in Richard K. Matthews, *The Radical Politics of Thomas Jefferson: A Revisionist View* (Lawrence: University Press of Kansas, 1986), 145 n. 44.

†Matthews, *The Radical Politics of Thomas Jefferson*, 67.

really knew, and certainly in the eighteenth century common law jurisprudence was more a legacy of suppression of the press than a liberating force. Common law defined libel and seditious libel very broadly to cast a chilling effect on even relatively innocuous criticism of government and public officials. In the private sphere, libel was easily proven against anyone who made virtually any statement that could damage the reputation of another. (See Discussion Box 6.2.)

Advocates of a bill of rights were intensely committed to their cause, though, and several state ratifying conventions considering the Constitution recommended amendments protecting civil liberties and civil rights. To attract the support of these forces for ratification, Madison promised that the new national legislature would consider adding amendments after ratification; following some delays, the first Congress proposed a short list of amendments. In the Bill of Rights, as ratified in 1791, the first eight amendments enumerate individual rights and liberties. The Ninth Amendment answers Hamilton's concern that the enumeration of some rights and liberties would imply the government's power to suppress others not listed. The Tenth Amendment reserves to the states or to the people those powers not delegated to the federal government. (See Zip Box 6.1.)

Like so many aspects of the Constitution, the Bill of Rights enumerates rather than defines its content. But unlike enumerated powers for the new governing branches, common law jurisprudence and the common law itself contained extensive precedents that provided the courts with a basis for defining parts of the Bill of Rights. As such, it is particularly the province and duty of the courts to say what the law is in the area of civil liberties and civil rights, and they have struggled to do so throughout American history.

## *NO COMPETITION AT ALL: THE SLOW DEVELOPMENT OF CIVIL LIBERTIES AND CIVIL RIGHTS AS ISSUES IN NATIONAL POLITICS*

The Bill of Rights originally limited Congress and the national government, not the state governments. In *Barron v. Baltimore* (1833), Chief Justice John Marshall held unequivocally that the Bill of Rights applied only to the national government (see BriefCase Box 6.1). Nor were rights a dominant part of the political culture through the nineteenth century. In *Democracy in America*, Alexis de Tocqueville devotes only a few sentences to private rights and the need to protect them, without specifying what they are. In *The American Commonwealth* (1888), Englishman James Bryce did not mention the Bill of Rights in any context, and his brief discussion of the judiciary and judicial review simply noted that the courts could overturn congressional laws that conflicted with constitutional principles.

Nor were First Amendment protections an important priority in the nineteenth century. National and state governments suppressed speech and press and the freedom to associate politically. Litigation failed to overturn repressive laws. The courts did not become the principal venue to resolve political

Hamilton's argument against the Bill of Rights encompassed the thoughts of many framers, who believed that an enumeration of rights was unnecessary and potentially dangerous. According to the following passage, why is any constitution an inappropriate location for a Bill of Rights? Why does the American Constitution, as originally drafted, not need a Bill of Rights? What dangers are posed by a Bill of Rights? Have these dangers come to pass? Are Hamilton's arguments relevant today, or do you find Hamilton's position unconvincing?

"WE, THE PEOPLE of the United States, to secure the blessings of liberty to ourselves and our posterity, do ORDAIN and ESTABLISH this Constitution for the United States of America." Here is a better recognition of popular rights, than volumes of those aphorisms which make the principal figure in several of our State bills of rights, and which would sound much better in a treatise of ethics than in a constitution of government.

But a minute detail of particular rights is certainly far less applicable to a Constitution like that under consideration, which is merely intended to regulate the general political interests of the nation, than to a constitution which has the regulation of every species of personal and private concerns. If, therefore, the loud clamors against the plan of the convention, on this score, are well founded, no epithets of reprobation will be too strong for the constitution of this State. But the truth is, that both of them contain all which, in relation to their objects, is reasonably to be desired.

I go further, and affirm that bills of rights, in the sense and to the extent in which they are contended for, are not only unnecessary in the proposed Constitution, but would even be dangerous. They would contain various exceptions to powers not granted; and, on this very account, would afford a colorable pretext to claim more than were granted. For why declare that things shall not be done which there is no power to do? Why, for instance, should it be said that the liberty of the press shall not be restrained, when no power is given by which restrictions may be imposed? I will not contend that such a provision would confer a regulating power; but it is evident that it would furnish, to men disposed to usurp, a plausible pretense for claiming that power. They might urge with a semblance of reason, that the Constitution ought not to be charged with the absurdity of providing against the abuse of an authority which was not given, and that the provision against restraining the liberty of the press afforded a clear implication, that a power to prescribe proper regulations concerning it was intended to be vested in the national government. This may serve as a specimen of the numerous handles which would be given to the doctrine of constructive powers, by the indulgence of an injudicious zeal for bills of rights. On the subject of the liberty of the press, as much as has been said, I cannot forbear adding a remark or two: in the first place, I observe, that there is not a syllable concerning it in the constitution of this State; in the next, I contend, that whatever has been said about it in that of any other State, amounts to nothing. What signifies a declaration, that "the liberty of the press shall be inviolably preserved"? What is the liberty of the press? Who can give it any definition which would not leave the utmost latitude for evasion? I hold it to be impracticable; and from this I infer, that its security, whatever fine declarations may be inserted in any constitution respecting it, must altogether depend on public opinion, and on the general spirit of the people and of the government. And here, after all, as is intimated upon another occasion, must we seek for the only solid basis of all our rights.

There remains but one other view of this matter to conclude the point. The truth is, after all the declamations we have heard, that the Constitution is itself, in every rational sense, and to every useful purpose, A BILL OF RIGHTS. The several bills of rights in Great Britain form its Constitution, and conversely the constitution of each State is its bill of rights. And the proposed Constitution, if adopted, will be the bill of rights of the Union. Is it one object of a bill of rights to declare and specify the political privileges of the citizens in the structure and administration of the government? This is done in the most ample and precise manner in the plan of the convention; comprehending various precautions for the public security, which are not to be found in any of the State constitutions. Is another object of a bill of rights to define certain immunities and modes of proceeding, which are relative to personal and private concerns? This we have seen has also been attended to, in a variety of cases, in the same plan. Adverting therefore to the substantial meaning of a bill of rights, it is absurd to allege that it is not to be found in the work of the convention. It may be said that it does not go far enough, though it will not be easy to make this appear; but it can with no propriety be contended that there is no such thing. It certainly must be immaterial what mode is observed as to the order of declaring the rights of the citizens, if they are to be found in any part of the instrument which establishes the government. And hence it must be apparent, that much of what has been said on this subject rests merely on verbal and nominal distinctions, entirely foreign from the substance of the thing.*

*Alexander Hamilton, *Federalist 84,* in *The Federalist Papers,* ed. Clinton Rossiter (New York: Mentor, 1961), 513–515.

### AMENDMENT I.

Congress shall make no law respecting an establishment of religion, or prohibiting the free exercise thereof; or abridging the freedom of speech, or of the press, or the right of the people peaceably to assemble, and to petition the Government for a redress of grievances.

### AMENDMENT II.

A well regulated Militia, being necessary to the security of a free State, the right of the people to keep and bear Arms, shall not be infringed.

### AMENDMENT III.

No Soldier shall, in time of peace be quartered in any house, without the consent of the Owner, nor in time of war, but in a manner to be prescribed by law.

### AMENDMENT IV.

The right of the people to be secure in their persons, houses, papers, and effects, against unreasonable searches and seizures, shall not be violated, and no Warrants shall issue, but upon probable cause, supported by Oath or affirmation, and particularly describing the place to be searched, and the persons or things to be seized.

### AMENDMENT V.

No person shall be held to answer for a capital, or otherwise infamous crime, unless on a presentment or indictment of a Grand Jury, except in cases arising in the land or naval forces, or in the Militia, when in actual service in time of War or public danger; nor shall any person be subject for the same offence to be twice put in jeopardy of life or limb, nor shall be compelled in any criminal case to be a witness against himself, nor be deprived of life, liberty, or property, without due process of law; nor shall private property be taken for public use without just compensation.

### AMENDMENT VI.

In all criminal prosecutions, the accused shall enjoy the right to a speedy and public trial, by an impartial jury of the State and district wherein the crime shall have been committed; which district shall have been previously ascertained by law, and to be informed of the nature and cause of the accusation; to be confronted with the witnesses against him; to have compulsory process for obtaining witnesses in his favor, and to have the assistance of counsel for his defence.

### AMENDMENT VII.

In Suits at common law, where the value in controversy shall exceed twenty dollars, the right of trial by jury shall be preserved, and no fact tried by a jury shall be otherwise re-examined in any Court of the United States, than according to the rules of the common law.

### AMENDMENT VIII.

Excessive bail shall not be required, nor excessive fines imposed, nor cruel and unusual punishments inflicted.

### AMENDMENT IX.

The enumeration in the Constitution of certain rights shall not be construed to deny or disparage others retained by the people.

### AMENDMENT X.

The powers not delegated to the United States by the Constitution, nor prohibited by it to the States, are reserved to the States respectively, or to the people.

disputes in the critical area of freedom of expression until World War I because politicization of the First Amendment freedoms had not yet taken place.

Moreover, until 1931 the Supreme Court exercised judicial self-restraint in virtually all of the very few cases that adjudicated civil liberties and rights claims. The Court presumed that laws passed by Congress were constitu-

## BriefCase Box 6.1
*Early Limits on the Bill of Rights:* Barron v. Baltimore *(1833)*

The plaintiff Barron sued the City of Baltimore, which is an agent of the state, for compensation under the Fifth Amendment provision "nor shall private property be taken without just compensation." Barron alleged that city action in paving a street had rendered his wharf useless by causing deposits of dirt beside the wharf, making formerly deep water too shallow for the vessels that used it. Chief Justice Marshall had to decide whether the "takings clause" of the Fifth Amendment applied to state action. He decided against Barron. In the following passage, why does Marshall refuse to apply the Constitution to the states' action? According to Marshall, is this a difficult case?

[The plaintiff] insists that this [fifth] amendment, being in favor of the liberty of the citizen, ought to be so construed as to restrain the legislative power of a state, as well as that of the United States. If this proposition be untrue, the court can take no jurisdiction of the cause.

The question thus presented is, we think, of great importance, but not of much difficulty. The Constitution was ordained and established by the people of the United States for themselves, for their own government, and not for the government of the individual States.

Each State established a constitution for itself, and in that constitution provided such limitations and restrictions on the powers of its particular government as its judgment dictated. The people of the United States framed such a government for the United States as they supposed best adapted to their situation and best calculated to promote their interests. The powers they conferred on this government were to be exercised by itself, and the limitations on power, if expressed in general terms, are naturally, and we think necessarily, applicable to the government created by the instrument. They are limitations of power granted in the instrument itself, not of distinct governments framed by different persons and for different purposes.

If these propositions be correct, the fifth amendment must be understood as restraining the power of the General Government, not as applicable to the States. In their several Constitutions, they have imposed such restrictions on their respective governments, as their own wisdom suggested, such as they deemed most proper for themselves. It is a subject on which they judge exclusively, and with which others interfere no further than they are supposed to have a common interest.*

\* *Barron v. Baltimore*, 7 Pet. 243 (1833).

tional. Not until the Carolene Products footnote in 1938 did the Supreme Court recognize an emerging judicial activism as appropriate to protect civil liberties and rights. That famous "Footnote Four" established the Court's position that different degrees of judicial deference were due to different types of laws. The footnote suggested that the courts might apply greater scrutiny in evaluating laws that restrict participation in the political process, and those that affect "discrete and insular minorities." In those cases, the presumption of a law's constitutionality might be lessened.

What we have, then, is a long history during which civil liberties and civil rights were not politicized. The Supreme Court did not finish extending most of the protections of the Bill of Rights to the states until the end of the 1960s. For much of the nineteenth and early twentieth centuries, judicial self-restraint was the order of the day in most cases that challenged government action.

## The Fourteenth Amendment

The short-lived exception to the absence of civil rights issues at the national level came in the years immediately following the Civil War, during which national politics focused briefly on political rights. The period 1868–1883 witnessed attempts to expand political rights through legislation. The Civil Rights Act of 1875, for example, was similar in many respects to the broad Civil Rights Act of 1964. It attempted to end racial discrimination by private parties in all "public accommodations," which were defined as inns, hotels, restaurants, theaters, and so on. Opponents of the law succeeded in overturning it through the courts, however. In the 1883 *Civil Rights Cases,* the Supreme Court ruled that the Fourteenth Amendment confined Congress's enforcement power to *state* action. It did not authorize Congress to regulate "public" accommodations in the private sphere.

More importantly, post–Civil War amendments to the Constitution prohibited slavery and state action that denied the political rights of former slaves. The Fourteenth Amendment, in particular, had the potential in 1868 to change the applicable scope of the first eight amendments. The Fourteenth Amendment has three central provisions that limit the states:

- No state shall abridge the *privileges or immunities* of citizens of the United States.
- No state shall deprive any person of life, liberty, or property without *due process of law.*
- No state shall deny any person within its jurisdiction the *equal protection of the laws.*

The amendment opened the door to the possible incorporation of most of the provisions of the Bill of Rights as privileges and immunities that states could not abridge. The congressional sponsors of the privileges and immunities clause saw it as doing just that, incorporating and nationalizing the Bill of Rights as privileges and immunities of national citizens that states could not deny. For the first time, depending upon how the courts interpreted the Fourteenth Amendment, some if not all of the Bill of Rights' provisions could limit state action.

### Privileges and Immunities: Victims of a First Round TKO

The Supreme Court interpreted the Fourteenth Amendment for the first time in the *Slaughterhouse Cases* (1873), which concerned the constitutionality of a Louisiana law creating a slaughterhouse monopoly and preventing competition from other companies within the state. Independent butchers in New Orleans challenged the law, arguing that it infringed upon their privileges and immunities as citizens of the United States. Supreme Court Justice Samuel F. Miller used textual and original-intent analysis as his method of judicial review. He concluded that the privileges and immunities clause applied only to citizens *of the United States*—not to individuals as citizens of the *states.* In other words, the responsibility for protecting individual rights against encroachment by state governments was still the responsibility of the states themselves, not of the federal government. Moreover, Miller concluded that the privileges and immunities clause did nothing to change the balance of national and state authority outlined in the Court's decision in *Barron v. Baltimore.* In effect, Miller nullified any force the clause was intended to have.

The Court's evisceration of the privileges and immunities clause from the Fourteenth Amendment left the due process and equal protection clauses as the only bases upon which to challenge state action that violated civil liberties and civil rights. Miller held that the butchers' due process rights had not been denied by the slaughterhouse monopoly; he thus left the Fourteenth Amendment's due process and equal protection clauses intact but as yet undefined. Judicial self-restraint would dominate Supreme Court reluctance to use the Fourteenth Amendment to expand the scope of the Bill of Rights well into the twentieth century, when a changing judicial philosophy and increasing pressure on the federal government would lead the Court to take a looser view of the Civil War Amendments' applicability.

## VOICES CARRY: COMPETING INTERESTS AND FIRST AMENDMENT CIVIL LIBERTIES

The Bill of Rights and the Fourteenth Amendment create three broad areas for the study of civil liberties and civil rights. The first of these areas looks at *civil liberties*, or the freedoms protected by the Bill of Rights. First Amendment freedoms of expression, for example, forbid Congress from abridging freedom of speech or freedom of the press.

In *Gitlow v. New York* (1925), the Supreme Court first applied provisions of the Bill of Rights to *state* governments—and it did so to protect First Amendment freedoms. The Court ruled, "We may and do assume that freedom of speech and of the press—which are protected by the First Amendment from abridgement by Congress—are among the fundamental personal rights and 'liberties' protected by the due process clause of the Fourteenth Amendment from impairment by the states."[3] Applying elements of the Bill of Rights as limits upon the actions of state and local governments through the Fourteenth Amendment is known as "incorporation." *Gitlow*'s incorporation of freedom of speech and of the press marked a sharp departure from the rule set down by the Court in *Barron v. Baltimore,* and following *Gitlow* the Court quickly began incorporating the remaining First Amendment liberties.

The Court recognized that the First Amendment's freedoms of expression are essential to free political discussion and hence to the democratic process. As we noted at this chapter's outset, however, these liberties are not absolute. The simple enumeration of a liberty of the press, for example, does not help define the scope of the liberty. In fact, even as it applied the First Amendment free speech protection to the states in the Gitlow case, the Court *rejected* Benjamin Gitlow's particular free speech claim. Gitlow had distributed pamphlets calling for the establishment of socialism by violent and other unlawful means. The Court ruled that "[A] state may punish utterances endangering the foundations of organized government and threatening its overthrow by unlawful means."

In addressing the competing claims of the public interest and individual freedom, the Supreme Court has relied upon a "balancing test," which weighs the needs of government against the rights of individuals to determine the proper balance between permissible government restraints and individual freedom. When the Supreme Court struck down parts of Congress's effort to regulate the transmission of indecent or obscene material to minors via the

ON THE WEB
www.aclu.org

ON THE WEB
www.epic.org

ON THE WEB
www.eff.org

ON THE WEB
www.freedomforum.
org

Internet, for example, they addressed squarely the difficult balance between government's interest in protecting the community and its citizens, and citizens' liberties under the First Amendment. In overturning the CDA, the Supreme Court did not say that there should be *no* regulation of the Internet, only that the nature of the Internet in 1997, together with the vague wording and criminal sanctions characterizing the CDA, made that particular Act

---

# DISCUSSION BOX 6.3
*A Burning Need for Free Speech? Brandeis's Impassioned Plea*

The great Supreme Justice <u>Louis D. Brandeis</u> best summed up our heritage of liberty of expression in his concurring opinion in *Whitney v. California* (1927). In the following passage, how does Brandeis defend protecting speech that could be false or have terrible consequences? What alone can justify repression? In the absence of that one condition, what is the remedy for dangerous speech? How would Brandeis's argument apply to contemporary free speech issues, such as laws that increase penalties for "hate" speech or the concept that burning the American flag is a protected form of free speech?

"[We] must bear in mind why a state is, ordinarily, denied the power to prohibit dissemination of social, economic and political doctrine which a vast majority of its citizens believes to be false and fraught with evil consequence. Those who won our independence believed that the final end of the state was to make men free to develop their faculties, and that in its government the deliberative forces should prevail over the arbitrary. They valued liberty both as an end and as a means. They believed liberty to be the secret of happiness and courage to be the secret of liberty. They believed that freedom to think as you will and to speak as you think are means indispensable to the discovery and spread of political truth; that without free speech and assembly discussion would be futile; that with them, discussion affords ordinarily adequate protection against the dissemination of noxious doctrine; that the greatest menace to freedom is an inert people; that public discussion is a political duty; and that this should be a fundamental principle of the American government. They recognized the risks to which all human institutions are subject. But they knew that order cannot be secured merely through fear of punishment for its infraction; that it is hazardous to discourage thought, hope and imagination; that fear breeds repression; that repression breeds hate; that hate menaces stable government; that the path of safety lies in the opportunity to discuss freely supposed grievances and

proposed remedies; and that the fitting remedy for evil counsels is good ones. Believing in the power of reason as applied through public discussion, they eschewed silence coerced by law—the argument of force in its worst form. Recognizing the occasional tyrannies of governing majorities, they amended the Constitution so that free speech and assembly should be guaranteed.

Fear of serious injury cannot alone justify suppression of free speech and assembly. Men feared witches and burnt women. It is the function of speech to free men from the bondage of irrational fears. To justify suppression of free speech there must be reasonable ground to fear that serious evil will result if free speech is practiced. There must be reasonable ground to believe that the danger apprehended is imminent. There must be reasonable ground to believe that the evil to be prevented is a serious one.

Every denunciation of existing law tends in some measure to increase the probability that there will be violation of it . . .

Those who won our independence by revolution were not cowards. They did not fear political change. They did not exalt order at the cost of liberty. To courageous, selfreliant men, with confidence in the power of free and fearless reasoning applied through the processes of popular government, no danger flowing from speech can be deemed clear and present, unless the incidence of the evil apprehended is so imminent that it may befall before there is opportunity for full discussion. If there be time to expose through discussion the falsehood and fallacies, to avert the evil by the processes of education, the remedy to be applied is more speech, not enforced silence. Only an emergency can justify repression. Such must be the rule if authority is to be reconciled with freedom. Such, in my opinion, is the command of the Constitution. It is therefore always open to Americans to challenge a law abridging free speech and assembly by showing that there was no emergency justifying it.*

*Whitney v. California, 274 U.S. 357 (1927).

unconstitutional. Justice O'Connor and Chief Justice Rehnquist explicitly noted that they would have upheld portions of the CDA.

Balancing tests require some framework for weighing competing claims. One of the more interesting issues involved in the regulation of speech on the Internet is the analogy the courts use to understand and assess government action. Proponents of restrictions on Internet speech often liken the Internet to television and radio broadcasting, which are governed by a long history of precedents upholding restrictions on the transmission of indecent material. But the courts have been less receptive to efforts to regulate speech in print, and they almost never allow prior restraint, or the censorship of material before it is printed. If the Internet is viewed as a vehicle for mass free speech more akin to print than broadcast speech—which looks increasingly like the standard the courts will use—then the courts will likely require government regulation to meet much more exacting standards to justify speech restrictions.

In addition to cases involving government regulation of First Amendment liberties, balancing tests are also used when protected freedoms compete with other rights guaranteed in the Constitution. A classic example of competing liberties and rights is the question of freedom of the press versus "the right to a speedy and public trial," guaranteed in the Sixth Amendment. A free press, by publicizing information about crimes and investigations, can prejudice potential jurors and turn the media spotlight on innocent people. Further, coverage of a trial itself can disrupt the judicial system and infringe on Sixth Amendment rights: the O.J. Simpson case is an extreme example, but live coverage of the Simpson trial helped slow the proceedings to a crawl. The Supreme Court has generally tried to balance the right to attend and report on criminal trials with the interests a judge might have in closing a trial to the public; the Court usually demands that the government have a compelling interest in security or confidentiality in order to justify limiting public access to trials.[4]

The Court has yet to establish a universal standard for evaluating civil liberties conflicts, since the political context of those claims and the competing interests at stake are so varied. In effect, though, the Court has supported balancing tests with informal adherence to the "preferred position doctrine," by which the Court approaches any limitations on protected forms of expression with a healthy skepticism. Freedoms of speech, press, and religion are so vital to the maintenance of democratic institutions that they enjoy a preferred position when weighed against competing interests and competing rights.

## The "Clear and Present Danger" Test

Preferred position civil liberties often face their strongest competition during times of war. At such times foreign powers could undermine the nation's fighting capability by encouraging espionage, sabotage, or the circulation of subversive propaganda. During wartime, the people are usually primed by the government to be suspicious of the enemy, looking for enemy agents even among loyal citizens. At the same time, citizens are more likely to sacrifice their own individual freedoms when this would aid a war effort. For example, even before the United States entered World War I, there was a great deal of pressure on Congress to pass legislation curtailing certain activities by disloyal individuals. In June 1917, two months after the United States entered the war, Congress passed the Espionage Act, which made anyone liable for punishment who circulated false statements that might interfere with military success, obstruct recruiting efforts, or encourage disloyalty in the armed forces.

To some individuals this act seemed in direct conflict with the freedoms of speech and press protected by the First Amendment. Charles Schenck and his associates had circulated a pamphlet among draftees that argued that the military draft violated the Thirteenth Amendment prohibition against involuntary servitude and suggested that the draft was a despotic, monstrous wrong against humanity committed in the interests of Wall Street. The pamphlet urged new recruits to assert their rights and oppose conscription. Although this appeal was couched in rather strong language, for the most part the form of resistance suggested by the pamphlet was not violent. After Schenck was convicted in a federal district court for violating the Espionage Act, he appealed to the Supreme Court on the grounds that his First Amendment freedoms of speech and press had been unconstitutionally abridged.

In *Schenck v. United States* (1919), the Supreme Court upheld Schenck's conviction. Justice Oliver Wendell Holmes's decision enumerated for the first time the clear and present danger test, which has guided decisions in similar cases ever since. Said Holmes:

> In many places and in ordinary times the defendants in saying all that was said in the circular would have been within their constitutional rights. But the character of every act depends upon the circumstances in which it is done. . . . The question in every case is whether the words used are used in such circumstances and are of such a nature as to create a clear and present danger that they will bring about the substantive evils that Congress has a right to prevent. . . . When a nation is at war, many things that might be said in time of peace are such a hindrance to its effort that their utterance will not be endured so long as men fight, and that no court could regard them as protected by any constitutional right.[5]

Thus Schenck's First Amendment freedoms of speech and press did not extend to the distribution of a pamphlet that constituted a clear and present danger by obstructing military recruitment during wartime.

In the years since *Schenck*, the Court has repeatedly modified the clear and present danger test. Rulings have sought to distinguish speech from action, for example, allowing government to punish the advocacy of illegal action only if "such advocacy is directed to inciting or producing imminent lawless action and is likely to incite or produce such action."[6] This linkage of speech and imminent harm (requiring both intent to incite action and the *likelihood* of actual action) now protects the advocacy of lawlessness in most circumstances.

## Freedom of Religion

Freedom of religion consists of two parts: the Establishment Clause ("Congress shall make no law respecting an establishment of religion") and the Free Exercise Clause, which forbids Congress from making law to prohibit the free exercise of religion.

In addressing cases dealing with the "free exercise" clause, the Court has generally tried to balance government interests with individual rights to ensure that government action remains "neutral" with respect to the free exercise of religion. This does not mean that free exercise of religion is an absolute freedom. Government may not interfere with religious opinions and beliefs, but religious actions may be regulated in many instances. Free exercise creates no problem until it conflicts with the rights of others or with the government's interest in upholding social order. Efforts to develop a consistent test for evaluating infringements of free exercise rights have been controversial in recent years. The Supreme Court for years used a "compelling interest" test, requiring that any law substantially burdening the free exercise of religion needed to be justified by a compelling government interest. In 1990, the Court ruled that this was the wrong test.[7] At issue in the case was the use of the hallucinogen peyote by two members of the Native American Church. The two members were dismissed from their jobs for ingesting peyote during off-duty religious rituals; they were subsequently denied unemployment benefits from the State of Oregon, because state law prohibited people who had been fired for "misconduct" from receiving benefits. While the two church members argued that the state was prohibited from denying benefits to people who refuse to give up activities mandated by their religion, Oregon rested its defense on a general state law which prohibited the use of peyote regardless of religious or nonreligious context.

The Court ruled that applying the compelling interest test in the case would have made it possible for citizens to ignore otherwise acceptable, neutral laws that *inadvertently* burdened the free exercise of religion. In effect, the Court ruled that if a law is valid and neutral, it must be obeyed—even if it interferes with an individual's free exercise of religion. Since the Oregon statute served a valid purpose (regulating drug use) and was neutral (it applied to all uses of peyote), its inadvertent infringement upon the two church members' activities was allowed. Dismayed at the ruling, Congress passed the Religious Freedom Restoration Act (RFRA) in 1993, an effort to legislate a return to the compelling interest test. Subsequently, the Court ruled the RFRA an unconstitutional attempt to circumvent its earlier ruling.[8] The Court's new standard for weighing competing interests in free exercise cases has, in the eyes of many civil libertarians, made government intrusion upon the free exercise of religion much more likely.

The Establishment Clause raises even trickier issues for the Court. The United States has always been a religious nation, using the phrase "In God We Trust" on currency and in courtrooms and opening formal government activities with official prayers. On the other hand, in a nation founded in part by people escaping officially sanctioned religious intolerance, people are justifiably wary of government involvement with religion. Two different interpretations of the meaning of the Establishment Clause fuel competition in this area of the law. *Accommodationists* argue that the framers and the nation's people have always accepted interactions between government and religion, as long as those interactions do not favor some religions over others and do not establish a national religion. *Separationists*, though, favor a "wall of separation between Church and State"—a phrase which does not appear in the Constitution but which was written by Thomas Jefferson, who along with James Madison authored the Establishment Clause. (For more on the use of the framers' intent as a guidepost to the Constitution's meaning, see Discussion Box 10.4 in chapter 10.)

The Supreme Court, especially since it incorporated the Establishment Clause in 1947,[9] has struggled to find a coherent approach to balancing the interests of government and religion, the interests of different religions, and the attitudes of accomodationists and separationists. The Court often relies on what is called the *Lemon* test, outlined in *Lemon v. Kurtzman* (1971).[10] Under this test, government action does not violate the Establishment Clause if it has a secular, rather than a religious, purpose; if its effect neither promotes nor inhibits religion; and if it does not foster excessive government involvement in religion. The three-pronged *Lemon* test is inexact, however, and even when the justices agree to use it (which they do not always do), they often disagree on how the details of specific cases meet, or fail to meet, the test's requirements. Chief Justice Rehnquist and Justice Scalia, in particular, have looked for alternatives to the *Lemon* test.

In general, though, the Court has relied on the *Lemon* test and other standards to set broad guidelines along three lines of rulings involving the Establishment Clause. The *tax exempt status* of religious institutions like churches has been allowed, under the reasoning that exemptions are neutral (other institutions like hospitals and libraries are also exempt from property taxes) and that lifting the exemption and allowing government to become deeply

---

## Zip Box 6.2
*When May Government Establish a Religion? American Indians, Civil Liberties, and Civil Rights*

American Indians stand in a unique position with respect to the United States and constitutional protections. In 1968, Congress passed the Indian Civil Rights Act (ICRA), a response to concerns that individuals living on reservations and under the jurisdiction of semi-sovereign tribal governments were not afforded the protections of the Constitution. The ICRA conferred certain rights on individuals who are subject to the jurisdiction of a tribal government, and it authorized federal courts to enforce those rights. Some were pleased to have constitutional protections extended into Indian country, but others saw the Act as an encroachment on tribal government sovereignty, because Congress unilaterally limited the power of tribes to regulate their own internal affairs.

The ICRA acknowledges that the Indian context creates unique issues with regard to civil liberties and civil rights. The Act confers every fundamental civil right in the Constitution, with several important exceptions:

- The ICRA does not contain an Establishment Clause, allowing tribes with close ties between religion and government to maintain theocracies.
- The ICRA does not prevent a tribe from discriminating in voting on account of race, which protects tribal governments' ability to prevent non-Indians from voting in tribal elections.
- Tribes are not required to convene juries in civil trials, to issue grand jury indictments in criminal cases, or to appoint counsel for indigent defendants.

*Source:* See Stephen L. Pevar, *The Rights of Indians and Tribes: The Basic ACLU Guide to Indian and Tribal Rights,* 2nd ed. (Carbondale, IL: Southern Illinois University Press, 1992), 242. See also Vine Deloria, Jr. and Clifford M. Lytle, *American Indians, American Justice* (Austin: University of Texas Press, 1983), 126ff.

In June 2000, the Supreme Court reinforced its series of rulings banning prayer in public schools. The case involved student-led prayers at high school football games. Here, Merian Ward says a prayer before Santa Fe High School's season opener in September 1999.

involved in assessing church properties and activities might lead to excessive government entanglement with religion.[11] Regarding *state aid for religious schools,* the court usually prohibits aid given directly to religious schools but allows both aid given directly to children or parents and aid that is "neutral," such as bus transportation and textbooks.[12] Finally, the Court has consistently banned *prayer in public schools,* holding that denominational prayers support one religion over others and nondenominational prayers promote religion over non-religion.[13] This last line of rulings runs sharply against public opinion, and the Court's original school prayer decision in 1962 upset many communities across the country that commonly included prayer in school proceedings. In June 2000, the Court reinforced its line of rulings in school prayer by forbidding official prayers at high school football games.[14]

## WHATCHA GONNA DO WHEN THEY COME FOR YOU? COMPETING INTERESTS AND DUE PROCESS

*Due process* is the second major area of study under the heading of civil liberties and civil rights. The Bill of Rights enumerates rights of the accused in the Fourth, Fifth, Sixth, Seventh, and Eighth Amendments. These provisions are the basis for "procedural due process," which demands that government adhere to fair procedures when dealing with the accused.

Including procedural rights within the Due Process Clause of the Fourteenth Amendment has taken longer than incorporating First Amendment liberties, but since the 1940s most of the procedural protections contained in the Bill of Rights have been applied to the states. Highlights of these rights include the Fourth Amendment's protections against unreasonable searches and seizures; the Fifth Amendment's right to counsel and its protections against self-incrimination and double jeopardy; the Sixth Amendment's guarantees of a speedy and public trial; and the Eighth Amendment's protection against cruel and unusual punishments.

In addressing due process considerations, the courts have sought balances between the interests of the accused, on the one hand, and government's interest in protecting community standards and safety, on the other. These balances are not always met with universal approval. Two issues are of particular interest here. First, the Fourth Amendment protects individuals against unreasonable searches and seizures, and in most cases law enforcement officers are required to obtain search warrants from impartial judges before they can conduct searches and seize evidence. The "exclusionary rule" bars evidence seized illegally from being used in criminal trials to demonstrate an individual's guilt, and as such the rule aims to enforce the due process restrictions of the Fourth Amendment by removing the government's motivation for violating due process rights. The Warren Court applied the exclusionary rule to the states in *Mapp v. Ohio* (1961).[15] Application of this decision, however, has angered some law enforcement and citizen groups that believe the Court protected the rights of the accused to the detriment of public safety and community concerns. Recent rulings have weakened the exclusionary rule's protections by allowing technically imperfect warrants obtained by the police in "good faith" and by allowing evidence obtained illegally that would have been uncovered "inevitably."[16]

Second, the Fifth Amendment states that no person "shall be compelled in any criminal case to be a witness against himself." To enforce this due process protection, the Warren Court ruled in *Miranda v. Arizona* (1966) that persons in police custody must be informed of their rights, including the right to remain silent.[17] This decision, too, sparked opposition from certain interests, particularly law enforcement officials who argued that the ruling complicated efforts to investigate crimes, convict criminals, and protect the public. Two years later, in 1968, Congress passed a law diluting the *Miranda* decision's application, but the law lay largely dormant for decades. In a closely watched case based on an effort to apply that law, the Supreme Court in June 2000 ruled that the *Miranda* warnings are protected by the Constitution: "We conclude that Miranda announced a constitutional rule that Congress may not supercede legislatively."[18]

### Substantive Due Process

The Constitution, then, protects certain individual rights by requiring the government to follow due process procedures. In addition to procedural rights, the Constitution protects certain substantive values, or those "fundamental" rights that are "implicit in the concept of ordered liberty."[19] Identifying, defining, and protecting the substance of these values involves "substantive due process."

Substantive due process is a controversial concept, involving the Supreme Court in clarifying the nature of fundamental rights and evaluating government activity that may or may not infringe upon those rights. In the early 1900s, the Supreme Court used substantive due process to define and protect liberty in economic contexts. In *Lochner v. New York* (1905), the most infamous application of substantive due process, the Supreme Court ruled that a New York state law that sought to protect bakers' health by regulating their work hours infringed on the liberty to contract. The Court ruled that the law was an "unreasonable interference with an employer's right of contract protected in the liberty guarantee of the 14th Amendment," and that the law was unconstitutional because it was not necessary to protect bakers. The Court's conclusion seemed to dismiss the fact that the New York state legislature had held extensive hearings on the health effects of flour dust on bakers, and had made a political and expert judgment that it should pass the legislation.[20]

In effect, substantive due process allowed the Court to substitute its own views regarding the reasonableness of public policies for the decisions made by the elected branches of government. (For excerpts from the opinions in *Lochner,* see Discussion Boxes 10.3 and 10.4 in chapter 10.) Substantive due process was used throughout the early decades of the twentieth century to strike down many laws that sought to regulate business activity. By the 1930s, though, as the public demanded greater government regulation of the economy during the New Deal and the Great Depression, the Court became more deferential to government economic policies and the use of substantive due process became discredited.

Substantive due process reemerged in the 1960s, though, in the context of individual privacy. In *Griswold v. Connecticut* (1965), the Supreme Court ruled that a right to privacy exists and that it is a fundamental right.[21] Laws that infringe upon fundamental rights are subject to "strict scrutiny," which means that the law is presumed unconstitutional unless the government can demonstrate that its action is the least restrictive means of accomplishing a "compelling" governmental interest. (See Discussion Box 6.7.)

The *Griswold* ruling attracted criticism because the Constitution does not explicitly mention a right to privacy. The opinion for the Court found the right in the "penumbras," or the existing but unspecified regions, surrounding the specific rights mentioned in the First, Third, Fourth, Fifth, and Ninth Amendments. Other justices emphasized specifically the Ninth Amendment, while still others found the right to privacy in the Fourteenth Amendment's concept of liberty. Two justices found no general right to privacy in the Constitution. Regardless of the right's location, the 7-2 ruling established that the right to privacy could not be infringed without due process.

Once the Court identified the right to privacy, questions arose as to what was encompassed by the right. In *Roe v. Wade* (1973), the Court ruled that the fundamental right to privacy encompasses a woman's decision whether or not to terminate a pregnancy by abortion. Restrictions on abortion, then, would be

The Supreme Court's ruling in *Roe v. Wade* continues to energize activists on all sides of the abortion issue. These pro-choice demonstrators stood outside the Supreme Court building in Washington, D.C.

ON THE WEB
www.now.org

ON THE WEB
www.nrlc.org

ON THE WEB
www.planned
parenthood.org

ON THE WEB
www.operationsave
america.org/index.
html

ON THE WEB
www.naral.org

subject to strict scrutiny, and in *Roe* the Court overturned a Texas statute that criminalized most abortions. The Court did not uphold an absolute right to abortion, however; it ruled that "the right of personal privacy includes the abortion decision, but that right is not unqualified and must be considered against important state interests in regulation."[22]

The Court complicated matters by stating that the government's interest in regulating abortion changes as a pregnancy moves forward in time. The Court devised the "trimester" system, under which the government had virtually no interest in regulating abortion decisions during the first three months of a pregnancy. In the second trimester, government could not prohibit abortions but could regulate abortion procedures to promote the state's interest in the health of the mother. After the point of the unborn child's viability, or roughly the beginning of the third trimester, the state had a compelling interest in protecting potential life as well as the life and health of the mother, and so it could regulate or even prohibit abortions except where necessary to preserve the life or health of the mother. (See Discussion Box 6.4.)

*Roe* has not been overturned, but it has been weakened by subsequent rulings altering the standards by which courts weigh competing interests and evaluate restrictions on abortion. In *Planned Parenthood v. Casey* (1992), for example, the Court eliminated the trimester system as the basis for evaluating government's interest in regulating abortion. More importantly, the Court altered its earlier reliance on strict scrutiny in evaluating abortion regulations. Under *Casey*, restrictions on abortion are evaluated according to the "rational basis" test as long as the restrictions create no undue burden on a woman's ability to make the abortion decision. The rational basis test requires that a gov-

Competing interpretations of rights are nothing new for the Supreme Court. Advocates on both sides of the abortion issue have tried to cast the issue as one of individual rights: pro-life advocates argue that they defend the right to life of unborn children, and pro-choice advocates argue that they defend the liberty and privacy rights of women. In *Roe v. Wade,* the Court ruled that "the word 'person,' as used in the Fourteenth Amendment, does not include the unborn," and that therefore the Court did not need to resolve the question of when life begins in order to evaluate the constitutional rights of the unborn.

The following passages are from oral arguments in *Roe v. Wade.* Robert Flowers represented Henry Wade, the Dallas, Texas, district attorney; Sarah Weddington represented Norma McCorvey, an unmarried pregnant woman using the pseudonym Jane Roe. Consider issues of governmental interests, due process, and court balancing tests involved with the abortion issue: Why is the question of whether or not a fetus is a "person" protected by the Constitution so important? In the passages below, how does Flowers frame the issue? Why is Flowers opposed to locating these decisions within the authority of a legislature? What is Weddington's position, on behalf of Roe? What does Weddington mean when she says that the state has shown no interest in interfering with a woman's right to make decisions to carry or terminate a pregnancy?

*Flowers:* I think that here is exactly what we're facing in this case: Is the life of this unborn fetus paramount over the woman's right to determine whether or not she shall bear a child? This Court has been diligent in protecting the rights of the minorities, and, gentlemen, we say that this *is* a minority, a silent minority, the true silent minority. Who is speaking for these children? Where is the counsel for these unborn children, whose life is being taken? Where is the safeguard of the right to trial by jury? Are we to place this power in the hands of a mother, in a doctor? All of the constitutional rights, if this person has the person concept. What would keep a legislature, under this grounds, from deciding who else might or might not be a human being, or might not be a person?

. . .

*Weddington:* No one is more keenly aware of the gravity of the issues or the moral implications of this case. But it *is* a case that must be decided on the Constitution. We do not disagree that there is a progression of fetal development. It is the conclusion to be drawn from that upon which we disagree. We are not here to advocate abortion. We do not ask this Court to rule that abortion is good or desirable in any particular situation. We *are* here to advocate that the decision as to whether or not a particular woman will continue to carry or will terminate a pregnancy is a decision that should be made by that individual. That in fact she has a constitutional right to make that decision for herself, and that the state has shown no interest in interfering with that decision.*

*Quoted in *May It Please the Court . . . ,* ed. Peter Irons and Stephanie Guitton (New York: New Press, 1993), 353.

ernmental action be reasonably related to a legitimate governmental interest. If an abortion regulation *does* create an undue burden, only then is the strict scrutiny standard invoked. This change makes it far easier for governmental restrictions on abortion to be upheld by the courts.[23] (See Discussion Box 6.7.)

# DO THE RIGHT THING: COMPETING VIEWS AND CONTROVERSIES SURROUNDING EQUAL PROTECTION

*Equality* is the third major area of study in the field of civil liberties and civil rights. Equality demands the equal protection of the laws and is the basis of political rights like the right to vote. The government's posture in this area is not *"hands off,"* as with civil liberties, but *"hands on,"* to guarantee political rights.

The congressional drafters of the Fourteenth Amendment designed its equal protection clause to protect the political rights of newly freed slaves in the South. Equal protection was a uniquely American concept that arose out of slavery and its aftermath. The meaning of the phrase *equal protection of the laws* is, of course, subject to interpretation, and the courts have applied different equal protection standards from one era to another.

According to Justice Samuel Miller in 1873, neither the framers nor ratifiers of the Fourteenth Amendment intended for the equal protection clause to protect any group outside of the former "slave class." In the *Slaughterhouse Cases* (1873), he refused to apply the equal protection clause to economic groups such as independent butchers in New Orleans. Miller wrote that, taking the Civil War Amendments together, "no one can fail to be impressed with the one pervading purpose found in them all [which is] the freedom of the slave race." Then Miller said something remarkable:

> We do not say that no one else but the Negro can share in this protection. Both the language and spirit of these [amendments] are to have their fair and just weight in any question of construction [of their meaning]. Undoubtedly, while Negro slavery alone was in the mind of the Congress which proposed the 13th [Amendment], it forbids any other kind of slavery, now or hereafter. If Mexican peonage or the Chinese coolie labor system shall develop slavery of the Mexican or Chinese race within our territory, this Amendment may safely be trusted to make it void. And so, if other rights are assailed by the states which properly and necessarily fall within the protection of these [amendments], that protection will apply though the party interested may not be of African descent.[24]

In other words, Miller stated that the Court should not narrowly construe the meaning of the Civil War Amendments. In the future it must look to their purpose, their "pervading spirit," the "evil which they were designed to remedy, and the process of continued addition to the Constitution until that purpose was supposed to be accomplished, as far as constitutional law can accomplish it." Miller, then, interpreted the equal protection clause more flexibly than he interpreted the privileges and immunities and due process clauses of the Fourteenth Amendment.

### Separate but Equal

Despite the Fourteenth Amendment provision that no state may "deny to any person within its jurisdiction the equal protection of the laws," racial segregation has a long history. After the Reconstruction era, some states began to pass "Jim Crow" laws that required racial segregation in a host of environments including public transportation and recreational facilities, residential areas, and public schools. Although "separate," these facilities were supposed to be "equal" in order to avoid violation of the Fourteenth Amendment's equal protection clause.

The Supreme Court established the "separate but equal" doctrine in *Plessy v. Ferguson* (1896). A Louisiana statute required that "all railroad companies carrying passengers . . . in this state shall provide equal but separate accommodations for the white and colored races." The Supreme Court upheld the statute, saying that the Fourteenth Amendment could not possibly

> have been intended to abolish distinctions based upon color, or to enforce social, as distinguished from political, equality, or a commingling of the two races upon terms unsatisfactory to either. Laws permitting, and even requiring their separation in places where they are liable to be brought into contact do not necessarily imply the inferiority of either race to the other, and have been generally, if not universally, recognized as within the competence of the State legislatures in the exercise of their police power.[25]

Thus, state laws requiring the separation of the races, the Court said, were perfectly legal. In its formal opinion the Court found that the state law requiring segregation in railroad cars did not create unequal transportation facilities; therefore the state law did not violate the equal protection clause of the Fourteenth Amendment. The Court added that the Louisiana law was "reasonable" because it reflected the dominant interests and traditions of its citizens.

It is, of course, impossible to speculate on what the consequences would have been if the Supreme Court had handed down a different decision in *Plessy v. Ferguson.* Because the nation was still recovering from the Civil War, it is quite possible that state segregation might have yielded. Racial separation had not yet become firmly entrenched by a century of tradition. To say this is not to overlook the difficulties that would have existed in overcoming the prevailing social attitudes, but it cannot be said that the *Plessy* decision was the only one possible in the late nineteenth century. The very fact that there was a vigorous dissent in the *Plessy* case indicates that another result might have been possible. (See Discussion Box 6.5.)

---

 **DISCUSSION BOX 6.5**
*A COMPETING VOICE: HARLAN'S DISSENT IN* PLESSY V. FERGUSON

In upholding the validity of separate but equal facilities in 1896, the Supreme Court itself reflected the customs and traditions of the time not only in the South but in most of the nation. The prevailing mores, however, did not prevent Justice John Marshall Harlan, a Kentuckian, from writing a vigorous and impassioned dissenting opinion, passages of which follow below. To Harlan, the separate-but-equal doctrine was clearly a violation of constitutional rights. According to Harlan, how does the *Plessy* decision fit into the Court's history of decisions on race? Does Harlan leave any room for a practical or political compromise on segregation? What does Harlan suggest is the greatest catalyst for hate based on racial distinctions? How does Harlan's reaction to segregation

differ from Jefferson's reaction to slavery (Discussion Box 6.1)? Why?

In my opinion, the judgement this day rendered will, in time, prove to be quite as pernicious as the decision made by this tribunal in the *Dred Scott* case. It was adjudged in that case that the descendants of Africans who were imported into this country and sold as slaves were not included nor intended to be included under the words "citizens" in the Constitution, and could not claim any of the rights and privileges which that instrument provided for and secured to citizens of the United States. . . . The recent amendments of the Constitution, it was supposed, had eradicated these principles from our institutions. But it seems that we have yet, in some of the states, a dominant race, a superior class of citizens, which assumes to regulate the enjoyment of civil rights, common to all citizens, upon the basis of race. . . . Sixty millions of whites are in no danger from the presence here of eight millions of blacks. The destinies of the two races in this country are indissolubly linked together and the interests of both require that the common government of all shall not permit the seeds of race hate to be planted under the sanction of law. What can more certainly arouse race hate, what more certainly create and perpetuate a feeling of distrust between these races, than state enactments which in fact proceed on the ground that colored citizens are so inferior and degraded that they cannot be allowed to sit in public coaches occupied by white citizens? That, as all will admit, is the real meaning of such legislation as was enacted in Louisiana. . . .

The arbitrary separation of citizens, on the basis of race, while they are on a public highway, is a badge of servitude wholly inconsistent with the civil freedom and the equality before the law established by the Constitution. It cannot be justified upon any legal grounds.*

*Plessy v. Ferguson, 163 U.S. 537 (1896).

Following the *Plessy* decision, many states took advantage of the Court's approval of the separate-but-equal doctrine and passed new laws providing for racial segregation. The inequalities of state segregation pointed out by Justice Harlan in 1896 soon became evident to an increasing number of people. As time passed, the Court became more and more insistent that the states provide equal facilities, at least in physical properties.

### The End of "Separate but Equal"

In 1954's landmark case *Brown v. Board of Education of Topeka, Kansas*—one of the most far-reaching decisions in Supreme Court history—the Supreme Court extended to all public education the principle that separate was not equal. The decision came in the wake of earlier decisions narrowing the scope of acceptable segregated facilities, and actually involved four separate cases in which black students were seeking admission to all-white public schools in the states of Kansas, South Carolina, Virginia, and Delaware. Because the four separate cases involved a single legal question, the Court determined that they should be heard and decided together.

The significance of the *Brown* case prompted the filing of amicus curiae briefs by a number of groups interested in civil rights. The cases on behalf of the students were argued by a legal team led by Thurgood Marshall of the NAACP. The decision of the Court was unanimous in finding that the school districts in the case had separate schools for blacks that were relatively equal with regard to "buildings, curricula, qualifications and salaries of teachers, and other 'tangible' factors." But tangible factors were not enough. The Court went on to say: "We must look instead to the effect of segregation itself on public education." Education, the Court said, is the very keystone of individual success in all endeavors today. It is "a principal instrument in awakening the child to cultural values, in preparing him for later professional training and in helping him to adjust normally to this environment." Even though the tangible properties may be equal among segregated schools, this does not mean that they will have an equal impact on children. The Court concluded that "separate educational facilities are inherently unequal" and that such segregation "is a denial of the equal protection of the laws."[26]

The Court was aware that its decision would provoke strong opposition, so it refrained from dealing with implementation of the ruling until the following year. In its 1955 *"Brown II"* decision, the Court said that desegregation

ON THE WEB
www.naacp.org/default.asp

ON THE WEB
www.nul.org

ON THE WEB
www.narf.org/

ON THE WEB
www.civilrights.org

was to be achieved with "all deliberate speed," but it permitted the federal district courts, more attuned to local circumstances, to determine the proper rate for desegregation. Consequently, the progress of school integration was slow, hindered by traditional restrictions and delaying tactics that perpetuated segregation for decades. In the 1970s, the courts began to require the busing of students within large metropolitan areas in both the North and the South to achieve ratios within the schools that approximated the racial balance existing within the larger communities. The busing decisions created an immediate backlash in white communities, and eventually in black communities, against forced busing, which became a major political issue. By the end of the twentieth century, court-ordered desegregation had waned as new educational alternatives, such as school choice through charter schools in inner cities, gained acceptance. (See Discussion Box 6.6.)

---

 ## DISCUSSION BOX 6.6
### BROWN II: *ANOTHER CONTROVERSIAL COMPROMISE*

Having overturned the "separate but equal" doctrine in *Brown v. Board of Education,* the Court a year later turned to the question of implementation. In *"Brown II,"* the Court ordered that desegregation be accomplished "with all deliberate speed," and authorized federal courts at lower levels to approve or disapprove of local desegregation plans. Opponents argued that the decision condoned continued segregation; supporters defended the Court's action as a realistic understanding of the obstacles imposed by deep-seated opposition to desegregation. The Court's compromise ruling helped spark the Civil Rights movement, as outlined in the following passage from legal scholar Lawrence M. Friedman. What do you think of the Court's ruling in *Brown II?* Should the Court have mandated a faster timetable (or *any* timetable) for desegregation? Did the Court overstep its bounds when it ruled against segregated schools? To what extent should the Court be concerned with the practical circumstances of implementing its rulings?

Enforcement of *Brown* was never easy. The South resisted, dragged its heels, dug in. "Massive resistance" was the slogan in the former Confederacy. In 1962, eight years after *Brown,* not a single black child went to school with whites in Mississippi, Alabama, or South Carolina. Even colleges and universities in these states were still rigidly segregated.

Civil rights had become, quite literally, a struggle. At times blood was shed. Civil-rights workers were ha-rassed, beaten, ostracized. Martyrs died for the cause, most of them black. A church was bombed and black children died. There were sit-ins, marches, petitions, riots; nonviolent protest spread throughout the South. Meanwhile, legal struggles went on in the law courts. Both modes of battle were vital. Neither was sufficient in itself: the marchers and battlers needed lawyers, and the work of the lawyers meant nothing without action on the streets. Perhaps a third element should be added: the civil-rights struggle was carried on in the age of TV. When civil-rights workers were beaten, and when howling mobs screamed at little black children marching to school under the protection of federal marshals, the whole country watched what was going on.

More than forty years have passed by since *Brown* was decided. School desegregation is still controversial, still an issue in the country. There are still hundreds of all-black (and all-white) schools. Most now are in the North, products of the neighborhood school system, segregated housing patterns, and "white flight"—that is, the migration of the white middle class to the suburbs. . . . Yet this does not mean that *Brown* has failed. All-black schools are not segregated schools, in the older sense. They have integrated staffs, and the school boards tend to treat them fairly. Indeed, in some cities, blacks control the boards of education. Black schools face immense problems, but they are not Jim Crow schools in the same sense that they were in the South.*

*Lawrence M. Friedman, *American Law: An Introduction* (New York: Norton, 1998), 303–304.

In chapter 4, we examined extensions of the right to vote during the Civil Rights era. The Civil Rights movement worked through the courts to achieve success in the *Brown* cases and other cases, but the movement's tactics also included pressuring Congress and the White House. The following is a list of major civil rights legislation.

*1957 Civil Rights Act:* Empowered the U.S. Civil Rights Commission to investigate any situation where the denial of suffrage due to race was suspected

*1960 Civil Rights Act:* Authorized the Justice Department to send voting referees to areas with a "pattern or practice" of discrimination in voting; referees were expected to encourage the registration of black voters

*1964 Civil Rights Act:* Forbids discrimination through voting procedures; establishes national criteria for ending discrimination in public accommodations; outlaws some discriminatory employment practices, such as the classification of employees into particular jobs due to race, the exclusion of such employees from labor unions, and discrimination against minorities in apprenticeship or job-training programs; bans discrimination in programs and activities receiving federal funds, which includes most public schools

*1965 Voting Rights Act:* Barred all discriminatory "tests and devices" wherever less than 50 percent of the eligible electorate had been registered to vote in 1964; Justice Department examiners were appointed to register qualified voters in these areas; requires "preclearance" by the Justice Department before these areas can change their voting procedures

*1968 Civil Rights Act:* Discrimination in the sale or rental of housing becomes illegal for roughly 80 percent of all housing; the Department of Housing and Urban development is authorized to investigate violations

*1972 Higher Education Act, Title IX:* Bans discrimination based on gender by colleges and universities receiving federal aid

*1990 Americans with Disabilities Act:* Bans discrimination, based on physical or mental disabilities, in transportation, employment, and public accommodations

## Equal Protection and Affirmative Action

**On the Web**
aad.english.ucsb.edu

**On the Web**
www.whitehouse.gov/
WH/EOP/OP/html/aa/
aa-lett.html

"Equality" can be interpreted in a variety of ways. In general, "equality under the law" is an uncontroversial position promoting the idea that government should treat everyone in the same way, regardless of race, gender, age, and so on. "Equality of opportunity" suggests that all people should have the same chances in life, and not be shut out of certain opportunities because of characteristics like race and gender. Finally, "equality of outcomes"—the most controversial view of equality—argues that all people should enjoy the same benefits in life.

Affirmative action programs seek to remedy past discrimination, for example by ordering government institutions to take positive steps toward recruiting minority workers and hiring contracting companies owned by minorities. In existence since the 1940s, affirmative action took off in the civil rights era of the 1960s. Many programs established numerical goals, or quotas, to guide hiring and contracting activity. Affirmative action expanded to encompass many private businesses, state and local governments, and institutions receiving funding or other support from the federal government.

## BriefCase Box 6.2
*Government by the People: Ordinary Citizens and Civil Liberties*

When we examined Jefferson and slavery (see Discussion Box 6.1), we looked at how a public leader in a position of power struggled to forge compromises between his beliefs and the demands of practical politics. But leaders aren't the only ones who face difficult questions. During World War II, the United States government relocated more than 100,000 Japanese Americans from their homes within the "military area" of the West Coast, sending them to "relocation camps" out of fear that some might threaten the United States war effort. In 1944, the Supreme Court upheld such action as legitimate under the Constitution's war powers. In *Korematsu v. United States*, a 6–3 decision upholding the government's actions, Justice Hugo Black wrote:

Korematsu was not excluded from the Military Area because of hostility to him or his race. He was excluded because we are at war with the Japanese Empire, because the properly constituted military authorities feared an invasion of our West Coast and felt constrained to take proper security measures, because they decided that the military urgency of the situation demanded that all citizens of Japanese ancestry be segregated from the West Coast temporarily, and finally, because Congress, reposing its confidence in this time of war in our military leaders—as it inevitably must—determined that they should have the power to do just this. There was evidence of disloyalty on the part of some, the military authorities considered that the need for action was great, and time was short. We cannot—by availing ourselves of the calm perspective of hindsight—now say that at that time these actions were unjustified.*

Observers then and now have condemned the government's action as a harsh and unconstitutional encroachment upon individual liberty, and Japanese internment continues to symbolize the darker side of American power in times of crisis. Yet it was not some unseen, evil force that relocated and imprisoned Japanese Americans; relocation was administered by ordinary people following the directions of their elected leaders. In a biography critical of the head of the War Relocation Authority, Dillon S. Myer, historian Richard Drinnon argues that the incident is all the more worrisome because it was headed by such an ordinary man:

Gray-green eyes, steel-gray hair, frequently gray-suited, Myer was a study in dull shades. A lifelong bureaucrat, he had achieved a certain distinction in gray office

buildings by having no distinguishing characteristics. In speech as in writing, his was the gray language of official memoranda. In appearance and outlook, he was the gray "normalcy" another Ohioan, Warren G. Harding, had wanted to get back to. Normality personified, Myer was empathically not a monster and not even an interesting villain and therein lies a difficulty. . . .

With such notable exceptions as Adolf Hitler and Joseph Stalin, our age has lacked easily identifiable villains of stature commensurate with their crimes against humanity. No longer the transgressions of exceptionally cruel individuals, evil has been bureaucratized by the twentieth-century state and made the charge of relatively faceless administrators, small in character and comprehension. In the West, in the East, and in the Third World, natty figures in suits or uniforms have carried out monstrous suppressions, uprootings, and scatterings without entering the pages of history as striking despots—considered individually, their outstanding characteristic is their mediocrity. As for political leaders with recognizable faces and some stature, the problem of identification remains. Though Franklin Delano Roosevelt signed the executive order for the great internment, who thinks of the debonair Hudson River squire as the commander in chief of concentration camps? Next to FDR, Henry L. Stimson was the official most responsible for that calamity, but he has been permanently typecast as a distinguished elder statesman. Stimson's right-hand man, John J. McCloy, comes close to being the only identifiable villain on the scene, but the undersides of his role have only recently been exposed. Myer and his associates in the WRA and the BIA were more like the gray president who ordered the bombing of Hiroshima, heard the outcome, and declared elatedly: "This is the greatest thing in history."†

What are the responsibilities of ordinary citizens when asked to perform acts that they believe might be unconstitutional? What would you have done if the president told you that imprisoning Japanese Americans was essential to the nation's survival during a time of war? Consider today's debates over abortion: What if you were opposed to abortion, yet were asked by your government to help protect access to abortions? What if you favored abortion rights, but the government asked you to force the closure of an abortion clinic that had been outlawed?

*Korematsu v. United States, 323 U.S. 214 (1944).

†Richard Drinnon, *Keeper of Concentration Camps: Dillon S. Myer and American Racism* (Berkeley: University of California Press, 1987), xxvii–xxviii.

Affirmative action programs rely on a belief in equality of outcomes and have inspired growing criticism from diverse elements of American society. On its face, affirmative action based on racial classifications is discrimination pure and simple. Proponents argue that it is benign discrimination necessary to overcome the effects of past racial discrimination, and that by doing so such programs in fact benefit the entire nation. Opponents of affirmative action, though, challenge these arguments and hold that affirmative action violates the nation's commitment to equal opportunity, stigmatizes its beneficiaries, and violates the Equal Protection Clause as well as parts of the Civil Rights Act of 1964.

The courts, of course, have the responsibility to determine whether federal and state affirmative action programs are based on constitutional or unconstitutional racial classifications—and as with First Amendment civil liberties and questions surrounding due process, the standards used by the courts to evaluate competing claims are significant. The Supreme Court's interpretation is operationalized through three different levels of "scrutiny," which provide a guideline for how the courts go about interpreting laws that separate people according to explicit classifications (see Discussion Box 6.7). *Strict scrutiny* requires governments to demonstrate a compelling interest to support a racial classification in law.

The 1970s witnessed efforts to apply the equal protection clause to prohibit affirmative action programs under which educational institutions admitted members of racial minorities on a preferential treatment basis. The landmark case in this area for years was *Regents of the University of California v. Bakke* (1978), in which the medical school application of a white man was rejected by the University of California Medical School at Davis. Sixteen of one hundred openings had been set aside for minority applicants; Bakke alleged reverse discrimination when he learned that his "objective" qualifications—undergraduate grades and his scores on the Medical College Admission Test—were better than the qualifications of some of the minority candidates who were admitted.

In a politically charged environment, the Supreme Court issued a complex decision that held that the racial quota system at the Davis Campus was unconstitutional, and that Bakke should be admitted; however, the Court also ruled that an applicant's race *could* be considered as one factor among many in admissions decisions. This part of the decision recognized that "the state has a substantial interest that legitimately may be served by a properly devised admissions program involving the competitive consideration of race and ethnic origin."[27]

For years, the Supreme Court did not apply strict scrutiny to racial classifications in federal government affirmative action programs. The Court held that Congress had broad authority to enact affirmative action policies that it viewed as necessary to remedy the effects of past societal discrimination. States and localities, however, could only enact affirmative action plans to remedy proven past or present discrimination by governmental entities. In other words, states and local governments had to prove that they had discriminated or were discriminating against a specific racial class in order to enact affirmative action programs that would pass the strict scrutiny review of the

The federal courts use different levels of "scrutiny" to evaluate governmental actions and classifications in order to support the Equal Protection Clause of the Fourteenth Amendment:

**Ordinary scrutiny:** Is a governmental action or classification "reasonably" related to a "legitimate" governmental interest? Most governmental classification schemes fall under this heading, including *social and economic* classifications, as well as those based on *age, sexual orientation,* and *physical or mental handicaps.* Courts presume that the challenged legislation or governmental action is constitutional, and the plaintiff has the burden of showing a constitutional violation. Also called the "rational basis" test.

**Heightened scrutiny:** Is a governmental action or classification "substantially" related to an "important" government interest? Classification based on *gender* falls under heightened scrutiny. Sometimes called "intermediate scrutiny."

**Strict scrutiny:** Is a governmental action "closely" related to a "compelling" governmental interest? Classifications based on *race* or that impinge on *fundamental constitutional rights* demand strict scrutiny. In contrast to ordinary scrutiny, *strict scrutiny assumes that legislation or constitutional action is unconstitutional*—and the *government* has the burden of demonstrating the compelling interest behind its action. The courts assess the action's *purpose,* and not just its effect.

Note that there are some gray areas among these levels of scrutiny: what is the difference, for example, between a "close" relationship and a "substantial" relationship to governmental interests? What is the difference between a "compelling" governmental interest and a "substantial" one? Lawyers and other interests fight over these issues, and over whether certain actions should be judged according to strict scrutiny or by lesser standards. Gender discrimination is one of these areas, and the Supreme Court in the 1970s came close to making gender a suspect classification invoking strict scrutiny. In *Craig v. Boren* (1976), Justice William Brennan devised the intermediate scrutiny test in order to evaluate an Oklahoma law that set different standards for beer sales to young men and women.

Why do you think physical handicaps are covered by ordinary scrutiny, gender by heightened scrutiny, and race by strict scrutiny? Do you think this classification scheme is fair? Would you move some of the issues to other levels of scrutiny? Why? Keep in mind that the presumption of constitutionality differs significantly: with strict scrutiny issues, the courts assume that governmental action is unconstitutional, and the government must show why classifications based on race, for example, serve a "compelling" governmental interest. Would you want the same assumption to be made when evaluating age or gender discrimination? Why, or why not?

courts; the federal government did not have to demonstrate discrimination to support its affirmative action programs.

In *Adarand Constructors, Inc. v. Pena* (1995), the Supreme Court for the first time held Congress to the same strict scrutiny of affirmative action racial classifications that it had applied to the states. Congress now has to prove it has a compelling interest to pass the constitutional test for affirmative action. The Supreme Court now holds that vague references to societal discrimination are insufficient and not compelling enough to justify racial classifications in national as well as state affirmative action laws. The *Adarand* rule makes it virtually impossible for Congress to continue its past affirmative action policies.[28]

## Conclusion

Civil liberties and civil rights in America are a complex, changing, and competitive issue area. Courts struggle to balance the interests and rights of diverse interests and groups, and they struggle to reconcile individual liberties and rights with government's interests in restraining certain behaviors for the good of the community. The Internet is only the latest new frontier for debates about competing rights and interests, as the government continues its never-ending search for adequate balances between its governing interests and the rights of individuals.

## Overnight Assignment

Turn to your media source. Are there examples of people making claims based on their liberties or rights, either formally or simply through rhetorical appeals? Are the claims persuasive? On what rights, specifically, are the claims based? Are the rights explicitly contained in the Bill of Rights, the Fourteenth Amendment, or elsewhere? Are opposing interests also making arguments based on rights?

## Long-Term Integrated Assignment

Consider your interest group and its issues; review the group's website or other materials, and search your media source for references to the group. Have they made claims based on liberties or rights to support their positions? Are the claims persuasive, and do they rely on provisions explicitly included in the Bill of Rights? Were these issues important parts of the most recent election, or are they playing a role in an upcoming election?

## Researching Civil Liberties and Civil Rights?

### Try These Authors:

| | | |
|---|---|---|
| Stephen L. Carter | Fred W. Friendly | Thomas G. Walker |
| Lee Epstein | Leonard W. Levy | |

### Try These Sources:

CRAIG, BARBARA HINKSON and DAVID M. O'BRIEN. *Abortion and American Politics*. Chatham, NJ: Chatham House Publishers, 1993.

*Eyes on the Prize: America's Civil Rights Years* [videorecording]. Alexandria, VA: PBS Home Video, 1995.

GLAZER, NATHAN. *Affirmative Discrimination: Ethnic Inequality and Public Policy*. New York: Basic Books, 1975.

GLENDON, MARY ANN. *Rights Talk: The Impoverishment of Political Discourse*. New York: Free Press, 1991.

LEWIS, ANTHONY. *Gideon's Trumpet*. New York: Vintage Books, 1989.

REGAN, PRISCILLA M. *Legislating Privacy: Technology, Social Values, and Public Policy*. Chapel Hill: University of North Carolina Press, 1995.

TRIBE, LAURENCE H. *Abortion: The Clash of Absolutes*. New York: Norton, 1990.

1. *Reno v. ACLU,* 521 U.S. 844 (1997).
2. Robert Allen Rutland, *The Birth of the Bill of Rights, 1776–1791* (Boston: Northeastern University Press, 1983 [1955]), 12.
3. *Gitlow v. New York,* 268 U.S. 652 (1925).
4. See *Nebraska Press Association v. Stuart,* 427 U.S. 539 (1976), *Gannett Company v. De Pasquale,* 443 U.S. 368 (1979), *Richmond Newspapers v. Virginia,* 448 U.S. 555 (1980).
5. *Schenck v. United States,* 249 U.S. 47 (1919).
6. *Brandenburg v. Ohio,* 395 U.S. 444 (1969).
7. *Employment Division, Department of Human Resources of Oregon v. Smith,* 494 U.S. 872 (1990).
8. *City of Boerne v. Flores,* 117 S.Ct. 2157 (1997).
9. *Everson v. Board of Education,* 330 U.S. 1 (1947).
10. *Lemon v. Kurtzman,* 403 U.S. 602 (1971).
11. *Walz v. Tax Commission,* 397 U.S. 664 (1970).
12. *Everson v. Board of Education,* 330 U.S. 1 (1947).
13. *Engel v. Vitale,* 370 U.S. 421 (1962).
14. *Santa Fe Independent School District v. Doe,*—U.S.—(2000).
15. *Mapp v. Ohio,* 367 U.S. 643 (1961).
16. *United States v. Leon,* 468 U.S. 897 (1984); *Nix v. Williams,* 467 U.S. 431 (1984).
17. *Miranda v. Arizona,* 384 U.S. 436 (1966).
18. *Dickerson v. United States,*—U.S.—(2000).
19. *Palko v. Connecticut,* 302 U.S. 319 (1937).
20. *Lochner v. New York,* 198 U.S. 45 (1905).
21. *Griswold v. Connecticut,* 381 U.S. 479 (1965).
22. *Roe v. Wade,* 410 U.S. 113 (1973).
23. *Planned Parenthood of Southeastern Pennsylvania v. Casey,* 505 U.S. 833 (1992).
24. *Slaughterhouse Cases,* 16 Wall. 36 (1873).
25. *Plessy v. Ferguson,* 163 U.S. 537 (1896).
26. *Brown v. Board of Education of Topeka, Kansas,* 347 U.S. 483 (1954).
27. *Regents of the University of California v. Bakke,* 438 U.S. 265 (1978).
28. *Adarand Constructors, Inc. v. Pena,* 515 U.S. 200 (1995).

# PART THREE

# Institutions and Governing

# The Bureaucracy

## CHAPTER OUTLINE

Running a government might look easy. You want a social security program to protect retired workers? Decide who will be eligible and hire some people to send out checks. You want to build highways or dams? Hire engineers, map some routes, pour some concrete. You want clean air and safe cars? Set standards, and then monitor factories and automakers to make sure they comply. You want a census of the nation's population? *Count people,* and leave politics out of it.

All of these are things people want or need from government, and because they look like straightforward projects, failures or controversies are often blamed on "politics" or on government inefficiency. Take the census, for example—perhaps the best example of a government task that looks pretty simple but that, in reality, is deceptively complex. In chapter 5 we looked briefly at the controversy over how the 2000 census would be taken—whether it would be a "traditional" headcount, or whether statistical measures would be used to address the vexing issue of the undercount of minorities and certain other populations. The battle over census-taking methods frequently faces the charge that the census should be "taken out of politics"—counting people is straightforward, the argument goes, and we only get controversy when political forces try to manipulate the count for partisan advantage.

Yet the census is, in fact, an inherently political activity. As political scientist Peter Skerry writes:

> In Aristotelian terms, the census is an aspect of the statesman's role of ordering the parts that make up the polis. Those parts are not to be taken as given: they are themselves shaped by political competition and conflict. This suggests that the census is not simply about counting in the abstract, but about counting certain group characteristics whose salience is determined through politics. The census is therefore concerned with establishing the boundaries that define the parts, or groups, that constitute the political community. This is inescapably a political undertaking.[1]

The same is true of most other government activities. Determining who will be eligible for social security, for example, and how big their checks will be and when they will receive them—all involve competing interests and competing interpretations of government's role and responsibilities. The same goes for building highways and dams: What are the goals of building them, exactly where should they be built, who will do the construction, and how much will they cost? Who will define "clean air" or "safe cars," and how will standards be enforced? Certainly, coal-mining companies or big automakers might have different answers to such questions than the Sierra Club or Consumers Union.

Before we can appreciate how difficult it is for the three main branches of government to make, execute, and interpret laws and policies, we need to understand the federal bureaucracy. Much of the competition among the three governing branches centers on trying to control the actions of the bureaucracy, which is composed of hundreds of agencies that not only implement congressional laws and presidential directives but also act as major forces in shaping presidential decisions and congressional legislation. Consider a quick example: If the Congress is controlled by Republicans and the presidency by Democrats, and the two parties have conflicting plans for the nation's environmental policy, then the two branches will compete not only in the making of environmental laws but also to influence the way the Environmental Protection Agency (EPA) interprets and implements those laws. Further, because the EPA, like many public agencies, is empowered to write regulations that have the force of law, elements on Capitol Hill, at the White House, and in the offices of government lobbyists will compete for influence over all of the EPA's decisions. And because agencies have so much power, they must satisfy certain demands that often conflict with each other and impair agencies' efforts to achieve their goals.

**The Bottom Line.** Congress delegates significant authority to administrative agencies and executive departments; these organizations combine important legislative, executive, and judicial powers. The bureaucracy's extensive influence over how the government designs and administers policies and programs encourages the three main branches of government to compete with each other and with interest groups to influence the behavior of individual agencies. Agencies utilize their own competitive defenses to protect their autonomy. All of this competition has particular effects on the nature of American administrative and regulatory agencies. Finally, the actions and the efficiency of public agencies are complicated by the conflicting demands we make on their behavior.

## *GOVERNMENT IN A SERIES OF BRAVE, NEW WORLDS: THE GROWTH AND DEVELOPMENT OF THE FEDERAL BUREAUCRACY*

The size of the federal government and the scope of its activities have grown throughout the nation's history, a result of expansion, new industries and technologies, and new public philosophies surrounding the proper role of government.

Early governmental departments and agencies focused on *national survival and expansion.* The founding fathers had considerable administrative experience in colonial government and during the Revolution, and they created executive departments and fledgling bureaucracies at the federal level to address issues facing the new national government. The federal government worked to manage the nation's expansion, control relations with formidable Indian nations, and establish the basic infrastructure for tax collection, mail delivery, and the disposition of lands. In the 1790s, Congress created the Departments of State, War, and the Treasury, as well as the Post Office and the Department of the Navy. Over the years, expansion created a need for more employees in the postal service, and Indian conflicts and the Civil War spurred growth in the military.[2]

In the latter part of the nineteenth century, *demands for the regulation of new industries* like the railroads *and demands for better representation from specific economic sectors* like agriculture encouraged more growth in the federal bureaucracy. Regulation from 1887 to World War I focused on monopolies that controlled certain economic sectors, such as the railroads, and business trusts, which controlled production from raw material stages to the final stages of shipping and selling refined products. The practices of trusts and monopolies created controversy and complaint because they severely limited competition, with harmful effects for workers and consumers. In response, Congress passed the Interstate Commerce Act in 1887, prohibiting price discrimination and creating the Interstate Commerce Commission, an independent regulatory agency empowered to strike down "unreasonable" railroad rates. Other actions included passage of the Sherman Antitrust Act in 1890 and the Clayton Antitrust Act in 1914. In 1906, Congress sought to protect consumers with passage of the Pure Food and Drug Act, and in 1914 it created the Federal Trade Commission. On the whole, though, these regulatory efforts were halting and did not stand at the center of expansion in the federal government's size and scope. This expansion was more closely tied to federal departments that were created to serve particular interests, or "clients." Client politics, for example,

ON THE WEB
www.state.gov/index.
html

ON THE WEB
www.ustreas.gov

ON THE WEB
new.usps.com/
cgi-bin/uspsbv/
scripts/front.jsp

ON THE WEB
www.navy.mil

ON THE WEB
www.doi.gov/bureau-
indian-affairs.html

ON THE WEB
www.ftc.gov

ON THE WEB
www.usda.gov

ON THE WEB
www.dol.gov

led to creation of the Department of Agriculture in 1862 to represent farmers and farming interests, and the Department of Labor in 1882 to represent workers.

The New Deal of the 1930s and 1940s brought a new public philosophy to federal government activity, and with it an explosion in administrative capacities to undertake new tasks and implement new initiatives.[3] President Franklin D. Roosevelt encapsulated the new philosophy in his 1936 acceptance speech:

> Governments can err, Presidents do make mistakes, but the immortal Dante tells us that divine justice weighs the sins of the cold-blooded and the sins of the warm-hearted in different scales. Better the occasional faults of a Government that lives in a spirit of charity than the constant omission of a Government frozen in the ice of its own indifference.[4]

ON THE WEB
www.ssa.gov

ON THE WEB
www.tva.gov

ON THE WEB
www.nlrb.gov

The Depression, the New Deal, and World War II sparked an explosion of federal agencies committed to *protecting citizens' economic security and controlling and regulating aspects of the economy.* The government focused on recovering from the Depression, providing jobs and services to citizens, and promoting infant industries like the airlines. The Roosevelt Administration created new programs, such as Social Security, unemployment compensation, and food stamps; it built new agencies and initiatives, such as the Civilian Conservation Corps, the Tennessee Valley Authority, and the National Labor Relations Board; it ran work programs and encouraged the arts. The federal government extended its influence over the economy, and it sought to protect workers and their families from exploitation. Historian William E. Leuchtenberg summarizes the impact of the New Deal this way:

> For the first time for many Americans, the federal government became an institution that was directly experienced. More than state and local governments, it came to be *the* government, an agency directly concerned with their welfare. It was the source of their relief payments; it taxed them directly for old age pensions; it even gave their children hot lunches in school. As the role of the state changed from that of neutral arbiter to a "powerful promoter of society's welfare," people felt an interest in affairs in Washington they had never had before.[5]

ON THE WEB
www.ed.gov

ON THE WEB
www.hud.gov

ON THE WEB
www.dot.gov

ON THE WEB
www.doe.gov

In the 1960s and 1970s, government continued to expand its scope and its size as it addressed social issues and created new government programs. In particular, President Lyndon Johnson's Great Society (1963–1969) saw the creation of federal departments dealing with Education, Transportation, Housing and Urban Development, and Energy; the era also saw new or expanded government initiatives in public health, welfare, civil rights, and urban development. New agencies like the Environmental Protection Agency, the Occupational Safety and Health Administration, and the Consumer Products Safety Commission emerged in the 1960s and 1970s to deal with "quality of life" issues. The government's attention focused on protecting the physical and moral well-being of the nation's citizens through *"social regulation."* Social regulation targets *physical harms* like pollution, risks from nuclear power, and dangers from unsafe consumer goods. Social regulation also targets *moral harms* like discrimination in education, housing, and the workplace.

ON THE WEB
www.epa.gov

ON THE WEB
www.osha.gov

ON THE WEB
www.cpsc.gov

Federal employees perform numerous and diverse jobs across the country and throughout the world. Here, federal workers from the Federal Emergency Management Agency (FEMA) and the Federal Bureau of Investigation (FBI) comb through the rubble of the Alfred Murrah Federal Building in Oklahoma City, Oklahoma following a 1995 bombing attack.

## *Zip Box 7.1*
*Government Employees*

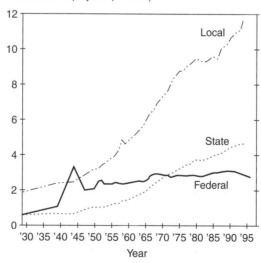

Number of employees (millions)

*Note:* No Annual Survey of Government Employment was conducted in 1996.

**Number of Government Employees: Federal, State, and Local, 1929–1997**

*Source:* Figure from *Vital Statistics on American Politics, 1999–2000,* ed. Harold W. Stanley and Harold Watkins (Washington, DC: CQ Press, 2000), 306.

All of this activity over more than two centuries has created a vast federal bureaucracy with enormous scope. New programs do not always increase the size of the federal workforce, which by some estimates held steady through the 1970s and 1980s, but evaluating such statistics is a tricky process because many federal programs pay for administrators and administration at state and local levels. Political scientist <u>Paul C. Light</u> estimates that there are roughly 12.7 million full-time equivalent jobs making up the "true" size of American government, by which he means federal employees as well as others who either work under contract to the government or whose jobs are directly related to federal grants and programs; adding 1.5 million uniformed military personnel and 850,000 postal workers brings the total to about 17 million people (see Zip Box 7.1).[6]

## ONE-STOP SHOPPING: THE CONCENTRATED POWER OF ADMINISTRATIVE AGENCIES

### Delegated Powers and Agency Activities

Bureaucracies are important to American government because they wield much of the real power in the system. The bureaucracy's strength comes from delegated powers received from Congress, and the extent of delegated power is critical to the bureaucracy's importance. In general, Congress must clearly state its intent when it delegates power, and it must establish the limits of administrative authority. In practice, though, the courts have upheld very vague declarations on these points, allowing Congress to delegate very broad and vaguely defined authority to the bureaucracy.

Congress creates most administrative bureaucracies through an enabling statute, which usually gives an agency three basic responsibilities. First, an agency is empowered to *set policy guidelines*, such as what the goals of government efforts to regulate certain activities will be and how resources will be distributed or redistributed to meet those goals. Second, agencies are empowered to *set procedural guidelines:* how rules will be made, how disputes will be examined, and so on. Third, agencies are empowered to *establish an organization and structures for being held accountable for their decisions.*

An administrative agency holds hearings, conducts studies, and works with interest groups, Congress, and the executive branch to write rules and regulations in its area of expertise. Under the most common practice of *informal rulemaking,* proposed rules have to be published, and the public has a specified amount of time to respond and make comments. In 1999 and 2000, for example, the U.S. Department of Agriculture (USDA) was deeply involved in setting rules that would regulate the production, sale, and labeling of "organic foods." The USDA's initial proposed rules generated much criticism during the public comment period, leading the department to develop a newer, revised set of guidelines. The Occupational Safety and Health Administration is currently involved in writing ergonomics rules to respond to workers' complaints about job-related repetitive stress injuries, and is working with industries as well as workers' representatives to do so. Once the rules become final, they have the same force of law as if they had been passed by Congress.

The agency then acts to execute and enforce the rules. For example, the Food and Drug Administration may inspect meat to ensure that meatpacking companies are following the FDA's safe food guidelines, or the EPA may test for the presence of chemicals in drinking water to make sure that the EPA's safety standards are being met.

## Zip Box 7.2
*There Are Agencies, and Then There Are Agencies*

Development of the federal bureaucracy has been haphazard, with different types of agencies being established to meet different needs at different points in history. Though each federal agency is unique, there are four general types of government agency:

### EXECUTIVE DEPARTMENTS

*Examples:*

- State Department
- Treasury Department
- Department of Labor
- Department of Commerce

*Characteristics:*

- Formal parts of the executive branch.
- Operate in line under the authority and direction of the president.

### INDEPENDENT AGENCIES

*Examples:*

- National Aeronautics and Space Administration (NASA)
- U.S. Postal Service
- Environmental Protection Agency (EPA)
- Central Intelligence Agency (CIA)

*Characteristics:*

- Not formally part of the executive branch.
- Some operate under considerable control by the president (CIA, EPA).
- Others are more autonomous (Postal Service).

### INDEPENDENT REGULATORY COMMISSIONS (IRCs)

*Examples:*

- Federal Communications Commission (FCC)
- Securities and Exchange Commission (SEC)
- Federal Trade Commission (FTC)
- National Labor Relations Board (NLRB)
- Nuclear Regulatory Commission (NRC)

*Characteristics:*

- Regulate important sectors of the economy.
- Formally outside of the traditional branches of government.
- IRCs have five or seven commissioners, not a single agency head.
- IRCs are bipartisan, with commissioners representing both major parties.
- Commissioners' terms are staggered, so that in a five-person commission, for example, each term is five years and the president (with Senate consent) appoints (or reappoints) one member each year.
- These characteristics are designed to insulate IRCs from the political branches. Two problems surround IRCs, however: because they ostensibly operate outside of political control, they lack accountability; and because they lack accountability, they are subject to "capture" by the industries they are supposed to regulate.

### GOVERNMENT CORPORATIONS

*Examples:*

- Amtrak
- Federal Deposit Insurance Corporation (FDIC)
- Export-Import Bank

*Characteristics:*

- Chartered by congressional statute.
- Operate like private corporations.
- President appoints the board of directors.

At this point, questions often arise as to how to apply rules and standards in specific cases. The agency holds quasi-judicial proceedings to address these questions. In most cases, the first step is *informal adjudication,* which includes most of the decisions made by civil servants every day. For example, if you were audited by the IRS, your initial meeting with an auditor would most likely be a matter of informal adjudication. You and the auditor would review your tax returns and other documents, and probably come to an agreement on whether or not you owed any money. If you disagreed with the IRS auditor, however, a more formal procedure might take place in Tax Court. Under *formal adjudication* the agency conducts a type of trial, addressing a specific case or controversy on the basis of a formal record.

In short, agencies are empowered to write policies, rules, and regulations; they are empowered to execute policies and enforce rules; and they are

## Zip Box 7.3
*Major Regulatory Agencies*

| Agency | Year Established | Agency Head Number | Agency Head Title | Number of Employees[a] |
|---|---|---|---|---|
| Consumer Product Safety Commission | 1972 | 3 | commissioner | 474 |
| Environmental Protection Agency | 1970 | 1 | administrator | 18,687 |
| Equal Employment Opportunity Commission | 1965 | 5 | commissioner | 2,564 |
| Federal Communications Commission | 1934 | 5 | commissioner | 1,968 |
| Federal Deposit Insurance Corporation | 1933 | 5 | board of directors | 7,841 |
| Federal Election Commission | 1971 | 6 | commissioner | 317 |
| Federal Energy Regulatory Commission | 1977 | 5 | commissioner | 1,310 |
| Federal Reserve System | 1913 | 7 | governor | 1,677 |
| Federal Trade Commission | 1914 | 5 | commissioner | 994 |
| Food and Drug Administration | 1906 | 1 | commissioner | 9,000[b] |
| National Labor Relations Board | 1935 | 5 | board of directors | 1,855 |
| Occupational Safety and Health Administration | 1970 | 1 | assistant secretary | 2,221 |
| Securities and Exchange Commission | 1934 | 5 | commissioner | 2,806 |

*Note:* The Interstate Commerce Commission, established in 1887, was terminated on December 30, 1995. It was succeeded by the Surface Transportation Board.

[a]As of November, 1998, except OSHA (February, 1999).

[b]Approximate number.

Table from *Vital Statistics on American Politics, 1999–2000,* ed. Harold W. Stanley and Harold Watkins (Washington, DC: CQ Press, 2000), 261.

## Hilarious Pranks To Play On The IRS

10. Tell an agent he's in charge of auditing the Gambino family.

9. Add check-off box that reads, "Do you want $3 to go to hooker fund for lonely IRS agents?"

8. Check box labeled "joint filing": enclose actual joint.

7. Open up competing country with lower taxes, drive IRS out of business.

6. Tell IRS agent you made a $50 "charitable donation" to his wife.

5. You know that squiggly line people draw through "7's"—draw them through "8's"!

4. Mail tax return in an envelope with return address "Kaczynski."

3. Call IRS—Ask, "Do you have Prince Albert's deductible mortgage interest in a can?"

2. Fake return from President Clinton made out to the "Intern Revenue Service."

1. The old poorly-grounded, high-voltage calculator trick.

Source: Reprinted by permission of CBS Worldwide, Inc.

empowered to adjudicate disputes. *In effect, then, individual agencies exercise legislative, executive, and judicial authority simultaneously.* This combination of powers and the vast authority delegated to administrative agencies worries some observers, especially as administrative agencies have grown in size and scope during the twentieth century. As we saw in chapter 5, the Constitution divides power among the three branches of government in order to create competitive incentives and provide checks and balances on the exercise of power—a theory that seems to be violated by the concentration of powers within agencies. Some observers worry that Congress has delegated too much power to the bureaucracy, abdicating its own responsibility to make difficult decisions and tough choices. We saw in chapter 1 that some critics believe that members of an unelected media wield too much power; critics make a similar charge against the bureaucracy. Agencies are not run by elected officials, and the accountability of agency decision makers is insulated from popular control.

### Wait a Minute—Why Delegate Power?

It might seem counterintuitive, in a system driven by competition for power and influence, for Congress to surrender important legislative powers and delegate them to administrative agencies. There are two good reasons for doing this, however. First, *members of Congress are often not expert* enough in certain areas to make informed policy choices. Many of the bureaucracy's functions—such as environmental regulation and food and drug safety—are complex and technical matters that require years of study and analysis to master. Congress delegates important decision-making powers to administrative agencies in the belief that experts at the agencies have the time and skills to make informed decisions.

The second reason Congress is willing to delegate important powers is a more political one. Delegating decision-making authority to an agency *shifts responsibility for making tough decisions* away from Congress. Representatives and senators often want to avoid making tough decisions on politically charged or important issues for fear of alienating key constituencies and supporters. Passing responsibility to a bureaucratic agency, and then helping constituents grapple with bureaucratic decision making, helps Congress respond to constituent demands in a cycle that subtly contributes to government expansion as well as to the reelection goals of members of Congress (see Scholar Box 7.1).

---

## *Scholar Box 7.1*
*Fiorina: Congress, Casework, and the Bureaucracy*

In a classic work published in 1989, political scientist Morris P. Fiorina outined the clever way in which Congress uses the bureaucracy to claim credit for activities undertaken on behalf of constituents. Fiorina noted that although the bureaucracy "serves as a convenient lightning rod for public frustration and a convenient whipping boy for congressmen," the relationship works for both sides—Congress gets a ready-made villain, and the bureaucracy receives ever larger budgets and ever more authority. According to the following passages, what effect does this relationship have on how Congress drafts legislation? How does the dynamic relate to the incumbency effect, which we studied in chapter 4? Does Fiorina's last sentence bring to mind Theodore Lowi's critique of interest group politics, which we examined in chapter 2?

[E]veryday decisions by a large and growing federal bureaucracy bestow significant tangible benefits and impose significant tangible costs. Congressmen can affect these decisions. Ergo, the more decisions the bureaucracy has the opportunity to make, the more opportunities there are for congressmen to build up credits [with constituents].

The nature of the Washington system is now clear. Congressmen . . . earn electoral credits by establishing various federal programs. . . . The legislation is drafted in very general terms, so some agency, existing or newly established, must translate a vague policy mandate into a functioning program, a process that necessitates the promulgation of numerous rules and regulations and, incidentally, the trampling of numerous toes. At the next stage, aggrieved and/or hopeful constituents petition their congressman to intervene in the complex (or at least obscure) decision processes of the bureaucracy. The cycle closes when the congressman lends a sympathetic ear, piously denounces the evils of bureaucracy, intervenes in the latter's decisions, and rides a grateful electorate to ever more impressive electoral showings. Congressmen take credit coming and going. They are the alpha and the omega.

. . . All of Washington prospers. More and more bureaucrats promulgate more and more regulations and dispense more and more money. Fewer and fewer congressmen suffer electoral defeat. Elements of the electorate benefit from government programs, and all of the electorate is eligible for ombudsman services. But the general, long-term welfare of the United States is no more than an incidental by-product of the system.*

*Morris P. Fiorina, *Congress: Keystone of the Washington Establishment*, 2nd ed. (New Haven: Yale University Press, 1989), 45–47.

Further, a host of rules and regulations are in place to make sure that agencies operate fairly and openly, in an attempt to control the potential for abuse that might come from delegating such broad authority to agencies headed by unelected officials. The most important of these is the 1946 Administrative Procedure Act (APA), which standardizes the ways in which agencies must conduct hearings and issue rules. The APA divorces agencies' adjudicatory proceedings from their rulemaking efforts, echoing the separation-of-powers theory. The APA also allows judicial review of many agency actions to take place in regular courts, even though the courts are supposed to show great deference to decisions made by experts at agencies as long as those decisions are supported by "substantial evidence" and are not "arbitrary and capricious." As we will see, the involvement of the courts in this way encourages agencies to create detailed records of their actions, slowing the process and resulting in relatively few, but very specific, rules.

ON THE WEB
www.law.cornell.edu/
topics/administrative.
html

ON THE WEB
www.lawfsu.edu/
library/admin/

ON THE WEB
www.nesl.edu/
research/RSGUIDES/
FEDAM.HTM

## COMPETING FOR CONTROL OF THE BUREAUCRACY: OUTSIDE PRESSURES AND AGENCY DEFENSES

Competition for influence over administration began in the late eighteenth century, as the new executive and the new Congress immediately began battling for control. To a great extent, this competition is a result of the separation of powers and the vagueness of the Constitution. Most of the framers believed, with Alexander Hamilton, that most details of administration would be carried out within the executive branch and under the supervision of the president; the Constitution's charge that the president "take Care that Laws be faithfully executed" speaks to this role. Congress acquiesced to some extent when, after extensive debate, it gave the president the important power to remove department heads. On the other hand, though, the Constitution endowed *Congress* with the power to create and structure the organization of the bureaucracy, and a Congress wary of presidential power rarely gives the executive branch full control of administrative agencies. Further, Congress can pass laws limiting or expanding the duties and authorities of administrative agencies.

For more than two hundred years, Congress and the president have competed to exercise influence over the bureaucracy. Interest groups also vie for influence, working through the White House and Congress and even directly lobbying the bureaucracy. All of these competing interests focus on three critical aspects of public agencies: the people who do the work, the amount of money available to do the work, and the ways in which that work gets done. In turn, public agencies defend themselves by trying to insulate their people, budgets, and actions from outside influence.

### Competition for Influence over the Bureaucracy

#### You Work for *Me!* Influence through People

People run agencies. Political appointees head agencies and act as the public face of government, while managers and "line workers" conduct much of an agency's day-to-day work. Competing interests vie to influence the people who work at public agencies.

Presidents rely on *the appointment process* to influence the activities of the bureaucracy. The president appoints several thousand people, and it makes a difference who gets appointed to what posts. Agency leaders come with agendas, and strong leaders can have a decided impact on the effectiveness and course of an agency's activities. Appointments also make important statements about the president's positions and his goals, and they send important messages about the seriousness with which a president is involved in a given issue area. Appointing a top confidante to a particular agency, or an individual with a high-profile agenda, indicates what the president has in mind and can build morale at an agency by sending a message to its employees that their work is considered important. On the other hand, appointing a lesser-known individual or one who does not have the president's ear can indicate that a particular agency's work will not be near the top of the president's priorities.

Congress must approve many presidential appointments, which gives Congress influence over who gets appointed. Interest groups also try to influence appointments, by lobbying for or against particular individuals. For

---

# DISCUSSION BOX 7.1
*"KICKING GLASS": WOMEN AT THE TOP OF THE BUREAUCRACY*

Developments that started decades ago, together with the Clinton Administration's aggressive efforts to appoint women to government positions, have resulted in a significant number of women holding leadership positions within the federal bureaucracy. Reporter <u>Dick Kirschten</u> reviews some of the developments in the following passage. Do you think having women in these positions makes a difference in the actions of agencies? How are Clinton's appointments to the bureaucracy related to political goals?

The highly publicized appointments of Secretary of State Madeleine Albright and Attorney General Janet Reno as the first women to hold those posts are merely the tip of the iceberg. Women also run a remarkable array of other government activities—from regulating the nation's airways to running the federal prison system—that previously were presumed to require leaders with a Y-chromosome. Even a space shuttle mission last July [1999] was commanded by a female astronaut, Air Force Col. Eileen Collins.

When White House senior staffers convene each morning for their daily strategy meetings, half the attendees are usually women. Counselor to the President, Ann

Lewis, in fact, recalls a recent planning session at which the lone male participant glanced around the room and somewhat sheepishly remarked, "Gee, I guess I represent the guys."

Secretary of Health and Human Services Donna Shalala goes a step further, boasting in an interview that "women control all of the major operating divisions" of her department. During Alice Rivlin's tenure as director of the Office of Management and Budget, Shalala said she told President Clinton "it was possible for a major policy issue to move through the government and never touch a man's hand until it got to his." . . .

Much, but by no means all, of the credit for the shattering of glass ceilings throughout the federal establishment goes to Clinton, who benefited mightily from the emerging "gender gap" that has seen women vote in disproportionate numbers for Democrats. The President has been more than happy to show his gratitude on the patronage front. Forty percent of Clinton's political appointees—including a third of his current Cabinet—are women.*

*Dick Kirschten, "Kicking Glass," online at GovExec.com (http://www.govexec.com/features/0200/0200s1.htm), retrieved February 13, 2000.

example, in 1999 Republicans pushed the White House to appoint Bradley Smith, a conservative law professor, to the Federal Election Commission. We saw in chapter 4 that Smith is not among those panicking over the current state of campaign finance (see Zip Box 4.6). Republicans were able to hold up Clinton's nomination of Richard C. Holbrooke to be chief American diplomat to the United Nations as they promoted Smith's nomination and other goals. Republican Senator Mitch McConnell noted, "The only leverage we have with the Administration is the power to confirm."[7] Finally, Congress also tries to influence people at agencies through *investigations* aimed at highlighting aspects of the bureaucracy's behavior or embarrassing and distracting agency leaders.

### I'm Not Paying for *That!* Influence through Money

Public agencies rely on funding to pay their workers and to pay for programs. Anyone who can influence the amount of money an agency receives, or the amount of money targeted for specific programs, can influence the bureaucracy. The president exercises influence over agency budgets through the *Office of Management and Budget* (OMB), which must approve proposed agency budgets before they are sent to Congress for authorization. This gives the president a significant amount of control and leverage not only over individual agencies, but also over the relative positions and priorities among those agencies within the government.

Congress *authorizes spending* for agencies, controlling and limiting what they can spend on specific programs. Such authorizations, which originate in congressional committees like the Agriculture or the Education and Labor Committee, may exist for a specified number of years, for only one year, or they may be permanent. Further, Congress must also *appropriate money* for the agencies before any money can actually be spent, meaning that Congress gets two chances to influence spending. The Appropriations Committee often acts as a budget cutter by appropriating less money than was authorized.

Getting authorizations and appropriations requires an agency's representative to appear before Congress to demonstrate why the agency and its programs deserve to be funded. The Appropriations Committee "marks up" an agency's budget request, affecting not only how much money is ultimately appropriated but also detailing the programs on which the money will be spent—which gives the Appropriations Committee considerable influence over which programs get funded and which don't. The fact that Congress has several committees involved in authorizing, appropriating, and overseeing agencies' spending means that agencies must argue their case and compete for dollars before a large number of Congress members, all of whom have their own contacts, relationships, obligations, and goals for what to do with public dollars. This gives interest groups another way of influencing the bureaucracy: by influencing members of Congress.

### Do *This!* Do *That!* Direct Influence on Agency Actions

Influencing personnel and budgets are indirect ways of controlling the bureaucracy. A much more direct way is to order an agency to take some action, or order it not to take some action. Each major branch of government has legitimate power in this area.

**ON THE WEB**
www.whitehouse.gov/
OMB/

**ON THE WEB**
www.ombwatch.org/

**ON THE WEB**
www.govexec.com

The president can influence agency actions through *executive orders and administrative changes.* President Reagan's executive orders, for example, affected the behavior of the EPA by encouraging deregulation at the federal level and by increasing the authority of states in some regulatory matters. For its part, Congress originally creates all agencies and thus is able to use an *enabling statute* to outline what an agency is supposed to do, how it is supposed to do it—and also what it is not supposed to do. Congress can also pass laws at any time giving agencies new responsibilities or withdrawing old ones.

The courts directly influence agency actions through exercise of judicial review; agencies must act consistently with congressional intent, and they must adhere to proper procedures when they take action. Courts have influence over agencies in two key ways: First, *courts can direct agency procedures,* affecting the way an agency goes about its business. A federal court, for example, mandated testing standards for automobile crash test dummies; the decision infringed on the National Highway Transportation and Safety Administration's ability to design the standards itself.[8] Second, *courts have sometimes mandated that agencies perform new tasks.* For example, a federal court required the EPA to "prevent significant deterioration" of clean areas. The court failed to define this phrase, and thus gave the EPA enormous new responsibilities in defining and enforcing the mandate.[9]

Interest groups influence agency actions by working directly with administrative agencies; groups offer technical expertise and they even help write many rules and regulations. Interest groups also influence the bureaucracy indirectly, by lobbying other parts of government. Finally, interest groups focus their efforts to influence agency actions on the courts. As we saw in chapter 2, the ability of groups to file suit in the federal courts challenging agency actions, or seeking to force agency actions, has greatly increased in recent decades.

As we might expect by this point, *the media* are an important part of influencing the bureaucracy's actions. Members of Congress, of the executive branch, and of interest groups all use the media to send messages about agency behaviors in order to influence actions. In particular, the media's hunger for conflict and novelty make the news media fertile ground for exposes of agency misbehavior or corruption. The tendency to personalize stories, too, has the effect of focusing stories of bureaucracy on individuals—usually people who have been hurt by red tape or by agency mistakes. Just as in other areas of media influence, stories of bureaucracy often overlook the complex political and administrative world of government agencies, and the long-term causes of the social and technical problems with which agencies struggle.

### Agency Defenses

We noted at the beginning of this chapter that bureaucracies exercise broad powers; in fact, they exercise all three of the basic kinds of powers of government: legislative, executive, and judicial. This concentrated power is why the major branches of government compete so fiercely to control and influence administrative agencies by influencing their personnel, their funds, and their actions. The agencies, though, are not mere puppets at the mercy of the major branches; rather, agencies have defenses that insulate them from outside influences and help protect their independence and autonomy.

## I Work for My *Agency* Now, Not for *You:* Agencies and People

Agencies defend against efforts to control their personnel in several ways. Leaders who are placed at the heads of agencies are often *"co-opted"* by the agency itself. In other words, agency heads come to see themselves as the representative, advocate, and defender of the *agency,* regardless of former political ties and regardless of a president's program. Presidents quickly find out that the bureaucracy's own need to protect itself can hinder presidential innovation. Presidents might see this as a betrayal, but the competitive system is designed to encourage each element in the governing system to promote and protect itself. If the head of the Immigration and Naturalization Service, for example, were to decide that her agency's budget would be better spent at the U.S. Customs Service, then she is probably not serving her own agency very well. Independent regulatory commissions are insulated from efforts to influence their members by *staggered terms of office,* which provide continuity across shifts in political power by preventing presidents from appointing entire commissions upon entering office.

---

### BriefCase Box 7.1
*With Friends Like These, Who Needs Enemies? Cabinet Appointments and Agency Allegiances*

Presidential appointees commonly see the focus of their loyalty to be their agencies—*not* the president who appointed them. According to the following passage by journalist Lou Cannon, what drove President Ronald Reagan's thinking in making appointments? How did he expect those appointments to help him govern? What aspect of public bureaucracies did he overlook? Do you think politically appointed agency leaders should be responsible to the president or to their agencies?

"Surround yourself with the best people you can find, delegate authority and don't interfere as long as the policy you've decided upon is being carried out," Reagan said in an . . . interview with *Fortune* [magazine]. . . . Reagan wrongly believed that the establishment of policy, both foreign and domestic, could be totally separated from its execution. He thought he had done everything he was supposed to do when he set broad policy outlines in meetings with his policy advisers. And he was encouraged in this fallacy by a commitment to "cabinet government," an idea that has beguiled nearly every modern president in his struggle to manage what governmental scholar Bradley H. Peterson Jr. has called "the

vast plurality" of the executive branch. Reagan came to office after declaiming for decades about the need to bring the federal government under control and make it the servant rather than the master of the people. He believed he could accomplish this by taking people of like mind and putting them in control of departments and agencies, then assembling them to make decisions. Despite his one-liners at the expense of bureaucrats, Reagan never really appreciated either the skill or the tenacity of the permanent government. He did not realize that cabinet secretaries, however conservative or strongminded, often are captured by the bureaucracies they are supposed to manage, as [Secretary of Defense Caspar] Weinberger ultimately would be at the Pentagon. "Cabinet members are vice presidents in charge of spending, and as such they are the natural enemies of the president," said Charles G. Dawes, the first director of the Bureau of the Budget. Reagan thought that the bureaucracy was the enemy. He did not know that this enemy was lurking in the cabinet, within the palace gates.*

*Lou Cannon, *President Reagan: The Role of a Lifetime* (New York: Simon & Schuster, 1991), 182.

*The civil service system* also protects agencies from efforts to exert influence over its personnel. A result of nineteenth-century changes culminating in the Pendleton Act of 1883, the civil service system ensures that most subordinate federal workers are hired and promoted on the basis of merit, not partisan or personal loyalty. It also provides tenure for workers regardless of political changes. This means that much of the federal workforce is not beholden directly to Congress or to the president for job security, but it also means that the bureaucracy can sometimes be unresponsive to political shifts in the elected branches of government.

### If You Cut *My* Budget, Watch *Your* Back: Agencies and Money

Agencies and agency leaders work very hard and use a variety of means to protect their budgets, in an effort to capture the funding they need to meet the demands made on them. First, agency representatives *make and keep alliances with powerful forces inside of government* that help an agency protect itself against budget cuts. Strong alliances with key members in Congress, for example, can come in handy if an agency needs to defend itself against actions by a president. Likewise, alliances with the White House can help an agency fend off efforts by Congress to exercise control, although White House ties are less stable because of regular turnover in the executive branch's personnel as presidents and administrations come and go.

Agencies also work to *ally themselves with powerful interest groups and constituencies.* The Department of Defense, for example, ties many of its programs to influential corporations involved in designing and building weapons systems. Work on these programs is spread across the country, maximizing the number of people and interests with a stake in maintaining the programs. Reducing the budget for a defense program, then, often requires Congress or OMB to reduce funds that ultimately go to key constituencies—a difficult path for elected officials to take.

*Tapping into hot issues* is another way of insulating, and even increasing, budgets. The Immigration and Naturalization Service, for example, has effectively used its role in fighting the drug war to help increase funding for the Border Patrol. With the drug war a perennially hot issue and one in which spending resources can be politically rewarding, the INS's effort is politically astute and helps ensure continued support and funding for its programs and initiatives.

### I'll Do It *My* Way: Agencies and Actions

Agencies have several ways of defending against outside efforts to control how they go about their business. First, agencies protect their autonomy by *compromising and cooperating with powerful interests* to improve agency performance; such actions can help deflect criticism and secure an influential role for the agency. For example, the Food and Drug Administration had long suffered criticism for delay in approving new drugs for sale. The FDA had built its reputation on its thorough examination of new drugs' safety, but by the 1990s its procedures were so slow that they had created a vicious cycle: Slow review of new drugs encouraged drug companies to apply for approval before *they* had done adequate research on the drugs themselves, and the FDA then had even *more* work to do, slowing the approval process to a crawl.

Under the innovative leadership of <u>David Kessler</u>, appointed by President Bush in 1992, the FDA promoted a system of user fees imposed on businesses: payment would guarantee review in a specified, and shorter, period of time. In the past, many interests had opposed such fees: some feared that they would erode the FDA's integrity and make the agency dependent on the companies it was supposed to be regulating; others, particularly the FDA itself, worried that the presence of user fees would encourage Congress to cut the agency's budget. Yet the FDA's skillful coordination with the executive branch, Congress, and the pharmaceutical industry in the early 1990s was able to satisfy those parties that user fees would not threaten their interests. With the fee system in place, the FDA improved its own processes, improved its reputation, protected its role in the review process, and made allies out of drug companies as well as advocacy groups that wanted to see experimental drugs for critical diseases more readily available to people at risk.[10]

A second way agencies protect their autonomy is through the creative use of varied resources. Agency heads, for example, are often just as savvy about *utilizing the media* as are Congress and interest groups. They defend against efforts to influence the actions of workers by publicly proclaiming that outside interests are meddling with the workings of the agency. Agencies also promote themselves and their programs through the media, and justify to the public directly why their actions are beneficial and worth paying for (see Discussion Box 7.2).

---

 ## DISCUSSION BOX 7.2
*LET ME TELL YOU A STORY: BUREAUCRACIES AND THE MEDIA*

Media coverage of the bureaucracy is spotty at best: agencies are rarely involved in newsworthy conflicts, and their personnel are often unfamiliar to the public. Further, many agency heads avoid the spotlight—public attention can make it harder for an agency to do its job, and favorable press can awaken the jealousies of other high-level officials, especially in the White House.

By communicating with the media, though, agency heads and administrators can educate the media and also point journalists toward particular aspects of issues and policies; communication can help define goals and expectations of agency actions. Savvy public servants build effective collaborative relationships with the media. Political scientist <u>Richard N. Haas</u> puts it this way:

Many who work in government—or elsewhere in the public or private sector—tend to see the media as something of an enemy, if only because at times they will publish or broadcast stories that complicate their lives. This temptation to demonize or avoid the media is understandable. But either would be a mistake. In most cases, those in the media are just doing their job, a part of which is explaining why you are not doing yours well. . . . The media are a central, permanent, and powerful element of the political environment. Like any other constituency, they need to be managed.*

How does Haas's point reflect the concept of news as a "coproduction" between the media and government, which we studied in chapter 1? Why might the media be interested in talking with an agency's representative? According to Haas, why might agency heads want to avoid the media?

*Richard N. Haas, *The Bureaucratic Entrepreneur: How to Be Effective in Any Unruly Organization* (Washington, DC: Brookings Institution Press, 1999), 156.

Agencies that lack carefully defined mandates and that are constrained by small budgets also *craft creative approaches* in order to do their jobs. The Consumer Products Safety Commission (CPSC) provides an excellent example. Formed in the 1970s with an extremely broad and vague mandate—to "protect the public against unreasonable risks of injury associated with consumer products"[11]—the CPSC struggled in its early years to define what, exactly, it was supposed to do and how it would do it. It lacked the funds to do very much, and so needed to focus on a few influential activities if it wanted to avoid being at the mercy of other interests. One of its central activities came to be the recall of unsafe products. But as tests and sensitive decisions about recalls worked their way through the CPSC bureaucracy, red tape caused delays that threatened consumer safety; delay and bureaucratic requirements also brought the agency into conflict with the business community. Through a clever strategy involving use of the media and cooperation with businesses, which generally *wanted* to see dangerous products recalled, the CPSC streamlined procedures and won the support of interests inside and outside of government. Cooperative, "fast-track" recalls helped businesses and protected consumers, and they generated important support for the CPSC from business and consumer groups. Most importantly, these actions enhanced the CPSC's reputation, allowing the agency to bring effective pressure on companies even in the absence of a large agency budget.

*Dynamics within agencies* also work to limit outsiders' influence over agency actions. The strategy of controlling the bureaucracy by influencing individuals assumes that those individuals can control the bureaucracy. Agency heads, though, are often unable to make significant or lasting changes at large, established agencies. An ingrained "organizational culture," or what political scientist James Q. Wilson defines as "a persistent, patterned way of thinking about the central tasks of and human relationships within an organization," can prevail at these agencies. Wilson writes, "Organizational culture is like an agency's personality: the way the agency and its personnel think about the world, its job, and what it is supposed to be doing; and like a personality, organizational culture can be very difficult to change." A sense of "mission" exists when culture is strong, widely shared, and warmly embraced throughout an agency.[12] A strong organizational culture can help an agency make sure its workers do what they're supposed to do, even when those workers can't be observed all the time. A strong and deeply ingrained culture can also inhibit change, though, even when change is in the best interests of the agency or public policy. Employees with a strong sense of mission can be reluctant to take on new tasks or to perform duties that they do not consider part of their central mission. As a result, new agency heads who have innovative ideas or who try to implement a president's program are often frustrated in their attempts to change the focus or activities of their agency.

## YOU THINK YOU'RE STRESSED: AGENCIES IN A COMPETITIVE SYSTEM

The competitive aspects of American politics have several important effects on administrative agencies, despite agency defenses and despite examples in which agencies have forged successful outside alliances. Agencies are torn between competing interests, they become legalistic, and they become hesitant to act.

## Agencies and the Separation of Powers

Competition affects the types of agencies we get, and it leads to "stressed" agencies caught between different interests. Divided government and political fragmentation brought on by the separation of powers provide incentives for "one-upsmanship" in the creation of new agencies. Government interests compete to respond to demands, promising more and more out of new agencies, but they sometimes wind up creating agencies with *inflated goals and expectations.* The legislation that created the Occupational Safety and Health Administration (OSHA), for example, was driven by a process of one-upsmanship among Democrats and Republicans courting blue-collar votes in the late 1960s. The National Highway Traffic Safety Administration (NHTSA) also was born of this style of one-upsmanship as Ralph Nader, Abraham Ribicoff, and Lyndon Johnson sought to apply the rhetorical force of the Civil Rights movement and the 1960s' hopes for technological achievement to the problems of automobile safety.[13]

One-upsmanship complicated both agencies' early years. The competition between the executive and the legislative branches in both the OSHA and the NHTSA cases resulted in strong but vaguely worded enabling statutes that lost much political support immediately following the agencies' creation. The acts' former supporters seemed to recognize that they had gone too far in their expectations of what the agencies could accomplish, and both agencies were left without strong political allies.[14] In turn, vague enabling statutes confused organizational missions, making it difficult for the agencies to clarify and pursue identifiable goals.

*Expectations about future competition* also affect how agencies are designed. Interests in Congress in the early 1970s, for example, believed that an agency designed to protect the environment would be opposed by polluting industries and by the Nixon White House. Congress responded to this expectation by drafting a highly *detailed* enabling statute for the EPA, mandating tough action by the agency in an effort to protect the agency from opponents and to promote its role in implementing clean air legislation. The EPA's strong mandate, though, invited challenges in the courts—so the effort to protect the EPA from executive influence wound up encouraging court influence instead.[15]

Once in action, the competitive design of American government continues to affect agencies as *interests with different goals pull agencies in different directions.* Opposition to OSHA from congressional constituencies, for example, created a series of bills calling either for changes to legislation or for the outright abolition of the agency. Congress came to OSHA's rescue, though, as the multiplication of committees within Congress enabled pro-OSHA members to tie the bills up in committee, preventing any changes.[16] But even though committee non-action saved OSHA from abolition, the flip side was that Congress was simultaneously unable to effect change that might have been beneficial to a troubled agency.[17]

Political scientist Martha Derthick captures many of the difficulties agencies face in the American system in her book *Agency under Stress: The Social*

*Security Administration in American Government.* Derthick writes of how the competitive political system gives agencies conflicting cues to influence behavior:

> The separated institutions of American government give separate guidance. In the absence of a coordinating force, their instructions [to agencies] often conflict, for the institutions are constituted on different principles and tend to have different policy biases. The president and Congress are separately accountable in their own ways to their particular electorates, and the courts are as nearly autonomous as any institution in a democratic society can be. At any particular time, the primary institutions also embody partisan or ideological preferences peculiar to that time (even if they do not do so in equal measure). Each has its own conception of what an important agency, deeply engaged in

---

 **BRIEFCASE BOX 7.2**
*Those Dam Politicians! The Competition between Politics and Expertise*

Political scientists have long understood that "policy" and "implementation" cannot be easily separated. Agency administrators and technicians face many of the same political pressures that legislators face, because the actual implementation of a policy can be just as important as the policy's original design. The Tennessee Valley Authority (TVA) was a grand New Deal–era government program designed to construct dams and power plants, developing the economic and social well-being of the Tennessee Valley region. In the passages below, TVA Chairman David E. Lilienthal acknowledges the role of politics in designing the TVA, but he defends the need for engineers and other experts to act without politics. Do you think Lilienthal's separation of politics and administration makes sense? Can experts do their jobs without being affected by political concerns? What is Lilienthal's attitude toward technicians who complain of politicians who delay administrators?

A river has no politics. Whether an engineer is a Democrat or a Republican, a conservative or a liberal, or indeed whether he has any interest in or knowledge of political matters at all, is entirely unrelated to his ability to design a dam. In this sense, experts as well as rivers have no politics. But the question of whether a river should be developed *is* a political question, and hence a proper subject of "politics." Whether a series of dams should provide only navigation, or instead should serve all the unified purposes to which the river can be put— this *is* a political question, and should be decided by Congress. The TVA Act is filled with such broad politi-

cal decisions, made, as they should and must be made, by the elected representatives of the whole people. . . .

Facts and experienced judgement, not political views, are the foundation of dependable technical decisions and action. Whether the rock at a particular site is a safe dam foundation or whether a certain kind of truck or transmission tower is best fitted for a job—these are not political questions and should not be decided politically or by political bodies. . . .

\* \* \*

But to find [the] deprecation of politics spreading is a danger sign. The strongest expressions of disgust and impatience with politics and with Congress I have ever heard have come recently from men of great executive or technical ability in government service and in business who tried to get an urgent defense job done quickly, only to be delayed and even frustrated by what they describe as "political pressure," by sometimes pointless, demagogic, or just plain stupid Congressional committee hearings, and endless conferences with legislators. This is trying, of course. And it is true that when the line I have tried to draw . . . is crossed—the line between political policymaking and administrative execution of that policy—there is ample cause for this discouragement. But genuine democrats are under a peculiarly heavy responsibility to recognize, with scrupulous care, the role of politics in the fixing of basic policies. They must be the first to see that, if the institution of politics becomes discredited, the enemies of democracy have won an important victory.*

*David E. Lilienthal, *TVA: Democracy on the March* (Chicago: Quadrangle Books, 1966 [1944]), 175–176, 185.

HON JANET RENO

Members of the federal bureaucracy, particularly heads of agencies and departments, are frequently called upon to testify to Congress about the federal government's operations. Here, Attorney General Janet Reno of the Justice Department testifies about campaign finance reform before the House Committee on the Judiciary.

direct relations with the public, ought to be doing. Each has a constitutional right to seek to influence the agency's conduct. Each has a particular set of weapons it uses to that end.[18]

Derthick concludes by noting how agencies get caught between the major branches and become the scapegoats for government's failures. "The default of the president, who is the agencies' putative leader, combines with the assertiveness of Congress and the courts to make administrative agencies the fall guys of American government. As every institution's subordinate, [agencies] are obliged to answer each and are permitted to talk back to none."[19]

## Legalistic Agencies

Agencies are increasingly affected by the courts, in part because the courts have made it easier for parties to file lawsuits to address regulatory and administrative issues, but also in part because of our national commitment to rights. Interests argue that businesses and others invade our rights to clean air and clean water, or our rights as consumers, or our rights as travelers; these claims support lawsuits and can garner public support for changes in regulations or for lawsuits.

The fear of litigation can slow the administrative process to a crawl. Court action and the threat of future litigation result in increased costs in time and money as an agency prepares itself for the inevitable court battle. Anticipating a court challenge also changes the dynamics involved in negotiations between a rulemaking agency and the interests that will be governed by those rules:

with the ability always to bring a court case challenging any rule outright, an industry has little incentive to negotiate or bargain at the rulemaking stage. On the other hand, the agency, which stands to lose time and scarce resources if a court challenge arises, has incentive to compromise with industry and reach a settlement before litigation begins. This often leads to less-stringent regulatory standards.[20] (See Discussion Box 7.3.)

Court decisions have a variety of effects on agencies. They can take power and autonomy out of an agency's hands; they can make the agency look weak and unable to control its own activities; and they can shift the balance of power *within* an agency. Agencies employ all types of people to do the numerous tasks required of them: technical experts to design and conduct research, lawyers to defend the agency in court, economists to figure out the costs and benefits of various agency actions on business and other interests, as well as advocates and politicians to promote certain goals. An increase in litigation

---

## DISCUSSION BOX 7.3
*AN OCEAN APART: REGULATION IN COMPARATIVE CONTEXT*

Many American agencies write and enforce regulations related to safety and risk in areas as diverse as the environment, the workplace, and the effects of scientific advances. The practice and results of American regulation, though, differ from regulation in many European countries. The separation of powers plays a crucial role in the United States, as it gives the American courts an important role in administrative policymaking through judicial review of agency actions. In the following passage by scholar Sheila Jasanoff, how does the American approach to managing risk differ from that in Europe? How has involvement by the courts in America influenced this difference? How do you think the courts' role impacts what goes on within American agencies?

Studies of public health, safety, and environmental regulation published in the 1980s revealed striking differences between American and European practices for managing technological risks. These studies showed that U.S. regulators on the whole were quicker to respond to new risks, more aggressive in pursuing old ones, and more concerned with producing technical justifications for their actions than their European counterparts. Regulatory styles, too, diverged sharply somewhere over the Atlantic Ocean. The U.S. process for making risk decisions impressed all observers as costly, confrontational, litigious, formal, and unusually open to participation. European decisionmaking . . . seemed by comparison almost uniformly cooperative and consensual; informal, cost conscious, and for the most part closed to the public. . . .

It takes little more than a nodding acquaintance with American politics to realize that courts in this country play a uniquely influential role in policy making. But even experienced U.S. court watchers could not have foreseen the impacts that courts would have on administrative thinking about scientific uncertainty and on national policies for controlling risk. Comparative analysis revealed striking disparities between America and Europe with respect to the judicial control of administrative decisions. Whereas European agencies could generally count on their decisions as being final no significant administrative action in America was assured of finality until it had undergone judicial review. Review by the courts not only delayed decisions relating to risk (as in licensing nuclear power plants or authorizing field tests for genetically engineered organisms), but also affected the character of administrative decision making in more subtle ways. The knowledge that their decisions would be subjected to judicial scrutiny drove agencies to adopt formal analytical procedures, such as quantitative risk assessment, and to build massive technical records to satisfy judicial demands for "reasoned decision making" and a "hard look" at the evidence. These records went far beyond any reports or explanations produced by European agencies concerned with risk.*

*Sheila Jasanoff, "American Exceptionalism and the Political Acknowledgment of Risk," *Daedalus* 119 (Fall 1990): 63, 66.

and the fear of future court challenges strengthened the position of lawyers within both NHTSA and EPA.[21]

## Gun-Shy Agencies

Agencies that are stretched between many competing interests—interests that do not hesitate to condemn an agency when they don't get their way—have a powerful incentive to become rule-bound and conservative. Vulnerable to charges of mismanagement or bad decision making, and subject to being dragged into court at any time, agencies fall back on established rules and guidelines to justify their behavior. They become reluctant to innovate or to design new policies for fear that lurking interests will drag the agency back into court to challenge the new activity.

Any new task can be a risk: it can upset established procedures and political relationships, and if not accomplished can be embarrassing. Thus, many agencies shy away from new tasks, fearing negative consequences. For years, the FBI resisted becoming involved with antidrug activities, for fear that agents might become corrupted. And though some have argued that welfare and employment fraud necessitate a better system of identifying individuals in the United States, the Social Security Administration—which keeps some of the nation's best personal records—resists becoming involved in proposals to issue a national identification card because it fears being drawn into complex and potentially divisive new issues surrounding individual privacy concerns.

## COMPETING DEMANDS AND PUBLIC ADMINISTRATION: WHY RUNNING A GOVERNMENT IS TOUGHER THAN RUNNING A BUSINESS

It is not only competition among interests and the separate branches of government that make life difficult for people at public agencies. Unlike private organizations, public agencies are tangled in a web of competing demands that affect how we judge what they do and how they go about their business.

Political scientist James Q. Wilson relates the story of how Donald Trump managed to rebuild the ice-skating rink in New York City's Central Park after years of failure by the city government.[22] Many observers looked on Trump's success, quick and efficient, as just another example of how the private sector is better managed and more efficient than the public sector: the skating rink story became an example of how government must struggle to achieve even the simplest tasks.

The lessons of the skating rink story go deeper than an easy comparison between private sector efficiency and public sector incompetence, however. Though some public agencies are indeed inefficient, and some make simple mistakes, many difficulties in public administration stem from agency efforts to meet all the demands we make on government. We demand that public agencies be fair, accountable, responsive, and efficient—but these demands have a stubborn tendency to compete and conflict with each other. Most private organizations don't face the same constraints as we place on government agencies, so it is often much easier to run a business than it is to run a government agency.

## Equity

We expect agencies to be fair and to treat people and interests equally; favoritism in awarding public contracts or in making rules or other decisions is one of the worst violations of our public ethics. But two problems follow the ideal of equity in public administration. First, efforts to be strictly fair create a morass of *red tape and oversight rules* aimed at ensuring fairness and demonstrating that fairness to observers, but red tape hampers an agency's ability to function. Red tape arises from charges that an agency has been unfair, and also from preemptive efforts by agencies to avoid those charges in the first place. The red tape that protects equity and fairness, then, simultaneously hampers the efficiency and responsiveness of public agencies.

Second, *defining equity* in the first place is tricky. If the government is to distribute one hundred million dollars in aid to cities with poverty-stricken populations, for example, how should the money be divided? Should the money be targeted to cities with the most severe problems, giving less to cities with small populations in poverty? Or should the money be divided equally among all cities, even if it means that less-needy areas receive as much as the most needy areas? Both answers seem to be "equitable," but for different reasons. In the first, the neediest get more than those less needy; in the second, everybody receives equal help. Such dilemmas are often exacerbated by the separation of powers, which gives different overseers of the bureaucracy different constituencies and interests to satisfy; agencies can be caught between two branches of government with different notions of what is "equitable" in a given situation. In such situations, it is almost inevitable that those who wind up losing—those cities that receive less money, for example—will charge the agency with unfairness or even incompetence.

## Accountability

As we have seen, the executive, legislative, and even judicial branches of the federal government each try to hold public agencies accountable for agency actions; citizens, special interest groups, and agency clients also try to hold the agencies accountable. The demand for accountability follows from our belief in government by the people: knowing that agencies are populated by unelected public servants, we rightly demand that they be accountable to duly elected representatives or to popular interests. Yet the competitive structure of the system—the fact that we have two elected branches sharing authority over the bureaucracy, for example—has effects on agency behaviors, as we saw above. Agencies become conservative, rule-bound, legalistic, gun-shy, and generally stressed out as so many interests try to hold them accountable to diverse and conflicting demands. Agencies' ability to pursue their goals are impaired, and even more red tape is created as agencies try to justify their actions to their many masters.

## Responsiveness

We want government agencies to be flexible enough to be responsive to outside interests and to new demands and concerns. We want the Federal Emergency Management Agency (FEMA), for example, to respond quickly with aid to areas damaged by floods or hurricanes, and we want the FDA to respond quickly and effectively to outbreaks of *E. coli* bacteria or other health hazards. Yet the red tape arising from efforts to be equitable and accountable hampers responsiveness, as we saw above when we examined the Consumer Products Safety Commission's efforts to streamline its product recall process.

Further, *too much* responsiveness raises questions about whether an agency is fulfilling its proper mission. Critics hit on this very point in worrying about the FDA's accelerated drug review process, discussed above. The FDA's accelerated review process garnered accolades from many drug companies and patients, yet some feared that the agency would become dominated by the drug companies. Moreover, a *Washington Post* editorial pointed out that speed, in this case, might be at odds with the FDA's role in ensuring that approved drugs are safe: "The most avid reformers do not appear to be giving enough attention to the risks involved. . . . Even when time is of the essence, is speed ever more important than safety?"[23] In short, the FDA's efforts to be responsive to demands for faster procedures caused concern about the agency's accountability.

## Efficiency

Efficiency in government agencies refers to eliminating waste, fraud, and abuse: We want the most "bang" for the buck, and as little waste as possible. Meeting the requirements of equity, though, reduces efficiency because red tape is time-consuming and expensive. Instead of giving a public works contract to a company that an agency knows has the expertise and the ability to do the job, for example, the demand for equity can require the agency to solicit bids on the project from all companies that might be interested. Not only is such a process lengthy and expensive, the agency could wind up with a different contractor than the one in which it has the most confidence. Because of the time and paperwork involved, and because the contractor might be incompetent despite (or even because of) its low bid on a project, the whole process can look inefficient.

The efficiency issue takes us back to Wilson's original example, the Central Park skating rink. One of the criticisms of the city's efforts was that the city was inefficient: its procedures were laden with paperwork and cumbersome bidding processes. But this "inefficiency" resulted from the city's efforts to be fair. The city needed to make sure it showed no favoritism in bidding on the project, for example, and it also needed to trace the ins and outs of money raising and spending to avoid any charges of waste, fraud, and abuse. Trump was free to hire who he wanted, when he wanted, and to oversee their work how he wanted; if he saved money, he got to keep it or give bonuses to diligent workers. The city did not have the same freedom: not because city government is necessarily inefficient, but because public administration needs to meet standards that compete with the efficiency goal (see Discussion Box 7.4).

One of the most important differences between government agencies and private sector companies is that public agencies do not have strong incentives to economize. According to political scientist James Q. Wilson in the following passage, what is the crucial difference between what public and private organizations can do with revenue surpluses? What effect does this have on public agencies at the end of the fiscal year? How do such restrictions illustrate the competition among governing branches that occurs under the separation of powers?

In the days leading up to September 30, the federal government is Cinderella, courted by legions of individuals and organizations eager to get grants and contracts from the unexpended funds still at the disposal of each agency. At midnight on September 30, the government's coach turns into a pumpkin. That is the moment—the end of the fiscal year—at which every agency, with a few exceptions, must return all unexpended funds to the Treasury Department.

Except for certain quasi-independent government corporations, such as the Tennessee Valley Authority, no agency may keep any surplus revenues (that is, the difference between the funds it received from a congressional appropriation and those it needed to operate during the year). By the same token, any agency that runs out of money before the end of the fiscal year may ask Congress for more (a "supplemental appropriation") instead of being forced to deduct the deficit from any accumulated cash reserves. Because of these fiscal rules agencies do not have a material incentive to economize: Why scrimp and save if you cannot keep the results of your frugality?*

*James Q. Wilson, *Bureaucracy: What Government Agencies Do and Why They Do It* (New York: Basic Books, 1989), 116.

Wilson summarizes the issue of efficiency in public administration this way:

> The economic definition of efficiency . . . assumes that there is only one valued output, the new [skating] rink. But government has many valued outputs, including a reputation for integrity, the confidence of the people, and the support of important interest groups. When we complain about skating rinks not being built on time we speak as if all we cared about were skating rinks. But when we complain that contracts were awarded without competitive bidding or in a way that allowed bureaucrats to line their pockets we acknowledge that we care about many things besides skating rinks; we care about the contextual goals—the constraints—that we want government to observe. A government that is slow to build rinks but is honest and accountable in its actions and properly responsive to worthy constituencies may be a very efficient government, *if* we measure efficiency . . . by taking into account *all* of the valued outputs.[24]

These four demands, then—equity, accountability, responsiveness, and efficiency—compete with each other and complicate the efforts and the evaluation of public agencies.

## Conclusion

Government activity faces a basic dilemma. We generally want government to be professional and nonpartisan: once the politicians have settled on a policy, administrators should carry it out without further influence from politicians or outside interests. This attitude explains why we flinch at the notion that the census count could be manipulated by one political party or the other. At the same time, though, we want government to be responsive to public opinion and to directives from our elected leaders—which is why we might want the Bureau of the Census to be responsive to demands from interest groups worried about the procedures for taking the census. Because we want so many things from government, and because we often overlook how difficult it is for public agencies to meet the demands of outside interests as well as the constraints imposed on their behavior, we have a tendency to forget what a complicated battle public agencies face.

## Overnight Assignment ▬▬▬▬▬▬▬▬▬▬▬▬▬▬▬

Pick a federal agency; what is the agency's mission? Usually, the agency's mission statement can be found on its webpage. Is the mission clear? What are the values that support the mission? What conflicts can you foresee in the issue area in which the agency is involved? Will it be difficult to determine whether or not the agency is fulfilling its mission? Is it likely that the president and Congress will want different things from that agency?

## Long-Term Integrated Assignment ▬▬▬▬▬▬▬▬▬▬

Pick a governmental agency related to your interest group or one of its issues. What is the agency's mission? How is the agency involved with your group's issue? What does the agency do to further or to regulate your issue? Has your interest group drawn connections between the agency and the issue? Has the agency appeared in your media source, either as the subject of debate or because someone from the agency gave an interview? What issues were discussed? How did the story reflect the tendencies of the media or the difficult position of agencies as discussed in this chapter? If the agency is being criticized, what is the subject of the criticism—equity, accountability, responsiveness or efficiency?

## Researching the Bureaucracy? ▬▬▬▬▬▬▬▬▬▬▬▬

**Try These Authors:**

Eugene Bardach            Donald F. Kettl            Paul J. Quirk
Martha Derthick           Kenneth J. Meier           James Q. Wilson

**Try These Sources:**

DONAHUE, JOHN D., ed., *Making Washington Work: Tales of Innovation in the Federal Government*. Washington, DC: Brookings Institution Press, 1999.
HARRIS, RICHARD A. and SIDNEY M. MILKIS. *The Politics of Regulatory Change: A Tale of Two Agencies*, 2nd ed. New York: Oxford University Press, 1996.
HOROWITZ, DONALD L. *The Jurocracy: Government Lawyers, Agency Programs, and Judicial Decisions*. Lexington, MA: Lexington Books, 1977.
KAUFMAN, HERBERT. *The Forest Ranger: A Study in Administrative Behavior*. Washington, DC: Resources for the Future, 1993.

LEVIN, MARTIN A. *Making Government Work: How Entrepreneurial Executives Turn Bright Ideas into Real Results.* San Francisco: Jossey-Bass, 1994.

MELNICK, R. SHEP. *Regulation and the Courts: The Case of the Clean Air Act.* Washington, DC: Brookings Institution, 1983.

SHAPIRO, MARTIN M. *The Supreme Court and Administrative Agencies.* New York: Free Press, 1968.

## Endnotes

1. Peter Skerry, *Counting on the Census? Race, Group Identity, and the Evasion of Politics* (Washington, DC: Brookings Institution Press, 2000), 9.
2. See, for example, Leonard D. White, *The Federalists: A Study in Administrative History 1789–1801* (New York: Free Press, 1965) and Leonard D. White, *The Republican Era 1809–1901: A Study in Administrative History* (New York: Macmillan, 1958).
3. Samuel H. Beer, "In Search of a New Public Philosophy," in *The New American Political System,* ed. Anthony King (Washington, DC: American Enterprise Institute for Public Policy Research, 1978).
4. Quoted in William E. Leuchtenberg, *Franklin D. Roosevelt and the New Deal* (New York: Harper Torchbooks, 1963), 333.
5. Ibid., 331.
6. Paul C. Light, *The True Size of Government* (Washington, DC: Brookings Institution Press, 1999), 1.
7. Quoted in Eric Schmitt, "When Nomination Turns to Wrangling to Impasse," *New York Times,* July 28, 1999: p. A16. Smith was nominated to the FEC by President Clinton in February 2000, and confirmed by the Senate in May 2000.
8. *Chrysler Corporation v. Department of Transportation,* 515 F.2d 1053 (C.A. 6, 1975).
9. *Sierra Club v. Ruckelshaus,* 344 F.Supp. 253 (D.D.C. 1972).
10. See John D. Donahue, ed., *Making Washington Work: Tales of Innovation in the Federal Government* (Washington, DC: Brookings Institution Press, 1999), chap. 13.
11. Quoted in ibid., 20.
12. James Q. Wilson, *Bureaucracy: What Government Agences Do and Why They Do It* (New York: Basic Books, 1989), 95.
13. Graham K. Wilson, *The Politics of Safety and Health: Occupational Safety and Health in the United States and Britain* (Oxford: Oxford University Press, 1985), 35–43; Jerry L. Mashaw and David L. Harfst, *The Struggle for Auto Safety* (Cambridge, MA: Harvard University Press, 1990), chap. 3.
14. Wilson, *The Politics of Safety and Health,* 35–43; Mashaw and Harfst, *The Struggle for Auto Safety,* chap. 3, also 67, 72, 158.
15. R. Shep Melnick, *Regulation and the Courts: The Case of the Clean Air Act* (Washington, DC: Brookings Institution Press, 1983), chap. 2, 253.
16. Wilson, *The Politics of Safety and Health,* 46.
17. Melnick, *Regulation and the Courts,* 252–261, 255.
18. Martha Derthick, *Agency under Stress: The Social Security Administration in American Government* (Washington, DC: Brookings Institution Press, 1990), 177.
19. Ibid., 181.
20. Ibid., 282–290.
21. Mashaw and Harfst, *The Struggle for Auto Safety,* chap. 9 and 87; Wilson, *The Politics of Safety and Health,* 282.
22. Wilson, *Bureaucracy,* chap. 17.
23. Quoted in Donahue, *Making Washington Work,* 170.
24. Wilson, *The Politics of Safety and Health,* 317–318.

# The Presidency

## CHAPTER OUTLINE

Two things stand out from the early days of Bill Clinton's presidency. First, Clinton rode to Washington on a surge of support for an overhaul of the nation's health care system. After much debate and competitive fighting, the Clinton health care plan fell apart. Second, Clinton had promised gay activists during the 1992 campaign that he would lift the ban on gays in the military. President Clinton lifted the ban almost immediately after his inauguration—but opponents rallied, and resistance from forces around the country, including the military, forced the new president to scale back his initiative. The retreat upset gay activists who had supported Clinton during the election, and the administration's compromise policy of "Don't ask, don't tell" continues to be a lightning rod for controversy.

Both cases—one dealing with a grand design for a major policy overhaul, the other a seemingly simple act changing specific rules for a limited part of the public service, and affecting a relatively small number of people— illustrate the fact that the president is only one of many forces in the vast machine of the American government. As much as the presidency remains the most visible and important single force in the constitutional system, the framers located the president within a system designed to check the power of that office and control the president's behavior.

**The Bottom Line.** Americans have high hopes and expectations for their presidents. At the founding, compromises regarding presidential selection aimed to satisfy diverse interests and create an office with a measure of independence and autonomy—but one that would nevertheless be checked in the exercise of its power. For the most part, the system has worked: today the office enjoys broad powers under the Constitution, the potential for energy, and a position of visibility and leadership without parallel in the American system. Yet other forces continue to limit the president's potential: Congress and the bureaucracy have their own interests and their own constituents, and they must be persuaded—not commanded—to work with the president toward his objectives. Leadership is more about bargaining and compromise with these forces than it is about striking out in new directions and hoping that the nation follows. Finally, presidents confront a fundamental dilemma in satisfying demands that the president serve simultaneously as the leader of the entire nation and as the leader of partisan initiatives.

## ANOTHER CREATIVE COMPROMISE: THE CONSTITUTIONAL PRESIDENCY

### It Might Look Simple, But It's Not: Selecting the President

From the earliest days, the presidency has seemed to want to be all things to all people. As we will see at the end of this chapter, the president today is caught between the responsibilities of being a national leader and the demands of being a partisan leader. Even at the Constitutional Convention, the framers resolved the most hotly debated aspect of the presidency—the method of selecting the president—with a compromise ingeniously designed to satisfy numerous diverse interests.

The trick facing the Constitution's framers was to create a government that was strong enough to be effective but not strong enough to threaten liberty. A related puzzle surrounded the design of the presidency: how to make the office strong enough to check the legislature, yet not so strong as to *dominate* that legislature. Having settled quickly on having a single executive, unlocking this puzzle relied on ensuring that the method of selecting the president would satisfy diverse interests without making the office subservient to any of those interests.

The original Virginia Plan, for example, gave to the legislature the power to select the executive, in the belief that legislators would have the knowledge and judgment necessary to make wise choices. Yet the involvement of the legislature raised a number of worries. In most schemes for selection by the legislature, for example, the president would not be eligible for reelection for fear that he might use the office's powers and patronage to bribe legislators for future support. In the absence of reelectability, legislative selection suggested a longer term of office for the president, usually six or seven years. The framers were not overjoyed with long terms and no reelectability, with some arguing that the longer term would distance the president from the people and others arguing that reelectability was an important incentive for good presidential performance.

Perhaps surprisingly, given the framers' wariness regarding popular passions and the dangers of true democracy, several influential delegates to the Constitutional Convention favored the direct election of the president by the public. Hamilton, Madison, Franklin, James Wilson, and Gouverneur Morris all supported popular election, with the president limited to a shorter term but generally eligible for reelection. Yet this too had its detractors: Skeptics, for example, worried that the public's limited knowledge and questionable judgment would result in poor choices. More importantly, representatives of smaller states feared that direct popular election would bias the selection process in favor of states with larger populations. Amid stalemate in choosing a selection method, delegate James Wilson remarked that this question was "in truth the most difficult of all on which we have had to decide."[1]

The compromise result was the electoral college system, in which each state would have a number of electors equal to its number of representatives plus the number of its senators. Each elector would cast two votes. If no individual received a *majority* of electoral votes—more than half—the Senate would select the winner from the top five electoral vote-getters; the second-place finisher would be vice president.

This system, which looks archaic now and which continues to attract ridicule and calls for reform, was an ingenious compromise. First, it gave both large and small states influence in the selection process. The framers believed that electors would generally use one of their votes to choose someone from their own state, and the other vote would be cast for someone from a different state. Under this method, the framers believed, only in very rare cases would any candidate actually receive a majority of electoral votes—meaning that most elections would be sent to the Senate, where small states had relatively greater influence. Because of concerns that the Senate already had too much power, the system was adjusted to give the final vote to the House, with each delegation voting as a state to maintain the small states' proportionate power. In effect, the electoral system gave the large states the first crack at "nominating" candidates, and it secured to the small states an important role in the ultimate choice.

The electoral college system also satisfied states' rights interests, because each state legislature—not the federal government—would establish its own mechanism for choosing electors. Finally, the system compromised between advocates and skeptics of popular choice. The people would still have an important role in choosing electors, yet the final selection of the president would be filtered through the electors. By 1832, almost all states allowed the public to vote for electors directly.

Beyond satisfying diverse interests, the electoral system cleverly protected the integrity of the president's selection in several other ways. Rather than have electors meet in one location, which would be expensive and vulnerable to corrupting influences, electors would cast their votes in their home states.

On the Web
www.fec.gov/pages/
ecmenu2.htm

On the Web
www.nara.gov/fedreg
/elctcoll/index.html#
top

This dispersal of electors, restrictions against electors holding national office, and the fact that they would gather briefly for this single purpose, all worked to limit the ability of corrupting forces to tamper with the presidential selection system.

With this system, the framers settled on a four-year term with eligibility for reelection (reelection was limited to two terms by the Twenty-Second Amendment, ratified in 1951). The system did, however, need some tinkering. Party development by 1800 had organized voting to the extent that interests allied with Thomas Jefferson cast their ballots for Jefferson and Aaron Burr, who was expected to serve as vice president. Yet because these delegations voted for both men, Jefferson and Burr received an equal number of votes—and tied. Only the influence of Hamilton, Jefferson's rival but a man who mistrusted Burr even more than he disagreed with Jefferson, gave the election to Jefferson. After this, the Twelfth Amendment provided for voting for president and vice president separately. Scholar William H. Riker has written of the presedential selection process, "It is astonishing that a compromise put together over a weekend to satisfy diverse, parochial, and temporary interests has, with only slight modification by the Twelfth Amendment, served adequately for two centuries."[2]

## Checks and Balances

The president was a new creation. As historian Max Farrand recognized in 1913, "When an institution has been in reasonably successful operation for . . . years, it is hard to conceive the attitude towards it of the men who lived before that institution existed. It was a new officer whom they were creating, and he loomed all the larger in their eyes that from the very limitations of their experience they were compelled to think of him in terms of monarchy, the only form of national executive power they knew."[3]

Balancing that "new officer" between competing interests, protecting his independence, and limiting his potential, was a masterful achievement.

A few features of the presidency insulate the office from outside pressure. The delegates at the Convention, for example, quickly and remarkably easily agreed that the president's salary could not be changed while he was in office. This aimed to prevent Congress from either punishing a president by cutting his salary or raising (or promising to raise) his salary in an effort to influence the president's behavior. The Constitution also prohibited members of Congress from holding the office of the presidency, and it forbade them from serving as presidential electors; together with the president's independent electoral base, these aspects gave the office a measure of independence and autonomy.

The checks-and-balances scheme dominates the Constitution, as we have seen, and the presidency is notable for the powers it shares with the legislature. Among the most important is the president's limited veto, subject to override only by a two-thirds vote in Congress. The veto gives the president an important influence in the passage of legislation, and it gives the office a weapon with which to defend itself against encroachments by the legislature. The veto's limits, though, mean that ultimate legislative authority still resides in the Congress. The president also has a "pocket veto," by which he can, in effect, reject legislation by not returning it to Congress if Congress goes into recess within ten days of passing a bill.

Several other aspects of the president's power involve the Congress, such as the Senate's involvement in the treaty process and in the appointment of judges. The commander-in-chief role is also checked by Congress's power to authorize funds and to declare war. Finally, of course, complete autonomy of the president is checked by Congress's power of impeachment (see BriefCase Box 8.1).

By the Convention's end, the framers had designed a presidency with some carefully enumerated powers and responsibilities. Note how many of

## BriefCase Box 8.1
### Presidents, Precedents, and Prescience: Impeachment at the Philadelphia Convention

The framers disagreed about how much power they wanted to give the executive, and in how much they feared the abuse of that power. Discussion over whether the president would be subject to impeachment, and who would control the impeachment power, illustrates one piece of this debate. The discussion was taken down by James Madison, whose notes remain the best source we have for the discussions at the Convention. In the following passages, note how Gouverneur Morris's view changes as a result of the discussion, suggesting the competing viewpoints and the power of persuasion at the Convention. Does Morris favor or oppose impeachment by the end of the discussion? What changed his mind? Why are the delegates worried about the legislature's role in an impeachment?

Mr. Gouverneur Morris: [The executive] can do no criminal act without Coadjutors who may be punished. In case he should be re-elected, that will be sufficient proof of his innocence. Besides who is to impeach? Is the impeachment to suspend his functions[?] If it is the impeachment will be nearly equivalent to a displacement, and will render the Executive dependent on those who are to impeach[.]

Colonel George Mason: No point is of more importance than that the right of impeachment should be continued. Shall any man be above Justice? Above all shall that man be above it, who can commit the most extensive injustice? When great crimes were committed he [Mason] was for punishing the principal as well as the Coadjutors. . . .

Mr. Gouverneur Morris admits corruption & some few other offences to be such as ought to be impeachable; but thought the cases ought to be enumerated & defined[.]

. . .

Mr. Charles Pinkney [sic] did not see the necessity of impeachments. He was sure they ought not to issue from the Legislature who would in that case hold them as a rod over the Executive and by that means effectually destroy his independence. His revisionary [veto] power in particular would be rendered altogether insignificant.

Mr. Elbridge Gerry urged the necessity of impeachments. A good magistrate will not fear them. A bad one ought to be kept in fear of them. He hoped the maxim would never be adopted here that the chief magistrate could do no wrong.

. . .

Mr. Edmund Randolph: The propriety of impeachments was a favorite principle with him. Guilt whenever found ought to be punished. The Executive will have great opportunitys [sic] of abusing his power. . . . [Randolph] is aware of the necessity of proceeding with a cautious hand, and of excluding as much as possible the influence of the Legislature from the business. . . .

. . .

Mr. Pinkney . . . presumed that [the executive's] powers would be so circumscribed as to render impeachments unnecessary.

Mr. Gouverneur Morris's opinion had been changed by the arguments used in the discussion. He was now sensible of the necessity of impeachments, if the Executive was to continue for any time in office. Our Executive was not like a Magistrate having a life interest, much less like one having an hereditary interest in his office. . . . This Magistrate is not the King but the prime-Minister. The people are the King. When we make him amenable to Justice however we should take care to provide some mode that will not make him dependent on the Legislature.*

*Adapted from *Notes of Debates in the Federal Convention of 1787 Reported by James Madison* (New York: W. W. Norton & Company, 1987), 331–335. The phrases are direct quotations; we have altered Madison's references to the speakers for convenience.

these powers are shared with other branches, and how many are fairly vague outlines of presidential responsibilities:

- The president is *commander in chief* of the military.
- The president possesses the power, with the advice and consent of the Senate, to *make treaties.*
- The president has the power to nominate and, with Senate advice and consent, *appoint ambassadors, Supreme Court judges, and public ministers and consuls.*

- The president is required to give to Congress information on the *state of the union*, and to *recommend measures* "as he shall judge necessary and expedient."
- The president is mandated to *receive ambassadors* and other public ministers.
- The president "shall take Care that the Laws be faithfully executed."
- The president "may require the Opinion, in writing, of the principal Officer in each of the executive departments, upon any subject relating to the Duties of their respective Offices."
- Finally, the president must affirm an oath in defense of the office and of the Constitution: "I do solemnly swear (or affirm) that I will faithfully execute the Office of President of the United States, and will to the best of my Ability, preserve, protect, and defend the Constitution of the United States."

## WHITE HOUSE, LEADERSHIP: PRESIDENTIAL STRENGTHS IN A COMPETITIVE SYSTEM

One of the most significant passages in the Constitution is the opening clause of Article 2, which invests the president with executive powers: "The executive Power shall be vested in a President of the United States." "Executive power" is a curious thing, though. John Locke had written that "the good of the society requires that several things should be left to the discretion of him that has the executive power. . . . For the legislators not being able to foresee and provide by laws for all that may be useful to the community, the executor of the laws, having the power in his hands, has by the common law of Nature a right to make use of it for the good of society."[4] The Constitution's vesting clause seems to imply that there are inherent powers in the office that go beyond those enumerated in the Constitution, and presidents throughout history have seized on the vague constitutional reference to executive power as justification for expanding the scope of the president's authority.

The president has become the focal point of the federal government. Alexander Hamilton argued that a single executive, tenured by fixed, regular elections and independent of legislative control would have the energy and accountability necessary to make the office effective in the new government. To some extent he was right: A single executive focuses attention and helps the president attract attention for his programs; the fixed term allows the president to pursue long-term objectives without being overly concerned about being removed from office; and the president's unique national constituency, his veto, and the grant of executive power have helped maintain the president's ability to function autonomously. Yet not all of the president's strength comes from constitutional factors; strong presidents have used institutional developments within the White House and the executive branch as well as opportunities to expand their leadership potential to build the office's competitive advantages in the political system.

# The Development of the Presidency I: Institutions

Over the years, one of the most significant developments in presidential power has been the expansion of the institutional arrangements surrounding the office. Political scientist <u>Sidney M. Milkis</u> writes, "[T]he institutionalization of the presidency established a formal organizational apparatus with which presidents and their appointees could short-circuit the separation of powers, accelerating the transfer of authority from Congress to the executive."[5] The foundation of the institutionalized presidency lies in Franklin D. Roosevelt's New Deal administrations.

 **ON THE WEB**
www.whitehouse.gov/
WH/EOP/html/EOP_
org.html

The 1939 Executive Reorganization Act redefined the executive's position and institutional strength by centralizing administrative control. This attempt to increase presidential power significantly by overhauling control of agencies and departments did not fully succeed, but the Act expanded executive power by creating the Executive Office of the President (EOP), which now includes the National Security Council and the Council of Economic Advisors, among others (see Zip Box 8.2). The centerpiece of the ever-changing EOP is the White House staff. Chosen directly by the president, the staff is loyal to the president and is often chosen, at least in part, from members of the president's

## Zip Box 8.2
*Institutional Support for the President*

### White House Staff and Executive Office of the President, 1943–1998

| Year | White House | OMB/ Bureau of Budget[a] | Council of Economic Advisers | National Security Council | Office of Economic Opportunity | Office of Science and Technology | Office of Adminis- tration | Special Rep- resentative for Trade Negotiations | Office of Policy Development/ Domestic Council | Total Executive Office[b] |
|------|-------------|--------------------------|------------------------------|---------------------------|--------------------------------|----------------------------------|----------------------------|------------------------------------------------|-------------------------------------------------|---------------------------|
| 1943[c] | 51 | 543 | | | | | | | | 703 |
| 1944[c] | 8 | 542 | | | | | | | | 683 |
| 1945[c] | 64 | 705 | | | | | | | | 820 |
| 1946[c] | 216 | 692 | 26 | | | | | | | 1,034 |
| 1947[c] | 228 | 549 | 26 | | | | | | | 1,077 |
| 1948[c] | 209 | 521 | 38 | 20 | | | | | | 1,205 |
| 1949 | 243 | 517 | 36 | 17 | | | | | | 1,240 |
| 1950 | 313 | 509 | 38 | 17 | | | | | | 1,408 |
| 1951 | 246 | 518 | 37 | 21 | | | | | | 1,326 |
| 1952 | 248 | 470 | 31 | 22 | | | | | | 1,296 |
| 1953 | 247 | 417 | 28 | 28 | | | | | | 1,183 |
| 1954 | 262 | 430 | 34 | 26 | | | | | | 1,078 |
| 1955 | 366 | 422 | 33 | 27 | | | | | | 1,221 |
| 1956 | 392 | 443 | 38 | 25 | | | | | | 1,228 |
| 1957 | 399 | 441 | 35 | 65 | | | | | | 1,255 |
| 1958 | 395 | 424 | 33 | 61 | | | | | | 2,605 |
| 1959 | 406 | 432 | 33 | 64 | | | | | | 2,735 |
| 1960 | 423 | 441 | 31 | 64 | | | | | | 2,779 |

| Year | White House | OMB/ Bureau of Budget[a] | Council of Economic Advisers | National Security Council | Office of Economic Opportunity | Office of Science and Technology | Office of Adminis- tration | Special Rep- resentative for Trade Negotiations | Office of Policy Development/ Domestic Council | Total Executive Office[b] |
|---|---|---|---|---|---|---|---|---|---|---|
| 1961 | 439 | 456 | 45 | 43 | | | | | | 1,586 |
| 1962 | 338 | 465 | 65 | 39 | | 63 | | | | 1,492 |
| 1963 | 376 | 485 | 57 | 43 | | 48 | | 30 | | 1,572 |
| 1964 | 328 | 493 | 46 | 41 | | 57 | | 29 | | 1,478 |
| 1965 | 292 | 506 | 45 | 39 | 1,768 | 75 | | 24 | | 3,307 |
| 1966 | 270 | 592 | 62 | 40 | 2,319 | 105 | | 26 | | 4,050 |
| 1967 | 271 | 570 | 56 | 38 | 2,951 | 58 | | 24 | | 4,747 |
| 1968 | 261 | 550 | 74 | 35 | 3,211 | 62 | | 22 | | 4,964 |
| 1969 | 341 | 576 | 34 | 66 | 2,282 | 75 | | 22 | | 4,116 |
| 1970 | 491 | 636 | 57 | 82 | 2,633 | 77 | | 26 | 26 | 4,808 |
| 1971 | 580 | 717 | 62 | 80 | 2,304 | 75 | | 33 | 44 | 4,809 |
| 1972 | 583 | 703 | 58 | 80 | 2,066 | 76 | | 38 | 53 | 5,721 |
| 1973 | 528 | 642 | 49 | 85 | 1,148 | | | 39 | 24 | 3,877 |
| 1974 | 560 | 646 | 46 | 87 | 1,090 | | | 45 | 32 | 2,868 |
| 1975 | 525 | 664 | 48 | 85 | | | | 56 | 55 | 1,801 |
| 1976 | 534 | 694 | 39 | 79 | | 19 | | 55 | 43 | 1,796 |
| 1977 | 387 | 721 | 36 | 68 | | 44 | | 52 | 41 | 1,637 |
| 1978 | 381 | 617 | 35 | 76 | | 46 | 197 | 58 | 55 | 1,679 |
| 1979 | 418 | 638 | 36 | 73 | | 44 | 180 | 70 | 60 | 1,918 |
| 1980 | 426 | 631 | 38 | 74 | | 50 | 182 | 131 | 68 | 2,013 |
| 1981 | 378 | 679 | 38 | 65 | | 13 | 190 | 139 | 48 | 1,674 |
| 1982 | 374 | 617 | 35 | 59 | | 20 | 196 | 138 | 46 | 1,608 |
| 1983 | 376 | 619 | 34 | 61 | | 23 | 213 | 139 | 39 | 1,622 |
| 1984 | 371 | 605 | 28 | 63 | | 21 | 196 | 147 | 40 | 1,593 |
| 1985 | 362 | 569 | 32 | 61 | | 17 | 193 | 152 | 38 | 1,549 |
| 1986 | 365 | 537 | 36 | 69 | | 11 | 200 | 144 | 40 | 1,526 |
| 1987 | 375 | 573 | 31 | 56 | | 11 | 199 | 155 | 37 | 1,604 |
| 1988 | 357 | 573 | 35 | 63 | | 10 | 232 | 162 | 32 | 1,594 |
| 1989 | 370 | 536 | 32 | 62 | | 20 | 213 | 164 | 37 | 1,640 |
| 1990 | 391 | 568 | 35 | 60 | | 22 | 215 | 172 | 37 | 1,729 |
| 1991 | 358 | 608 | 36 | 61 | | 39 | 241 | 181 | 33 | 1,797 |
| 1992 | 392 | 553 | 34 | 62 | | 47 | 247 | 185 | 42 | 1,869 |
| 1993 | 392 | 522 | 31 | 52 | | 35 | 185 | 177 | 42 | 1,570 |
| 1994 | 381 | 544 | 29 | 49 | | 36 | 182 | 166 | 38 | 1,577 |
| 1995 | 387 | 522 | 28 | 44 | | 34 | 182 | 165 | 30 | 1,555 |
| 1996 | 387 | 527 | 30 | 43 | | 33 | 185 | 161 | 28 | 1,582 |
| 1997 | 389 | 507 | 28 | 43 | | 34 | 178 | 154 | 29 | 1,591 |
| 1998 | 291 | 509 | 27 | 42 | | 34 | 170 | 169 | 30 | 1,604 |

*Note:* In almost all instances when no figures are shown, the office did not exist as a separate entity. Data as of December of the year indicated, except 1947 (January), 1960 (October).

[a]The Bureau of the Budget became the Office of Management and Budget in 1970.

[b]Includes offices not shown separately.

[c]Total executive office excludes personnel in war establishments or emergency war agencies.

Table from *Vital Statistics on American Politics, 1999–2000*, ed. Harold W. Stanley and Harold Watkins (Washington, DC: CQ Press, 2000), 250–251.

successful campaign team. Other advisers are chosen for their expertise in certain areas and for their loyalty to the president. Presidents have used a variety of staff arrangements, but most choose either a hierarchical, pyramid arrangement, with access to the president carefully restricted by a chief of staff, or a looser arrangement involving six or seven chief advisors with greater access to the president. Presidents Eisenhower, Nixon, Reagan, and Bush all favored a pyramid style; FDR, Kennedy, and Johnson relied on looser arrangements.

The EOP and the White House staff are designed to be political extensions of the presidency and to give the president enhanced control over other aspects of the bureaucracy. Perhaps the most influential executive office is the *Office of Management and Budget* (OMB). The OMB dates to President Nixon's reorganization of the Executive Office in 1970, during which Nixon replaced a statutory agency (the Bureau of the Budget), with duties outlined by Congress, with an agency (OMB) designed by and at the service of the president alone. The OMB develops the executive budget; this is an enormously complicated task that invests the OMB with extraordinary power over the bureaucracy and over administrative initiatives and procedures. These agencies must have their budgets approved through the OMB before the budgets are sent on to Congress, at which time the fighting over funding and priorities begins again. This process gives the president, through the OMB, extensive authority over the bureaucracy's priorities.

### The Development of the Presidency II: Personal Leadership

While institutional developments have helped consolidate the president's power, an evolving understanding of the president's role has helped concentrate power—and, more importantly, expectations—in and around the White House. Twentieth-century presidents capitalized on the presidency's visibility, utilizing the media to nurture the office's place at the center of national leadership.

Early presidents used constitutionally mandated State of the Union addresses and other messages to Congress to suggest or promote specific policy directions. Washington's early messages to Congress, for example, outlined federal policy toward American Indians, a critical aspect of the new republic's plans to survive in the years after the Revolution. Only rarely, though, did presidents aim messages past Congress and directly at the public.

In the twentieth century, presidents began to speak more directly to the public. Advances in communication technologies aided presidents in getting their messages out to a broad audience, and the media's desire to build stories around familiar individuals helped presidents free themselves from party constraints and from the limitations of formal messages. As the twentieth century unfolded, of course, the direct primary and the rise of candidate-centered organizations further focused attention away from the parties and onto individual candidates and presidents.

A succession of presidents found new ways to communicate with the public and attract attention to themselves. Theodore Roosevelt cultivated his "rough and ready" image, taking the president onto a nationally publicized

ON THE WEB
www.pbs.org/
newshour/character/
index.html

ON THE WEB
www.cspresidency.
org

Photos of the presidents are often carefully prepared to highlight certain aspects of a president's personality or image. Images of the John F. Kennedy administration often highlighted the youth and playfulness of the Kennedy family, as in this photo showing John F. Kennedy, Jr. and the president in the Oval Office.

Richard M. Nixon's presidency ended when he resigned the office in the face of a possible impeachment proceeding, following the White House's cover-up of a break-in at the Democratic Party's national campaign headquarters at the Watergate hotel in Washington, D.C. Intentionally or not, many of the images from the Nixon era seem to evoke the isolation of the Nixon White House during the Watergate scandal.

When party ties provided a strong link between the president, party officials, and the general public, party loyalty and organization went far toward supporting the president during crisis situations. These supports were also critical in helping to stabilize presidential leadership over the course of a four-year term, and they gave presidents some security when the president pushed necessary but unpopular policies.

Candidate-centered campaigns, the direct primary, and a professionalized bureaucracy have helped free the president from the control of political parties. Yet this independence comes with a price: personal leadership separates the president from party support, resting the potential of the office on popular opinion of the president as an individual.

According to the following passage by presidency scholar Sidney M. Milkis, what tools do modern presidents use to forge ties to the public? What risks surround the new dynamics of presidential support? Why is the connection between the president and the parties important?

[I]t might be unreasonable, indeed, dangerous, to rely so heavily on presidents to determine the contours of political action. The modern presidency operates in a political arena that is seldom congenial to meaningful political debate. . . . With the liberation of the executive from many of the constraints of party leadership and the rise of the mass media, presidents have resorted to rhetoric and administration, tools with which they have sought to forge new, more personal ties with the public. But, as the nation has witnessed all too clearly during the past twenty-five years, this form of "populist" presidential politics can all too readily degenerate into rank opportunism. Moreover, it risks exposing the people to the kind of public figures who will exploit citizens' impatience with the difficult tasks involved in sustaining a healthy constitutional democracy.

Presidents who enjoy prominent places in history have justified their reform programs in constitutional terms, claiming to restore the proper understanding of first principles, even as they have attempted to transfuse the Declaration [of Independence] and the Constitution with new meaning. But they have done so as great party leaders, in the midst of major partisan realignments. Critical partisan elections have enabled each generation to claim its right to redefine the Constitution's principles and reorganize its institutions. The New Deal continued this unending task to ensure that each generation could affirm its attachment to constitutional government. The burden of this generation is to hold the modern presidency to account, to recapture the understanding of democracy that has made such momentous deliberation and choice so central to the pursuit of America's political destiny.*

*Sidney M. Milkis, "The Presidency and Political Parties," in Peter Woll, ed., *American Government: Readings and Cases*, 13th ed. (New York: Longman, 1999), 309.

---

stage. Woodrow Wilson actively worked to free the presidency from party constraints by organizing support around the individual candidate. Using popular appeals and travel much more extensively than Roosevelt did, Wilson used the "bully pulpit" to mobilize public opinion behind his initiatives. In turn, Franklin D. Roosevelt standardized popular communication through regular fireside chats. Speaking directly to the people and capitalizing on radio just as Theodore Roosevelt had capitalized on the fledgling national media, FDR connected more closely with the people than any previous president had. His personal leadership, together with the institutional development of the presidency and the federal bureaucracy during the New Deal, made the Roosevelt era a watershed in the development of the office. Historian William E. Leuchtenberg summarizes FDR's influence on the presidency this way: "Under Roosevelt, the White House became the focus of all government—the fountainhead of ideas, the initiator of action, the representative of the national interest."[6]

The presidency exists in a system of shared powers and institutional competition for power and influence, but strong presidents have taken advantage of constitutional and implied powers to take actions they felt were necessary. The following is a brief list of some notable executive actions, followed by a few key efforts to check the use of executive power.

### EXECUTIVE ACTIONS . . .

*George Washington*

- establishes the office's independence and legitimacy
- with advisors, develops argument for executive privilege protecting executive-branch documents from congressional investigation (although Washington did not utilize the privilege)

*Andrew Jackson*

- uses veto extensively to block legislation
- uses patronage extensively to place political supporters in government jobs

*Abraham Lincoln*

- suspends the writ of habeas corpus during the Civil War (habeas corpus, guaranteed by the Constitution, requires that a person being held for trial be brought before a judge; the protection is designed to prevent the authorities from detaining people indefinitely without a trial)
- blockades southern ports
- spends funds for unauthorized purposes
- issues the Emancipation Proclamation without congressional approval

*Theodore Roosevelt*

- utilizes the growing national media to build the president's visibility and to mobilize public support for policies
- establishes the first White House press room

*Woodrow Wilson*

- builds on Roosevelt's model, attracting attention to the presidency
- works to free the president from party control

*Franklin D. Roosevelt*

- uses regular radio addresses—"fireside chats"—to build a personal relationship with a mass public
- commits U.S. funds to support Allies prior to official U.S. entry into World War II
- establishes the Executive Office of the President by Executive Order 8248, and oversees a tremendous expansion in institutions supporting the president
- directs the internment of Japanese Americans during World War II by Executive Order 9066
- attempts to "pack" the Supreme Court with new justices supportive of New Deal programs; the attempt fails
- oversees further separation of the president and the executive bureaucracy from party influences
- crafts and promotes a new conception of the federal government as the protector of economic security and the initiator of national programs

*Harry S Truman*

- commits troops to the Korean conflict without a congressional declaration of war
- attempts to nationalize most of the nation's steel mills to avert a workers' strike which Truman argued would harm the nation's military involvement in Korea
- integrates the armed forces with Executive Order 9981

*Dwight D. Eisenhower*

- uses federal troops to facilitate the integration of public schools

*Lyndon B. Johnson*

- commits troops to the Vietnam War without a congressional declaration of war

*Richard M. Nixon*

- continues the war in Vietnam without a formal declaration of war
- attempts to impound, or refuse to spend, funds appropriated by Congress

*Ronald Reagan*

- orders the bombing of Libya following Libyan terrorist attack
- orders a military invasion of the island of Grenada
- requires that major government regulations be justified by cost-benefit analysis by Executive Order 122291

*George Bush*

- leads the deployment and use of force in the Gulf War without a formal declaration of war
- mobilizes the military to remove Panamanian strongman Manuel Noriega from power

*Bill Clinton*

- uses military force in Bosnia and Kosovo without a formal declaration of war
- uses military force to restore Jean Bertrand Aristede to power in Haiti, without a congressional declaration of war

. . . AND REACTIONS

- 1952 *Steel Seizure Case:* Supreme Court rules, in *Youngstown Sheet and Tube v. Sawyer,* that President Truman's executive order directing the Secretary of Commerce to take possession of and operate most of the nation's steel mills oversteps the president's authority.
- 1973 *War Powers Act:* Congress attempts to limit the president's ability to fight wars without involving Congress. The Act requires the president to consult Congress "in every possible instance" before deploying forces abroad; report to Congress within forty-eight hours, and then periodically afterwards, about the deployment; and terminate deployment within sixty days unless Congress has specifically approved or the president has requested a thirty-day extension to protect the safety of personnel. Congress is also empowered to direct the withdrawal of troops by a veto-proof concurrent resolution. Largely untested in court, this Act has generally been ignored by presidents and its enforcement has been weak.
- 1974 *U.S. v. Nixon:* The Supreme Court rules that executive privilege does not apply to particular documents and audiotapes held by President Nixon, which had been subpoenaed as evidence in the Watergate investigation. The Court did, however, acknowledge the validity of executive privilege in general, especially in matters of national security.
- 1974 *Budget and Impoundment Act:* Congress responds to Nixon's impoundment of funds by legislating that all funds must be spent for their intended purpose.
- 1996 *Chamber of Commerce v. Reich:* Federal court overturns an executive order issued by Bill Clinton barring federal contractors from hiring permanent workers to replace workers on strike.

More recently, presidents have continued to increase their public appeals. John F. Kennedy, Ronald Reagan, and Bill Clinton have each used the media to build popular support for themselves as well as for their public initiatives. Kennedy and Reagan in particular used press conferences to build alliances through—and with—the media. The White House Press Office and the Office of Communications have become essential parts of the White House's activities, and daily briefings, background reports, and even leaks have become regular events for the White House press corps.

Interestingly, it is in coverage of the president that we can best see the news media serving both as government's adversary and as a helpful "coproducer" working with interested parties. Presidents are, by nature, policy advocates and partisan competitors; they thus tend to see the media either as aids in their battles or as obstacles. For the media, their desire for full information stands in direct opposition to the president's desire to control and manage information. It is natural, then, that the media and presidents tend to see each other as adversaries, and they often are. At the same time, though, the president can be the king of newsworthiness: familiar, personalized, current, easily set against some opponent for drama, and sometimes even relevant. Even as they stand as natural adversaries, then, the president and the media both benefit from co-producing stories and laying the adversarial relationship aside.

## *HAVEN'T WE MET BEFORE? SOME FAMILIAR COMPETITION IN THE CONSTITUTIONAL SYSTEM*

Not many years ago, observers of American politics echoed the framers' concerns in worrying about an "imperial presidency." In the wake of FDR's four terms, the charismatic leadership of Eisenhower and Kennedy, the strong executive leadership of Lyndon B. Johnson, and the White House scandal of Nixon's Watergate, critics feared that the presidency had become too powerful. Balancing an energetic and accountable president with the philosophy of the separation of powers is a tricky business. A president with too much power risks destroying the balance of competition in the system and threatens the kind of tyrannical despotism against which the founding generation fought in the first place.

In spite of Hamilton's hopes for an energetic president, and in spite of institutional advances and the increasing attention paid to the president as a national leader, major initiatives and simple orders emanating from the White

President Ronald Reagan's confidence and sense of humor endeared him to millions of Americans in the 1980s. Here, Reagan seemed to laugh in the face of surgery, showing off his half-shaved head to reporters as First Lady Nancy Reagan stands in the background.

House still fail. Why? In the competitive constitutional system, presidents regularly confront other interests that compete with the White House for power and influence. Presidential power, checked at almost every turn, is rarely as extensive as it appears. Bill Clinton's inability to pass major health care reform and the tangled implementation of his policy on gays in the military are just two examples of how the American system of divided power limits the executive's potential.

## President, Congress, and the Courts

When Bill Clinton entered the White House in 1993, with firm Democratic majorities in both houses, expectations were so high that Democrats had a difficult time agreeing on priorities and initiatives. Congressional incentives disorganize and fragment the legislative branch; a president can be at the mercy of those forces, even when his party controls both houses. Though Clinton wanted to push for health care reform, for example, a significant number of Senate members led by New York's Daniel Patrick Moynihan wanted to push first for welfare reform. The Democrats here and on other issues fought

---

### Zip Box 8.4
*Presidents and Interest Groups*

We noted in chapter 2 that interest groups tend to focus their action on congressional subcommittees, the bureaucracy, and the courts. In part, interest groups' decisions not to focus on the presidency are a function of the presidency's position in a competitive system, which makes it no more attractive a center of power than the other branches. In part, too, the fact that the president has a national constituency with diverse supporters, and limited control over budgets and implementation, makes him a less-than-optimal target for lobbying efforts.

Interest groups, though, do not ignore the White House completely. White House support can augment other lobbying techniques, and the president's visibility on issues and his power in designating certain issues for attention makes him a valuable resource in the right circumstances. Interest groups are deeply involved in campaigns and elections, both in influencing candidates' positions and in working to raise money and mobilize voters. After being elected, presidents continue regular contacts with interest groups, particularly those that helped get them elected. Fi-

nally, interest groups and the presidency are involved in "reverse lobbying," in which the president enlists the support of interest groups on a particular issue. Though official lobbying activity is limited by the Anti-Lobbying Act of 1919, presidents coordinate and help focus interest group activity on behalf of specific measures. President Clinton, for example, enlisted groups' input and support on behalf of his health care reform proposal. Clinton also carefully coordinated lobbying efforts on behalf of his 1992 campaign promise to put one hundred thousand new police officers on the streets. Groups not only provided active lobbying support, pressuring Congress and mobilizing individuals and public opinion; they also were involved in designing the legislation and in building compromises that ensured wide support among diverse law enforcement interests and organizations.

*Source:* See Ronald G. Shaiko, "Reverse Lobbying: Interest Group Mobilization from the White House and the Hill," in *Interest Group Politics*, 5th ed., ed. Allan J. Cigler and Burdett A. Loomis (Washington, DC: CQ Press, 1998).

among themselves and quarreled over which congressional committees and which members would take the lead in these important areas. Clinton was unable to persuade sufficient forces within Congress that supporting his health care reform plan was in their interest.

Congress's *independence from presidential control* establishes that branch as the president's major competitor for influence and leadership, and Clinton's failure on health care reform demonstrates how the independence of Congress and the shared legislative powers across the two branches limit the power of even a popular president with a popular issue. Members of Congress have their own constituencies, which have their own interests and agendas; these often differ from those of the president. The weak ties between individual presidents and members of Congress fail to provide a reliable means of coordinating these interests and presidential-congressional relations. Clinton, like many presidents before him, failed to pass his primary policy initiative because he failed to secure Congress's help.

Because of Congress's independence, the powers it shares with the presidency, and its ability to counter expansions of executive authority, the president needs to work carefully with Congress when acting to make public policy. The president must persuade members of Congress that they and the president have mutual interests. In a narrowly divided Congress, presidents often need to court members of the opposition party to ensure legislative majorities; presidents in that situation are always in danger of losing a few votes from party members and being embarrassed on the national stage.

Congress has also taken *direct actions* over the years to limit or check expansions in presidential power. For example, the War Powers Act of 1973 sought to limit the president's ability to use military force by mandating that he report to

Time will tell which image of the Clinton presidency will endure: the victorious Bill Clinton, with First Lady Hillary Clinton and daughter Chelsea, who swept the Democrats into the White House—or the downcast, scandal-ridden Clinton, shown here in 1998 after delivering a short statement related to Congress's impeachment inquiry.

Congress when troops are used in areas where hostilities are occurring or imminent; by requiring Congress to provide for continued action by such troops after sixty days; and by providing that if Congress does not grant a continuance, the president must withdraw the troops. The Act also stipulated that the president must abide by any concurrent resolution ordering the removal of troops. The courts later struck down parts of the War Power Act, and no president has formally acknowledged the Act (it passed despite President Nixon's veto). The provisions for notifying Congress remain untested in court. (See Zip Box 8.3.)

The president must also compete with the courts, which have also taken *direct action* to limit executive power. Because the courts are a point of resolution for conflicts between the branches of government, they are often the appropriate place for resolving issues over where, exactly, power lies in the constitutional system. Courts try to avoid "political questions," but they have at times weighed in on important matters. For example, the Supreme Court ruled that President Truman's 1952 seizure of steel mills to avoid a strike by steel workers was unconstitutional (see Zip Box 8.3). The courts also *can impose significant new duties* on the presidency. For example, the Supreme Court's school desegregation rulings in the 1950s imposed new demands on the presidency's time and resources. The courts, then, can vie with the presidency for leadership and they can put checks on executive actions.

## Competition for Control of the Bureaucracy

We have seen how expansions in the federal bureaucracy increase the power and authority of the executive branch. Presidents focus their efforts to influence the bureaucracy on their *ability to appoint leaders* to administrative agencies, on their *ability to influence agency budget requests* through the OMB, and through the *signing of executive orders*. Unfortunately for presidents, numerous other factors complicate their efforts to direct the actions of the bureaucracy: because a vast number of career civil servants are not subject to presidential appointment or removal, and because it often takes years to make major changes in the budgets of federal programs, even these powers are limited. And as we saw in chapter 7, agencies, Congress, and the courts all compete for influence over administrative actions.

Presidents can appoint agency heads, but *agencies have their own competitive weapons* to use against interference by the president. Agencies have their own agendas and they promote their own interests, and agencies' agendas are often at odds with one another—these dynamics limit the president's ability to control the bureaucracy. The president can also become caught between battling bureaucracies as they compete with each other for resources and for attention. For example, in the late 1990s the president's official AIDS czar, Sandra Thurman, promoted a needle-exchange program designed to reduce AIDS infections among drug users. This effort ran counter to opinion in the president's Office of National Drug Control Policy, headed by retired General Barry McCaffrey. Within the executive branch itself, then, the president had advisors and underlings on different sides of a key issue. With only so much money and time to go around, the president must oversee bureaucratic competition and must weather criticism from his own agencies that he is overlook-

ON THE WEB
www.whitehouse.gov/
WH/Services/

ing important aspects of government or taking the wrong positions on controversial issues.

Congress and the courts also compete with the president for control of the bureaucracy. When the president and the Congress have divergent programs, both work through the bureaucracy to influence policy and its implementation. Even though many federal agencies are formally in the line of authority extending down from the White House, *Congress* has an important and influential role as overseer of the bureaucracy, as the dispenser of federal funds for agency programs, and also as an ally for agencies seeking to protect and promote their own interests. *The courts* also have a say in the competition for control of the bureaucracy: they have an important role in condoning or condemning the actions agencies take, and they can order agencies to take actions or *not* to take actions—regardless of the president's desires.

Finally, the *separation of powers* limits the ability of the executive branch to create long-term change independently. Any changes accomplished by executive order are subject to reversal by a later president with different views. Further, executive orders are not guaranteed to affect the way administrative agencies function, even during the signer's administration. Consider the example of gays in the military: When President Clinton signed the executive order lifting the ban, he provided a catalyst for opposition and a focus for debate. The military itself opposed the measure and worked to block its implementation. Having failed to alter policy effectively with the stroke of a pen, the president was suddenly in the position of needing to *persuade* the military and the public not only that the measure was proper, but that it would be effective without sacrificing the integrity of national defense. Changing an agency's actions or priorities can be difficult even when that agency *wants* to follow an executive order; it is considerably more difficult if the bureaucracy—like the military—opposes the goal of the order.

## C'mon, It'll Be Good for You!: The Power to Persuade

Despite the vast powers and potential of the presidency, the president is usually unable to unilaterally dictate courses of action and policies of government. He is at odds with Congress, the courts, the bureaucracy—and increasingly, he lacks the stability and strength that once emanated from his ties to a political party. Political scientist Richard E. Neustadt, in his classic book *Presidential Power,* writes that although the president is still a leader in form, in actual practice he is more like a clerk than a king: "His services are in demand all over Washington. His influence, however, is a very different matter." The reason for this is that all other actors in the political system have their own goals and agendas—they represent their own interests, not those of the president. Neustadt continues:

> Since everyone depends on [the president] why is he not assured of everyone's support? The answer is that no one else sits where he sits, or sees quite as he sees; no one else feels the full weight of his obligations. Those obligations are a tribute to his unique place in our political system. But just because it is unique they fall on him alone. *The same conditions that promote his leadership in form preclude a guarantee of leadership in fact.* No man or groups at either end

of Pennsylvania Avenue shares his peculiar status in our government and politics. That is why his services are in demand. By the same token, though, the obligations of all other men are different from his own. His Cabinet officers have departmental duties and constituents. His legislative leaders head *congressional* parties, one in either House. His national party organization stands apart from his official family. His political allies in the States need not face Washington, or one another. The private groups that seek him out are not compelled to govern. And friends abroad are not compelled to run in our elections. Lacking his position and his prerogatives, these men cannot regard his obligations as their own. They have their jobs to do; none is the same as his. As they perceive their duty they may find it right to follow him, in fact, or they may not.[7]

Because all of the other forces have their own interests, presidential power often rests on the president's success in persuading others that their interests are the same as his own. The need for a president to persuade others to see things his way—and the ineffectiveness of *commanding* loyalty—compels the president to participate in the competitive political system and to interact with forces challenging the White House for power and influence. The number of forces checking the president prevents the president from getting his way without the help of others, so competition places a premium on the president's ability to bargain and negotiate. (See Scholar Box 8.1.)

## Scholar Box 8.1
### *Neustadt: The Power to Persuade*

A tale from the years after World War II neatly captures the difficulty of being president, and the way in which the leader of the strongest, most prosperous nation on earth is not nearly as powerful as we might expect. Americans elected Dwight "Ike" Eisenhower president in 1952. Eisenhower, a career military man, the leader of victorious Allied forces in World War II, and the architect of the D-Day invasion at Normandy in 1944, was a popular and respected general. His predecessor in the White House, Harry Truman, once predicted how surprised Ike would be to find out that being president was not like being a general. Truman said of Eisenhower, "He'll sit here, and he'll say, 'Do this! Do that!' *And nothing will happen.* Poor Ike—it won't be a bit like the Army."*

The following passage comes from Richard E. Neustadt's classic analysis of the president's need to utilize the power of persuasion in our competitive political system. According to Neustadt, what role do charm and reason play as a president tries to persuade others? How do shared powers influ-

ence a president's tasks? What is the best way to persuade others? Why?

The separateness of institutions and the sharing of authority prescribe the terms on which a President persuades. When one man shares authority with another, but does not gain or lose his job upon the other's whim, his willingness to act upon the urging of the other turns on whether he conceives the action right for him. The essence of a President's persuasive task is to convince such men that what the White House wants of them is what they ought to do for their sake and on their authority.

Persuasive power, thus defined, amounts to more than charm or reasoned argument. These have their uses for a President, but these are not the whole of his resources. For the men he would induce to do what he wants done on their own responsibility will need or fear some acts by him on his responsibility. If they share his authority, he has some share in theirs. Presidential "powers" may be inconclusive when a President commands, but always remain relevant as he persuades. The status and authority inherent in his office reinforce his logic and his charm. . . .

The essence of a President's persuasive task with congressmen and everybody else, *is to induce them to believe that what he wants of them is what their own appraisal of their own responsibilities requires them to do in their interest, not his.* Because men may differ in their views on public policy, because differences in outlook stem from differences in duty—duty to one's office, one's constituents, oneself—that task is bound to be more like collective bargaining than like a reasoned argument among philosopher kings. Overtly or implicitly, hard bargaining has characterized all illustrations [of presidential persuasion] offered up to now. This is the reason why: persuasion deals in the coin of self-interest with men who have some freedom to reject what they find counterfeit.[†]

*Quoted in I. M. Destler, *Presidents, Bureacrats, and Foreign Policy: The Politics of Organizational Reform* (Princeton: Princeton University Press, 1974), p. 52 [emphasis in original].
[†]Richard E. Neustadt, *Presidential Power: The Politics of Leadership* (New York: Signet, 1964), 43, 53.

---

# DISCUSSION BOX 8.2
### DUMB AND DUMBER: HOW SMART SHOULD A PRESIDENT BE?

Are intellectual presidents good presidents? Historian and presidential expert Richard Brookhiser recently examined this question, focusing on Theodore Roosevelt, William Taft, and Woodrow Wilson. His analysis raises questions about the qualities and characteristics of individual presidents. According to the passages below, what advantages do intellectual politicians enjoy? What factors, besides intellectualism, affect a president's performance? Think about how American government operates: what benefits and drawbacks might an intellectual president face in a political system driven by competition, bargaining, and compromise?

How smart is it to put smart guys in power?

The first time America tried to do such a thing, it worked very well. The Founding Thinkers—Franklin, Jefferson, Hamilton, Madison, Adams, Gouverneur Morris—belong on any all-time short list of political immortals, and their success gave the idea of ideas a special place in American politics. America, it could plausibly be argued, was a nation of ideas—"dedicated to a 'proposition,' " as Lincoln put it at Gettysburg.

We are in another era of political intellectuals now, admittedly less glittering. For four years the Speaker of the House was Newt Gingrich, a former history professor with a didactic streak, who bristled with pet ideas, from the scholarship of the American Revolutionary historian Gordon S. Wood to the futurism of Alvin and Heidi Toffler. One of his assignments to the Republican freshmen of the 104th Congress was a reading list. Probably not all of them plowed through Tocqueville's *Democracy in America,* but I know at least one middle-aged activist who did. Last year Gingrich was deposed, but his number two man in the House remains: Dick Armey, a former economics professor. Meanwhile at the White House there is Bill Clinton, no scholar (though he was a Rhodes scholar) but as fond as Gingrich of spritzing ideas.

. . . To the extent that they are wordsmiths, intellectual politicians can be effective press agents for their ideas and for themselves. This can give them a quick start in the race for office and success.

Whether they go on to victory and achievement depends in part on their character. Perhaps the success of the early American smart guys relied on the steadying presence of a George Washington in their midst. Washington, though smart, would have been the first to say that he was no intellectual (he called his own education, which included no time in college, "defective"). Socrates, who first recommended philosopher kings—let us "appoint as Guardians," he argued in *The Republic,* ". . . those who have learned to know the ideal reality of things"—added that the right ideas were not enough; the philosopher king should also possess "experience" and "virtue," areas in which everyone gave Washington the highest marks. The three philosophers who followed him in the White House—Adams, Jefferson, and Madison—served five terms altogether, of which only one (Jefferson's first) was a success. Perhaps the wise leader should strive to have intellectuals on tap and not be one himself.*

*Richard Brookhiser, "How Smart Should a President Be?" *American Heritage,* September 1999, pp. 59–60, 65.

*ONE FOR ALL AND ONE FOR SOME:*
*THE COMPETING ROLES AND*
*RESPONSIBILITIES OF THE PRESIDENT*

### It Might Look Simple, But It's Not (Reprise): Being the President

When six firefighters were killed in the line of duty in Massachusetts, President Clinton went to the city of Worcester to attend the funeral. To redirect the nation's foreign affairs, President Richard Nixon visited Communist China at the height of the cold war. President George Bush rallied domestic and international support, directing the deployment and use of military force against Saddam Hussein's aggression in Kuwait. The president's responsibilities as chief of state, leader of foreign affairs, and commander in chief of the military place the president at the head of the nation's people, representing the interests of all Americans regardless of partisan conflict and interest group competition.

Yet presidents also attend party fundraisers and appoint party loyalists to government posts, they work to enact controversial and sometimes divisive legislative initiatives, and they execute policies through a bureaucratic structure at least partially responsive to political—and partisan—leadership.

In short, some of the president's roles and responsibilities place the president at the head of all the nation's people, unifying the population and its leadership in the person of a single individual. When the president acts as chief of state, as the leader of foreign affairs, and as commander in chief of the military, he is, for the most part, representing the American people. At other times, however, the president is called upon to fulfill roles that divide interests and people: when he acts as his party's leader, for example, or when he acts as the chief executive or as legislative leader. These roles encourage the president to promote certain goals and interests to the detriment of others. Political scientist <u>Thomas Cronin</u> puts it this way:

> [T]here exists a kind of public schizophrenia that deeply complicates the task of presidential leadership. Americans want a government that is isolated and protected from the worst aspects of partisan politics. But they also want a government that is controlled not by 'faceless bureaucrats' but by elected leaders who will keep it responsive to popular concerns. Those are contradictory goals. How is it possible to have a government that is simultaneously free of politics and under political control? The answer, of course, is that it is not possible.[8]

Just as Americans want their political parties to reconcile interests and bring order to political competition, all the while battling for partisan advantage and electoral success, the demands Americans make on the presidency are fundamentally conflicted. These competing views make it easy to criticize the president, and they fill the atmosphere around the president with a sense of conflict, hope, and inevitable disappointment.

## The President as National Leader

The president is the nation's *chief of state,* acting as the focal point of ceremonial functions in the United States related to both foreign and domestic affairs. Representing the entire nation and its people to interests abroad, the president receives ambassadors and heads of state and leads formal gatherings like state dinners. Related to these duties are practical functions like signing treaties and making key appointments to the foreign service. The president is also expected to represent the American people at domestic ceremonial events, such as the lighting of the national Christmas tree. As chief of state, the president is also expected to appear at the sites of, or at least respond to, national tragedies. Thus the president tours flood-ravaged areas in the Midwest and visits the scenes of national tragedies like the bombing of the Murrah Federal Building in Oklahoma City. These duties are important: they draw together a nation conditioned to competition and the promotion of self-interest, and they reflect the importance of the United States to foreign interests. Snubbing an ambassador can upset and even anger foreign nations, just as inattention to an unexpected national crisis can alienate large segments of the general population.

The president is also the *leader of the nation's foreign affairs.* In many ways, this role is connected with that of chief of state and with the president's role as commander in chief. The president represents the American people when travelling abroad, and acts as a primary force in the design and implementation of foreign policy. Finally, the president's role as *commander in chief* makes the president the visible head of military affairs for the entire nation.

## The President as Partisan Leader

In stark contrast to the president's roles as national leader, the president is the most visible member of his political party—and head of all of its partisan positions and actions. The contradiction between the president's role as *party leader* and his role as chief of state could not be more insoluble. The dilemma, in short, is this: When the president acts to promote the goals of his party and his supporters, he risks running afoul of those who interpret such actions as being against the national interest; opponents can always make this case when the president promotes a specific position on an issue. At the same time, though, a president who fails to support the goals and beliefs of his party and supporters not only risks being seen as a wavering president with no vision or positions, he risks losing the support of the people who put him in the White House in the first place.

The president is also a *legislative leader,* using the attention and clarity of the single executive to be an influential catalyst in the design and promotion of legislation. There are several constitutional sources for this role. The Constitution gives the president the authority to recommend legislation to Congress. Further, the Constitution requires the president to address Congress on the state of the union—this is, and always has been, a golden opportunity for the president to propose new measures and promote (or criticize) existing ones. As the most visible member of a political party, the president has a responsibility to the members of that party to organize and promote a legislative plan reflecting the party's goals. Finally, as head of the bureaucracy, the president can call on agencies to help design legislation in their specific areas before it is sent to Congress.

The Constitution assigns to the president the responsibility of seeing that the laws are faithfully executed. The role of *chief executive* is one of the president's primary functions, and also one of the most difficult. How is one person supposed to see that the laws are faithfully executed? A major answer to this is through the bureaucracy. As we saw in chapter 7, the Constitution places the president at the head of the bureaucracy, even though important appointment powers and influence over funding the departments and agencies are shared with Congress.

The nationally oriented chief-of-state role and the partisan chief executive role compete with each other for the president's time and attention, and they can sometimes create dilemmas. Many other nations split the roles of chief of state and chief executive, assigning the ceremonial duties of a head of state to a monarch or a royal personage and giving responsibility for executive duties to a prime minister. The notion that the American president can meet all of the office's responsibilities simultaneously to the satisfaction of all citizens creates unrealistic expectations for the office and its inhabitant, as the president struggles to be all things to all people (see Discussion Box 8.3).

## Politics, Expectations, and the Presidency

Political scientist Thomas Cronin neatly summarizes the paradoxes surrounding Americans' expectations of the presidency:

> The presidency will surely remain one of our nation's best sources for creative leadership. Indeed, a strong, effective President is a necessity if we are to make our system work. Hamiltonian energy in the Presidency is needed to make our Madisonian system of checks and balances work in such a way as to allow us to achieve those cherished Jeffersonian ends of liberty, freedom, and social justice. The paradoxes of the Presidency do not lie in the White House so much as in our own feelings and exalted hopes. There continues to exist some element in the minds of Americans that it is possible to find a savior-hero who will deliver us to some promised land. And then when this pseudo-messiah fails us, we inflict upon him the wrath of our vengeance. It is almost a ritual purifying or savaging—we venerate the Presidency and the White House though we punish the President. Perhaps this is to be expected when we elevate flawed and very human politicians who lust after fame and glory to an office we fill with our hopes and our fears and about which we remain of so many minds.[9]

Even without unusual dynamics like those characterizing the 2000 election, presidents face these paradoxes from the moment they take office. A sitting Vice President who wins the White House will be expected to maintain the political momentum built up by the previous president, to duplicate the predecessor's successes, or to overcome the previous administration's failures. An out-party challenger winning the White House will generate high expectations

Reliant on polls during campaigns, Bill Clinton used polls extensively as a governing tool. Governance by poll raises uneasy images of leaders too beholden to popular support—something scholars of president-party relationships as well as the framers themselves have worried about since the design of the office took shape in 1787.

The competition between leadership and responsiveness lies at the core of any elected official's responsibilities. In particular, the "perpetual campaign" raises worries that presidents will make leadership decisions based on what public opinion polls say the public wants—whether or not the public knows what it's talking about. In the passages below, James Madison and former Clinton advisor Dick Morris comment on the relationships between public opinion and government activity. According to Madison, what relationship exists between a country's size and the ability to know public opinion? How might Morris respond to Madison's last statement, about facilitating "a general intercourse of sentiments"? How can a president know when to respond to the public and when to lead against the tide of public opinion?

### Madison

Public opinion sets bounds to every government, and is the real sovereign in every free one.

As there are cases where the public opinion must be obeyed by the government; so there are cases, where not being fixed, it may be influenced by the government. . . .

The larger a country, the less easy for its real opinion to be ascertained, and the less difficult to be counterfeited; when ascertained or presumed, the more respectable it is in the eyes of individuals. This is favorable to the authority of government. For the same reason, the more extensive a country, the more insignificant is each individual in his own eyes. This may be unfavorable to liberty.

Whatever facilitates a general intercourse of sentiments, as good roads, domestic commerce, a free press, and particularly a *circulation of newspapers through the entire body of the people,* and *Representatives going from, and returning among every part of them,* is equivalent to a contraction of territorial limits, and is favorable to liberty, where these may be too extensive.*

### Morris

The emphasis on polling . . . naturally gives rise to the question of whether it has become a substitute for leadership. Voters have never much liked the idea that candidates merely spout what pollsters have told them the public wants to hear. It smacks of opportunism. But Clinton used polling for a different purpose: as a tool for governing, as a technique to facilitate progress in a democracy. Polling for him was not a onetime test of opinion. It was a way of conducting an extensive dialogue with the public. . . . When the polls indicated that his position on an issue was unpopular, he would usually ask for a study of how he could convince people of his point of view.†

*James Madison, *National Gazette,* December 19, 1791, reprinted in James Madison, *Writings* (New York: Library of America, 1999), 500–501 [italics in original].

†Dick Morris, *Behind the Oval Office: Getting Reelected Against All Odds* (Los Angeles: Renaissance Books, 1999), 338.

---

from followers too long estranged from power, as well as demands that the tone and priorities of government be reversed quicky and successfully.

Ironically, the unusual circumstances of the 2000 election may lower expectations for the presidency as an institution, at least temporarily. Given the final breakdown of the popular vote and the confusion surrounding the electoral vote in the 2000 race, together with the close margins of control in both houses of Congress, few will expect much effective energy to emanate from the White House any time soon. The 2000 election produced a lot of things, but it did not produce a new pseudo-messiah.

The final story of the 2000 election and its unique effects on the country, however, has yet to be written. Americans often look to assign responsibility when the nation passes through a crisis or when presidents fail to deliver the country to the promised land, and the American people may still gorge on the ritual savaging of the president. Neither candidate could have emerged from the 2000 election with the kind of veneration that citizens reserve for the office of the president. The best any new president can hope to achieve, even under normal circumstances, is to control the transition process.

A new president's earliest decisions help set the tone and the expectations that surround a new administration. First, the transition from campaigning to governing sets themes that can stay with an administration for years. As presidency scholar Charles O. Jones writes, transitions are a chance to establish credibility, adaptability, and organizational agility. The transition is a launching point for first impressions and future expectations surrounding the new administration. Transitions are also important because of the "theme" that they convey to the public about the incoming administration. Jones argues that if a transition team fails to advance its own theme, one will be provided for it by observers and by the media.[10] As part of the transition, the appointment process exemplifies the president's need to satisfy diverse political interests while establishing the direction and priorities of his administration (see BriefCase Box 8.2).

Second, a new president faces questions about the move from running a campaign to running an administration. The "perpetual campaign" of the Clinton administration, in which the transition and Clinton's two administrations seemed to be extensions of his original campaign for the office, has made the transition period an even more significant bridge between the campaign and governing. Critics will be ready to capitalize on partisan activities undertaken by the new administration, and they will be quick to condemn exercises in leadership as pandering to public opinion polls (see Discussion Box 8.3).

---

## Zip Box 8.5
*Five More Mean Things People Said about the Presidents*

1. **H. L. Mencken, on Franklin D. Roosevelt:** "If [President Roosevelt] became convinced tomorrow that coming out for cannibalism would get him the votes he sorely needs, he would begin fattening a missionary in the White House backyard come Wednesday."

2. **Harry S Truman, on Richard M. Nixon:** "Richard Nixon is a no-good lying bastard. He can lie out of both sides of his mouth at the same time, and if he ever caught himself telling the truth, he'd lie just to keep his hand in."

3. **Lyndon B. Johnson, on Gerald R. Ford:** "He's a nice fellow but he spent too much time playing football without a helmet."

4. **Jim Hightower, on George Bush, 1988:** "If ignorance ever goes to $40 a barrel, I want the drilling rights on George Bush's head."

5. **New York Times, endorsing Bill Clinton prior to the 1992 presidential election:** "Bill Clinton, though highly regarded by other governors, has not previously been tested on the national stage. He has, when pressed, shown a discomfiting tendency to blur truthful clarity."

*Source:* Adapted from William A. DeGregorio, *The Complete Book of U.S. Presidents: From George Washington to George Bush* (New York: Wings Books, 1991); except for the last entry, which is from "George Bush's Failure—Bill Clinton's Promise" [editorial], *New York Times,* October 25, 1992: p. D14.

| | Political experience | Clientele or ethnic group identification | Technical expertise | Pre-tenure friendship |
|---|:---:|:---:|:---:|:---:|
| **INNER CABINET** | | | | |
| Defense | | | | |
|   Les Aspin | ✔ | | ✔ | |
| Justice | | | | |
|   Janet Reno | | ✔ | ✔ | |
| State | | | | |
|   Warren M. Christopher | ✔ | | ✔ | |
| Treasury | | | | |
|   Lloyd Bentsen | ✔ | | ✔ | |
| **OUTER CABINET** | | | | |
| Agriculture | | | | |
|   Mike Espy | ✔ | ✔ | | |
| Commerce | | | | |
|   Ronald H. Brown | ✔ | ✔ | | |
| Education | | | | |
|   Richard W. Riley | ✔ | | | ✔ |
| Energy | | | | |
|   Hazel O'Leary | | ✔ | ✔ | |
| Health and Human Services | | | | |
|   Donna E. Shalala | | ✔ | | ✔ |
| Housing and Urban Development | | | | |
|   Henry G. Cisneros | ✔ | ✔ | | |
| Interior | | | | |
|   Bruce Babbitt | ✔ | | | |
| Labor | | | | |
|   Robert B. Reich | | | ✔ | ✔ |
| Transportation | | | | |
|   Federico Peña | ✔ | ✔ | | |
| Veterans Affairs | | | | |
|   Jesse Brown | | ✔ | | |
| **CABINET-LEVEL POSITIONS** | | | | |
| EPA Administrator | | | | |
|   Carol M. Browner | ✔ | ✔ | ✔ | |
| OMB Director | | | | |
|   Leon E. Panetta | ✔ | | ✔ | |
| United Nations Ambassador | | | | |
|   Madeleine K. Albright | | ✔ | ✔ | |
| U.S. Trade Representative | | | | |
|   Michael Kantor | | ✔ | | |

The cabinet consists of the major executive department heads; presidents can raise other departments to the cabinet level to reflect their interests and priorities. Presidents must consider a number of factors in making appointments, including satisfying political debts and building ties to important consituencies, reflecting goals like diversity, ensuring that appointees are skilled administrators or experts in particular areas, and recognizing the important role of Congress in approving nominations and in future interactions with the appointees. The table on p. 251, developed by political scientists Norman C. Thomas and Joseph A. Pika, illustrates these considerations in Bill Clinton's initial cabinet appointments. Which criteria seem to be the most common? Which are the least common? Do you notice any relationship between the positions and the criteria used to select nominees?

*Source:* Table from Norman C. Thomas and Joseph A. Pika, *The Politics of the Presidency,* 4th ed. (Washington, DC: CQ Press, 1996), 258.

## Conclusion

The president operates in a system of shared powers, relying as much on the powers of persuasion as on the institutional strengths and leadership opportunities enjoyed by the White House. A president's successes, as well as his failures, are intimately related to his ability to operate in a complex and crowded political system. Among the most important players in that system is the United States Congress, to which we turn in the next chapter.

## Overnight Assignment

Review the president's appearances in the news recently. Has the president appeared on television? Why? Do you think it was a necessary appearance? Has the president responded to any events or occurrences lately? What role or roles was the president fulfilling? Did the president's actions come in for criticism or approval by other aspects of the system? What were these reactions, and why were they made?

## Long-Term Integrated Assignment

Consider the issue you've chosen and the interests involved in it. Do they expect or demand different things from the executive? If so, what demands are the interests making? Do these demands appeal to different aspects of the president's job, as discussed in the text? For example, does one interest make demands that call for the president to exercise popular leadership, while another makes demands that rest on the constitutional duties of the office? Do any interests argue that the president has exceeded the powers granted to the office by the Constitution?

In the previous chapter, you looked at how a public agency was involved in your chosen issue. Why was the agency's head appointed to the post? Is the agency head's position on this issue different from the president's? If so, why?

**Try These Authors:**

Thomas E. Cronin          Sidney M. Milkis          Richard E. Neustadt
Charles O. Jones          Michael Nelson          Clinton Rossiter

**Try These Sources:**

BARBER, JAMES DAVID. *The Presidential Character: Predicting Performance in the White House.* Englewood Cliffs, NJ: Prentice-Hall, 1977.

BOND, JON R. and RICHARD FLEISHER, eds. *Polarized Politics: Congress and the President in a Partisan Era.* Washington, DC: CQ Press, 2000.

BROOKHISER, RICHARD. *Founding Father: Rediscovering George Washington.* New York: Free Press, 1996.

GREENSTEIN, FRED I. *The Presidential Difference: Leadership Style from FDR to Clinton.* New York: Free Press, 2000.

PFIFFNER, JAMES P., ed. *The Managerial Presidency.* Pacific Grove, CA: Brooks/Cole Publishing, 1991.

SCHLESINGER, ARTHUR M. JR. *The Imperial Presidency.* Boston: Houghton Mifflin, 1973.

SKOWRONEK, STEPHEN. *The Politics Presidents Make: Leadership from John Adams to George Bush.* Cambridge, MA: Belknap Press, 1993.

THURBER, JAMES, ed. *Rivals for Power: Presidential-Congressional Relations.* Washington, DC: CQ Press, 1996.

WALSH, KENNETH T. *Feeding the Beast: The White House versus the Press.* New York: Random House, 1996.

WILLS, GARRY. *Lincoln at Gettysburg: The Words that Remade America.* New York: Simon & Schuster, 1992.

*Endnotes* ▬▬▬▬▬▬▬▬▬▬▬

1. Quoted in Max Farrand, *The Framing of the Constitution of the United States* (New Haven: Yale University Press, 1967 [1913]), 164.

2. Quoted in R. Gordon Hoxie, "The Presidency in the Constitutional Convention," in *The American Presidency: Historical and Contemporary Perspectives,* ed. Harry A. Bailey, Jr., and Jay M. Shafritz (Pacific Grove, CA: Brooks/Cole, 1988), 12.

3. Farrand, *The Framing of the Constitution,* 162.

4. Quoted in Hoxie, "The Presidency in the Constitutional Convention," 10.

5. Sidney M. Milkis and Michael Nelson, *The American Presidency: Origins and Development, 1776–1990* (Washington, DC: CQ Press, 1990), 269.

6. William E. Leuchtenberg, *Franklin D. Roosevelt and the New Deal* (New York: Harper Torchbooks, 1963), 327.

7. Richard E. Neustadt, *Presidential Power: The Politics of Leadership* (New York: Signet, 1964), 20–21.

8. Thomas Cronin, "How Much Is His Fault?," The New York Times Magazine, October 16, 1994; for more on the diverse roles and responsibilities of the president as discussed in this section, see Clinton Rossiter, *The American Presidency,* revised ed. (New York: Mentor, 1960), chs. 1–2.

9. Thomas Cronin, "How Much Is His Fault?" *New York Times Magazine,* October 16, 1994.

10. Charles O. Jones, *Passages to the Presidency: From Campaigning to Governing* (Washington, DC: Brookings Institution Press, 1998), 179, 186.

# Congress

## CHAPTER OUTLINE

With few exceptions, no building in downtown Washington, D.C. may be built to stand higher than the Capitol dome. This symbolizes the dominance of Congress over the other branches of the government—a dominance clearly foreseen by the framers of the American Constitution. Congress is the Lockean institution that embodies popular sovereignty. It is the Madisonian branch that checks the president, representing the people in the House and the states in the Senate.

Maybe Americans want taller buildings in the nation's capital. The American people hold Congress, as an institution, in low esteem. They question the ethics and efficiency of Congress, feeling that most members of Congress are self-serving and out to enrich themselves and their friends at the expense of the public. The president, the media, and even members of Congress themselves fortify this popular distrust of Congress. Presidents accuse Congress of acting selfishly and against the national interest when Capitol Hill fulfills its constitutional responsibility of checking the White House. National media coverage of Congress as an institution is more often negative than positive; the media aggressively investigate congressional scandals and ethics questions, sometimes accusing members of Congress of improprieties before there is evidence to support the accusations. Finally, and most ironically, members of Congress "run against" Congress itself in their reelection campaigns, separating themselves from the institution and accusing it of inefficiency, neglect of duty, and even malfeasance. They know all too well the popularity of the anti-Congress theme.

Despite popular disdain for Congress and perennial calls for reform, however, people tend to give high marks to their individual representatives and, as we saw in chapter 4, constituencies reelect incumbents to both houses year after year after year. And although at times it is overshadowed by the presidency, Congress valiantly attempts to control the reins of power in Washington. By any measure it is a critical part of the Washington power establishment, perhaps more important than the presidency in its ability to shape the development and implementation of policy. Congress has more permanency and more expertise than the president and his personal staff, who tend to leave their jobs just as they reach the threshold of understanding the complexities as well as the important limits of presidential power.

**The Bottom Line.** Congress is the cornerstone of American government; its roles in representation, lawmaking, and overseeing government activities involve virtually every aspect of American politics. Congress's authority is ex-

*Zip Box 9.1*
*Don't Hate the Player, Hate the Game*

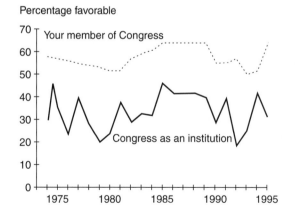

**Public Opinion of Congress and Members**
*Source:* Figure from Roger H. Davidson and Walter J. Oleszek, *Congress and Its Members,* 5th ed. (Washington, DC: CQ Press, 1996), 426.

pansive, a function of enumerated constitutional powers and helpful rulings from the Supreme Court, yet it is also checked and balanced by other institutions and by its own bicameral structure. Members strive for reelection, especially early in their careers, and for power and policy influence within Congress. In many ways, the activities and structure of the modern Congress are designed to maximize members' ability to meet these goals. Congress's lawmaking and oversight responsibilities endlessly multiply competition and the need for compromise across Capitol Hill, creating an open public policy process that produces change only incrementally.

## COMPETITION ALL OVER THE PLACE: BICAMERALISM AND REPRESENTATION IN AMERICA

James Madison emphasized, in *Federalist 51*, that "In republican government, the legislative authority necessarily predominates." It predominates because the legislature represents popular sovereignty, which is supreme. Congress's powers under Article 1 of the Constitution—such as the powers to tax and provide for the general welfare, regulate commerce among the states, declare war, and raise and support armies—constitute the very core of national power. Despite the independent executive and the Supreme Court, Congress is the cornerstone of the constitutional government. Its powers are the most extensive the Constitution delegates to any branch of the national government. Further, the constitutional powers of Congress gave it potentially vast authority over the states—authority confirmed and sanctioned by the Supreme Court under Chief Justice John Marshall, which cemented the foundation for a vast expansion of national and congressional power over the states through a "loose" interpretation of Congress's enumerated powers.

### The Bicameral Framework: Institutional Competition within the Legislative Branch

The American national legislature consists of two houses: the House of Representatives, with seats apportioned to states according to their populations, and the Senate, in which each state holds two seats. This bicameral, or two-house, legislature fulfilled two purposes at the framing. First, bicameralism reflects the framers' wariness of concentrated power. Because of its role as primary lawmaking authority, the framers believed, Congress would be the dominant, and therefore most dangerous, branch of the federal government. So even as the framers distributed powers among the branches of government to prevent tyranny, they designed special mechanisms to thwart this threat by fragmenting and checking legislative power *within the legislative branch itself.* (See Discussion Box 9.1.)

Bicameralism helped prevent the arbitrary exercise of power by Congress by establishing checks and balances between the House and the Senate. Madi-

ON THE WEB
thomas.loc.gov

ON THE WEB
www.house.gov

ON THE WEB
www.senate.gov

son wrote, "The remedy for [dominant legislative power] is to divide the legislature into different branches; and to render them, by different modes of election and different principles of action, as little connected with each other as the nature of their common functions and their common dependence on the society will admit."[1] He also noted this check in *Federalist 62:* "Another advantage accruing from . . . [a separated] Senate is, the additional impediment it must prove against improper acts of legislation. No law or resolution can now be passed without the concurrence, first, of a majority of the people [represented in the House] and then, of a majority of the States [represented in the Senate]."

Second, the bicameral framework served as a nifty compromise to satisfy competing interests at the Constitutional Convention. As we saw in chapter 4, the Great Compromise satisfied large states' interest in representation based on population, and also the small states' desire not to be overrun by the larger states. The bicameral structure achieves popular representation in the House and accommodates federalism by giving each state the same number of senators, regardless of population.

**ON THE WEB**
www.access.gpo.gov/
congress/index.html

**ON THE WEB**
congress.nw.dc.us/
c-span/

**ON THE WEB**
congress.nw.dc.us/
nyt/

**ON THE WEB**
congress.indiana.edu

**ON THE WEB**
www.congresslink.org

---

### DISCUSSION BOX 9.1
*DON'T WORRY, BE HAPPY: GRIDLOCK BY DESIGN*

In the introduction to this book, we noted that competition and compromise create perpetual motion in American government. Among the common criticisms of Congress, though, is the claim that the system is *gridlocked*—infected by special-interest influence and partisanship, and paralyzed by an institutional structure that is too large, too complex, and too unwieldy to legislate effectively. Yet what sometimes looks like gridlock masks the behind-the-scenes competitive effort necessary to maintain the status quo. Further, former United States Representative Bill Frenzel (R-MN) suggests that gridlock can be a good thing for policy reasons. According to the following passage by Frenzel, what are the roots of gridlock? Why is gridlock good? What risks might the country run if the government were able to act on the public's wishes more readily?

[A]s to the theory of gridlock, there are some of us who think gridlock is the best thing since indoor plumbing. Gridlock is a natural gift the Framers of our Constitution gave us so that the country would not be subjected to policy swings resulting from the whimsy of the public. And the competition—whether multibranch, multilevel, or multihouse—is important to those checks and balances and to our ongoing kind of centrist government. Thank heaven we do not have a government that nationalizes this year and privatizes next year, and so on ad infinitum.

If we wanted a government that could stand dynamic transcending leadership, we could get ourselves a parliament and a prime minister. We have not wanted that kind of government. Our Framers gave us a government built in the depths of distrust of government. They gave us a government that could not give us more than very little government. And I suspect that, other than the Swiss, we have probably been rewarded as well as any country with very small amounts of government. I do not mind gridlock. I think the country knows when it needs a change and will call for it, so I do not wring my hands over gridlock.*

*Bill Frenzel, "The System is Self-Correcting," in *Back to Gridlock? Governance in the Clinton Years*, ed. James L. Sundquist (Washington, DC: Brookings Institution, 1995), 105–106.

## Wrestling or the Symphony Tonight, Dear? The Different Characters of the House and Senate

The House and the Senate were carefully crafted to highlight and promote their different roles, encouraging the two houses to work at cross-purposes. As intended by the framers, the House of Representatives was to be the forum of popular representatives, dealing with matters of local concern and popular passion, whereas the Senate was to be the forum for state governments, concerned with state and national interests. The House was designed to be closer to the people, with the Senate placed at a greater distance from the popular will and therefore better able to reflect and deliberate upon issues of greater import and long-term significance. To achieve this separation, the houses appeal to different constituencies, differ in the number and characteristics of their members, and possess different powers.

### Separate Constituencies

The original constitutional formula for selecting members of Congress was based on the constituency and purpose that each house was to serve. The framers provided that members of the House of Representatives would be elected directly by the people of relatively small congressional districts every two years. The frequent election of representatives aimed to ensure that representatives would always be responsive to the constituents of their local districts. Alexander Hamilton emphasized this point in *Federalist 52:* "[I]t is essential to liberty that the government in general should have a common interest with the people, so it is particularly essential that the branch of it under consideration should have an immediate dependence on, and an intimate sympathy with, the people. Frequent elections are unquestionably the only policy by which this dependence and sympathy can be effectually secured."

Elections for the Senate, by contrast, were placed at greater intervals—six years rather than two—giving them greater distance from popular whims and fluctuations in public opinion, and allowing senators to be more thoughtful and deliberative public servants. Further, senators were originally chosen by state legislatures, reflecting the framers' expectation that the primary responsibility of the upper house would be to represent the interests of the states as sovereign entities. Only in 1913 did the Seventeenth Amendment provide for the direct popular election of senators. Even with that change, senators serve statewide constituencies, not local districts.

### Different Members

The framers provided that senators should be at least thirty years old, as opposed to representatives, who could be elected at the age of twenty-five. Senators had to have been citizens for at least nine years, two years longer than the time required for representatives. The framers expected the older members of the Senate to act with wisdom and moderation, offsetting the more enthusiastic approach to legislation that might come from the popularly elected House. *Federalist 62* describes "the nature of the senatorial trust" as that which, "requiring greater extent of information and stability of character, requires at the same time that the senator should have reached a period of life most likely to supply these advantages." The presentation of the Senate in *Federalist 62* leaves no doubt that the "upper" body was indeed to rule over the House. (See Zip Box 9.2.)

### Separated Powers

The framers of the Constitution assigned different powers to the House and the Senate based upon the character of the two bodies. Although both the House and the Senate vote to *enact* tax bills, for example, only the House was given the authority to *originate* revenue or tax legislation, because it alone was to represent the people. Given that "no taxation without representation" was a rallying cry of the Revolution, the state-centered Senate was an inappropriate source of tax or revenue legislation.

Other differences in responsibilities between Congress's two branches also result from the framers' view that the House would be the people's body and the Senate would be more politically detached from popular will and more deliberative than the House. The Senate's exclusive authority to approve treaties and its role in approving presidential appointments to high posts and federal judgeships, for example, reflect its deliberative nature and its connection to affairs of state. The impeachment process also reflects this separation. Under

---

## Zip Box 9.2
*The House and Senate: Members' Characteristics*

### Members of Congress: Female, Black, Hispanic, Marital Status, and Age, 1995–1999

| | | | | | Age | | | | | |
|---|---|---|---|---|---|---|---|---|---|---|
| Congress | Female | Black | Hispanic | Not Married[a] | Under 40 | 40–49 | 50–59 | 60–69 | 70–79 | 80 and Over |
| *Representatives* | | | | | | | | | | |
| 104th (1995) | 49 | 39 | 18 | — | 53 | 153 | 136 | 80 | 12 | 1 |
| 105th (1997) | 51 | 37 | 18 | — | 47 | 145 | 147 | 82 | 10 | 2 |
| 106th (1999) | 58 | 39 | 19 | — | 32 | 131 | 171 | 80 | 20 | 0 |
| *Senators* | | | | | | | | | | |
| 104th (1995) | 8 | 1 | 0 | — | 1 | 14 | 41 | 27 | 16 | 1 |
| 105th (1997) | 9 | 1 | 0 | — | 1 | 21 | 39 | 26 | 12 | 1 |
| 106th (1999) | 9 | 0 | 0 | — | 2 | 16 | 42 | 27 | 11 | 2 |

*Note:* "—" Indicates not available. As of beginning of first session of each Congress. Figures for representatives exclude vacancies. The counts above exclude nonvoting delegates and commissioners from American Samoa, Guam, Puerto Rico, the Virgin Islands, and Washington, D.C.

[a]Single, widowed, or divorced.

*Source:* Table adapted from *Vital Statistics on American Politics, 1999–2000*, ed. Harold W. Stanley and Harold Watkins (Washington, DC: CQ Press, 2000), 201.

Lockean theory, the people can dissolve a government that acts without its consent; a president who violates the rule of law commits a "High Crime and Misdemeanor," a "political crime" that is an impeachable offense. Popular sovereignty resides in the House, and the House alone has the power to bring an impeachment against the president. Yet the deliberative body, the Senate, actually conducts the impeachment trial—to ensure that the people's allegations of political wrongdoing reach a sufficient level of importance to justify removing the nation's highest elected leader. The framers did not want politics to control impeachments. If a House majority could simply remove a president at will, the Madisonian system and the Lockean ideal would have been destroyed.

---

## DISCUSSION BOX 9.2
*IT CAN DO ONLY SO MUCH: THE NATURAL LIMITS OF AN ELECTED LEGISLATURE'S ABILITIES*

The United States is not a "democracy"; rather, it is a republic in which the public delegates its power to elected representatives in Congress. In chapter 7, we saw how Congress, in turn, delegates significant authority to administrative agencies. According to the following passages, written by political theorist John Stuart Mill in 1861, what are the limits of a representative body's abilities, and why? What are the implications of those limits? What is the legislature's responsibility to its constituents?

The meaning of representative government is, that the whole people, or some numerous portion of them, exercise through deputies periodically elected by themselves the ultimate controlling power, which, in every constitution, must reside somewhere. This ultimate power they must possess in all its completeness. They must be masters, whenever they please, of all the operations of government. . . .

But while it is essential to representative government that the practical supremacy in the state should reside in the representatives of the people, it is an open question what actual functions, what precise part in the machinery of government, shall be directly and personally discharged by the representative body. Great varieties in this respect are compatible with the essence of representative government, provided the functions are such as secure to the representative body the control of everything in the last resort.

There is a radical distinction between controlling the business of government and actually doing it. The same person or body may be able to control everything, but cannot possibly do everything; and in many cases its

control over everything will be more perfect the less it personally attempts to do. . . .

[A] popular assembly is [not] fitted to administer, or to dictate in detail to those who have the charge of administration. Even when honestly meant, the interference is almost always injurious. Every branch of public administration is a skilled business, which has its own peculiar principles and traditional rules, many of them not even known, in any effectual way, except to those who have at some time had a hand in carrying on the business, and none of them likely to be duly appreciated by persons not practically acquainted with the department. I do not mean that the transaction of public business has esoteric mysteries, only to be understood by the initiated. Its principles are all intelligible to any person of good sense, who has in his mind a true picture of the circumstances and conditions to be dealt with: but to have this he must know those circumstances and conditions; and the knowledge does not come by intuition. . . .

Instead of the function of governing, for which it is radically unfit, the proper office of a representative assembly is to watch and control the government: to throw the light of publicity on its acts: to compel a full exposition and justification of all of them which any one considers questionable; to censure them if found condemnable, and, if the men who compose the government abuse their trust, or fulfil it in a manner which conflicts with the deliberate sense of the nation, to expel them from office, and either expressly or virtually appoint their successors. This is surely ample power, and security enough for the liberty of the nation.*

*John Stuart Mill, *Considerations on Representative Government* (London: Longmans, Green, Reader, and Dyer, 1878), 35–37.

The Constitution provides that each state shall have two senators; the number of representatives allotted to each state depends on the size of its population, with each state having at least one representative. The Constitution mandates that a census be taken within ten years of the previous census, the main purpose of which is to apportion representatives fairly. The framers assumed that each of the houses of Congress would be small enough for all members to participate directly in the enactment of legislation, with the smaller size of the Senate especially conducive to reasoned debate and deliberation. During the early years of the republic, the House and Senate were small bodies in comparison to their present size. The first Senate, which had twenty-six members, was not much larger than legislative committees are today; the House of Representatives in the first session of Congress had sixty-five members. Madison warned that under no circumstances should the size of the House be indiscriminately increased, because "in all legislative assemblies, the greater the number composing them may be, the fewer will be the men who will in fact direct their proceedings."[2]

Little did the framers realize that the United States would grow to have a population approaching three hundred million, spanning the North American continent and including the noncontiguous states of Alaska and Hawaii. In 1929, fearing an endless growth in the size of the House, Congress permanently fixed the number of representatives at 435; with fifty states, the Senate's elected membership stands at one hundred. As the population has increased since 1929, of course, the number of citizens represented by each member has also increased. Each House member now represents more than 600,000 people.[3]

## *I'LL BE THERE FOR YOU: REELECTION AND THE CONSTITUENCY*

Because Congress is the principal lawmaking body in the country, its members naturally consider the lawmaking function to be an important responsibility. However, as representatives of the people, they must respond to numerous constituent demands and perform many functions that are only indirectly related, or are even *un*related, to making laws.

Even the Senate ain't what it used to be: Today, political forces, more than constitutional prescriptions, dictate the character of the Senate. Senators, like representatives, are popularly elected and must respond to constituent demands. And senators are much more likely to be challenged at the polls than are members of the House, where incumbency is an almost certain guarantee of reelection. The Senate no longer occupies its exalted constitutional perch, which was meant to be above day-to-day political pressures. Though reelection is just one of the incentives driving members of Congress, it is a prerequisite for pursuing other goals like gaining power within Congress or producing good public policy. Especially for junior members, reelection is a driving concern. (See Zip Box 9.3.)

**Activities of Members of Congress: Actual and Ideal (in percentages)**

| Activity | Members actually spending time | | | | Members Preferring to Spend More Time |
| | Great Deal | Moderate Amount | A Little | Almost None | |
|---|---|---|---|---|---|
| *Representation* | | | | | |
| Meet with citizens in state/district | 68% | 30% | 1% | 0% | 17% |
| Meet in Washington with constituents | 45 | 50 | 5 | 0 | 17 |
| Manage office | 6 | 45 | 39 | 10 | 13 |
| Raise funds for next campaign, for others, for party | 6 | 33 | 45 | 16 | 7 |
| *Lawmaking* | | | | | |
| Attend committee hearings, markups, other meetings | 48 | 46 | 6 | 0 | 43 |
| Meet in Washington on legislative issues | 37 | 56 | 6 | 0 | 31 |
| Study, read, discuss pending legislation | 25 | 56 | 17 | 2 | 78 |
| Work with informal caucuses | 8 | 43 | 36 | 13 | 25 |
| Attend floor debate, follow it on television | 7 | 37 | 44 | 12 | 59 |
| Work with party leaders to build coalitions | 6 | 33 | 43 | 18 | 42 |
| Oversee how agencies are carrying out policies/programs | 5 | 22 | 43 | 29 | 53 |
| Give speeches about legislation outside state/district | 5 | 23 | 49 | 23 | 16 |

*Source:* Table from Roger H. Davidson and Walter J. Oleszek, *Congress and Its Members,* 5th ed. (Washington, DC: CQ Press, 1996), 133.

Note how much time is spent meeting with constituents in relation to the time spent lawmaking. Note also how time spent in certain lawmaking activities reflects the importance of committee action, with considerably less time spent on floor debates, working with party leaders to build coalitions, and overseeing administrative agencies.

## *I Try to Walk Away and I Stumble: The Evolution of Congress as a Career Path*

In its two-hundred-plus years, Congress has evolved considerably. For almost the first hundred years of its existence, Congress was essentially an amateur body composed of citizen legislators who rarely stayed in Washington for more than two terms of office. The House was particularly prone to turnover from the very beginning, but the Senate, too, was not a place for political careers until the latter part of the nineteenth century.

Members of Congress spend considerable time talking with constituents and helping them pursue their concerns through the federal government. Representative Paul McHale (D–Pennsylvania) set aside an "Open Till Midnight" evening every few weeks to allow constituents to call him directly at his Washington, D.C. office.

Some of the framers of the Constitution feared that senators might entrench themselves for life, but perhaps they need not have worried—at least during the first decades of the republic. Between 1789 and 1801, 33 of the 94 men who served as senators resigned before their terms were up; 6 did so to take other federal offices. Between 1801 and 1813, 35 more senators resigned. Such resignations reflected the low esteem in which the Senate was held as a place to advance political careers. Along with voluntary resignations, there was also an extremely low rate of reelection in both the House and the Senate until well after the Civil War—a trend owing more to incumbents choosing not to stand for reelection than to the fluctuating choices of fickle electorates.

The emergence of Congress as an arena for developing political careers began in the 1870s, illustrated in part by a decreasing rate of turnover in Congress in the latter decades of the nineteenth century. In the House, for example, the percentage of freshman representatives dropped from 50 percent in the 1870s to only 30 percent by 1899. In Congress as a whole, freshman members dropped from close to 60 percent in the 1870s to between 20 and 30 percent by the 1890s.

The turnover rate continued to decline steadily in the twentieth century. In sharp contrast to its early years, Congress today provides rewarding and often profitable careers for its members. And as being in Congress becomes a career, the incentives driving members' behavior shift. As members strive to advance their political careers on Capitol Hill, they might or might not advance the broader constitutional purposes of Congress or the interests of the citizens whom they are elected to represent.

New members of the House make *reelection* their first objective because they know they must serve for at least three or four terms before they can be

## DISCUSSION BOX 9.3
*A NOTE ON THE JOB DESCRIPTION: REPRESENTING THE RIGHT INTERESTS*

Citizens usually love their own representatives and condemn Congress as an institution. One reason for this is the representative's relatively narrow focus—constituents appreciate their representative's actions because they reflect the interests of the constituency, but they condemn the actions of others who appear to act selfishly. In the following passage from James Fenimore Cooper's *The American Democrat* (1838), Cooper offers his view of the nature of representation in the United States. According to Cooper, what is the primary responsibility of a representative? What is the "express compromise" Cooper says lies at the foundation of the union? How does this system of government affect the sacrifices a representative should make for the good of the country or of other states?

Although the principle that the representative chosen by a few, becomes the representative of all, is sound as a general principle, it is not an unqualified rule any where, and still less so in the federal government. The constitution requires that the representative should reside in the state from which he is sent, expressly to identify him with its particular interests, and in order to prevent that concentration which exists in other countries. Half the French deputies are from Paris, and a large por-

tion of the English members of parliament are virtually from the capital. Their systems are peculiarly systems of concentration, but ours is as peculiarly a system of diffusion. It may be questioned, therefor, how far the American representative ought to sacrifice the good of his particular state, in order to achieve the general good. Cases may certainly occur, in which the sacrifice ought to be made, but the union of these states is founded on an express compromise, and it is not its intention to reach a benefit, however considerable, by extorting undue sacrifices from particular members of the confederacy. All cases to the contrary should be clear, and the necessary relations between the good and evil, beyond cavil.

In identified governments, the principle that a few shall be sacrificed to the general good, must always, in a greater or less degree, prevail; but it is not the intention of the American compact that any one state should ruin itself, or even do itself any great and irreparable injury, that the rest of the Union should become more prosperous. In this sense, then, the member of congress represents his immediate constituents, or perhaps it would be better to say his immediate state, and although he has no right to further its interests at the expense of the interests of other states, he is not called on to sacrifice them for the benefit of the sisters of the Union.*

*James Fenimore Cooper, *The American Democrat* (Baltimore: Penguin, 1969 [1838]), 165–166.

---

**ON THE WEB**
www.congress.org

**ON THE WEB**
www.vote-smart.org

**ON THE WEB**
www.campaignline
.com//

**ON THE WEB**
www.capweb.net/
classic/index.morph

seriously involved in congressional decision making as subcommittee chairs, ranking minority party members of subcommittees, or party leaders. Senators can achieve power far earlier on Capitol Hill than representatives because the Senate is smaller, more collegial, and more a body of equals than the House. Freshmen senators in the majority party generally chair subcommittees and, unlike in the past, begin early to participate fully in Senate proceedings. Yet senators, especially freshmen, are prime targets for serious and well-financed challengers; in recent decades, even senators have had to focus considerable time and resources on keeping their seats.

## Say Anything . . . : How Legislators Get Reelected

Political scientist David Mayhew, in a study of the House of Representatives, found that members seek reelection not only by adopting positions they believe will be supported by their constituents but, more importantly, through advertising and "credit claiming." House members seeking reelection make every effort to present a favorable image to their constituents and to avoid going out on a limb on controversial issues.

James Fenimore Cooper is right to argue that representatives in America are charged with serving their constituents and protecting their interests in a competitive system (Discussion Box 9.1), but the framers also tried to establish a deliberative government that would be concerned with the national interest. In particular, the Senate was to function as a deliberative and thoughtful body protective of the nation's long-term well-being. Edmund Burke was elected in 1774 to represent the city of Bristol in England's House of Commons, and he delivered the classic statement of the parliamentary legislator's duty. As you read the following passage, note that Burke's view is, in a sense, the anithesis of Cooper's. Where do they differ? According to Burke, what is the legislator's duty when a constituent's interest is at odds with the good of the larger community? What would Cooper say? Assuming that members of the U.S. Congress feel the pull of both Cooper and Burke, which interests do you think should take precedence in a conflict?

Parliament is not a *congress* of ambassadors from different and hostile interests; which interests each must maintain, as an agent and advocate, against other agents and advocates; but parliament is a *deliberative* assembly of *one* nation, with *one* interest, that of the whole; where not local purposes, not local prejudices ought to guide, but the general good, resulting from the general reason of the whole. You choose a member indeed; but when you have chosen him, he is not a member of Bristol, but he is a member of *Parliament*. If the local constituent should have an interest or should form a hasty opinion evidently opposite to the real good of the rest of the community, the member for that place ought to be as far as any other from any endeavor to give it effect. . . .

"We are now members for a rich commercial *city*; this city, however, is but a part of a rich commercial *nation*, the interests of which are various, multiform, and intricate. We are members for that great nation, which, however, is itself but part of a great *empire*, extended by our virtue and our fortune to the farthest limits of the East and of the West. All these wide-spread interests must be considered—must be compared—must be reconciled, if possible.*

*Edmund Burke, "Speech to the Electors of Bristol," reprinted in *American Government: Readings and Cases*, 13th ed., ed. Peter Woll (New York: Longman, 1999), 374–375.

## Position Taking: Here's What I *Think*

Mayhew defines position taking as "the public enunciation of a judgmental statement on anything likely to be of interest to political actors."[4] Legislators have many forums in which they can take positions, including committee hearings and roll call voting on Capitol Hill, radio and television appearances, speeches before their constituents, press releases, newsletters, and ghostwritten books and articles.

Legislators would prefer not to have to take stands on emotionally charged and controversial issues, such as abortion, school prayer, busing of schoolchildren to achieve racial balances, and Social Security or Medicare tax increases and benefit reductions. However, these and many other controversial issues are frequently raised in legislation and floor amendments to bills introduced by members with strong views who want to see government action taken one way or another. Position taking can therefore be informative, giving voters knowledge of their representatives' views on major public policy issues.

House members usually cannot avoid taking *some* positions that could make them electorally vulnerable. A wide variety of liberal and conservative interest groups, such as Americans for Democratic Action, the Consumer

Federation of America, the National Rifle Association, and Americans for Constitutional Action rate members of Congress on the basis of the positions they have taken on issues that are of concern to these groups. Interest group leaders work diligently to defeat legislators who have consistently opposed them. Further, Mayhew suggests that "marginal" members of the House—those in danger of electoral defeat—often innovate in position taking to broaden their appeal to the voters. Congressional marginals might "fulfill an important function here as issue pioneers, experimenters who test out new issues and thereby show other politicians which ones are usable."[5]

Representatives, though, are generally less likely than senators to be held politically accountable by their constituents for the positions they take. Position taking is particularly dangerous to senatorial incumbents, who are more likely to be challenged than representatives and who, due to the size of their constituencies, have less opportunity to build the solid constituent relationships, often based on personal contacts, that help ensure the reelection of an overwhelming majority of House incumbents. The visibility and exalted status of senatorial office make senators prime electoral targets.

In contrast, as we will see shortly, representatives cultivate close ties with their constituents through advertising, credit claiming, and casework, helping to resolve voters' grievances with government. Senators do the same, but for most of them the large numbers of voters in their states make it difficult to develop the kinds of contacts with influential individuals and groups that characterize House members' relationships with their constituents. Constituents know "their" representative is working for them, and an unpopular position or two will not undermine the ongoing good relationship between members of the House and their electorates. House members also find it easier than senators to equivocate on the positions they take. The media, both back home and in Washington, closely scrutinize the votes and the legislative activities of senators. A senator's stand is generally considered to be relatively more important than that of a House member. For example, the foreign policy views of members of the Senate Foreign Relations Committee can make headlines, but the activities of the House International Relations Committee and its members are more often than not forgotten. For the most part, the local press reports dwell less on members' issue positions and more on their activities on behalf of constituents. Still, Mayhew concludes, "The best position taking strategy for most congressmen at most times is to be conservative, to cling to their own positions of the past where possible, and to reach for new ones with great caution where necessary."[6]

### Credit Claiming: Here's What I *Did*

While position taking can be electorally hazardous, claiming credit for the concrete benefits of government that flow directly to a legislator's district serve to enhance a member's popularity. Mayhew defines credit claiming "as acting so as to generate a belief in a relevant political actor (or actors) that one is personally responsible for causing the government, or some unit thereof, to do something that the actor (or actors) considers desirable."[7] Legislators claim credit for particularized benefits bestowed on districts, such as "pork barrel" projects like dams, bridges, federal buildings, grants to local communities, colleges, and schools, defense contracts and military bases, and government funds for disaster relief. Members also claim credit for casework that benefits individual constituents.

Credit claiming affects the representative role of legislators in several ways. First, members use effective credit claiming to build almost impenetrable legislative bases in their respective districts. The overwhelming incumbency advantage of members of the House is largely based upon their credit-claiming activities. Senators claim credit too, but the large size of their constituencies and their greater vulnerability in position taking makes it impossible for them to rely upon credit claiming for electoral support. Second, because House members can rely to such a large extent upon credit claiming for reelection, they do not have to depend upon electoral appeals based upon policy positions. Their representative role becomes one of channeling particular benefits to constituents rather than representing the policy preferences of voters. (See Zip Box 9.4.)

## Advertising: Here's Who I *Am*

Members of Congress advertise to sell themselves to constituents. Mayhew defines advertising as "any effort to disseminate one's name among constituents in such a fashion as to create a favorable image, but in messages having little or no issue content. A successful congressman builds what amounts to a brand name, which may have a generalized electoral value for other politicians in the same family."[8]

Advertising is carried out through newsletters, opinion columns in newspapers, and radio and television broadcasts (which are often conveniently recorded in Capitol Hill studios at public expense), and by engaging in news-

---

### Zip Box 9.4
*When Constituents Attack!*

#### High Approval for Members and Low Approval for Congress

| Individual members | Congress as institution |
| --- | --- |
| Serve constituents | Resolves national issues only with difficulty or not at all |
| Run against Congress | Has few defenders |
| Emphasize personal style and outreach to constituents | Operates as collegial body that is difficult for citizens to understand |
| Covered by local media in generally positive terms | Covered by national media, often negatively (with focus on scandals and conflicts) |
| Respond quickly to most constituent needs and inquiries | Moves slowly with cumbersome processes that inhibit rapid responses |
| Are able to highlight personal goals and accomplishments | Has many voices but none can speak clearly for Congress as a whole |

*Source:* Table from Roger H. Davidson and Walter J. Oleszek, *Congress and Its Members*, 5th ed. (Washington, DC: CQ Press, 1996), 425.

Congress is a fragmented and often uncoordinated collection of members. Even when both houses are controlled by the same party, individuals representing diverse state and local constituencies must still forge compromises to move affairs forward. Federal budget negotiations in 1999, for example, involved Senate Majority Leader Trent Lott (R–Mississippi), Speaker of the House Dennis Hastert (R–Illinois), and House Majority Leader Dick Armey (R–Texas).

worthy activities. Incumbents have considerable advantages over challengers in advertising because they have the staff, facilities, and expenses to engage in advertising, and because the news media are more likely to publicize incumbents than challengers.

Effective advertising, like credit claiming, tends to ensure the reelection of House incumbents, and it benefits Senate incumbents as well. Challengers find it difficult, if not impossible, to unseat incumbents by waging a campaign based on issues. They know that before even beginning to deal with issues, they must attract attention to themselves to gain recognition among voters. The links among challengers' campaign spending, media advertising, and name recognition are strong, which is one reason why Senate campaigns, as we saw in chapter 4, can be so expensive.

### Home Style: *Trust* Me

Political scientist <u>Richard F. Fenno, Jr.</u> points out that a legislator's Washington career inside Congress and her or his constituency career in the home district are often separated. Representatives are rarely reelected solely because of what they accomplish on Capitol Hill, and so members must build a district organization and personal image: a "home style" that will ensure reelection.[9] A successful home style can free members to pursue their congressional careers, to build power as committee chairs or party leaders, and to achieve policy goals. (See Scholar Box 9.1.)

## Scholar Box 9.1
### Fenno: Home Style

Political scientist Richard F. Fenno, Jr. offers an insightful analysis of the importance of congressional members' "home style" and how members' Washington careers and constituency careers compete for scarce time, attention, and resources. Younger members pursue reelection intensely, especially House members who face high obstacles to gaining inside power and policy influence early in their careers. Goals change with time, though, as home style assures reelection and the member's Washington career starts to take off. Resources can then be shifted to support power and policy goals inside Congress. In the following passage, Fenno describes how the pull of these two careers tears at legislators and impacts their ability to represent constituents. According to Fenno, how have relations between members and constituencies changed in recent years? What effect has this had on some congressional careers?

The congressman's home activities are more difficult and taxing than we have previously recognized. Under the best of circumstances, the tension involved in maintaining constituency contact and achieving legislative competence is considerable. Members cannot be in two places at once, and the growth of a Washington career exacerbates the problem. But, more than that, the demands in both places have grown recently. The legislative workload and the demand for legislative expertise are steadily increasing. So is the problem of maintaining meaningful contact with their several constituencies. Years ago, House members returned home for months at a time to live among their supportive constituencies, soak up the home atmosphere, absorb local problems at first hand. Today, they race home for a day, a weekend, a week at a time. [Few] maintain a family home in their district. [Many] stay with relatives or friends or in barely furnished rooms when they are at home. The citizen demand for access, for communication, and for the establishment of trust is as great as ever. So members go home. But the quality of their contact has suffered. "It's like a one-night stand in a singles bar." It is harder to sustain a genuine two-way communication than it once was. House member worries about the home relationship—great under any circumstances, but greater now—contribute to the strain and frustration of the job. Some cope; but others retire. It may be those members who cannot stand the heat of the home relationship who are getting out of the House kitchen. If so, people prepared to be more attentive to home . . . are likely to replace them.*

*Richard F. Fenno, Jr., *Home Style: House Members in Their Districts* (Boston: Little, Brown and Company, 1978), 222–223.

To build a home style, members and their aides spend a considerable amount of time maintaining direct contact with constituents. General mailings inform all constituents of a representative's activities, but letters of a more personal nature often must be written to respond to particular constituents. Sometimes these letters explain legislation, but they are also written to congratulate new mothers, to extend holiday greetings, or to offer sympathy to the bereaved. Senators and representatives also attend groundbreaking ceremonies, college and high school commencements, and parades; they appear on local television programs and attend meetings of all types in their home district. They might make policy speeches on some of these occasions, but more often they simply attend because their constituents expect it of them.

Junior members of Congress, in particular, spend much of their time building a home style in their constituency careers. One member, near the end of his second term, described the position of the junior member: "I haven't been a congressman yet. The first two years, I spent all of my time getting myself reelected. The last two years, I spent getting myself a district so that I could get reelected. So I won't be a congressman until next year."[10]

Home style builds on the fact that constituents are often unaware of members' positions or the votes they've taken. One congressman described the result of effective constituency relations:

> It's a weird thing how you get a district to a point where you can vote the way you want to without getting scalped for doing it. I guess you do it in two ways. You come back here [to the district] a lot and let people see you, so they get a feel for you. And, secondly, I go out of my way to disagree with people on specific issues. That way, they know you aren't trying to snow them. And when you vote against their views, they'll say, "Well, he's got his reasons." They'll trust you. I think that's it. If they trust you, you can vote the way you want, and it won't hurt.[11]

### Casework: Put Me to Work for *You*

An overwhelming majority of voters agree that *their* representatives are doing a good job. Effective casework is one of the most important ways incumbents buttress their reelection chances, because casework can provide

---

## BRIEFCASE BOX 9.1
*Home Style in Cyberspace: Legislators and the Internet*

E-mail and the Internet are inexpensive and versatile new tools for legislators. Yet as much as Congress has revolutionized popular access to government by placing extensive collections of documents, transcripts, and other data online, individual members of Congress have used websites to promote more traditional goals. Legislators use websites as an extension of their home style, focusing efforts on the web's advertising capabilities. How do the authors of the following passages tie their findings to Mayhew's analysis of congressional incentives and Fenno's focus on the importance of home style? Why would a member of Congress be likely to use the web in this way? What other opportunities, like electronic town hall meetings or soliciting casework, might the web offer to legislators?

David Mayhew once concluded that members of Congress engage in three categories of reelection-related activities: advertising, position taking, and credit claiming. . . . Electronic resources, particularly Web sites, offer the opportunity for members of Congress to influence each of the categories defined by Mayhew. Users who access a Web site, and who likely will never encounter the member personally, can see statements about the member's personal qualities—such as personal background, family, hobbies, interests—as well as the member's issue positions. They may also be able to

judge legislative achievements through the member's particularized credit claiming. . . .

. . .

By using their Web sites to present themselves as attractive, approachable, and helpful public servants, members of Congress effectively use the Internet to advertise themselves. Their advertising clearly reflects a home style designed to impress their constituents. However, members of Congress are less effective in using their Web sites to accomplish the purposes of position taking and credit claiming. Congressional sites are replete with information. That information consists generally of items that the members have already made available publicly. For example, 75 percent of House members and 65 percent of senators included on their Web sites the texts of releases that they had already sent to the press.

However, the abundance of on-line information has a predominantly innocuous nature. Most members' sites contain no discussion of legislation—not even legislation that the member has sponsored or co-sponsored. In general, members avoid discussing substantive issues on their Web pages. . . . Nonetheless, the sites mimic some aspects of home style, as members use their sites to place emphasis on the safest aspects of their relationship to their constituents.*

*Diana Owen, Richard Davis, and Vincent James Strickler, "Congress and the Internet," *Harvard International Journal of Press/Politics* 4, no. 2 (Spring 1999): 14–15, 25.

opportunities for credit claiming and can help build a home style. In doing casework members serve as advocates for constituents as they take up voter complaints against government agencies; how members handle constituent grievances can impress (or alienate) voters. Political scientist <u>Morris P. Fiorina</u> observes:

> As the years have passed, more and more citizens and groups have found themselves dealing with the federal bureaucracy. They may be seeking positive actions, eligibility for various benefits, and awards of government grants. Or they may be seeking relief from the costs imposed by bureaucratic regulations on working conditions, racial and sexual quotas, market restrictions, and numerous other subjects. While not malevolent, bureaucracies make mistakes, both of commission and omission, and normal attempts at redress often meet with unresponsiveness and inflexibility and sometimes seeming incorrigibility. Whatever the problem, the citizen's congressman is a source of succor. The greater the scope of government activity, the greater the demand for his services.[12]

As a convenience to legislators, many administrative departments maintain liaison groups within the House of Representatives for the sole purpose of answering congressional inquiries about decisions the agencies have made. For example, Congress members receive so many inquiries about actions of the military regarding servicemen and their families that the Pentagon maintains a special office in the House Office Building to deal with these matters.

Fiorina argues persuasively that the programmatic, or policy oriented, activities of Congress members "are dangerous (controversial) on the one hand, and programmatic accomplishments are difficult to claim credit for, on the other. While less exciting, casework and pork barreling are both safe and profitable. For a reelection oriented congressman the choice is obvious."[13] As we saw in chapter 7, Fiorina traces the rise of a permanent Washington establishment with Congress linked closely to administrative agencies and interest groups: the growth of the federal bureaucracy facilitates the reelection of incumbents by making casework popular and endless.

## MANY KINGS OF THE HILL, MANY ROUND TABLES: COMPETITIVENESS INSIDE THE CONGRESS

So you're a member of Congress, and you want to be reelected. You know what you have to do: try to avoid taking positions unless they're safe ones, claim credit, advertise, and do casework on behalf of constituents. But you also might be interested in gaining power within Congress and making good public policy, especially once you've got that reelection thing sewn up. No problem—in fact, Congress itself is conveniently structured to enhance your opportunities. Congress is decentralized, with fragmented power centers and numerous opportunities for individuals to assert influence. Political parties and individuals in leadership positions play important roles in organizing activity on the Hill, as do institutional rules that favor the majority power in the House and protect the influence of minority members in the Senate. Nevertheless, the committee and leadership systems ultimately facilitate the narrower, individualized concerns of members. This dynamic complicates, without necessarily crippling, the efficiency with which Congress can execute legislative and oversight functions.

## Get a Grip: Organizing the Congress

### Party Organization

The Constitution provides only the sketchiest of outlines for House and Senate organization, and the framers did not envision the important role that parties would play in the political system. They sought to restrain the role that factions and parties could play in directing government activity, and instead build a thoughtful Congress that would define the national interest through a deliberative, not a partisan, process. But parties were inevitable, and party rule came to Congress in the nineteenth century. Congressional parties were never the governing or programmatic parties found in many European states, as we saw in chapter 3, and they were rarely disciplined enough to follow well-defined party policies. Rather, congressional parties were organized to control power within Congress.

Today, congressional parties have elaborate organizations to arrange committee assignments and control legislation on Capitol Hill. Committee assignments, for example, are the result of bargaining among separate party panels in each house, approval of each party's caucus, and a pro forma election in each house. These assignments help the parties control which bills get introduced, which are dealt with in committees, and which are ignored.

The continuing relevance of parties on the Hill is evident in the extent to which high levels of partisanship in Congress today recall the heyday of party control a century ago. Nearly two-thirds of all floor votes in Congress, for example, are party unity votes in which a majority of voting Democrats oppose a majority of voting Republicans. Further, the average member of Congress votes with her party roughly 80 percent of the time (see Zip Box 9.5). Party voting is linked to several factors, including the shared policy goals of party members, socialization within Congress, and pressure from party leaders to stick together. Party loyalty also reflects *"constituency differences,"* or the simple argument that "Partisans vote together . . . because they reflect the same kinds of political and demographic areas." Members break with the party only when the party's position will not suit the member's constituency.[14] (See Discussion Box 9.5.)

### Officers of Congress

Helping the parties influence the behavior of members are the leadership positions in both the House and Senate. Article 1 of the Constitution provides for the House to choose its Speaker and other officers, for the vice president of the United States to be president of the Senate, and for the members of the Senate to choose other officers, including a president pro tempore to serve in the absence of the vice president. As the political parties grew in importance, these posts became the rewards of the dominant party in each house of the legislature. Party leaders influence committee appointments and help shepherd legislation through each house with an eye toward the ways in which particular rules can work to the party's advantage. (See Discussion Box 9.5.)

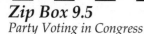

## Zip Box 9.5
### Party Voting in Congress

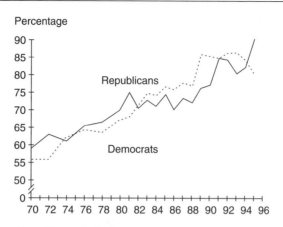

Percentage

*Note:* The graph shows the percentage of times the average Democrat or Republican in Congress voted with his or her party majority in partisan votes for the years listed. These *composite party unity scores* are based on votes that split the parties in the House and Senate a majority of voting Democrats opposing a majority of voting Republicans. Scores have been recomputed by authors to correct for absences.

**Levels of Party Voting in Congress, 1970–1996**

Figure from Roger H. Davidson and Walter J. Oleszek, *Congress and Its Members,* 5th ed. (Washington, DC: CQ Press, 1996), 272.

**Speaker of the House.** Leadership positions are more important in the House than they are in the Senate. The Speaker of the House presides over the House chamber, recognizes members who wish to speak, and appoints members to select and special committees. More importantly, the Speaker influences committee assignments, refers bills to committees, and controls the critically important Rules Committee—all of which gives the Speaker considerable influence over the course of legislation.

The Speaker's exercise of power, though, varies according to the priorities and character of the individual holding the post. Recently, Republican <u>Newt Gingrich</u> exercised strong leadership and extensive influence over the House and its members, and he gave the office of Speaker an uncommonly high public profile; yet immediately following Gingrich, Republican speaker <u>Dennis Hastert</u> of Illinois stepped back from the spotlight. In his classic 1885 work, *Congressional Government,* then-graduate student and future president <u>Woodrow Wilson</u> recognized the variability inherent in the Speaker's role:

> The most esteemed writers upon our Constitution have failed to observe, not only that the standing committees are the most essential machinery of our governmental system, but also that the Speaker of the House of Representatives is the most powerful functionary of that system. So sovereign is he

On the Web
speakernews.house.
gov/default.htm

On the Web
democratic
leader.house.gov

On the Web
majoritywhip.
house.gov

On the Web
hillsource.
house.gov

On the Web
dcaucusweb.
house.gov/home/

273

In chapter 3, we examined the weak nature of American political parties in the electorate and in their role in designing and implementing programmatic policies. Parties are hardly irrelevant on Capitol Hill, however, and individual competitiveness does not mean that members cast their votes erratically. In the following passages, political scientist Roger H. Davidson reviews some of the ways today's party activity, and heightened levels of partisanship, echo the party battles of the past. What mechanisms allow parties to be influential in Congress? How do the parties use the different rules in the House and Senate to exercise influence? How did the Republicans' "Contract with America" reflect parties' role in today's Congress?

Despite the widely proclaimed death of traditional political parties, partisanship and factionalism are very much alive on Capitol Hill. By dint of party mechanisms, leaders are selected, committee assignments made, and floor debates scheduled. Parties also supply members with voting cues. Today the parties' formal apparatus is extensive. There are policy committees, campaign committees, research committees, elaborate whip systems, and countless task forces. Nearly 200 staff aides are employed by party leaders and perhaps an equal number by assorted party committees. Party-oriented voting bloc groups—such as the Conservative Democratic Forum or the Republicans' Tuesday Lunch Bunch, "class clubs" (such as the Republican Freshman Class or the Democratic First Term Class), and social groups complement and reinforce partisan ties.

On the House and Senate floor, party affiliation is the strongest single predictor of members' voting behavior, and in recent years it has reached levels nearly as high as a century ago. Of the nearly 2,000 floor votes cast by representatives and senators on articles of impeachment against President Clinton, for example, 92 percent followed partisan battlelines—Republicans favoring impeachment, Democrats resisting it.

. . .

[P]arty leaders exploit each chamber's rules and procedures to encourage favorable outcomes. House procedures sharpen partisanship, inasmuch as a cohesive party majority can normally work its will. By controlling key committees, employing scheduling powers, and using special rules to structure floor debate and voting, majority party leaders can arrange votes they are likely to win and avoid those they are apt to lose. Senate leaders have fewer opportunities to engineer victories because that chamber's rules and procedures distribute power more evenly between the parties and among individual senators. Yet Senate floor leaders can regulate the timing of debates to their advantage and (through their right to be recognized first to speak or offer amendments on the floor) shape the order and content of floor deliberations.

Partisanship is underscored by events of the 1990s. Despite the public's professed antipathy toward partisanship (and toward the two major parties in particular), recent elections have had distinctly partisan results. One outgrowth of robust partisanship is the advent of congressional party "platforms" designed to attract voters and validate the party's bid for power. The House Republicans' manifesto, the "Contract with America," was far from the earliest such document, but it was shrewdly drafted, aggressively marketed, and then employed as the party's working agenda during their first months in power. Five years later, the Clinton impeachment became a pitched battle along party lines, dividing not only lawmakers but also their constituents. With visible party differences and bitter personal battles, Capitol Hill political alignments are rigorous, even with recent tenuous majorities. Current appeals to partisan loyalty would be understood by politicians and voters of a century ago.*

*Taken with permission from CONGRESSIONAL LEADERS, PARTIES, AND COMMITTEES, 1900 AND 2000, Roger H. Davidson, University of Maryland, College Park, Prepared for "The Turn of the Century Congress and American Governance: Then and Now," Seminar of the Woodrow Wilson International Center for Scholars, June 25, 1999. See http://wwics.si.edu/FORTHCOM/congress/david.htm.

within the range of his influence that one could wish for accurate knowledge as to the actual extent of his power. But Mr. Speaker's powers cannot be known accurately, because they vary with the character of Mr. Speaker.[15]

Wilson was describing a nineteenth-century Congress in which the Speaker had the potential to dominate the legislative business of the House through control of the Rules Committee (of which the Speaker had been *ex officio* chair

since 1858) and by dominating floor proceedings through rulings on parliamentary procedure. This power became particularly important in 1890 when, under the speakership of Thomas B. Reed of Maine, the House formally adopted rules that gave the Speaker almost dictatorial authority to control the proceedings on the House floor.

Complementing the power of the Speaker at that time was his authority to appoint both the chair and the members of all the standing committees of the House. At the time of Wilson's writing, seniority was the customary criterion in bestowing committee chairmanships; however, powerful speakers such as Thomas Reed (1889–1891, 1895–1899) and Joseph Cannon (1903–1911) ruled the House by unhesitatingly manipulating both parliamentary procedures and their power to appoint loyal followers as committee chairs.

The "1910 revolt" against the excessive power of the Speaker, particularly against his authority to appoint the members of committees and his domination of the Rules Committee, succeeded in greatly reducing the Speaker's influence. These reforms dispersed authority to the committees and reduced the Speaker's power to control floor proceedings; since 1910, Speakers have had to rely more heavily on their informal powers of persuasion to exercise influence over the House. Twentieth-century Speakers were not, however, without influence; behind the scenes the modern Speaker retains extraordinary power over the scheduling of legislation on the floor and over committee legislative activity in which he is particularly interested. Speakers periodically assume considerable control of the House, as demonstrated by the strong speakership of Sam Rayburn of Texas (1940–1947, 1949–1953, and 1955–1961), the dominant force of Speaker Thomas ("Tip") O'Neill, Jr., of Massachusetts in the 1970s and 1980s, the bold leadership of Texas Democrat Jim Wright (1987–1989), and Newt Gingrich's short but effective tenure as speaker in the 1990s.

**President of the Senate and the Senate Majority Leader.** The constitutional provision that the vice president is to serve as president of the Senate makes this leadership position ineffective, particularly compared to that of the Speaker of the House. The vice president is not a member of the Senate and can vote only in case of a tie. Whenever the vice president is unable to attend Senate meetings, a president pro tempore or, as is usually the case, one of the senators taking over the chair on a rotating basis, acts as the presiding officer. Although the presidency pro tempore of the Senate is elective, like the Speakership of the House, it is a pro forma office without any inherent power. The president pro tempore has not traditionally been given any independent powers to direct the floor proceedings of the Senate.

If individual power exists in the Senate, it is exercised through the position of the *majority leader,* who is elected by and is directly under the control of the majority party's members in the body. In effect, the majority leader directs the presiding officer, whether that officer is the vice president, the president pro tempore (for a limited time), or a senator presiding on a pro tempore basis in his disposition of parliamentary matters. In the Senate, though, individuals are much more independent than in the House; the majority leader, more so than leaders in the House, must rely on the power of persuasion.

The lack of a powerful presiding officer in the Senate is due not only to the constitutional assignment of the vice president as the chief presiding officer but also to the nature of the Senate itself. From time to time strong party leadership and discipline have emerged in the upper house, but for the most part each senator acts and is treated as an independent sovereign power within the body.

### The Grip Slips: Committees and Individualism in a Decentralized Congress

Though the parties and the leadership in both houses exercise some important influences over the location of power, the direction of votes, and the progress of legislation, Congress remains a decentralized governing branch characterized more by fragmented power and individualism than by coherent party control. The committee system, which distributes responsibility for the myriad issues facing the federal government to numerous smaller groups, is the real heart of congressional activity.

In some ways, the committee system helps the government deal with numerous complex topics by allowing members to gain expertise in a few policy

**ON THE WEB**
www.senate.gov/
learning/learn_leaders
_leadership _
responsible.html

**ON THE WEB**
www.senate.gov/
~rpc/

**ON THE WEB**
www.senate.gov/
~dpc/

Congressional hearings and investigations provide a formal opportunity for members to question experts and gather information. Here, Chairman and CEO of Microsoft Bill Gates testifies in March 1998.

ON THE WEB
www.house.gov/
house/Committee
WWW.html

ON THE WEB
www.senate.gov/
committees/index.
cfm

ON THE WEB
lcweb.loc.gov/
global/legislative/
housecomm.html

ON THE WEB
lcweb.loc.gov/
global/legislative/
senatecomm.html

ON THE WEB
lcweb.loc.gov/
global/legislative/
jtcomm.html

ON THE WEB
www.lcweb.loc.gov/
global/legislative/bill.
html # conference

areas. Committees handling issues like budgeting and appropriations work to give the system a measure of centralized control. Nevertheless, the committee system fragments the system and splinters the government's focus on issues. As one representative put it, "In order to attain legislative efficiency, we say that we have to break down into committees with specialized jurisdictions. When you do that, you lose your ability to grapple with the big problems."[16]

The committee system disperses power throughout both houses, multiplying competing interests within the legislature and multiplying the access points for forces coming from outside government. Committees compete for jurisdiction over issues, and committees and their members must negotiate compromise solutions to problems with fellow members and members of other committees in both houses. This process recurs throughout every stage in the legislative process, including the seemingly endless hearings, reports, markup sessions of committees (in which bills are taken up item by item and amendments are made and voted upon by the committee), investigations, and the informal meetings and machinations of all sorts that inevitably surround the performance of legislative functions—and that often substantially alter the substance of legislation after its initiation. Failure to recognize and understand the slow, negotiation- and compromise-driven nature of the legislative process can have ruinous effects. (See BriefCase Box 9.3.)

The decentralized committee system feeds the incentives of individual members by helping junior members deliver projects and pork barrel benefits to their districts, and by serving more senior members as power bases within

- STANDING COMMITTEES: permanent committees, including
  - *authorizing committees,* which define the content of policy and formally empower government agents to act
  - *appropriations committees,* which allocate funds to pay for authorized activities
  - *taxing committees,* which exercise control over revenue-raising
  - *budget committees,* which coordinate revenues and spending

- SELECT OR SPECIAL COMMITTEES: established from time to time to address temporary problems or conduct investigations
- JOINT COMMITTEES: created to study matters of special concern to both the House and the Senate; joint committees lack legislative authority
- CONFERENCE COMMITTEES: temporary committees made up of House and Senate members serving to draft compromise versions of similar House and Senate legislation; conference committees are an important stage near the end of the legislative process

the institution and as venues for policymaking. Further, as we saw in chapter 3, weak parties and the rise of candidate-centered parties as the vehicles for electoral success and career stability in Congress mean that individuals are only loosely beholden to their parties and can rarely be *compelled* to act in accord with party goals.

The decentralization of the committee system also provides numerous opportunities for members to act as policy entrepreneurs—taking on issues for individual reasons that might have little to do with party agendas or the involvement of organized interest groups. Individuals can use the committee system, personal organizations, and media access to raise and promote issues in which they are personally interested, like campaign finance reform or housing for the homeless, or issues they think will serve their ends, like current popular causes. This independence chips away at the control of committee chairs and party leadership.

## MILES TO GO BEFORE THEY SLEEP: CONGRESS IN A COMPETITIVE SYSTEM

None of this means that Congress cannot act, pass laws, or effectively oversee government—it means only that decentralization, weak party control, and individualism complicate those efforts. Congress can, and does, act; most of those acts are incremental adjustments and compromise solutions rather than major reforms, but on recent issues from budget reform to welfare reform Congress remains a major player in American government.

How is this possible if Congress is so fragmented—how does anything get done? Consider the wide range of motives and incentives we've examined in this chapter, and that we've seen throughout the book. Any member of Con-

## Zip Box 9.7
*The Committee System in the House and Senate*

### House and Senate Committee Comparison

| Category | House | Senate |
|---|---|---|
| Number of standing committees | 19 | 16 |
| Committee assignments per member | About 5 | About 7 |
| Power or prestige committees | Appropriations, Budget, Rules, Ways and Means | Appropriations, Armed Services, Finance, Foreign Relations[a] |
| Treaties and nominations submitted by the president | No authority | Committees review |
| Floor debate | Representatives' activity is somewhat confined to the bills reported from the panels on which they serve | Senators can choose to influence any policy area regardless of their committee assignments |
| Committee consideration of legislation | More difficult to bypass | Easier to bypass[b] |
| Committee chairmen | Subject to party and speakership influence that limits their discretionary authority over committee operations | Freer rein to manage committees |
| Committee staff | Less assertive in advocating ideas and proposals | More aggressive in shaping the legislative agenda |
| Subcommittee chairmanships | Representatives of the majority party usually must wait at least one term | Majority senators, regardless of their seniority, usually chair subcommittees |

[a]Almost every senator is assigned to one of these four committees.
[b]For example, by allowing "riders"—unrelated policy proposals—to measures pending on the [floor.]
*Source:* Table from Roger H. Davidson and Walter J. Oleszek, *Congress and Its Members,* 5th ed. (Washington, DC: CQ Press, 1996), 208.

gress might take up an issue in order to help build support for reelection, to have an impact on public policy, or because the issue has the potential to increase the member's visibility and power within Congress. Other members will join the fight on one side or another, and for their own individual reasons. Some members will join in because they want to satisfy party positions or the leadership in either house, but others will join to promote their independent reelection, power, or policy incentives. Just as we've seen interest groups form alliances to push the same measure for different reasons, so too members of Congress will work together to attain the same goal for different reasons. As they do so, adjustments to existing laws, the introduction of new measures, and investigations and oversight of the government's activities move forward.

As members weigh in with opposing viewpoints, positions and initiatives are shaped by compromises in committees, subcommittees, and throughout the whole of either house. All of these dynamics come together in Congress' law-making, oversight, and investigatory activity.

## There Oughta Be a Law: Competition and Compromise in the Legislative Process

In the abstract, the process of how a bill becomes a law is fairly straightforward. As illustrated in Zip Box 9.8, bills are introduced in the House or the Senate and then directed to a committee. The committee might send the bill to a subcommittee for review. The committee and subcommittee hold hearings, solicit testimony, mark up or revise the bill, vote, then send it to the floor for a vote by the full House or Senate. If the other house has passed a similar bill, a conference committee of members of both houses works to forge compromises in areas where the bills differ. If they can agree on one bill, it returns for a vote in both houses. If it passes by a majority vote, it goes to the president for his signature. If the president vetoes the bill, a two-thirds vote can override the veto.

In practice, of course, even this straightforward, if cumbersome, process is much more complicated. First, an issue must find its way onto the government's agenda, a process influenced by long-term lobbying, sudden crises, and political entrepreneurship. Competition and compromise infuse every stage of the process and involve virtually all of the forces we've examined throughout this book (see BriefCase Box 9.3).

### The President

The president is the most important and concentrated source of demands on Congress in matters of major public policy, a result of the president's unique institutional position and of the popular expectations surrounding the office. The president is able to focus attention on his proposals by outlining them publicly in his annual State of the Union message and in subsequent budgetary proposals and special messages. The president not only has at his command a potentially vast range of information flowing from the bureaucracy and from his own staff, but he also can make direct appeals to the people for support of his programs. The White House thus can act with greater dispatch and unity in developing legislative proposals than can Congress.

Moreover, the president and vice president are the only nationally elected officials, and the White House is therefore the focus of popular expectations about the proper role of the government. The president is the symbolic leader of his own political party, and his program is supposed to reflect and make concrete party views regardless of how vaguely and ambiguously they might have been stated in party conventions and platforms.

Despite these advantages, there are great variations in presidents' success in shepherding legislative proposals through Congress. The president must rely on his powers of persuasion, as we saw in the previous chapter, and his efforts usually face obstacles thrown up by the nature of party control in Congress. For example, a president's legislative proposals usually have greater difficulty getting through Congress when the body is dominated by the op-

## Zip Box 9.8
### How a Bill Becomes a Law

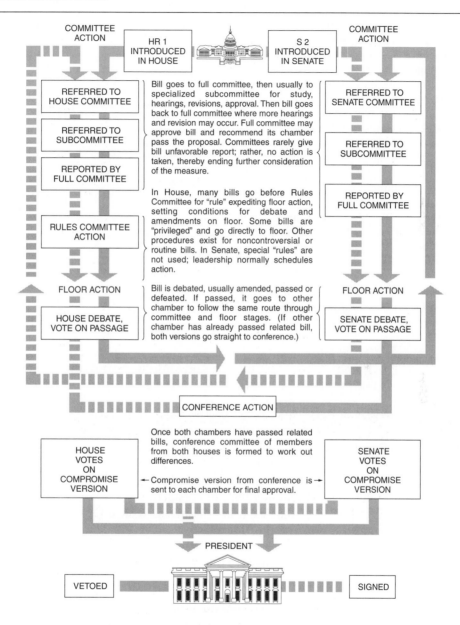

COMMITTEE ACTION

HR 1 INTRODUCED IN HOUSE

S 2 INTRODUCED IN SENATE

COMMITTEE ACTION

REFERRED TO HOUSE COMMITTEE

REFERRED TO SUBCOMMITTEE

REPORTED BY FULL COMMITTEE

RULES COMMITTEE ACTION

Bill goes to full committee, then usually to specialized subcommittee for study, hearings, revisions, approval. Then bill goes back to full committee where more hearings and revision may occur. Full committee may approve bill and recommend its chamber pass the proposal. Committees rarely give bill unfavorable report; rather, no action is taken, thereby ending further consideration of the measure.

In House, many bills go before Rules Committee for "rule" expediting floor action, setting conditions for debate and amendments on floor. Some bills are "privileged" and go directly to floor. Other procedures exist for noncontroversial or routine bills. In Senate, special "rules" are not used; leadership normally schedules action.

REFERRED TO SENATE COMMITTEE

REFERRED TO SUBCOMMITTEE

REPORTED BY FULL COMMITTEE

FLOOR ACTION

HOUSE DEBATE, VOTE ON PASSAGE

Bill is debated, usually amended, passed or defeated. If passed, it goes to other chamber to follow the same route through committee and floor stages. (If other chamber has already passed related bill, both versions go straight to conference.)

FLOOR ACTION

SENATE DEBATE, VOTE ON PASSAGE

CONFERENCE ACTION

HOUSE VOTES ON COMPROMISE VERSION

Once both chambers have passed related bills, conference committee of members from both houses is formed to work out differences.

← Compromise version from conference is → sent to each chamber for final approval.

SENATE VOTES ON COMPROMISE VERSION

PRESIDENT

VETOED

SIGNED

The "Republican Revolution" of 1994 restored Republicans to control of the House for the first time in forty years. The Republicans, though, were more than a little unfamiliar with being in the majority. They also believed that they had a mandate to overturn politics as usual. In the following passage, political scientist Richard F. Fenno, Jr., examines how Republicans in the 104th Congress misunderstood the competition and compromise at the heart of the legislative process. According to Fenno, what mistake did the House Republicans make? What opportunities to fulfill member and party incentives did they miss? What was the alternative plan put forth by veteran legislator Bob Dole, and what does the failure of the House to take his advice indicate about the power of leadership positions in our bicameral legislature?

[The House Republicans'] unsuccessful budget confrontation with the president demonstrated beyond any doubt how little the new majority knew about the legislative process, about its inevitable incrementalism, trade-offs, compromises, negotiations, and public resonances. For one thing, budget politics is *always* incremental politics. It is never apocalyptic politics. You can't possibly run a revolution through the budget process. But you can use budget increments to demonstrate that you have taken some steps to change the direction of government and the terms of public debate. You can then declare victory on that account and take an overall record of forward motion to the electorate. . . .

. . .

By contrast, Senate [majority] leader Bob Dole, who had experienced majority party power and leadership from 1981 to 1986, advocated . . . a series of small steps and small claims. For him, legislation should always be considered work in progress. "You get something this year," he advised, "and you get more next year." And he insistently pressed his House counterparts with the question, "What's your end game?" But as the president's budget negotiator knew, [Speaker of the House Newt] Gingrich had given no thought to what, in the end, he might settle for or what he could deliver. As [Clinton's budget director] Leon Panetta said, "He came to the table not to negotiate, but to dictate the terms of surrender."

From the beginning their electoral interpretation had pointed the Republicans toward a narrow, short-run view of governing. And because of that view, they were not positioned to settle for—and take credit for—incremental steps that would keep them in control of the public debate and keep them moving toward a goal of a unified Republican government. What a party can effectively claim in governing is related to the expectations it sets, and the Republicans' electoral interpretation set expectations that effectively ruled out incrementalist and gradualist governing claims.*

*Richard F. Fenno, Jr., *Learning to Govern: An Institutional View of the 104th Congress* (Washington, DC: Brookings Institution Press, 1997), 39–40, 41.

posing party, because even members of weak parties can agree to say no to a president's initiatives. Republican President Ronald Reagan was a brief exception to this rule, enjoying unusual success with a Democrat-controlled Congress at the beginning of his administration. Reagan's "honeymoon" with Capitol Hill lasted for almost an entire year, during which his sweeping proposals for reductions in taxes and government spending were enacted. Reagan's early success on Capitol Hill soon deteriorated, however, emblematic of a much more typical divided government relationship.

Even same-party control of the White House and both houses of Congress cannot ensure the passage of presidential initiatives, as we saw throughout the first part of this book when we looked at the failure of President Clinton's health plan. Clinton's failures with a same-party Congress echoed the problems that faced the administrations of John F. Kennedy (1961–1963) and Jimmy Carter (1977–1981). Despite the extraordinary legislative success of the administrations of Lyndon Johnson (1963–1969) and Franklin Roosevelt

Lawmaking in the United States is a difficult business, in large part because there are so many individuals and interests involved. This photo of the president with congressional leaders in February 2000 suggests the numerous interests throughout the government that often must be satisfied in order to pass new laws. From left to right are Senate Minority Leader Tom Daschle (D–South Dakota), Senate Majority Leader Trent Lott (R–Mississippi), President Bill Clinton, and Speaker of the House Dennis Hastert (R–Illinois).

(1933–1945), then, presidents have a tough time navigating the labyrinth of Congress regardless of party control.

A major reason for this difficulty is that the loose organization of parties is unable to provide a bridge between the president and Congress that will guarantee the success of legislative proposals coming from the White House. The presidential wings of the parties are loosely knit organizations that come together every four years to nominate and elect their candidates. The rise of candidate parties in presidential elections has further disintegrated party organization and isolated the White House's party support. Congressional parties are also not cohesive organizations in themselves; their independent organizations and policies reflect not only narrower constituencies than the broad national constituency of the presidency, but also the adversary position of Congress in relation to the president under the constitutional system.

### Interest Groups and the Media

Interest groups also play an important role in making demands on members of Congress, as we saw in chapter 2. Lobbying and other tactics to pressure Congress can be very influential, and groups play major roles both in supplying information to Congress and in helping to draft legislation. Interest groups also influence congressional committees and individual members indirectly through the administrative agencies. Private groups are important supporters of such agencies, and some of their demands are transmitted to Congress by the agencies. The Department of Defense, for example, wins support from the armaments industry when it obtains money from Congress for developing a new tank or fighter plane. The amount of attention a legislator pays to the views of a particular interest group is often based on the influence that group might have in future elections. If the group has considerable strength in the constituency, the senator or representative might be more than normally attentive to its wishes.

The influence of the news media on Congress's agenda is limited. We saw in chapter 2 that lobbying is a long-term endeavor, beginning well before issues capture the public's attention and continuing far past the signing of bills into law, as lobbyists work to influence implementation and congressional oversight of administration. The same is true of forces in Congress and the White House, with policy entrepreneurs and others carefully laying foundations and building support for new initiatives or for adjustments to existing laws. Much of this work takes place away from the media spotlight. Political scientist John Kingdon quotes one committee staffer in Congress as saying, "The media has some importance, but it's slight. Either media people are reporting what we're already doing, or they're reporting something we're already aware of."[17] Moreover, stories are usually newsworthy only for a brief period and often towards the end of the policy making process. As we saw in chapter 1, the media are more important for the ways in which news coverage affects what we learn about the issues Congress addresses. Issues already on the agenda are often presented in terms of two competing, polarized options, and then linked to the fortunes of familiar individuals. Topics are addressed in dramatic, crisis terms. These dynamics can narrow the policy options given serious consideration by lawmakers and oversimplify public discussion of complex topics and long-term problems.

## Behind the Music: Staff and Other Help for Congress

Lawmaking, then, is not simply competition and compromise among members of Congress and between the two houses; rather, it involves the president, political parties, interest groups, administrative agencies, and virtually anybody else interested in politics. Further, these forces are involved from the agenda-setting stage through the drafting of bills and hearings, floor votes, conference committees, the decision to use the presidential veto, and, as we saw in chapter 7, agencies' implementation of the laws. So it makes sense that even after dividing responsibilities through the committee system, members of Congress cannot fulfill their duties and function effectively in the competitive system without help.

While members of Congress attract the media spotlight, sit up front at hearings, and provide a face for congressional representation, behind all representatives and senators are their own *personal staff aides*; moreover, *special committee staffs* serve each congressional committee. The personal and committee staffs of the House and Senate now include more than 15,000 people. These staffs play a tremendously important role in Congress. They develop legislative proposals and often guide them through the intricate maze of the legislative process in Congress. It is also the staffs who generally provide senators and representatives with positions on particular pieces of legislation or legislative proposals, and who write most of the speeches given by representatives and senators, including many of the statements inserted in the *Congressional Record*. In a very real sense, staff aides operating behind the scenes often act as surrogate members of Congress.

Because the extent to which members of Congress rely on their staffs to supply them with information necessary for legislation makes the staffs influential, the staffs' information sources are also very important. The landmark Legislative Reorganization Act of 1946 increased the staffs of legislators and congressional committees so that members would no longer have to depend as heavily on administrative agencies for research and information. Members of Congress and their staffs now receive substantial amounts of information from private interest groups and from institutions established specifically to work for Congress.

*Congressional institutions,* such as the Congressional Budget Office (CBO), the Library of Congress, its Congressional Research Service (CRS), the Office of Technology Assessment, and the General Accounting Office (GAO), aid members and staffs with research. The CRS, for example, answers congressional requests for information of all kinds, whether or not the questions relate to pending legislation. More than 30 percent of all congressional requests to the CRS come originally from constituents, and Congress members simply transfer these constituent requests to the service for an answer. The Congressional Budget Office employs hundreds of professionals involved in making economic

ON THE WEB
www.cbo.gov

ON THE WEB
www.loc.gov

ON THE WEB
www.senate.gov/
~daschle/services/
reptsubj.html

ON THE WEB
gwis2.circ.gwu
.edu/~gprice/crs.htm

ON THE WEB
www.gao.gov

### Zip Box 9.9
*Congressional Staff*

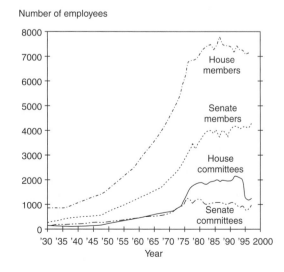

Figure from *Vital Statistics on American Politics, 1999–2000,* ed. Harold W. Stanley and Harold Watkins (Washington, DC: CQ Press, 2000), 203.

projections and assessing the budgetary impact of legislation. The GAO reviews government programs and provides top-quality, in-depth research.

Many *interest groups,* especially larger ones like the Farm Bureau Federation, the AFL-CIO, and the National Association of Manufacturers, maintain research staffs that are available to members of Congress. Lawmakers can call on such organizations to provide information regarding legislative proposals. Congressional use of such facilities is by no means universal; many members of Congress rely only slightly, if at all, on information supplied by private interest groups.

When Congress formulates legislation on a particular matter, it still tends to rely substantially on the experience of those who deal directly with the area concerned rather than on its own sources of information. The staff of the Congressional Research Service can reply only to factual questions. It cannot advise legislators on general questions of policy, such as these: Which changes should be made in the weapons system to ensure proper balance of offensive and defensive capabilities? Which changes should be made in the securities laws to protect the public against fraud and unnecessary stock market fluctuations? Which kind of fiscal policy will promote employment, reduce inflation, and spur expansion of the economy? Which type of labor legislation is needed

## Zip Box 9.11
*Information, Please: Congress and the Agencies*

The exchange of information between Congress and the bureaucracy takes place on several levels.

Formal Channels

- The president's Office of Management and Budget (OMB) acts as the chief clearinghouse for legislative and budgetary proposals from administrative agencies. When the OMB approves these proposals without major changes, it is evident to the Congress that the president agrees with the purpose and performance of the agency initiating the proposal.
- The president's political appointees, particularly cabinet secretaries and undersecretaries, present the administration's viewpoint in written statements to Congress. These must first be cleared by the OMB, which ensures that the opinions presented are in line with presidential policies. Committee members also question administration witnesses at live hearings. Political appointees who wish to survive politically try to make their public pronouncements accord with the wishes of the president.

Informal Channels

- Informal channels of communication with the bureaucracy often give Congress the most revealing information on legislative matters. Whereas political appointees who support the administration are heard at such formal occasions as committee hearings, career civil servants might not have the same opportunity to make their views heard. And Congress is interested in the opinions of both. In their informal contacts with members of Congress by telephone and at parties, luncheons, and the like, subordinate administrative officials might express opinions on legislation or even provide aid on the actual drafting of bills. Even though presidents might wish to prevent such informal contacts, it is almost impossible for them to do so.

Constraints and Competition

- Members of Congress who oppose a presidential program that is being vigorously supported by the White House will find it difficult to acquire information from the bureaucracy. Formal testimony before congressional committees, whether given by cabinet appointees or lower-level career bureaucrats, must be cleared in advance by the OMB. And even though informal channels of communication can circumvent the censorship of the OMB, lower-level officials in particular are taking risks if they go behind the president's back to Congress. Further, some administrators will defend presidential policy whether they personally like it or not. For example, members of Congress have found it difficult to get information from the armed forces, even when the military has opposed the policies of the president and the secretary of defense. Military officials are usually reluctant to testify in open committee hearings, where their views and plans could be aired before the public. The views of the military chiefs regarding defense policy are usually conveyed, if at all, through informal channels.

to reduce employer–employee conflict? Should agricultural supports be expanded or modified in any way? Information relevant to such questions is generally in the hands of the *administrative agencies* and the private interest groups concerned, and they pass it on to legislators. (See Zip Box 9.11 and Discussion Box 9.6.)

There is a common bond of purpose between Congress and the administrative agencies. Many agencies, particularly the independent regulatory commissions, are agents of Congress. Among other things, they are supposed to recommend legislation to Congress when needed; it is highly unlikely that any

The committee system helps Congress oversee the activities of government by allowing members to concentrate on a limited number of particular issues. In chapter 7, though, we saw how agency administrators sometimes bristle when "political" forces meddle with administration (see Discussion Box 7.2). In the following passage from his *Congressional Government* (1885), <u>Woodrow Wilson</u> argues that Congress's oversight responsibilities help ensure both public awareness and proper implementation of congressional initiatives. According to Wilson, how does congressional oversight promote a self-governing people, and how does it affect administrative efficiency? How does Wilson's view reflect the competition inherent in American government? What comparisons can you draw between Wilson's view and the position taken by John Stuart Mill in Discussion Box 9.2?

It is the proper duty of a representative body to look diligently into every affair of government and to talk much about what it sees. It is meant to be the eyes and the voice, and to embody the wisdom and will of its con-stituents. Unless Congress have and use every means of acquainting itself with the acts and the disposition of the administrative agents of the government, the country must be helpless to learn how it is being served; and unless Congress both scrutinize these things and sift them by every form of discussion, the country must remain in embarrassing, crippling ignorance of the very affairs which it is most important that it should understand and direct. The informing function of Congress should be preferred even to its legislative function. The argument is not only that discussed and interrogated administration is the only pure and efficient administration, but, more than that, that the only really self-governing people is that people which discusses and interrogates its administration. The talk on the part of Congress which we sometimes justly condemn is the profitless squabble of words over frivolous bills or selfish party issues. It would be hard to conceive of there being too much talk about the practical concerns and processes of government. Such talk it is which, when earnestly and purposefully conducted, clears the public mind and shapes the demands of public opinion.*

*Woodrow Wilson, *Congressional Government: A Study in American Politics* (New York: Meridian Books, 1960 [1885]), 198.

regulatory legislation will pass Congress without the approval of the agency that has jurisdiction over the area. Congress may veto legislative proposals from the commissions, but it rarely supports regulatory legislation that has not been cleared by the commission concerned.

These tools and resources help Congress keep up with the diverse interests competing for influence over legislation and implementation. As the cornerstone of American government and the focus of much popular disaffection with government, Congress needs all the help it can get.

## Conclusion

The competition and compromise inherent in Congress's activities reflect the framers' intent to fragment power and check the potential of both institutions and individuals. Congress competes and compromises with other aspects of the government, even as individual members of Congress balance their individual goals with their responsibilities as representatives, lawmakers, and overseers of government's activities. In the next chapter, we turn to a final force competing for influence in American government: the judiciary, which possesses the authority to negate all of the hard work and the difficult compromises made by elected representatives.

## Overnight Assignment ▬▬▬▬▬▬▬▬

Find your representative's webpage. Does the page reflect any of the activities discussed in this chapter, such as position-taking, credit claiming, or advertising? How? What information does the page have regarding your representative's legislative work, such as committee assignments or work on particular issues?

## Long-Term Integrated Assignment ▬▬▬▬▬▬▬

How has Congress addressed the issues related to the interest group you chose in chapter 2? Which representatives or senators are leaders on a particular current issue? What seems to be their motivation? Which subcommittee or subcommittees oversee key aspects of the issue? How are the president, administrative agencies, and your interest group involved in working with Congress? Have representatives from your group or your agency testified before Congress on the issue? This information may be available on the website of the agency or group, or on the website of the committee/subcommittee or representatives/senators involved. How has media coverage of the issue in Congress reflected the themes discussed in this chapter and in chapter 1?

## Researching Congress? ▬▬▬▬▬▬▬▬

**Try These Authors:**

Roger H. Davidson          Morris P. Fiorina          Walter J. Oleszek
Richard F. Fenno, Jr.       David R. Mayhew

**Try These Sources:**

BINDER, SARAH A. *Minority Rights, Majority Rule: Partisanship and the Development of Congress.* New York: Cambridge University Press, 1997.
*Congressional Quarterly Weekly Report.* Washington, DC: Congressional Quarterly, Inc.
CONLAN, TIMOTHY J. *Taxing Choices: The Politics of Tax Reform.* Washington, DC: CQ Press, 1990.
DODD, LAWRENCE C. and BRUCE I. OPPENHEIMER, eds. *Congress Reconsidered,* 6th ed. Washington, DC: CQ Press, 1997.
MAYER, KENNETH R. and DAVID T. CANON. *The Dysfunctional Congress? The Individual Roots of an Institutional Dilemma.* Boulder, CO: Westview Press, 1999.
WEISBERG, HERBERT F. and SAMUEL C. PATTERSON. *Great Theater: American Congress in the 1990s.* Cambridge: Cambridge University Press, 1998.
WILSON, WOODROW. *Congressional Government: A Study in American Politics.* New York: Meridian Books, 1960 [1885].

## Endnotes ▬▬▬▬▬▬▬▬

1. *Federalist 51.*
2. *Federalist 58.*
3. Roger H. Davidson and Walter J. Oleszek, *Congress and Its Members,* 5th ed. (Washington, DC: CQ Press, 1996), 26, Table 2-1.

4. David Mayhew, *Congress: The Electoral Connection* (Yale University Press, 1974), 61.

5. Ibid., 67ff.

6. Ibid., 67.

7. Ibid., 52–53.

8. Ibid., 8.

9. Richard F. Fenno, Jr., *Home Style: House Members in Their Districts* (New York: HarperCollins, 1978).

10. Ibid., 215.

11. Ibid., 154.

12. Morris Fiorina, *Congress: Keystone of the Washington Establishment* (New Haven: Yale University Press, 1977), 46–47.

13. Ibid., 46.

14. Taken with permission from CONGRESSIONAL LEADERS, PARTIES, AND COMMITTEES, 1900 AND 2000, Roger H. Davidson, University of Maryland, College Park, Prepared for "The Turn of the Century Congress and American Governance: Then and Now," Seminar of the Woodrow Wilson International Center for Scholars, June 25, 1999. See http://wwics.si.edu/FORTHCOM/congress/david.htm.

15. Woodrow Wilson, *Congressional Government: A Study in American Politics* (New York: Meridian Books, 1956 [1885]), 83.

16. Representative George E. Brown, Jr. (D-CA), quoted in Davidson and Oleszek, *Congress and Its Members*, 226.

17. Quoted in John W. Kingdon, *Agendas, Alternatives, and Public Policies* (Boston: Little, Brown, 1984), 62.

# The Judiciary

## CHAPTER OUTLINE

Litigation is politics. Despite the temptation to see legal battles and lawsuits as somehow outside the traditional boundaries of politics—as if going to court were a crafty way of circumventing "the system"—litigation is a familiar and effective means of pursuing political goals through influential government institutions. In fact, litigation is often at the cutting edge of politics and public affairs. Consider the Internet and emerging Internet law. Internet litigation already is a complicated maze of complex political issues, and Congress and the White House are way behind the action in the courts. A quick sampling from just a few days in winter 2000 illustrates the rapid development of Internet politics through the courts:[1]

- AMAZON SUB FACES FTC INVESTIGATION AND LAWSUITS. Amazon subsidiary Alexa is facing two legal actions alleging the company invaded the privacy of its users as well as an informal investigation on the matter by the FTC. (February 9, 2000)
- INJUNCTION ISSUED AGAINST ICRAVETV. A U.S. district court yesterday issued an injunction prohibiting iCraveTV from streaming TV broadcasts into the U.S. The court will revisit the issue in roughly 90 days. (February 9, 2000)

- MICROSOFT LOSES ROUND ONE IN CALIFORNIA ACTIONS. Microsoft yesterday lost an attempt to move 25 cases pending against the software maker for unfair business practices out of Silicon Valley. (February 8, 2000)
- EBAY SUED OVER AUCTION BOT POLICIES. Ebay rival Bidder's Edge has filed an antitrust action against the company over the availability of eBay listings on other sites. (February 8, 2000)
- MP3.COM STRIKES BACK WITH LAWSUIT AGAINST RIAA [Recording Industry Association of America]. MP3.com has fired back in its legal battle with the RIAA by launching its own lawsuit that alleges that the association engaged in unfair business practices. (February 8, 2000)
- AS LONG AS IT DOESN'T HAPPEN AT MY LAW SCHOOL. The debate over the liability for linking will be tested in a California action over a Web site that posts student reviews of professors. An angry professor is suing both the site and a site that links to the site. (February 8, 2000)
- NORTHWEST AIRLINES SEARCHES COMPUTERS IN EMPLOYEE HOMES. Northwest Airlines has obtained a court order permitting it to search the computers of up to 20 employees who the company believes helped organize a sickout. (February 10, 2000)
- 2ND CIRCUIT COURT OF APPEALS RULES ON ANTICYBERSQUATTING LAW. The 2nd Circuit Court of Appeals became the first appellate court to uphold the anticybersquatting law in ruling that a domain name was registered in bad faith in violation of the Act. (February 3, 2000)
- DOUBLECLICK RESPONDS TO PRIVACY SUIT. In the wake of a privacy suit launched late last week against online advertiser Doubleclick, the company responded by noting its commitment to user privacy and arguing that its activities were fully disclosed months ago. (January 31, 2000)

Note the diversity of interests involved in these cases: major airlines, software producers, online merchants, corporate employees, law school students and professors, the music and television industries. Everyone is suing; it's the American way. As Congress and the president slowly grapple with Internet policy issues like privacy and ownership of domain names, the courts become the venue for Internet politics—just by other means. Litigation is ubiquitous in our society as a means of resolving conflict. Injured parties can get to court far faster than they can mobilize to influence the elected branches of the government.

Litigation replaces traditional electoral politics in so many cases in large part because of the Madisonian system of competition and compromise. That system multiplies interests and participants in government, as we have seen throughout this book, and it fragments political power. The inability of traditional electoral politics to resolve so many important issues gives private interests incentives to seek judicial resolution of their conflicts, and the power vacuum created by fragmenting authority encourages the courts to enter the fray. Despite certain limitations which we will examine later in this chapter, judges have a great deal of discretion in legal interpretations—and thus a great deal of real power.

**The Bottom Line.** With the courts as the venue for so many political disputes, the judiciary is as important, and sometimes more important, to the political process, than the president or Congress. The courts can defer to or accommodate the compromises reached in the regular political process, or replace those compromises with judicially made compromises that weigh interests differently. The role of the federal judiciary and its considerable independence in a competitive system become important aspects of American politics. In turn, the means by which judges receive and decide cases, and their political role in policy making, place the courts squarely within—and not outside—the American system of competition and compromise.

## BUILDING A STURDY BENCH: THE STRUCTURE AND SIGNIFICANCE OF THE COURTS

### The Federal Judiciary at the Founding

The Constitution makes public policy the outcome of the system of separation of powers and checks and balances. Balancing the president and Congress assures that neither the executive nor the legislature will dominate; both are forced to deliberate to produce the compromises necessary for governance in the national interest. The Supreme Court and the federal judiciary—separated and independent from the "political" branches—were not originally part of the checks-and-balances system.

The framers at the Constitutional Convention did not devote much discussion to the Supreme Court. The limited discussion of the proposed Supreme Court and the judiciary dealt primarily with protecting states' rights and interests from interference by federal courts, with how judicial appointments would be made, and with how the judiciary could be made independent of the legislature. Proponents of a strong federal judiciary wanted to establish lower federal courts in the Constitution; on the other side, states' righters and those wary of federal power feared that any such lower federal courts might threaten the autonomy of state courts.

As we might expect, the delegates reached very simple and effective compromises: First, Article 3 of the Constitution restricts the jurisdiction of the federal judiciary to cases that concern federal questions. The makeup of state judiciaries, and cases that arise under the laws of a particular state, must be settled by state courts. The federal courts become involved only in federal cases and those cases involving conflict between state and federal law or between state law and the U.S. Constitution. The Constitution also establishes only the Supreme Court and outlines its jurisdiction, while giving to Congress the authority to establish other federal courts later. Thus the Convention arguments concerning the scope and size of the federal judiciary were deflected away from Philadelphia and made a subject for politics in the new government.

# The Federal Judiciary Today

Following these compromises, the federal government today has two general classes of courts. *Constitutional courts* consist of the Supreme Court and other courts created by Congress pursuant to Article 3 of the Constitution, which grants judicial power to "such inferior Courts as the Congress may from time to time ordain and establish." *Legislative courts,* on the other hand, are established by Congress through its power, under Article 1 of the Constitution, to make whatever laws are necessary for carrying out its enumerated powers and the other powers of the federal government; these include courts in U.S. territories like Guam and Puerto Rico, the United States Tax Court, and the Court of Military Appeals.

With time, the federal judiciary has developed into a three-tiered, hierarchical system (see Zip Box 10.1).

**ON THE WEB**
www.uscourts.gov

**ON THE WEB**
www.supremecourtus
.gov

**ON THE WEB**
www.uscourts.gov/
allinks.html # all

**ON THE WEB**
lcweb.loc.gov/
global/judiciary.html

- At the lowest level, *United States District Courts* hear cases and operate largely as trial courts. District courts have original jurisdiction in most federal cases. There is at least one district court for each state and for the District of Columbia; some of the larger states have several district courts.
- The *United States Courts of Appeals,* or circuit courts, receive appeals from the District Courts and review some cases involving the quasi-judicial functions of administrative agencies. Although they are often overlooked, the courts of appeal are very powerful, because only a small percentage of their decisions are ever heard on appeal by the Supreme Court. There are twelve "circuits," eleven for the states and one for the District of Columbia.

Justices of the United States Supreme Court: front row (l. to r.): Antonin Scalia, John Paul Stevens, Chief Justice William H. Rehnquist, Sandra Day O'Connor, and Anthony M. Kennedy. Back row (l. to r.): Ruth Bader Ginsburg, David H. Souter, Clarence Thomas, and Stephen G. Breyer.

- The *United States Supreme Court* and its nine justices stand atop this system, serving as the court of final appeal. Lower courts, by deciding federal constitutional questions, can force the Supreme Court to exercise its appellate authority to either ratify or nullify the action that has already been taken. When lower courts have issued conflicting decisions, their opinions might be reviewed by the Supreme Court in order to establish uniform legal principles. The Supreme Court makes final determinations of constitutional law. Aside from its appellate jurisdiction, the Supreme Court under Article 3 exercises original jurisdiction "in all cases affecting ambassadors, other public ministers and consuls, and those in which a state shall be a party."

We will return occasionally to the lower courts throughout this chapter, but clearly the centerpiece of the federal judiciary is the Supreme Court. Alexis de Tocqueville, who devoted only a few pages to the Supreme Court in *Democracy in America,* nevertheless stressed its unique position and vast political power. He wrote:

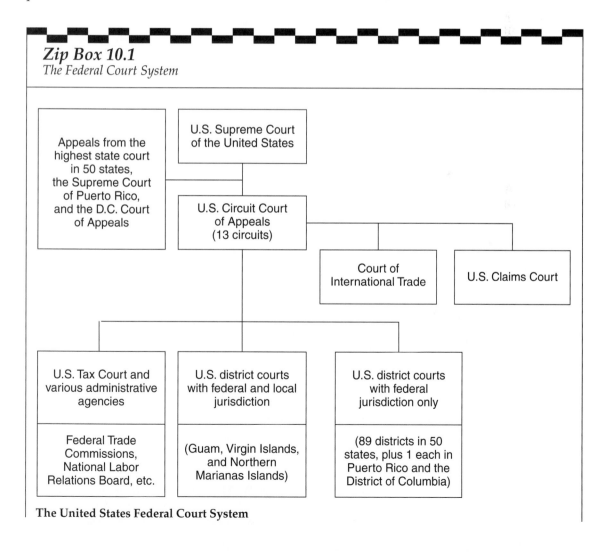

### Zip Box 10.1
*The Federal Court System*

**The United States Federal Court System**

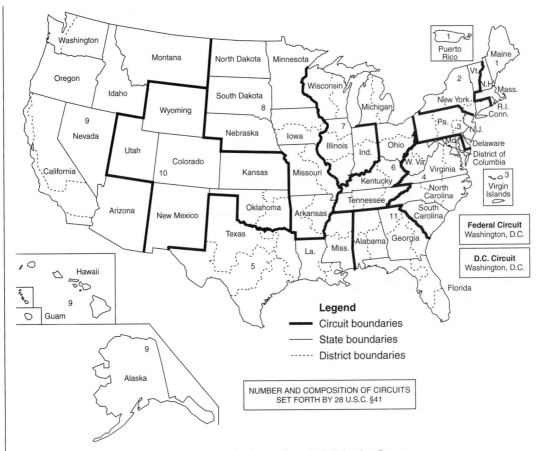

## The Thirteen Federal Judicial Circuits and Ninety-four U.S. District Courts

**Legend**
— Circuit boundaries
— State boundaries
----- District boundaries

NUMBER AND COMPOSITION OF CIRCUITS
SET FORTH BY 28 U.S.C. §41

## Cases Filed in the U.S. Supreme Court, 1938–1997.

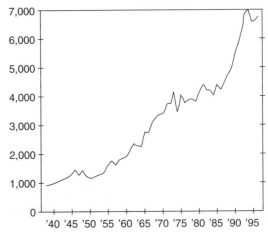

Number of cases

*Source:* Figures from *Vital Statistics on American Politics, 1999–2000,* ed. Harold W. Stanley and Harold Watkins (Washington, DC: CQ Press, 2000), 265, 266, 279.

When we have examined in detail the organization of the Supreme Court and the entire prerogatives which it exercises, we shall readily admit that a more imposing judicial power was never constituted by any people. . .

The peace, the prosperity, and the very existence of the Union are vested in the hands of the [Supreme Court Justices]. Without them the Constitution would be a dead letter; the executive appeals to them for assistance against the encroachments of the legislative power; the legislature demands . . . protection against the assaults of the executive; they defend the Union from the disobedience of the states, the states from the exaggerated claims of the Union, the public interest against private interests, and the conservative spirit of stability against the fickleness of the democracy.[2]

Whether the outputs of the Supreme Court are "liberal" or "conservative," then, one fact about the Court's operation stands out in stark contrast to most domestic policy making by coordinate branches—its independence and ability to act without going through a laborious political process. The judicial process is complicated and slow, but far more politically independent than decision making through the White House or Congress. The president, the House, and the Senate must agree to legislate, and each can check the other somehow in most major areas of policymaking. The Supreme Court, on the other hand, can hand down decisions the political process cannot make. For example, its ruling in *Brown v. Board of Education* in 1954 was the beginning of the end of school segregation in southern and border states. Congress, controlled by southern Democratic committee chairmen, had not passed major civil rights legislation since 1875; it could not politically have made such a sweeping policy change. President Eisenhower's failure to embrace and vigorously enforce the *Brown* decision illustrates the political constraints on the executive on such a charged political subject. But in *Brown* and the decisions that preceded it, the Supreme Court was able to end school segregation in law and shift the political environment surrounding the Civil Rights movement.

The last sentence in the Tocqueville passage above points to a final, and often overlooked, aspect of the judiciary's importance in the constitutional system. In many ways, the courts are a force operating against the will of the majority. In chapters 5 and 6, we saw that several aspects of the Madisonian system are antimajoritarian—for example, the president's veto, the requirement that super majorities be assembled in order to take certain legislative actions, and the Bill of Rights' protections of individual and minority interests against majority tyranny. The courts are a powerful antimajoritarian force. In evaluating legislation and adjudicating controversies, the courts are uniquely suited to defy majority interests and thwart popular will (see Discussion Box 10.1). The Court's decisions prohibiting prayer in public schools, for example, have run against the tide of prevailing public opinion for decades.

## Judicial Review

The evolution of a dynamic Supreme Court has been the most surprising area of expansion in the federal government's power. The key to the federal judiciary's unexpected power lies in its use of judicial review to evaluate whether or not the actions of other governmental branches and bodies conform to constitutional or statutory requirements. Judicial review as exercised by the federal courts in the United States extends to presidential, congressional, administrative, and state actions. It is the broadest form of review to be found in any government because it covers legislative acts. Judicial review serves to enhance the power of the federal judiciary in relation to the executive and the legislature, and it also has served to enhance the power of the federal judiciary over the states.

Although it was not a significant topic at the constitutional convention, judicial review in the federal courts was not completely unforeseen. The silence of Article 3 of the Constitution on the important issue of judicial review was clarified first by <u>Alexander Hamilton</u>'s interpretation of judicial authority in *Federalist 78*. In explicitly stating that the federal judiciary would have the power to overturn congressional laws that were repugnant to the Constitution, Hamilton clearly expressed the view of the majority of the delegates at the Constitutional Convention.

---

# DISCUSSION BOX 10.1
*HIGHER LAW VERSUS POPULAR WILL: A TOUGH COMPETITION*

The higher-law background of the Constitution and the national commitment to popular sovereignty often conflict, and it is up to the courts to protect the individual against what Madison called "the tyranny of the majority." In the following passage, legal scholar <u>Robert G. McCloskey</u> outlines the competition between higher law and popular sovereignty. According to the passage below, how does the separation of powers support these competing ideals? Are American attitudes about popular sovereignty and higher law evidence of the *absence* of compromise? What are the consequences of these attitudes?

Popular sovereignty suggests *will;* fundamental law suggests *limit.* The one idea conjures up the vision of an active, positive state; the other idea emphasizes the negative, restrictive side of the political problem. It may be possible to harmonize these seeming opposites by logical sleight of hand, by arguing that the doctrines of popular sovereignty and fundamental law were fused in the Constitution, which was a popularly willed limitation. But it seems unlikely that Americans in general achieved such a synthesis and far more probable, considering our later political history, that most of them retained the two ideas side by side. This propensity to hold contradictory ideas simultaneously is one of the most significant qualities of the American political mind at all stages of national history, and it helps substantially in explaining the rise to power of the United States Supreme Court.

For with their political hearts thus divided between the will of the people and the rule of law, Americans were naturally receptive to the development of institutions that reflected each of these values separately. The legislature with its power to initiate programs and policies, to respond to the expressed interest of the public, embodied the doctrine of popular sovereignty. The courts, generally supposed to be without will as Hamilton said, generally revered as impartial and independent, fell heir almost by default to the guardianship of the fundamental law. . . .

The consequences of all this were several. For one thing the Constitution itself could not become the certain and immutable code of governmental conduct that some of its latter-day idolators imagined it to be. Conceived in ambiguity as well as liberty, it could never escape that legacy. The framers had said in effect: with respect to certain questions, some of them very momentous, the Constitution means whatever the circumstances of the future will allow it to mean. But since those circumstances were almost sure to vary, the result was that alterability became the law of the Constitution's being: it might mean one thing in 1855, something else in 1905, and something still different in 1955, depending upon what circumstances, including popular expectations, warranted.*

*Robert G. McCloskey, *The American Supreme Court* (Chicago: University of Chicago Press, 1960), 13, 15.

More importantly, the Supreme Court, from its inception, assumed the authority to declare congressional acts unconstitutional. As early as 1792 the justices of the Court had refused to accept what they considered to be nonjudicial responsibilities delegated to them by Congress on the ground that the law violated Article 3 of the Constitution. In 1803, under Chief Justice John Marshall, the Supreme Court unequivocally stated its power of judicial review over congressional laws in the landmark case *Marbury v. Madison.* Newly elected president Thomas Jefferson had refused to deliver a justiceship-of-the-peace commission to William Marbury, who had been appointed to that position by outgoing Federalist president (and Jefferson rival) John Adams. Marbury

---

 ## DISCUSSION BOX 10.2
*FASTER THAN A SPEEDING BULLETIN: RAPID CHANGES IN TECHNOLOGY AND APPELLATE COURTS' STRUGGLE TO KEEP UP*

Not only are issues surrounding the Internet being addressed in the courts faster than in Congress or the White House—issues surrounding the Internet and other high-tech concerns are *changing* faster than the courts can deal with them. The facts in a lawsuit are determined by trial courts; appellate courts determine issues of law based on the facts presented at the original trial. But the pace of technological advance presents the very real possibility that critical facts will have altered by the time an appeals court is ready to issue a ruling. Legal scholar Stuart Minor Benjamin outlines this problem in the following passage. How does such a prospect affect the traditional understanding of an appellate court's function? How might such changes affect other actors' efforts to implement court rulings that might be obsolete the day they are handed down?

In the Supreme Court oral argument in *Reno v. ACLU*—the case that struck down a federal statute regulating Internet indecency—Justice Scalia asked:

"This is an area where change is enormously rapid. Is it possible that this statute is unconstitutional today, or was unconstitutional 2 years ago when it was examined on the basis of a record done about 2 years ago, but will be constitutional next week? . . . Or next year or in two years?"

. . . Commentators have largely ignored . . . the questions raised by Justice Scalia . . . : How should a court respond if, in the case before it, the factual findings from a previous opinion are no longer valid? . . .

We can also easily imagine future instances of factual transformations during the appellate process. The

computer industry, for example, provides some nice hypotheticals of continual factual change. Market share in the computer software industry has proved quite volatile—much more volatile than most any other industry. One year Lotus had the dominant spreadsheet program; the next year its market share was plummeting at a furious rate. The same is true of other companies and products that once had seemingly commanding market shares and then suddenly faded away—names from long ago (*i.e.,* the early- and mid-1990s) like Prodigy, Visi-Calc, and Borland. Similarly, changes in underlying technology can have dramatic effects. The recent litigation between Sun Microsystems and Microsoft over the latter's use of Sun's Java programming language, for example, relies heavily on the current configuration of Microsoft's programs in concluding that Microsoft is violating a contract with Sun. As those configurations change, the existence of any contractual violation may change with it. . . .

The larger issue . . . is that neither the appellate process nor our vision of precedent is terribly well equipped for rapidly changing facts. These situations confound not only our understanding of the role of appellate courts but also the seeming permanence of appellate decisions. . . . Where such transformations [of facts] occur, formerly "current" appellate rulings will be out of date. Ultimately, whether we like it or not, judicial opinions are written in sand.*

*Stuart Minor Benjamin, "Stepping into the Same River Twice: Rapidly Changing Facts and the Appellate Process," *Texas Law Review,* 78, no. 2 (December 1999), available on the World Wide Web at http://www.acusd.edu/~stuartb/article.html, retrieved March 7, 2000 [internal references omitted].

sought an original writ of mandamus from the Supreme Court to compel Secretary of State James Madison to give him his commission.

Marshall, though, faced a quandary: the Judiciary Act of 1789 granted the Supreme Court the authority, in its original jurisdiction, to issue writs of mandamus—yet if Marshall gave the order, Madison was almost sure to ignore it, making Marshall and the Court look powerless at a critical point in the Court's early development. *Not* issuing the writ, though, would play into the hands of Marshall's political opponents, giving the Jeffersonians a political victory and allowing Jefferson to make new appointments.

Judicial review provided the path out of this dilemma. Marshall ruled that the Judiciary Act giving the Court power to issue the writ was unconstitutional, because it conflicted with Article 3 of the Constitution. Because the Constitution had not included this power within the Court's original jurisdiction, Marshall wrote, *Congress* certainly could not do so. In effect, Marshall ruled that the Supreme Court was not empowered to solve Marbury's problem. At the same time, though, Marshall established the Court's role in reviewing laws and its power to overturn laws that conflicted with the Constitution. Marshall held that "it is emphatically the province and duty of the judicial department to say what the law is. Those who apply the rule to particular cases, must of necessity expound and interpret that rule. If two laws conflict with each other, the courts must decide on the operation of each."[3]

When Marshall stated that the last word on interpretation of the Constitution resides in the hands of the Supreme Court, he established an important precedent: the High Court assumed the power and responsibility to define constitutional law. The Constitution is the supreme law of the land; therefore the power to define the Constitution gives the Supreme Court power over Congress and the states, as well as the president, executive and administrative agencies, and their state counterparts.

Fewer than 150 congressional enactments have contained provisions held to be unconstitutional by the Supreme Court, out of a total of over 100,000 public and private bills that have been passed over the course of our history. However, approximately 1,200 state laws and provisions of state Constitutions have been overturned by the Supreme Court since 1789. Especially in the nation's formative years, judicial review more commonly overturned state actions, not federal ones.

## NIBBLES AROUND THE EDGES: THE COURTS IN A COMPETITIVE SYSTEM

As Tocqueville pointed out, the power of judicial review inevitably involves courts in politics as both governmental branches and private interests seek, through litigation, judicial resolutions of political conflicts. The Supreme Court, and the federal judiciary in general, can be extremely powerful political forces—but, of course, no power in the American system is ever exercised without limits and competitive challenges. Shared political influence and the difficulty of implementation limit the independence of the courts. Yet these limitations operate around the edges of judicial power, permitting influence primarily before and after rulings are made.

The system of shared powers gives the president and Congress some limited influence over the judiciary. The president, for example, is responsible for appointing judges to the federal bench. Some presidents, like <u>Ronald Reagan</u>, make appointments based largely on compatibility with their own philosophies and ideologies. In his two terms, Reagan appointed 368 judges to the federal district and appeals courts: 92 percent of the appointees were Republican, 93 percent were white, and 92 percent were male. Moreover, 46 percent had a net worth of more than $500,000, more than 20 percent were millionaires, and almost all had solidly conservative political records.[4] Other presidents, like <u>Bill Clinton</u>, pay greater attention to party affiliation and loyalty and less to ideological compatibility. When presidents choose judges based on ideology, have the political clout to get those choices through the Senate's approval process, and have the opportunity to fill a significant number of vacancies on the bench, presidents can influence the substance of the judiciary's rulings (see Zip Box 10.2).[5]

Still, the system of shared powers limits the influence the president alone can have over the judiciary. Presidential nominations must be approved by the Senate, for example. A Democrat-controlled Senate rejected the nomination of Judge Robert Bork to the Supreme Court in 1987, and interest groups were almost able to derail the nomination of Clarence Thomas in 1991 after charges arose that he had sexually harassed a coworker (see BriefCase Box 10.1). The pace of Senate confirmations slowed dramatically at the end of the 1990s, a function of divided government and partisan politics.[6] Further, once judges have been appointed to the bench, their independence limits the

The federal judiciary is not completely independent from the other branches of government. Here, the Senate holds hearings on the nomination of Ruth Bader Ginsburg to the Supreme Court.

*Zip Box 10.2*
*Recent Appointments to the Federal Judiciary*

## Characteristics of Federal District and Appellate Court Appointees (percent)

|  | Reagan Appointees | Bush Appointees | Clinton Appointees |
|---|---|---|---|
| **District Court** | | | |
| Political affiliation | | | |
| Democrat | 4.8 | 5.4 | 89.1 |
| Republican | 91.7 | 88.5 | 4.8 |
| Independent or other | 3.4 | 6.1 | 6.1 |
| Past party activism | 59.0 | 60.8 | 52.4 |
| Race/ethnicity | | | |
| White | 92.4 | 89.2 | 73.8 |
| Black | 2.1 | 6.8 | 19.0 |
| Asian-American | 0.7 | 0.0 | 1.6 |
| Hispanic | 4.8 | 4.0 | 5.2 |
| Native American | — | — | 0.4 |
| Sex | | | |
| Female | 8.3 | 19.6 | 28.2 |
| Number of appointees | 290 | 148 | 248 |
| **Court of Appeals** | | | |
| Political affiliation | | | |
| Democrat | 0.0 | 5.4 | 85.4 |
| Republican | 96.2 | 89.2 | 6.3 |
| Independent or other | 3.9 | 5.4 | 8.3 |
| Past party activism | 65.4 | 70.3 | 56.3 |
| Race/ethnicity | | | |
| White | 97.4 | 89.2 | 77.1 |
| Black | 1.3 | 5.4 | 10.4 |
| Asian-American | 0.0 | 0.0 | 2.1 |
| Hispanic | 1.3 | 5.4 | 10.4 |
| Sex | | | |
| Female | 5.1 | 18.9 | 33.3 |
| Number of appointees | 78 | 37 | 48 |

*Note:* "—" indicates not available.
*Source:* Table adapted from the *Vital Statistics on American Politics, 1999–2000*, ed. Harold W. Stanley and Harold Watkins (Washington, DC: CQ Press, 2000), 276–277.

president's influence. Chief Justice <u>Earl Warren</u>, for example, surprised President Eisenhower and other Republicans with a string of liberal decisions in the 1950s and 1960s.

Congress also has some authority over the judiciary. Senate approval is required to ratify presidential nominations, and senators of the president's party exercise "senatorial courtesy" in blocking unacceptable appointments to lower federal judgeships. Congress is empowered to decide the nature of the federal judiciary's organization, the number of courts and judges, their location, and their appellate jurisdiction. And though Congress cannot legislatively overrule

## BriefCase Box 10.1
*Interest Groups and Supreme Court Appointments: Bork and Thomas*

We saw in chapter 2 that interest groups use a variety of tactics and resources to compete for influence over government actions. Supreme Court appointments are no exception, bringing out interest groups from all parts of the political spectrum in support of or opposition to specific nominees. Are you surprised at the relatively little effort interest groups put into "external" activities, like maintaining a presence in the media or writing Op-Ed articles? Why would "internal" and "intergroup" activities be better tactics when trying to influence the progress of a nomination to the Supreme Court?

### Priority Tactics as Employed by Advocates in the Bork and Thomas Confirmation Processes

| Tactics | Total (N = 109) | Bork Priority (N = 59) | Thomas Priority (N = 50) |
|---|---|---|---|
| **Internal Group Activities** | | | |
| 1. Lobbying Senate | 65.0% | 59.3% | 72.0% |
| 2. Holding strategy sessions with members of Congress or staff | 13.0 | 13.6 | 12.0 |
| 3. Preparing witnesses | 13.0 | 10.2 | 16.0 |
| 4. Reaching out to group members | 40.4 | 57.6 | 16.0[a] |
| 5. Coordinating internal group efforts | 33.9 | 33.9 | 34.0 |
| **Intergroup Activities** | | | |
| 1. Coordinating activities with other groups | 44.4 | 42.4 | 46.0 |
| 2. Participating in strategy sessions with other groups | 30.0 | 37.3 | 22.0[a] |
| **External Group Activities** | | | |
| 1. Writing op-ed pieces, appearing on talk shows, etc. | 20.0 | 20.3 | 20.0 |
| 2. Conducting polls or other research toward building mass appeal | 4.6 | 6.8 | 2.0 |
| 3. Networking to keep presence in media | 18.3 | 22.0 | 14.0 |

*Note:* Respondents assigned each activity a value: "1" through "4" indicating first, second, third, and fourth priority rating, respectively. These are collapsed into two columns labeled "priority" above. The tactics that were employed but not ranked as a priority and the tactics that were not employed at all make up the unreported balance in each cell.
The row percentages do not sum to 100 because the figures in each column reflect only the proportion of participants who assigned the activity a priority rating: overall, in the case of Bork, or the case of Thomas, respectively.
[a]$p < .05$.

### Sample of Interest Groups

| Pro-Bork | Anti-Bork |
|---|---|
| Ad Hoc Committee in Defense of Life | Alliance for Justice |
| American Conservative Union | American Civil Liberties Union |
| American Farm Bureau Federation | American Federation of State, County, and |
| American Legislative Enchange Council | Municipal Employees |
| Americans for Tax Reform | Americans for Religous Liberty |
| Center for Judicial Studies | Center for Population Options |
| Christian Action Council | Citizen Action |

Christian Voice
Coalitions for America
College Republican National Committee
Concerned Women for America
Conservative Leadership PAC
Council for National Policy, Inc. (CNP, Inc.)
Federal Criminal Investigators Association
Fraternal Order of Police
Free the Court
International Association of Chiefs of Police
International Narcotics Enforcement Officers
   Association
Moral Majority
National District Attorneys Association
National Jewish Coalition
National Law Enforcement Council
National Republican Heritage Group's Council
National Sheriffs' Association
National Troopers' Association
Renaissance Women
Victims Assistance Legal Organization
We the People

Communications Workers of America
Epilepsy Foundation of America
Federally Employed Women
Federation of Women Lawyers
Friends of the Earth
International Association of Machinists
Mexican-American Women's National
   Association
National Abortion Rights Action League
National Association of Social Workers
   Associations
National Coalition to Abolish the Death Penalty
National Conference of Women's Bar Associations
National Council of La Raza
National Gay and Lesbian Task Force
National Lawyer's Guild
National Urban League
National Women's Health Network
9 to 5, National Association of Working Women
People for the American Way
Rainbow Lobby
Sane/Freeze
Sierra Club
United States Student Association
YWCA/USA

*Note:* Two names have been omitted in deference to the respondents' requests for complete anonymity.

## Sample of Interest Groups

| Pro-Thomas | Anti-Thomas |
| --- | --- |
| American Road and Transportation Builders Association | AFL-CIO |
| Americans for Tax Reform | American Association for Affirmative Action |
| Aqudath Israel of America | American Federation of Teachers |
| The Associated General Contractors of America | Americans for Democratic Action |
| Association of Christian Schools International | Equal Rights Advocates |
| Association of Retired Americans | The Gray Panthers |
| Citizens for Educational Freedom | Human Rights Campaign Fund |
| Coalitions for America | National Abortion Rights Action League |
| Concerned Women for America | National Association of Commissions for Women |
| Congress of Racial Equality | National Black Caucus of State Legislators |
| Conservative Caucus | National Conference of Black Lawyers |
| Conservative Victory Committee | National Council of Churches |
| International Narcotic Enforcement Officers Association | National Council of Jewish Women |
| | National Council of La Raza |
| National Black Nurses Association | National Council of Senior Citizens |
| National Deputy Sheriffs Association | National Federation of Business and Professional Women's Clubs |
| National District Attorneys Association | National Lawyers Guild |
| National Federation of Independent Business | Older Women's League |

| | |
|---|---|
| National Jewish Coalition | People for the American Way |
| National Small Business United | Service Employees International Union |
| National Tax Limitation Committee | United Church of Christ |
| Seniors Coalition | United Auto Workers |
| Students for America | Women's Employed Institute |
| Traditional Values Coalition | |
| U.S. Business and Industry Council | |
| U.S. Chamber of Commerce | |

*Source:* Figures from Christine DeGregorio and Jack Rossotti, "Campaigning for the Court: Interest Group Participation in the Bork and Thomas Confirmation Processes," in *Interest Group Politics,* 4th ed., ed. Allan J. Cigler and Burdett A. Loomis (Washington, DC: CQ Press, 1994), 223, 237, 238.

a Supreme Court decision based on the Constitution, it does have the power to change unpopular rulings by amending the Constitution.

Congress also exercises some influence over judicial review, as it is authorized by Article 3 of the Constitution to make regulations concerning the Supreme Court's appellate authority. After the Civil War, in fact, Congress, worried about the prospect of the Court overturning its Reconstruction laws, rescinded the Supreme Court's authority to decide a particular case *after* the Court had heard the case, but before it ruled.[7] The Court accepted the action as a legitimate exercise of Congress's authority over its jurisdiction.

In general, though, efforts to use power over appellate jurisdiction to bring the Supreme Court into line with Congress's views have failed. Congress also cannot delegate nonjudicial executive or legislative powers to the courts without violating the constitutional separation of powers. In 1792, the Court rejected a congressional statute delegating to the circuit courts the responsibility for settling claims of disabled Revolutionary War veterans, and making the courts' decisions subject to review by the Secretary of War. Chief Justice John Jay declared the statute unconstitutional because

> neither the legislative nor the executive branches can constitutionally assign to the judicial [branch] any duties but such as are properly, judicial, and to be performed in a judicial manner. . . . [T]he duties assigned to the circuit courts by this Act are not of that description, and . . . the Act itself does not appear to contemplate them as such, inasmuch as it subjects the decisions of these courts, made pursuant to those duties, first to the consideration and suspension of the secretary of war, and then to the revision of the legislature. . . . [B]y the Constitution, neither the secretary of war, nor any other executive officer, nor even the legislature, are authorized to sit as a court of errors on the judicial acts or opinions of this court.[8]

*Hayburn's Case* was the first in which Supreme Court justices, riding circuit and acting in the capacity of circuit court judges, held an act of Congress to be unconstitutional.

Finally, federal judges enjoy life tenure and their salaries cannot be reduced. Only through a cumbersome impeachment process, rarely used, can Congress remove judges from the bench. So even though Congress and the executive can exercise some influence over the nature and makeup of the judicial system, the characteristics of judges, and the jurisdictions of particular courts, they have only limited influence over the actions of the judiciary.

## The Problem of Implementation

The influence of the federal courts is affected in a more significant way by the fact that court decisions need to be implemented, or carried out, by other actors in the system. The courts have no armies, they do not control budgets and funds, and they cannot force other political actors to follow their dictates. The most famous example of this judicial weakness is captured in an anecdote involving President Andrew Jackson. In *Worcester v. Georgia* (1832), the Supreme Court ruled that Georgia's extension of state laws to Indian territory was repugnant to the Constitution. The decision supported Indian nations' political independence in relation to the states, and in so doing it complicated efforts by the states and the Jackson administration to remove eastern Indians to the

---

## DISCUSSION BOX 10.3
*REPORTER IN THE COURT! REPORTER IN THE COURT!*
*COMPROMISES AND AMBIGUITY IN COMMUNICATING COURT OPINIONS*

The Supreme Court must be able to communicate its rulings to the public, and coverage in the news media can be an important dynamic in garnering implementation cooperation and public support for decisions. Supreme Court expert David M. O'Brien notes that the Court has become slightly more cognizant of the media in recent decades. The Court now distributes copies of the "headnotes," or case summaries, to the media, and it has expanded its Public Information Office.* Still, O'Brien points out that time and other constraints facing news outlets affect their ability to cover the Court's rulings: only the most controversial rulings are reported, for example, and journalists must condense complex and lengthy opinions into brief reports that can be understood by an inexpert public. According to the following passages, what aspects of the judicial process affect the clarity of Supreme Court rulings? Considering what we know about the news media, why would they have trouble communicating the kinds of decisions O'Brien refers to here?

Some problems in communicating decisions are of the Court's own making. Since opinions of the Court must meet the approval of a majority of the justices, ambiguity results from the negotiations and compromises necessary to reach agreement. [Justice Charles Evans] Hughes, for example, met opposition to one of his opinions because of the "insertion of the word 'reasonable' in

certain places," even though he "put in the word out of abundant caution" to qualify the Court's holding. Since it was not "worth while to have a division in the Court over its use in the present case," he omitted the word from the opinion. . . .

Misunderstanding also results when opinions include extraneous matter, statements of personal philosophy, and other forms of obiter dicta—words entirely unnecessary for the case. These problems are exacerbated by longer, more heavily footnoted opinions. The justices are particularly confusing when they divide five to four and issue numerous concurring and dissenting opinions. . . .

Justice Stewart's opinion in *Gannett Co. v. De-Pasquale* (1979) illustrates these problems. His opinion not only invited sharp criticism from four dissenters but also caused confusion in the press and lower courts. . . .

[Justices] Burger, Powell, Brennan, Marshall, and Stevens later sought publicly to clarify and defend the ruling. Their extra-judicial explanations merely exacerbated the confusion. Reporters found the decision "cloudy," "confused," "mushy," and a "muddle." As the media lawyer James Goodale summed it up, "*Gannett* Means What It Says: But Who Knows What It Says?"†

*David M. O'Brien, *Storm Center: The Supreme Court in American Politics* (New York: Norton, 1986), 281ff.
†Ibid., 284–286 [internal footnotes omitted].

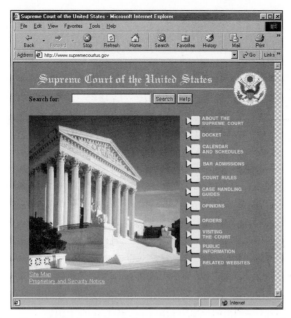

The Supreme Court's website includes information on upcoming court cases, previous opinions, and links to related websites.

West. Yet Georgia, unwilling to abide by the ruling, took advantage of legal loopholes and ignored it; the Jackson administration, sympathetic to Georgia, was unwilling (and not bound by law) to press the issue. Jackson declared, "[T]he decision of the supreme court has fell still born, and they find that they cannot coerce Georgia to yield to its mandate." In other words, Marshall and the Court were at the mercy of other forces responsible for implementing and enforcing the Court's edicts. If these forces refused, there was little the Court could do.[9]

Decisions about implementation and enforcement of Court decisions continue to limit the Court's ability to act independently. Recently, the cooperation of police and law enforcement officials has been necessary to implement the Court's many decisions regarding due process and the protection of procedural rights. Police, for example, are charged with implementing the Court's *Miranda* ruling requiring that suspects be notified of their rights. After the *Brown* desegregation decisions, the Court relied on numerous forces at state and local levels, as well as on the president and Congress, to begin the process of desegregation. A key event in the process of implementing the Court's ruling was President Eisenhower's nationalization of the Arkansas National Guard to enforce a federal court order desegregating Little Rock's Central High School.

Finally, court decisions that affect the bureaucracy must be carried out by officials at administrative agencies. As court review of agency actions becomes less deferential to decisions made by expert administrators, judges—who often lack technical expertise or knowledge of implementation problems—give agencies complicated new responsibilities and difficult goals to meet in implementing court orders.

# CALLING 'EM AS THEY SEE 'EM: COMPETING INTERESTS AND NEGOTIATED COMPROMISES IN JUDICIAL DECISION MAKING

## No Harm, No Foul: Getting and Selecting "Justiciable" Cases

The judiciary formally operates within much more closely defined procedural limits than the other branches of government. First and most importantly, the Constitution limits the federal judiciary to *cases and controversies* arising under the Constitution, laws, and treaties. Judges cannot initiate cases. Unlike the president and Congress, the courts must wait for issues to be brought to them, and they cannot make decisions in the absence of a concrete case or controversy. In *Muskrat v. United States* (1911), the Supreme Court refused to accept jurisdiction that Congress had conferred upon it to rule upon the constitutionality of congressional acts regulating lands possessed by Cherokee Indians. The Court rejected jurisdiction, holding that the issue did not contain a case or controversy.

Another criterion affecting the courts' selection of cases and controversies is *"standing."* To have standing to sue in court, generally

- a plaintiff must have suffered an *injury in fact,* meaning an actual or imminent invasion of a particular and concrete legally protected interest—not an injury that is conjectural or hypothetical;
- there must be a *causal connection* between the injury and action by the defendant;
- it must be *likely*—not merely speculative—that the *injury will be redressed by a favorable court decision.*

Rules governing standing prevent people or interests from bringing cases in which they are not directly involved, and the Court will not hear hypothetical cases designed to test what the Court might do in an actual case.

Cases must be *"ripe"* in order to be justiciable; the courts will not hear cases regarding a controversy that might only arise in future. In *United Public Works v. Mitchell* (1947), for example, the Court refused to issue an injunction against enforcement of the Hatch Act, which prohibited federal employees from participating in political activities. The plaintiffs had sought the injunction even though they had yet to engage in any political activities; the Court declined to rule on the "hypothetical threat" the Hatch Act posed. Moreover, cases that have been resolved and in which the plaintiff no longer has a complaint are rendered "moot," and also will not be heard.

The justiciability concepts of standing, ripeness, and mootness, and the case and controversy requirement of Article 3 are fused. A matter is justiciable when there is a case and controversy, which in turn automatically gives the involved parties standing. But because all of these conditions must be met before the courts will hear a case, access to the judiciary is limited.

Judges' decisions about these matters are subjective. Supreme Court justices and their colleagues in the lower courts often disagree, for example, on whether or not a case is ripe or whether a plaintiff has met the conditions for standing. Activist judges who want to address a particular issue find standing in places where other judges, who might want to avoid tackling a difficult case, do not. Since the 1970s, Congress and the federal courts have allowed far greater access to interest groups and others seeking redress through the courts by loosening the requirements for standing. This trend has encouraged the proliferation of interest groups and the use of the courts to pursue political ends.

## Supreme Court Independence and Political Questions

Decisions regarding the case-and-controversy rule, ripeness, and standing give judges some leeway in determining what cases they will, and will not, hear. The Supreme Court, in particular, has taken advantage of the vagueness of the Constitution to control the issues it addresses. Article 3's brevity makes it necessary for the courts to interpret the precise meaning of such terms as *judicial power* and what constitutes a justiciable case and controversy. And because litigation is simply politics by other means, cases involve wide-ranging interests and issues; this creates for the Supreme Court a broad docket from which it can select the issues it wants to address and those it wishes to bypass.

In fact, the Supreme Court can refuse, and has refused, to hear cases that clearly arise within its *original* jurisdiction. Although Chief Justice Marshall stated in *Cohens v. Virginia* (1821) that "we have no more right to decline the exercise of jurisdiction which is given than to usurp that which is not given,"[10] the Supreme Court has at times declined to hear cases that it did not consider appropriate. *Ohio v. Wyandotte Chemicals Corp.* (1971), for example, presented the Court with complex pollution issues involving a state and citizens of another state, as well as a state and foreign citizens; the case clearly fell within the Court's original jurisdiction. Nevertheless, the Court stated: "While we consider that Ohio's complaint does state a cause of action that falls within the compass of our original jurisdiction, we have concluded that this Court should nevertheless decline to exercise that jurisdiction."[11]

Various reasons were given by the Court for refusing to exercise its jurisdiction in the *Wyandotte* case. The "difficulties" of the case were cited, and the "sense of futility that has accompanied this Court's attempts to treat with the complex technical and political matters that inhere in all disputes of the kind at hand." The Court believed that this was a matter for resolution by other parts of the government, whether federal, state, or local. In concluding its opinion, the Court stated:

> To sum up, this Court has found even the simplest sort of interstate pollution case an extremely awkward vehicle to manage. And this case is an extremely complex one, both because of the novel scientific issues of fact inherent in it and the multiplicity of governmental agencies already involved. Its successful resolution would require primarily skills of fact finding, conciliation, detailed coordination with and perhaps not infrequent deference to other adjudicatory bodies, and close supervision of the technical performance of local industry. We have no claim to such expertise, nor reason to believe that, were we to adjudicate this case, and others like it, we would not have to reduce drastically our attention to those controversies for which this Court is a proper and nec-

Supreme Court Justices are not isolated from politics. Here, Chief Justice William Rehnquist addresses the American Bar Association.

essary forum. Such a serious intrusion on society's interest in our most deliberate and considerate performance of our paramount role as the supreme federal appellate court could in our view be justified only by the strictest necessity, an element which is evidently totally lacking in this instance.[12]

This is a clear-cut example of the way the Court can avoid involvement in a major policymaking area, even though it has jurisdiction and could set the directions of policy if it wanted to become involved.

A final factor involved in court decisions about hearing particular cases involves the *political question* doctrine. "Political questions" are questions that are best suited to be decided by the other two branches of government—especially public policy questions, which should be answered by the elected, and politically responsible, branches of government. The courts generally refuse to hear cases involving controversies on political questions in order to insulate themselves from dangerous political battles. Yet what is a political question to one justice is justiciable to another as a matter of law.

Two cases, *Baker v. Carr* (1962) and *Reynolds v. Sims* (1964) exemplify the way the Supreme Court can become involved in political questions if it so desires. The Court divided sharply on whether or not it should accept these cases, which involved the apportionment of electoral districts for state legislatures. Given that state electoral and representational plans were the result of prior competition and compromise in the political system, the question was whether the Court should accept those outcomes or supercede them, replacing the results of the regular political process with Court action. Were the issues constitutional and hence justiciable, or were they political and beyond the

Court's power to decide? The Supreme Court decided to become involved in these cases, but only over the vehement objections of justices who felt the questions were political and best left to other governmental institutions. (See BriefCase Box 10.2 and Zip Box 10.3.)

---

 ## BriefCase Box 10.2
*Does This Look Like a Job for a Judge? Competing*
*Applications of the Political Question Doctrine*

In *Marbury v. Madison* (1803), Chief Justice John Marshall stated that courts should not interfere with matters that are constitutionally placed within the jurisdiction and discretion of the president and Congress, the "political" branches of the government. The political question doctrine, though, is an accordian that can be expanded and contracted at the will of judges.

One of the most controversial cases in which the Court intervened in the political process was *Baker v. Carr* (1962), in which it held that the Fourteenth Amendment's Equal Protection Clause applied to the electoral districts for representation in state assemblies. Two years later, the Court applied equal protection to the upper bodies of state legislatures in *Reynolds v. Sims* (1964). At the time of the *Baker* case, no state had equal apportionment in either its legislative assembly or its senate; many states' districts advantaged rural areas over populous, and growing, urban areas. The Court's decisions spawned massive litigation to overturn existing state electoral apportionment plans across the country.

Justice William Brennan defended the Court's decision to rule in apportionment decisions; Justice Felix Frankfurter wrote that the Court should refrain from getting involved. Judging from the following passages, why does Brennan think the case is appropriate for Court action? How does he dismiss the claim that the subject is a nonjusticiable "political question"? How does Frankfurter distinguish this case from other equal protection cases? According to Frankfurter, what is at risk if the Court enters the fray on state electoral apportionment? Why, specifically, is the Court vulnerable if it addresses the question, and why is it particularly ill-suited to provide a satisfactory remedy in this case?

### Brennan, for the Majority:

We come, finally, to the ultimate inquiry whether our precedents as to what constitutes a nonjusticiable "political question" bring the case before us under the umbrella of that doctrine. A natural beginning is to note whether any of the common characteristics [of political questions] which we have been able to identify and label descriptively are present. We find none: The question here is the consistency of state action with the Federal Constitution. We have no question decided, or to be decided, by a political branch of government coequal with this Court. Nor do we risk embarrassment of our government abroad, or grave disturbance at home if we take issue with Tennessee as to the constitutionality of her action here challenged. Nor need the appellants, in order to succeed in this action, ask the Court to enter upon policy determinations for which judicially manageable standards are lacking. Judicial standards under the Equal Protection Clause are well developed and familiar, and it has been open to courts since the enactment of the Fourteenth Amendment to determine, if on the particular facts they must, that a discrimination reflects no policy, but simply arbitrary and capricious action.*

### Frankfurter, dissenting:

The Court today reverses a uniform course of decision established by a dozen cases, including one by which the very claim now sustained was unanimously rejected only five years ago. The impressive body of rulings thus cast aside reflected the equally uniform course of our political history regarding the relationship between population and legislative representation—a wholly different matter from denial of the franchise to individuals because of race, color, religion or sex. Such a massive repudiation of the experience of our whole past in asserting destructively novel judicial power demands a detailed analysis of the role of this Court in our constitutional scheme. Disregard of inherent limits in the effective exercise of the Court's "judicial Power" not only presages the futility of judicial intervention in the essentially political conflict of forces by which the relation between population and representation has time out of mind been and now is determined. It may well impair the Court's position as the ultimate organ of "the supreme Law of the Land" in that vast range of legal problems, often strongly entangled in popular feeling, on which this Court must pronounce. The Court's authority—possessed of neither the purse nor the sword—ultimately rests on sustained public confidence in its moral sanction. Such feeling must be nourished by the Court's complete detachment, in fact and in appearance, from political entanglements and by abstention from injecting itself into the clash of political forces in political settlements.

. . . In effect, today's decision empowers the courts of the country to devise what should constitute the proper composition of the legislatures of the fifty States. If state courts should for one reason or another find themselves unable to discharge this task, the duty of doing so is put on the federal courts or on this Court, if State views do not satisfy this Court's notion of what is proper districting.

We were soothingly told at the bar of this Court that we need not worry about the kind of remedy a court could effectively fashion once the abstract constitutional right to have courts pass on a state-wide system of electoral districting is recognized as a matter of judicial rhetoric, because legislatures would heed the Court's admonition. This is not only a euphoric hope. It implies a sorry . . . confession of judicial impotence in place of a frank acknowledgement that there is not under our Constitution a judicial remedy for every political mischief, for every undesirable exercise of legislative power. The Framers carefully and with deliberate forethought refused so to enthrone the judiciary. In this situation, as in others of like nature, appeal for relief does not belong here. Appeal must be to an informed, civically militant electorate. In a democratic society like ours, relief must come through an aroused popular conscience that sears the conscience of the people's representatives.[†]

*Baker v. Carr, 369 U.S. 186 (1962).

[†]Ibid.

In the final analysis, the Supreme Court is not a monolithic abstraction, but a reflection of its justices, their philosophies of the law, and the realities of politics. *Judicial activists* dive into the political waters, immersing the Court in political battles and eagerly addressing hot issues with the conviction that the Court has a proactive role to play in the political system. Justices exercising *judicial restraint* shy away from those battles, avoiding controversial topics, ruling with narrow interpretations of law, avoiding major constitutional issues whenever possible, and generally attempting to keep the Court from entering too deeply into legislative and other political issues. Justiciability, jurisdiction, and political questions serve as tools by which the courts can, to some extent, dismiss or embrace the cases that they want to hear.

## Judges in a Competitive Environment: Making Decisions

A number of factors affect the latitude enjoyed by judges crafting decisions on specific issues. First, judges decide cases on constitutional grounds only if they feel it is absolutely necessary. Virtually all cases are *construed narrowly*, or settled without having to resort to the Constitution. One reason for this is that courts are involved in the policymaking process through interpretations of statutory and administrative law that might not raise constitutional issues at all. For example, the Supreme Court can decide that an administrative agency has unreviewable discretion to act when an important policy decision is being made. Such an issue is decided not on the basis of the Constitution, but rather upon interpretation of legislation and administrative practice, as well as prior judicial precedent. (See Discussion Box 10.4.)

## Zip Box 10.3
*Can the Court Come Out to Play? Judicial Involvement in the Political Process*

The Supreme Court decides for itself whether or not an issue represents a "political question" best left to the elected branches of government. Here are some cases in which the Court chose between accepting and rejecting cases involving the political process.

- *Luther v. Borden* (1849): The first famous political question case in which the Supreme Court refuses to accept jurisdiction. The case would have required the Court to decide whether the legitimate "republican" government of Rhode Island, guaranteed to citizens by the Constitution's guaranty clause, was the state's original charter government or a new rebellious group trying to seize power. The Court holds that enforcement of the guaranty clause is within the discretion of Congress and the president, not the courts.
- *Mississippi v. Johnson* (1868): If the Court accepted jurisdiction, its decision might have enjoined the president from enforcing post–Civil War reconstruction acts on the ground that they were unconstitutional. Complicating the Court's action was a radical Republican majority in Congress that might have impeached any court that stood in the way of its post–Civil War reconstruction policies. The Court conveniently holds that it has no jurisdiction to enjoin what it holds to be a discretionary presidential power.
- *Steel Seizure Cases* (1952): President Truman ordered the Secretary of Commerce to seize the nation's steel mills, in order to prevent a strike that might have crippled the nation's war effort during the Korean War. The Court rules Truman's order an unconstitutional exercise of power. Chief Justice Frederick Moore Vinson writes an impassioned dissent arguing that the

Court should not intervene because the president is following constitutional precedent in unilaterally seizing the mills.
- *Powell v. McCormack* (1969): The Court overrules a congressional vote to refuse to seat controversial Harlem representative Adam Clayton Powell because of ethics violations. The Constitution provides that "Each House shall be the Judge of the Elections, Returns, and Qualifications of its own Members"—yet the Court rules that Powell has been duly elected and meets the constitutional qualifications of age, residence, and citizenship, and should therefore be seated.
- *U.S. v. Nixon* (1974): At the height of the Watergate investigation, the Court rejects President Nixon's claim of executive privilege and orders him to honor a district court subpoena for Oval Office audiotapes of conversations between the president and his aides. The Court dismisses the claim by Nixon's attorney that the separation of powers precludes a court from intervening in an area of discretionary presidential actions.
- *Immigration and Naturalization Service v. Chadha* (1983): The Court rules that the legislative veto, used in more than two hundred other laws, is unconstitutional because it allows Congress to legislate without following all of the constitutional requirements for lawmaking, particularly the presentment clause under which the president must sign laws.
- *Bowsher v. Synar* (1986): The Court overturns a complex budget-balancing law known as the Gramm-Rudman-Hollings Act. Chief Justice Warren Burger's majority opinion held that the law violated the separation of powers because it gave what were essentially executive powers over budgetary decisions to an officer controlled by Congress.

Even in cases that approach a constitutional issue, though, the Court will usually try to find a way of deciding the case without reaching constitutional issues. For example, at several points in this book we have examined the issue of the decennial census. The Constitution requires that censuses be taken for the purpose of apportioning representatives in Congress, making it a process with clear and explicit constitutional importance. Interests that oppose using statistical sampling methods to address the undercount of minorities have argued that such methods are unconstitutional because the Constitution requires an "enumeration," not an estimation, of the population. In ruling on such challenges, the Supreme Court has avoided the constitutional question involved. Addressing challenges to the 1990 census, the Court ruled that the Secretary of Commerce was within his administrative discretion to decide *against* using statistical methods in the census; the Court did not address whether or not these methods were *permitted* under the Constitution. Faced with a more difficult issue in 1999, because the Census Bureau planned to use statistical methods in the 2000 census, the Court again managed to avoid the constitutional question. The Court ruled that the Census Act, passed by Congress and governing the taking of the census, prohibits using such methods

---

## Discussion Box 10.4
### *That Was Then, This Is Now—But So What?*
### *Competing Visions of Constitutional Interpretation*

The Supreme Court usually tries to decide cases without invoking constitutional principles, but some cases demand interpretation of the document's provisions. Many of the conflicts discussed in this chapter center on how judges interpret the Constitution. A key issue that arises in such cases is the deference to be paid to the framers' original intentions. Which of the following brief passages do you find more compelling? Can both be right? Is there room for compromise between the two, or must a judge choose one interpretation or the other?

### Judge Robert H. Bork:

The progression of political judging, judging unrelated to law . . . has greatly accelerated in the past few decades and now we see the theorists of constitutional law urging judges on to still greater incursions into Americans' right of self-government.

This is an anxious problem and one that can be met only by understanding that judges must always be guided by the original understanding of the Constitution's provisions. Once adherence to the original understanding is weakened or abandoned, a judge, perhaps instructed by a revisionist theorist, can reach any result, because the human mind and will, freed of the constraints of history and "the sediment of history which is the law," can reach any result. . . . [N]o set of propositions is too preposterous to be espoused by a judge or a law professor who has cast loose from the historical Constitution.*

### Justice William J. Brennan, Jr.:

It is arrogant to pretend that from our vantage we can gauge accurately the intent of the Framers on application of principle to specific, contemporary questions. All too often, sources of potential enlightenment such as records of the ratification debates provide sparse or ambiguous evidence of the original intention. Typically, all that can be gleaned is that the Framers themselves did not agree about the application or meaning of particular constitutional provisions, and hid their differences in cloaks of generality. Indeed, it is far from clear whose intention is relevant—that of the drafters, the congressional disputants, or the ratifiers in the states—or even whether the idea of an original intention is a coherent way of thinking about a jointly drafted document drawing its authority from a general assent of the states. . . .

We current Justices read the Constitution in the only way that we can: as Twentieth Century Americans. We look to the history of the time of framing and to the intervening history of interpretation. But the ultimate question must be, what do the words of the text mean in our time? For the genius of the Constitution rests not in any static meaning it might have had in a world that is dead and gone, but in the adaptability of its great principles to cope with current problems and current needs. What the constitutional fundamentals meant to the wisdom of other times cannot be their measure to the vision of our time.†

*Robert H. Bork, *The Tempting of America: The Political Seduction of the Law* (New York: Free Press, 1990), 351–352.

†William J. Brennan, "For 'Loose' Construction," reprinted in *American Government: Readings and Cases,* 12th ed., ed. Peter Woll (New York: Harper Collins, 1996), 472–474.

for congressional apportionment—thus solving the immediate issue of how to take the census without needing to address the constitutional question. If the Act itself were changed, a new case might be brought that would touch the constitutional issue, but chances are that the Court would again look for a nonconstitutional means of answering whatever specific challenge was brought.[13]

Second, judicial rulings are constrained by the text and intent of legislation, and by the doctrine of *stare decisis,* or a reliance and adherence to precedent in deciding cases. The Supreme Court tries not to overturn established precedent, in an effort to impart stability and continuity to its decisions. At times, of course, the Court will reverse itself; the most prominent example here is the landmark reversal in *Brown v. Board of Education,* in which the Court reversed its earlier commitment to the constitutionality of "separate but equal" facilities for blacks and whites. But the Court has shied away from overturning *Roe v. Wade,* even as later rulings have narrowed the original decision's scope.

Third, judges are constrained by *the hierarchical nature of the judicial system.* Nowhere is there a more rigid chain of command than in the federal and state judiciary. Lower courts must operate within the framework of policies set forth by the Supreme Court or face almost certainly being overturned on appeal. The lower the level of court, the less likely it is to establish broad policy principles.

Finally, judges' decisions are constrained by *the views and interpretations of other judges.* In the Supreme Court, for example, reaching a decision requires writing and rewriting draft opinions, discussing issues and interpretations, negotiating positions, and bargaining for support. This does not take the form of legislative bargaining, in the sense that judicial bargaining is not a quid pro quo exchange where one Justice agrees to support another on one case in exchange for support on another case. Rather, judicial bargaining is a process of refining and smoothing interpretations in order to satisfy individuals who are attuned to very subtle differences in language and interpretation. A justice drafting an opinion can attract support from other Justices by shifting emphasis or even changing word usage. Chief Justice Earl Warren, for example, carefully crafted the *Brown v. Board* opinion to ensure a unanimous ruling from the Court overturning the separate-but-equal doctrine. (See Discussion Box 10.5.)

## WHY THE COURTS? COMPETITIVE POLITICS BY OTHER MEANS

There are good reasons why the parties involved in the Internet cases we reviewed at the start of this chapter race to the courts to promote or defend their interests. Nor are they the first band of interests to flood the courts with competitive demands and challenges. They know that, in the right circumstances, the courts can be influential actors on new or controversial issues. They know that the independence of the courts, together with judges' latitude over what cases to hear and how to decide them, makes the courts open to new arguments and interpretations of law—and thus the courts are potential policy-

"Collegial courts," like the Supreme Court, are courts in which more than one judge is involved in making rulings. Judges in collegial courts must negotiate and bargain with the other judges in order to reach decisions and build majorities. The following passages are from Justice William J. Brennan; a state supreme court justice; and judicial scholar Walter F. Murphy. According to these passages, are difficult cases likely to incur more or less negotiating? Is conflict and competition surrounding the court evidence of a judicial system in trouble? Why do judges work so hard to garner support for their positions? Why do you think a unanimous court is "best," as the second passage suggests? What risks do you think might arise from the bargaining process?

**Justice Brennan:**

There are . . . very few cases where the constitutional answers are clear, all one way or all the other, and this is also true of the current cases raising conflicts between the individual and government power—an area increasingly requiring the Court's attention. . . .

How conflicts such as these ought to be resolved constantly troubles our whole society. There should be no surprise, then, that how properly to resolve them often produces sharp division within the Court itself. When problems are so fundamental, the claims of the competing interests are often nicely balanced, and close divisions are almost inevitable.*

**State Supreme Court Justice:**

You might say to another judge that if you take this line out, I'll go along with your opinion. You engage in a de-

gree of compromise and if it doesn't hurt the point you're trying to make in an opinion, you ought to agree to take it out. . . . The men will write an opinion and circulate it. And then the other judges will write a letter or say at conference, can you change this or that, adjust the language here, etc. . . . Your object is to get a unanimous court. That's always best.†

**Walter F. Murphy:**

For [Supreme Court] Justices, bargaining is a simple fact of life. Despite conflicting views on literary style, relevant proceedings, procedural rules, and substantive policy, cases have to be settled and opinions written; and no opinion may carry the institutional label of the court unless five Justices agree to sign it. In the process of judicial decision-making, much bargaining may be tacit, but the pattern is still one of negotiation and accommodation to secure consensus. Thus how to bargain wisely—not necessarily sharply—is a prime consideration for a Justice who is anxious to see his policy adopted by the Court. A Justice must learn not only how to put pressure on his colleagues but how to gauge what amounts of pressure are sufficient to be "effective" and what amounts will overshoot the mark and alienate another judge. In many situations a Justice has to be willing to settle for less than he wants if he is to get anything at all. As [Justice] Brandeis once remarked, the "great difficulty of all group action, of course, is when and what concession to make."‡

*William J. Brennan, "For 'Loose' Construction," reprinted in *American Government: Readings and Cases,* 12th ed., ed. Peter Woll (New York: HarperCollins, 1996), 456.

†Quoted in Robert A. Carp and Ronald Stidham, *The Federal Courts,* 3rd ed. (Washington, DC: CQ Press, 1998), 161.

‡Quoted in ibid., 162.

makers. Litigation is simply politics by other means; outside interests as well as judges traditionally have used the judicial system to pursue and promote political ends.

## *How You Doin'? The Attractiveness of the Courts*

The nature of political majorities and of the American system affects the behavior of the courts and their willingness to become involved in certain issues. From its earliest days, the Supreme Court has heard or been asked to hear cases involving major political disputes. The Court in such instances can dive

**Signs Your Judge Is On Drugs**

10. In middle of trial points to defendant and says, "Dude, you are so guilty."

9. Shrieks that spiders are crawling all over the gavel.

8. When an undercover policeman testifies, judge yells "Narc!"

7. The bailiff: a bearded guy in a Santana t-shirt selling rope bracelets.

6. Perks up whenever someone uses phrase "joint custody."

5. Wants to replace closing arguments with "Laser Zeppelin."

4. Every time lawyer objects, judge replies, "Quit harshing my mellow!"

3. Instead of Bible, has witness swear on copy of "Fear and Loathing In Las Vegas."

2. When bailiff says "Order in the court," judge shouts "I'll have Doritos, lots of Doritos!"

1. Always citing the landmark case of "Cheech V. Chong."

*Source:* Reprinted by permission of CBS Worldwide, Inc.

into troubled waters by exercising judicial activism, or stay safely on shore by exercising self-restraint.

The Court tests the political waters to choose between activism and restraint. When a strong majority exists nationally, the Court, to protect its credibility and authority, often backs off by practicing self-restraint. Certainly the Supreme Court of the latter nineteenth century was not a bold innovator, upholding vested property rights and inventing the "separate-but-equal" doctrine to avoid challenging deep-seated discrimination after the Civil War. No one would argue that the Supreme Court was being particularly independent of the dominant political interests of society in ruling as it did during this period.

At many times and on many issues throughout our political history, though, cohesive majorities have not existed. The absence of cohesive majorities and the fragmentation of power throughout the political system account for much of the extraordinary power of the Supreme Court. When the Court confronts a power vacuum arising from the lack of a political majority, it is freer to act and to resolve political controversies. Further, when the executive and legislative branches are unable to make political decisions, either because they are in conflict or because the political will necessary to make tough choices is absent, the Supreme Court can step into the void.

Finally, stalemate between the "political" branches and the inability to build national majorities makes the courts attractive to groups or individuals pursuing political interests; the courts emerge as more promising avenues for action. The Madisonian system is antimajoritarian and it has worked well. Madison wrote in *Federalist 10* that a large republic would put obstacles in the path of majority rule. In *Federalist* papers 47, 48, and 51 he argued that the separation of powers would impede majority rule by preventing the accumulation of legislative, executive, and judicial power in the same hands. But blocking majority rule encourages minority power; and in the judicial process, factions or interest groups find a venue that often favors their interests.

### From the Marshall Era through the Civil War: Federalism and National Power

On the Web
www.law.cornell.edu/
supct

On the Web
www.findlaw.com/
casecode/index.html

On the Web
www.usscplus.com/
current/index.htm

On the Web
www.fedworld.gov/
supcourt/csearch.htm

On the Web
www.law.cornell.edu/
journals.html

On the Web
www.usc.edu/dept/
law-lib/legal/journals
.html

The Supreme Court has generally tended to hear and address cases that embody the political spirit and major issues of particular eras. In the nation's early years, questions of federalism and the proper boundaries of state and national power dominated politics at the national level. Chief Justice John Marshall's strong Federalist interpretations of the Constitution and his support for federal power mark the Supreme Court's early years. The Court broadly interpreted the many political compromises of the Constitutional Convention in Federalist terms, to the disappointment of states' rights advocates. In *McCulloch v. Maryland* (1819) and *Gibbons v. Ogden* (1824), for example, the Court upheld national supremacy and broad national powers over the competing claims of the states. *McCulloch* denied the state of Maryland's authority to tax a branch of the national bank created by Congress, settling a long-standing political dispute regarding Congress's constitutional authority to create such a bank. In *Gibbons,* as we saw in chapter 5, the Court cemented the national government's supremacy over state governments, laying the foundation for interpreting questions of federalism.

The fact that John Marshall succeeded in getting the Supreme Court to uphold the Federalist interpretation of the Constitution gave to the new republic the necessary legal authority to withstand attacks from proponents of state sovereignty that would have undermined the national government. Marshall's decisions certainly did not demonstrate judicial servility to the president or Congress, from which numerous threats of impeachment issued because of the course of action taken by the Court. With the possible exception of the Warren Court, the Supreme Court has never been as innovative over such an extended period of time as it was during Marshall's tenure.

After its early activist period under Marshall, whose tenure ended in 1836, the Court largely retreated from politics. It returned to the political foreground two decades later with an inauspicious choice—an attempt to resolve the complex and irreconcilable interests in support of and opposition to slavery. The Court ruled in *Dred Scott v. Sandford* (1857) that Congress could not ban slavery in the nation's territories, and that slaves were property protected by the Constitution. In *Dred Scott,* the Court entered a stalemated political thicket; its effort to resolve questions surrounding slavery jeopardized the Court's own legitimacy because it could not enforce its ruling. The *Dred Scott* ruling crystallized opposing forces on the issue, and some historians have gone so far as to blame the Civil War on the Court's political meddling. Of course, far broader influences than the Court caused the war, but attacks on the Court at the time reflected the widespread recognition that it had become deeply involved in politics.

## Competition in the Courts: Judicial Activism in the Lochner Era and the New Deal

From 1865 to 1937, issues of economic regulation dominated the Court's activities, and activity surrounding the courts continued to represent politics by other means. Following the Civil War, the Court again intervened in politics, this time to negate congressional efforts to carry out responsibilities under the Fourteenth Amendment to enforce the equal protection of the laws. The Court held in the *Civil Rights Cases* (1883) that Congress could not prohibit racial discrimination in public accommodations such as hotels, restaurants, and theaters under its Fourteenth Amendment, Section 5, enforcement authority. The decision overturned the Civil Rights Act of 1875, which was the only important legislative effort to ban racial discrimination in the decade following the Civil War. In these cases, the Court's decisions replaced the outcomes of democratic electoral and majoritarian politics.

Each time the Court becomes active, it shapes political compromises in ways that change the hard-fought outcomes of electoral politics. The Court hindered the federal government's efforts to regulate monopolies when it limited the enforcement of the Sherman Antitrust Act of 1890. In *United States v. E. C. Knight Co.* (1895), the Court held that Congress did not have the constitutional authority under its commerce power to apply antitrust policy to manufacturing. The Court used the Commerce Clause to overturn congressional statutes in other cases, as well. For instance, in *Hammer v. Dagenhart* (1918), the Court declared unconstitutional a statute that banned products in interstate commerce that had been made by child labor. The Court ruled that Congress cannot indirectly regulate child labor under its commerce power, for child labor is not by itself part of commerce. (See BriefCase Box 5.1 in chapter 5.)

Perhaps the most infamous example of politics by other means is the case of *Lochner v. New York* (1908). Following extensive hearings to determine the health effects of long exposure to flour dust, the New York state legislature concluded that the protection of bakers' health required limits on the number of hours they were permitted to work. In *Lochner*, the Supreme Court overturned the New York law, ruling that it violated the Fourteenth Amendment because it was state action that infringed without due process of law on both employers' and employees' liberty to contract. The law was not, wrote Justice Rufus Peckham, a "reasonable" state regulation. Over the stern objections of Justices Oliver Wendell Holmes and John Harlan, the *Lochner* opinion facilely replaced New York's legislative judgment with what, in effect, was a legislative determination of its own. In short, the Court rejected the results of competition and compromises between employer and employee interests in the political process, and substituted its own substantive due process preferences couched as a constitutional interpretation. (See BriefCase Boxes 10.3 and 10.4.)

The New Deal Court continued politics by other means. In a series of cases beginning with *Schechter v. United States* (1935), the Court held unconstitutional the core of Franklin Roosevelt's New Deal legislation. With Chief Justice <u>Charles Evans Hughes</u> leading the charge of conservative justices against liberal New Deal programs, the Court ruled that Congress did not have the power it had claimed under the Constitution's Commerce Clause to enact economic legislation designed to save the country from the Great Depression.

This was an extraordinary period in the Court's history. The president and Congress during the New Deal had engaged in a lengthy political process of compromise and bargaining, analogous to the state political process that preceded the *Lochner* case legislation. The *Schechter* case, for example, challenged the legitimacy of the National Industrial Recovery Act. This Act included codes of fair competition drawn up by major corporations in a wide variety of industries, and sought to reduce unemployment and unfair practices. The codes tended to favor big business, but they still embodied considerable compromises among competing organizations and interests.

Nevertheless, the Supreme Court substantively or legislatively defined Congress's Article 1 commerce power in cases that overturned New Deal leg-

---

## BRIEFCASE BOX 10.3
*Just Doing Our Job: Justice Peckham's Ruling in* Lochner v. New York

The most commonly cited example of the Supreme Court overstepping its bounds is *Lochner v. New York* (1905), in which the Court ruled that a New York State law regulating bakers' hours was unconstitutional because it was an unnecessary infringement on the liberty to contract. Justice <u>Rufus Peckham</u>'s decision stated that the Court must look "beyond the letter of the law" in the case and judge the statute's effects, not its proclaimed purpose. Peckham's opinion, though, squarely addresses the charge that the Court was inappropriately substituting its judgment for that of the legislature. Judging from the following passages, do you find Peckham's reasoning convincing? In a case such as this, in which a statute appears to infringe upon individual liberty, how can the Court *avoid* evaluating whether or not the law is "necessary"? Does the Court make such an evaluation whenever it weighs the competing interests of the government and the individual? Or should the Court studiously avoid rendering judgments based on the "reasonableness" of fairly enacted laws?

In every case that comes before this court, . . . where legislation of this character is concerned, and where the protection of the federal Constitution is sought, the question necessarily arises: Is this a fair, reasonable, and appropriate exercise of the police power of the State, or is it an unreasonable, unnecessary, and arbitrary interference with the right of the individual to his personal liberty or to enter into those contracts in relation to labor which may seem to him appropriate or necessary for the support of himself and his family? . . .

This is not a question of substituting the judgment of the court for that of the legislature. If the act be within the power of the State it is valid, although the judgment of the court might be totally opposed to the enactment of such a law. But the question would still remain: Is it within the police power of the State [to protect and promote the health, safety, and welfare of individuals]? and that question must be answered by the court. . . .

We think the limit of the police power has been reached and passed in this case. There is, in our judgment, no reasonable foundation for holding this to be necessary or appropriate as a health law to safeguard the public health, or the health of the individuals who are following the trade of a baker.*

*\*Lochner v. New York,* 198 U.S. 45 (1905).

islation based on the Constitution's Commerce Clause. In effect it said to Congress: "Hey, you may be representatives of the people and the constitutionally designated policymaking body, but you can't do that! Why not? Because your commerce power does not permit it." But the Constitution does not textually define what constitutes "commerce among the states," which Congress has the authority to regulate; nor does it define all of the boundaries between state and federal authority. The Court, in effect, replaced Congress's legislative judgment of what the country needed with its own substantive definition of legislative power. The Court's New Deal opinions were akin to *Lochner*'s substantive due process. Significantly, the Court soon recognized that it faced a cohesive pro–New Deal political majority; it reversed its actively obstructionist trend soon after *Schechter* and in the wake of FDR's effort to pack the court with pro–New Deal justices. For the remainder of the New Deal, the Court exercised much more restraint and validated major portions of Roosevelt's agenda.

## Since the New Deal: The Supreme Court and Competing Interests

Since the New Deal, the Court's role in evaluating the outcomes of competition and compromise in the political system continues to be controversial. Many of the battles now are between the rights of individuals and the interests

---

### BRIEFCASE BOX 10.4
*Except That That's Not Our Job: Justice Holmes's Dissent in* Lochner

Justice Oliver Wendell Holmes's dissent in *Lochner v. New York,* passages from which follow below, is a sharp criticism of the Court's foray into substantive due process, or substituting its own interpretation of what the law should be for the determinations made by competing interests in the legislative process. What is the Court's role, according to Holmes, when facing a law that resulted from a fair political compromise but that the Justices believe to be tyrannical? To what extent should the Court rely on justice, reason, and wisdom to reach decisions?

It is settled by various decisions of this court that state constitutions and state laws may regulate life in many ways which we, as legislators, might think as injudicious, or, if you like, as tyrannical, as this, and which, equally with this, interfere with the liberty to contract. Sunday laws and usury laws are ancient examples. A more modern one is the prohibition of lotteries. The liberty of the citizen to do as he likes so long as he does not interfere with the liberty of others to do the same, which has been a shibboleth for some well known writers, is interfered with by school laws, by the Post Office, by every state or municipal institution which takes his money for purposes thought desirable, whether he likes it or not. . . .

The responsibility therefor rests upon legislators, not upon the courts. No evils arising from such legislation could be more far-reaching than those that might come to our system of government if the judiciary, abandoning the sphere assigned to it by the fundamental law, should enter the domain of legislation, and upon grounds merely of justice or reason or wisdom, annul statutes that had received the sanction of the people's representatives. We are reminded by counsel that it is the solemn duty of the courts in cases before them to guard the constitutional rights of the citizen against merely arbitrary power. That is unquestionably true. But it is equally true—indeed, the public interests imperatively demand—that legislative enactments should be recognized and enforced by the courts as embodying the will of the people unless they are plainly and palpably, beyond all question, in violation of the fundamental law of the Constitution.*

*\*Lochner v. New York,* 198 U.S. 45 (1905).

of government. In *Griswold v. Connecticut,* for example, Justice <u>William O. Douglas</u> found that a fundamental due-process right to privacy emanated from penumbras of rights in the First, Fourth, and Fifth amendments to the Constitution. Dissenting Justice <u>Hugo Black,</u> however, found the majority's discovery of a constitutional right to privacy to be equivalent to substantive due process. Likening the majority's reasoning to the *Lochner* decision, he wrote:

> I do not to any extent whatever base my view that this Connecticut law [prohibiting the private use of contraceptives] is constitutional on a belief that the law is wise, or that its policy is a good one. In order that there may be no room at all to doubt why I vote as I do, I feel constrained to add that the law is every bit as offensive to me as it is to my Brethren of the majority and my Brothers HARLAN, WHITE and GOLDBERG, who, reciting reasons why it is offensive to them [in concurring opinions], hold it unconstitutional. There is no single one of the graphic and eloquent strictures and criticisms fired at the policy of this Connecticut law either by the Court's opinion or by those of my concurring Brethren to which I cannot subscribe—except their conclusion that the evil qualities they see in the law make it unconstitutional.[14]

The right to privacy remains highly controversial because it is the constitutional basis for the Court's decision in *Roe v. Wade,* which found that a Texas statute criminalizing abortion unconstitutionally infringed on a woman's privacy rights. Justice <u>Harry Blackmun</u> wrote in *Roe* that the right to privacy is founded in the Fourteenth Amendment's concept of personal liberty, and that therefore a state may regulate abortion only when its interests are "compelling": when the woman's health requires it or when necessary to protect the life of a viable fetus. Dissenting, Chief Justice <u>Rehnquist</u> wrote:

> While the Court's opinion quotes from the dissent of Mr. Justice Holmes in *Lochner v. New York,* . . . the result it reaches is more closely attuned to the majority opinion of Mr. Justice Peckham in that case. As in *Lochner* and similar cases applying substantive due process standards to economic and social welfare legislation, the adoption of the compelling state interest standard will inevitably require this Court to examine the legislative policies and pass on the wisdom of these policies in the very process of deciding whether a particular state interest put forward may or may not be "compelling."[15]

In other words, Rehnquist argued that the *Roe* decision would force the courts to rule on whether or not states' interests in regulating abortions were "compelling," thus entangling the courts in substantive determinations about the merits of legislative decisions. The Court would thus be involved in passing judgement, again and again, on the outcome of competition and compromise in other parts of the political system. And since *Roe,* the Court has indeed been asked to rule on the constitutionality of everything from parental notification requirements to waiting periods for women wanting abortions.

The nationalization of the Bill of Rights was also highly controversial in both procedural and substantive areas. The Court has defined due process to incorporate most of the procedural protections of the Bill of Rights, such as protections against double jeopardy, self-incrimination, and unreasonable searches and seizures, as well as Sixth Amendment rights to a speedy and public trial as well as jury trials in criminal cases. This process was "substantive" because the Court went beyond common law and settled usages in the law to expand traditional due process; it was politics by other means, as the Court overruled state legislatures and constitutions that had not adopted for their own citizens all of the rights in the national Bill of Rights. As a result of these decisions, courts at all levels are constantly asked to decide whether specific actions violate due process standards.

Two final examples illustrate ongoing controversies involving the Court. In 1961, the Court banned school prayer in *Engle v. Vitale* (1962), despite widespread public support for prayer in schools. Religious groups attacked the decision and supported efforts to amend the Constitution to overrule the *Engle* decision. Efforts continue to test the limits of the standard and to provide opportunities to overturn the decision, but the Court has stood firm: in June, 2000 the Court ruled that prayers at high school football games violate the Establishment Clause of the First Amendment.[16]

The Court has also ruled in recent years that states did not need to have a compelling interest to intrude upon the free exercise of religion; otherwise neutral laws that burden free exercise are allowable and do not violate the First Amendment. Strong opposition to the Court's position ensued, and Congress passed the Religious Freedom Restoration Act (RFRA) of 1993; this act restored the "compelling interest" test as the proper standard for evaluating state actions that infringe upon the free exercise of religion. As we saw in chapter 6, the Court overturned the RFRA, explicitly noting that Congress could not directly and openly overrule the Court with such legislation. The Court had once again thwarted the outcome of political competition in the legislature.

The history of the Court's involvement in politics suggests one important rule of thumb: "activism" is often in the eye of the beholder. Though the *Lochner* decision stands as a clear example of the Court substituting its views for those of government's elected branches, later cases like *Griswold* and *Roe* are more complicated. Nevertheless, opponents of the Court's willingness to engage in political issues and justices dissenting from the Court's rulings will continue to condemn the Court by invoking the discredited judicial activism involved in *Lochner*.

## Conclusion

Although the Supreme Court by the end of the New Deal had adopted judicial self-restraint in interpreting congressional authority under the Commerce Clause, in the 1990s the Court again became active in Commerce Clause litigation. In fact, since 1992 the Court has overturned more than a half-dozen statutes as exceeding congressional powers under the Commerce Clause or other parts of the Constitution, in a shift toward limiting the federal government's authority vis-à-vis the states. Dissents in these cases, most of which have been decided with very narrow majorities, criticize the Court for becoming too active in areas like state sovereign immunity, which are at best only vaguely defined by the terms of the Constitution. (See Zip Box 10.4.)

The Supreme Court has reined in the power of Congress in more than a half-dozen decisions since 1992. The court ruled in the following cases that Congress exceeded its power under the Constitution:

**1992** *New York v. United States.*
The justices struck down, 6–3, portions of a federal law (PL 99-240) making states liable for nuclear waste created by commercial reactors. The court cited the 10th Amendment, which limits Congress to powers enumerated in the Constitution and leaves other powers to the states, in ruling that Congress had exceeded its authority. (*1992 Almanac, p. 329*)

**1995** *United States v. Lopez.*
The justices struck down, 5–4, portions of an anti-crime law (PL 101-647) that aimed to ban guns within 1,000 feet of schools. The court said Congress had exceeded its authority under the "commerce clause," which allows Congress to regulate interstate commerce. (*1995 Almanac, p. 6–40*)

**1996** *Seminole Tribe of Florida v. Florida.*
The justices struck down, 5–4, a law (PL 100-497) that allowed tribes to file federal suits when states failed to negotiate gambling compacts. The court cited the 11th Amendment, which prohibits federal courts from adjudicating cases brought against a state by citizens of another state or country. (*1996 Almanac, p. 5–51*)

**1997** *City of Boerne v. Flores.*
The justices ruled, 6–3, that Congress exceeded its powers under the 14th Amendment with a law (PL 103-141) barring states from enacting laws interfering with citizens' First Amendment rights of religious expression, unless states had a "compelling interest." The 14th Amendment allows Congress to implement equal protection laws. (*1997 Almanac, p. 5–23*)

**1997** *Printz v. United States; Mack v. United States.*
The justices struck down, 5–4, a major portion of the Brady Act (PL 103-159) ordering local sheriffs to check the backgrounds of would-be gun buyers. The court cited the 10th Amendment in saying Congress had exceeded its authority. (*1997 Almanac, p. 5–21*)

**1999** *Alden v. Maine.*
The justices cited the 11th Amendment in ruling, 5–4, that Congress exceeded its authority in allowing individuals to sue a state over overtime wages for violations of the 1938 Fair Labor Standards Act. (*1999 CQ Weekly, p. 1527*)

**1999** *Florida v. College Savings Bank; College Savings Bank v. Florida.*
The justices cited the 11th Amendment in ruling, 5–4, that Congress exceeded its authority in enacting two laws (PL 102-560, PL 102-542) permitting lawsuits against state agencies alleging violations of federal patent and trademark laws. (*1999 CQ Weekly, p. 1527*)

*Source:* From *Congressional Quarterly Weekly Report,* January 15, 2000: 81, with references to CQ's *Weekly Report* and CQ's *Almanac of American Politics.*

The judiciary, then, continues to play a central role in defining public policy. Litigation becomes a political process as interests challenge congressional, presidential, and administrative actions that do not go their way. The long tradition of judicial review guarantees that litigation will continue to present an attractive venue for politics by other means. Political pluralism buttresses federalism and the constitutional separation of powers, helping to prevent the formation of cohesive and continuous political majorities—just as Madison predicted. Competition and compromise remain cornerstones of the American system. In the absence of cohesive majorities and stable centers of political power, the courts will continue to be a major political force.

## Overnight Assignment ▬▬▬▬▬▬▬▬▬

In the media or through one of the websites listed in this chapter, locate a federal court ruling that interests you. Your instructor might recommend a recent case or a landmark ruling for you to study. What were the details of the case? What was the specific case or controversy involved? What was the nature of the ruling? Was there a dissent in the case and, if so, did the dissent involve any of the topics covered in this chapter, such as standing, political questions, or the role of the judiciary?

## Long-Term Integrated Assignment ▬▬▬▬▬▬▬

Consider the issues and groups you've followed through this book. What role has the judiciary played? Is your group or issue involved in any federal litigation? What are the details of the case? Does you group have "standing," and is the case "ripe" for adjudication? What is the specific case or controversy involved? Have important rulings affected your group? Who brought the cases to the courts, and why? Did the effort in the courts follow failed efforts in other political venues, or did the court cases parallel efforts to lobby Congress or influence elections, for example? How did the media cover the cases? Was coverage affected by any of the dynamics we studied in chapter 1 or in this chapter?

## Researching the Judiciary? ▬▬▬▬▬▬▬▬

### Try These Authors:

Robert H. Bork
David M. O'Brien

John P. Roche
Bernard M. Schwartz

Robert G. Scigliano

### Try These Sources:

BAUM, LAWRENCE. *The Supreme Court,* 6th ed. Washington, DC: CQ Press, 1998.

CARP, ROBERT A. and RONALD STIDHAM. *Judicial Process in America,* 4th ed. Washington, DC: CQ Press, 1998.

EPSTEIN, LEE AND JACK KNIGHT. *The Choices Justices Make.* Washington, DC: CQ Press, 1998.

HOROWITZ, DONALD L. *The Courts and Social Policy.* Washington, DC: Brookings Institution, 1977.

JOST, KENNETH. *Supreme Court Yearbook: 1998–1999.* Washington, DC: CQ Press, 2000.

KATZMANN, ROBERT A. *Courts and Congress.* Washington, DC: Brookings Institution Press, 1997.

MCCLOSKEY, ROBERT G. *The American Supreme Court,* 2nd ed., revised by Sanford Levinson. Chicago: University of Chicago Press, 1994.

WILKINS, DAVID E. *American Indian Sovereignty and the U.S. Supreme Court: The Masking of Justice.* Austin: University of Texas Press, 1997.

YARBROUGH, TINSLEY E. *The Rehnquist Court and the Constitution.* New York: Oxford University Press, 2000.

# *Endnotes* ▄▄▄▄▄▄▄▄▄▄▄▄▄▄▄▄▄▄▄▄▄▄▄▄▄▄▄▄▄▄▄▄▄▄▄▄▄▄▄▄▄▄▄▄▄▄▄▄▄▄▄▄▄▄▄▄

1. From *The Internet Law Newsletter*, compiled by Professor Michael Geist, University of Ottawa Law School. To subscribe to this free service, send an email to michael-geist@yahoo.com with the message "subscribe netlaw". Reprinted with permission.
2. Alexis de Tocqueville, *Democracy in America* (New York: Vintage, 1945), I:155–157.
3. *Marbury v. Madison*, 1 Cranch 137 (1803).
4. Robert A. Carp and Ronald Stidham, *The Federal Courts*, 3rd ed. (Washington, DC: CQ Press, 1998), 89.
5. Ibid., 110–111.
6. See, for example, Stuart Taylor, Jr., "Why It's Getting Harder to Appoint Judges," *National Journal*, October 2, 1999.
7. *Ex Parte McCardle* 7 Wall. 506 (1869).
8. *Hayburn's Case*, 2 Dall. 409 (1792).
9. Jackson quoted in Francis Paul Prucha, *The Great Father: The United States Government and the American Indians* (Lincoln University of Nebraska Press, 1984), 212. See the discussion there for more on the technicalities of the Court's decision in *Worcester v. Georgia*.
10. *Cohens v. Virginia*, 19 U.S. 264 (1821).
11. *Ohio v. Wyandotte Chemicals Corp.* 401 U.S. 493 (1971).
12. Ibid.
13. *Wisconsin v. City of New York et. al.*, 517 U.S. 1 (1996); *Department of Commerce v. United States House of Representatives*, 525 U.S. 316 (1999). The census cases are also interesting because, as they were litigated before the census was taken, the question of standing arose. Parties favoring sampling and opposing the litigation argued that because the census had not yet been taken, the Court should not grant standing to plaintiffs and should determine the case to be nonjusticiable. Other arguments centered on the case as a political question inappropriate for the courts.
14. 381 U.S. 479, 507 (1965).
15. *Roe v. Wade*, 410 U.S. 113 (1973).
16. *Sante Fe Independent School District v. Doe*, 168 F.3d 806 (2000).

# Photo Credits

# Index